The Drug-Free Workplace: How to Get There and Stay There

John J. Fay, CPP

Butterworth-Heinemann
Boston Oxford Auckland Johannesburg Melbourne
New Delhi

Copyright © 2000 by Butterworth–Heinemann

 A member of the Reed Elsevier group

 Recognizing the importance of preserving what has been written,
Butterworth–Heinemann prints its books on acid-free paper whenever
possible.

GLOBAL
RELEAF
2000
Butterworth–Heinemann supports the efforts of American
Forests and the Global ReLeaf program in its campaign for the
betterment of trees, forests, and our environment.

ISBN 0-7506-7187-4

British Library Cataloguing-in-Publication Data
A catalogue record for this book is available from the British Library.

The publisher offers special discounts on bulk orders of this book.
For information, please contact:
Manager of Special Sales
Butterworth-Heinemann
225 Wildwood Avenue
Woburn, MA 01801-2041
Tel: 781-904-2500
Fax: 781-904-2620

For information on all Butterworth–Heinemann publications available,
contact our World Wide Web home page at: http://www.bh.com

10 9 8 7 6 5 4 3 2 1

Printed in the United States of America

Table of Contents

1

The Rationale for a Drug-Free Workplace

If I told you that the cost of drug abuse in the American workplace amounts to $140 billion per year you'd likely reply, "Oh, really?" and then go on about your business. But if I told you that the elimination of workplace drug abuse would provide enough money to buy you and every other American adult a spanking new Cadillac, you'd probably say, "Hmm," and think for a moment or two. To be honest with you, I don't know how many dollars it would take to buy that many Cadillacs, but the number has to be enormous, just as $140 billion dollars is enormous. Why is that number so high? Let's look at some facts.

An employee who arrives late for work or not at all reduces the organization's overall productivity, causes work to be transferred to others, and generates overtime. A rule of thumb says that on average a lost workday costs the employer 2.5 times the worker's daily pay. A worker who earns $20 an hour will cost the employer $400 for every day he or she is absent from the job. If the frequency of absence for that worker is one day per week (which is not high for a chronic abuser), the cost per year is $20,800. The Bureau of Labor Statistics

THE RATIONALE FOR A DRUG-FREE WORKPLACE

(BLS) reports that about 16 percent of the average workforce has a drug abuse problem. Thus, if you own a small company having 25 employees, 4 of them are possibly abusers. Your absenteeism cost would be $83,200 per year. If your company is large and has 1,000 employees, your cost would be $3,328,000.

- According to the Occupational Safety and Health Administration (OSHA), drug abusers are responsible for 35 percent of all absenteeism, are absent 10 times more often than non-abusers, and that the average abuser performs at 67 percent of productivity potential. The Research Triangle Institute announced a similar conclusion; drug-abusing employees are one-third less productive than other employees. General Motors (GM) determined that 70 percent of employee absences were due to abuse. The average abuser, in the year prior to undergoing treatment, was absent 100 days out of a 240 days per year work schedule. Drug-using employees averaged 40 days sick leave each year compared to 4.5 days for non-abusers. GM determined that abuse among its 472,000 workers and their dependents cost $600 million in one year alone.

Consider these other numbers:

- Seventy-one percent of illegal drug users are employed.

- Of those who called a national cocaine helpline, 75 percent reported using drugs on the job, 64 percent admitted that drugs adversely affected their job performance, 44 percent sold drugs to other employees, and 18 percent had stolen from co-workers to support their drug habit.

- Employees testing positive on pre-employment drug tests at Utah Power & Light were 5 times more likely to be involved in a workplace accident than those who tested negative.

- The State of Wisconsin estimates that expenses and losses related to drug abuse average 25 percent of the salary of each worker affected.

Then there is safety. The BLS, in looking at statistics for workers under the age of 44, found that 54 percent of work-related deaths, such as from falls, electrocutions, and vehicle crashes, involved workers who tested positive for drug abuse. In a study of fatally-injured truck drivers, as reported in *The Journal of Forensic Sciences*, 35 percent of the drivers had drugs and/or alcohol in their body systems when the accidents occurred, and the investigative findings in 89 percent of those accidents concluded that drugs and/or alcohol were contributing factors. The National Transportation and Safety Board found that 1 of every 4 drivers killed in a work-related accident had in the body system at least one drug (not including alcohol) which contributed to the accident. In a police study in Tennessee, 59 percent of drivers who had been stopped for reckless driving and agreed to be tested for drugs gave urine samples that were positive for drugs. At a Baltimore accident treatment center, 34 percent of victims tested positive for marijuana. After Walmart initiated a post-accident drug testing program, the accident rate fell 10 to 15 percent each month in the first 18 months of testing. Tropicana's drug testing program slashed the accident rate by 55 percent. For AT&T it was 81 percent.

Absenteeism and accidents also drive up the costs of medical benefits and workers' compensation. The U.S. Department of Labor concludes that drug-abusing employees generate medical costs three times that of non-abusing employees. The National Council on Compensation Insurance says that a drug abuser makes claims five times more frequently than non-abusers and that upward to 50 percent of all claims involve employees who use drugs or alcohol.

Then there are the individual horror stories. A truck driver under the influence of cocaine struck a lady on a sidewalk. She lost the use of her legs for 2 years. She sued. The court noted that the driver's employer knew or should have known that the employee had an abuse problem. The employer settled the case for $16 million.

HIDDEN COSTS

Don't forget the hidden costs. The morale of the non-abusing employees takes a nosedive when management demonstrates little concern about correcting an abuse problem. A Gallup poll revealed

THE RATIONALE FOR A DRUG-FREE WORKPLACE

that more than two-thirds of Americans view drugs as a serious workplace problem and want workplace drug testing. Study after study has shown that non-abusing workers are deeply concerned about drug abuse on the job. They don't like it; they expect management to stop it. They are resentful when required to pick up the slack created by drug abusing co-workers, they sue when they suffer on-the-job injuries resulting from accidents caused by the abusers, and when they happen also to be investors in the company, they are angry with management for not improving profits by controlling costs related to drug abuse.

Public image, reputation, and customer goodwill are damaged by perceptions that the company has an abuse problem. Whether selling a product or a service, management has to be seriously concerned about what the public and the consumer think about the organization. A food service company can be significantly damaged by any suggestion that drug-afflicted employees are contaminating the products; a temporary employee agency can be blackballed if a client believes the provided temps are drug abusers. A loss of public confidence in a major airline showed up in ticket sales shortly after the media reported that one of its pilots had a cocaine problem; reports of marijuana use by railroad employees continues to hurt railroad passenger ticket sales.

Other losses that tend to escape attention include friction between the abusing and non-abusing employees, time lost by managers and supervisors in dealing with problems created by abuse such as accidents, leaving the job without permission, disorderly conduct, damage to equipment and property, wastage of supplies and materials, and theft. What is the dollar value of time spent cleaning up an accident site, repairing equipment, settling workers down and restoring their attention to productivity, conducting an investigation, writing a report, imposing corrective and disciplinary actions, responding to a grievance complaint, and testifying at a hearing or a trial? Costs like these are difficult to put a handle on but are substantial.

We tend to stereotype illicit drug users. While it is true that many of the seriously addicted users are homeless persons and criminals, the majority of illicit drug users manage to hold jobs. The Department of Labor estimates that 73 percent of illicit drug users are employed. The

4

chances are good that one or more of these 8 million abusers work for you. No workplace is immune. When you assume that drug abuse is not present in your workplace, and you therefore choose not to initiate a drug-free workplace program, you are exactly the type of employer to attract drug-abusing job applicants. Job applicants who can't or don't want to be free of drug abuse naturally migrate to companies where anti-drug programs are not in place.

THE GOOD NEWS

Despite recent news reports about the increased use of drugs, we continue to be encouraged that workplace drug abuse is a problem for which a solution exists. When the issue is addressed by establishing comprehensive programs, it is a win-win situation for both employers and employees. The following examples are illustrative.

- A study of the economic impact of drug abuse treatment in Ohio found these significant improvements in job-related performance:

  - A 91 percent decrease in absenteeism

  - An 88 percent decrease in problems with supervisors

  - A 93 percent decrease in mistakes in work

  - A 97 percent decrease in on-the-job injuries

- At Southern Pacific railroad, injuries dropped 71 percent.

- An electric supply company with 150 employees experienced a 39 percent decrease in absenteeism and a 36 percent increase in productivity.

- A construction company with 60 employees reduced workers compensation claims by $50,000.

THE RATIONALE FOR A DRUG-FREE WORKPLACE

- A manufacturer with 560 employees experienced a 30-35 percent decrease in industrial accidents.

Statistics such as these suggest not just that workplace drug abuse is an issue that all employers need to address but also that it is an issue for which there is an answer. Taking steps to identify those with abuse problems and offering a helping hand will not only improve worker safety and health but also increase workplace productivity and competitiveness.

WHEN A DRUG-FREE WORKPLACE IS MANDATORY

In certain cases, a drug-free workplace is mandatory. For example, the Drug-Free Workplace Act of 1988 requires some federal contractors and all federal grantees to agree that they will provide drug-free workplaces as a condition of receiving a contract or grant from a federal agency. The requirements of the Act vary based on whether the contractor or grantee is an individual or an organization. The requirements for organizations are stiff. They include comprehensive, programmatic steps, and a failure to carry them out can be penalized by suspending payments, suspending the contract or grant, or prohibiting the contractor or grantee from receiving or participating in any future federal contracts or grants for a period of 5 years.

An employer subject to regulation by the Department of Defense, Nuclear Regulatory Commission, or Department of Transportation is required to maintain a drug-free workplace. The requirement is rooted in Executive Order 12564, issued by President Ronald Reagan, which mandated a drug-free federal workplace. The Secretary of the Department of Health and Human Services (DHHS) developed implementing guidelines. Each head of a federal agency is required to follow the guidelines and develop its own plan and set of rules for carrying out the order. Department of Transportation (DOT) rules were issued in 1988 and came to be accepted as a model for all federal agencies. The rules prescribe detailed procedures for operating a drug-free workplace program that includes drug and alcohol testing, and extend to employers in 6 transportation industries that fall within DOT's regulatory purview.

President Reagan's initiative to establish a drug-free federal workplace encouraged many non-federal employers to do the same, effectively launching a major trend that continues today, particularly in safety-sensitive work environments. The experiences of companies that have opted to go the drug-free route have been positive in many respects: lower costs, higher productivity, fewer accidents, happier employees. Simply stated, employers across the nation have learned that operating a drug-free organization makes good business sense.

In addition, the non-federal sector employers act against drug abuse because they have been stimulated by the realities of modern living. In spite of miraculous medical advances that create possibilities for well-being and long life for more people than ever before, the possibilities are tragically decimated by the use and effect of drugs. Health, happiness, and social order are often stifled in families, communities, schools, and workplaces because abuse eats at the very fabric of society. In a country where abuse is among the highest of any industrial country, employers can find themselves unable to compete effectively in the marketplace.

Clearly, employers have been stimulated by President Reagan's 1986 Executive Order. Five elements of the Order stand out:

- Development of a comprehensive written policy

- Supervisory training

- Employee education

- Availability of employee assistance programs

- Identification of illegal drug users through drug testing on a controlled and carefully monitored basis

While stating that use of illegal drugs will not be tolerated, the Order offers a helping hand and provides flexibility in its application.

THE RATIONALE FOR A DRUG-FREE WORKPLACE

DAMAGE REDUCTION

Drug abuse inflicts very serious societal damage. The lives of abusers and their families are destroyed; hospitals and treatment centers strain under the burden of drug-related admissions; courts and prisons overflow with dealers, traffickers, and offenders who committed their crimes while under the influence; and businesses are burdened with substandard work performance and higher-than-necessary operating costs. Studies made within the criminal justice system clearly show that drug abuse is the single largest contributor to the frequency and intensity of crime in all varieties. Studies made in American workplaces clearly show that abuse is a major contributor to accidents, theft, damage, poor productivity, and red ink on the bottom line.

We know very well the cause and effect of abuse, but have a lesser understanding of how to prevent and correct it. This gloomy observation, however, is offset by a few positive developments in the business sector. Intervention by drug testing of employees and referral to treatment are examples. Businesses have had a long history with abuse. The earliest programs for curbing it began in the workplace. Successes in those programs have led in recent years to an emulation of them in the criminal justice system.

Scientific techniques for assessing impairment are evolving rapidly. One of the oldest techniques, urinalysis, approaches one hundred percent accuracy. Urinalysis is a double-edged tool. One edge deters and the other detects. Drug-abusing employees who face testing are motivated to discontinue abuse, and when detected, are moved one step closer to treatment. Like all tools, testing works best when skillfully applied and when used in conjunction with other tools such as employee education, supervisor training, counseling, treatment, and rehabilitation.

THE CHANGING FACE OF DRUG ABUSE

While drug abuse overall has shown a steady move upward, the nature of the problem has changed in two respects. The first has to do with the drugs of choice, and the second has to do with the people who use them.

Not long ago the commonly abused drugs were relatively few in number, such as heroin, marijuana, and LSD. Today they include these plus cocaine, crack, PCP, methamphetamine, and a whole range of synthetic drugs.

The abusers have also changed. The abusers are no longer a small class of society's dropouts, but come from the mainstream. Drug abuse is practiced in all segments of society and in all forms of human activity. It is practiced by poor and rich, young and old, Blacks and Whites, farmers and city dwellers; it occurs in homes, in public, in sports.

Is drug abuse present at work? You can bet on it. The reality is that the workplace is just like every place else, and use of drugs at work is not limited to just the line workers, but includes specialists, supervisors, and managers. Use is likely to be higher among line workers but only because there are more of them.

Employers cannot blindly assume that drug abuse occurs only in the workforces of other companies. The idea that drug abuse is someone else's problem is to ignore reality, and an organization that ignores reality is at risk of sustaining losses so serious that it may be forced out of business.

A misleading facet of abuse at work is that many people who have problems, including problems with alcohol, seem to be productive, contributing employees. They successfully manage to meet or appear to meet the minimum standards, and they do so for years. An employee whose drug abuse reduces personal work capacity by twenty or thirty percent deprives the organization of significant value. The dollar value of lost productivity is enormous when you factor in the total number of abusing employees and the length of their employment.

But productivity is only a part of the problem. Drug-abusing employees, when compared with non-abusers, have higher accident rates, higher absence rates, higher medical insurance costs, and higher rates of theft and insubordination. Drug abusers are also a cause of low morale. Co-workers don't like having to work alongside people

THE RATIONALE FOR A DRUG-FREE WORKPLACE

who cause accidents, who don't carry their share of the workload, and who ask others to cover up for them.

2

An Overview of a Drug-Free Program

The first thing you need to know about a drug abuse program is that there is no such thing as a "one size fits all" model. Programs often have similar features, but they differ markedly in what they are designed to do and how they perform. Think sports cars and the similarity of overall features: sports cars are compact, built low to the ground, and have sleek lines. But Ferraris and Miatas perform very differently, as do drug abuse programs.

The details of a program will depend largely on the organization's circumstances, needs, location, culture, resources, and experiences with abuse. Just as importantly, a program will reflect in its design and administration the strength of the leadership's commitment to establish and maintain a workplace free of abuse.

AN OVERVIEW OF A DRUG-FREE PROGRAM

A drug-free program will typically include five essential components. In action terms, they are:

- Writing a policy that lays down the rules.

- Making employees aware of the negatives associated with alcohol and drug abuse.

- Training supervisors to carry out the policy.

- Conducting alcohol and drug testing to deter and detect.

- Assisting employees overcome their abuse problems.

WRITING A POLICY

A few important steps have to be taken before sitting down to write a drug abuse policy. First is to define the problem that the policy will address. A needs assessment survey, however informal, may help to better understand the true situation. An important ancillary objective is to enlist allies in this effort. The assistance and input of employees, particularly the line supervisors, will both help obtain usable information and secure the support of the workforce.

A written policy should provide:

- Unambiguous definitions of terms used in the policy.

- An explanation of why the program is being implemented. An important consideration may be the safety of employees, customers, and the general public. Other reasons may include maintaining the health of workers and their dependents, product quality, productivity, meeting contractual obligations, protecting sensitive material, such as trade secret and national defense information, and legal concerns such as public liability.

- A clear description of drug-related behaviors that are prohibited. At a minimum is the prohibition of the use, possession, and transfer or sale of illegal drugs. Unacceptable behavior may also forbid employees from being at work while under the influence of a drug.

- A thorough explanation of the consequences for violations of the policy.

- Amnesty and appeal procedures.

- The manner of alcohol and drug testing and the expectations placed on employees to cooperate with testing.

- Benefits available to employees who are in need of drug abuse treatment.

RAISING EMPLOYEE AWARENESS

A critical and early step is to inform employees, from top to bottom, of what the program entails and how it affects them individually. The awareness effort will, at a minimum, focus on these objectives:

- Educate employees about the health and social dangers of drugs, and how abuse can destroy the lives of individuals and their friends and families.

- Demonstrate as vividly as possible the negative impact that abuse can have on safety, productivity, product quality, and the overall bottom line.

- Explain in detail how the policy applies to every employee of the company, the prohibited behaviors, and the consequences for violations.

AN OVERVIEW OF A DRUG-FREE PROGRAM

- Describe the steps the company will take to enforce the policy such as supervisor attention to the indicators of abuse, workplace inspections, and drug testing.

- Identify treatment benefits offered both by the company and the community.

INVOLVING SUPERVISORS

The level of support supervisors give to the drug-free program, combined with the fairness of the program and the firmness of the commitment, will greatly influence the potential for success. Start-up problems are avoided or mitigated when full support and participation of supervisors are attained.

It is very reasonable to expect supervisors to spot and correct poor performance as it occurs. It is not reasonable, however, to expect supervisors to diagnose the reasons that underlie poor performance. Diagnosis should be the exclusive function of qualified treatment professionals. The supervisor's function is to bring the affected employee and the treatment professional together.

Each supervisor should be expected to:

- Know the policy and understand his or her role in carrying it out.

- Recognize the indicators of abuse and intervene in conformance to policy.

- Confront and counsel workers about unsatisfactory job performance.

- Refer to diagnosis or treatment those employees whose performance indicates drug abuse.

PROVIDING EMPLOYEE ASSISTANCE

Some employers will be unwilling or unable to provide assistance to employees who have drug problems. The unwilling employer may be philosophically opposed to using company resources to treat an employee's self-induced condition, especially when the condition is discovered after repeated warnings. An employer may have a limited choice or no choice at all when the company lacks the financial capacity to provide assistance.

A strong argument can be made for not automatically terminating employees with drug problems. Hiring and training replacement workers may not be a cost-effective answer, particularly when jobs demand workers with special skills. Helping an employee where help is merited may cost less than obtaining a comparable replacement. Another value, called workforce morale, is at play as well.

An employee assistance program (EAP) assists workers to resolve personal problems that stand in the way of acceptable job performance. Problems can be numerous and vary widely. In addition to being a stand-alone problem, abuse is often a contributing factor in other problems such as debt, divorce, and mental depression.

Before deciding on employee assistance, an employer would do well to:

- Research the issue by learning from other employers who have gone the EAP route; confer with the industry's professional association; and consult with EAP providers.

- Perform a cost versus benefit analysis. Look at all the angles, e.g., put together a package of assistance benefits the costs of which fall within the company's comfort zone.

- Explore the possibility of joining or forming an EAP consortium.

It is no longer true that EAPs are prohibitively expensive and therefore affordable only by large and profitable corporations. Companies with wide-ranging financial strengths and sizes can and do operate EAPs of all descriptions. Coming up with the right EAP is largely a matter of tailoring services to the company's unique needs at a reasonable cost level.

EAPs vary widely. At the minimum level, an EAP can be administered by an in-house human resources specialist acting like a traffic cop. The specialist directs employees to outside treatment resources that are provided free or with minimal fees picked up by the employees. The cost to the company is the salary of the human resources specialist who may perform other HR functions in addition to operating the EAP. At the maximum level, an EAP can be administered by an entire in-house department or by an outside vendor contracted to provide a full range of services at no cost or at nominal cost to the users. Between the minimum and maximum levels can be plans of varying combinations.

In a very important sense, the failure or success of an EAP will be determined by users. A program judged as successful will provide quality service, maintain strict confidentiality, and pose absolutely no threat to the employee's employment and potential advancement. The employee must be made to understand, however, that participation in the EAP does not shield against disciplinary action for continued poor performance or violations of policy.

DRUG TESTING

Prior to the development of the modern urine drug test, conscientious employers confronted workplace drug abuse with strong rules, diligent supervisors, and treatment benefits. Many employers were dissatisfied with results. Their anti-drug programs lacked a mechanism for identification, and without identification, enforcement of the rules was not possible. Along came advances in the scientific analysis of urine; employers found themselves with an accurate and reliable tool. Today a company seriously determined to rid its workplace of drug abuse can turn to drug testing.

Testing alone does not constitute a program; it is a component or a sub-part of a drug-free program. When used alone or used out of harmony with other program components, testing is problem-prone.

Program objectives tend not to be met and grievances and legal challenges arise. However, when testing is administered synchronously with other components, the program can hum along smoothly. The EAP component, for example, is facilitated when abusers who have been identified by testing are referred to treatment and who are subject to further testing as a means of monitoring their recovery.

For some companies, to test or not test is a decision made by a regulatory agency such as the U.S. Department of Transportation. For others, the decision is aided by incentives in the form of reduced premiums offered by insurance providers or workers' compensation agencies. But for many companies that test, the motivators are lower costs and higher profits.

The following checklist can be helpful in thinking about a drug testing program.

DRUG TESTING CHECKLIST

Who will be tested?

- Job applicants?

- All employees?

- Selected employees?

- Contractor employees?

Under what circumstances will tests be conducted?

- After an accident or near miss?

- Some but not all accidents?

AN OVERVIEW OF A DRUG-FREE PROGRAM

- When there is reason to believe an employee is under the influence?

- In conjunction with periodic physical examinations?

- Randomly?

- As a job qualifier?

What drugs will the testing look for?

What will be the testing methodologies and which lab will do the testing?

Will positive test results be reviewed by a medical review officer?

What will the company do when a person subject to testing fails to cooperate?

Who in the company will supervise or coordinate testing?

3

Assess the Problem

Your car's engine has started making a weird sound, it bucks when idling, and acrid smoke curls out from under the hood. Since you're not a Mister Goodwrench mechanic, you drive to a car repair business, describe the symptoms, sign a paper, and hand over the ignition key. An hour later, you are told the piston rings are worn and need to be replaced. You gulp when you hear the cost and then ask a few questions. You learn that you don't need to change the timing belt or adjust the carburetor, and the cooling system works just fine. Finally you say, "Okay, fix it." In this little scenario, you defined the problem, determined the appropriate problem-solving action, and made a decision to act.

The same approach can be applied in developing a drug-free workplace program. Start by looking for and evaluating the symptoms of drug abuse. What is the nature of the abuse and where does it exist? How widespread and deep-rooted is it? What can be done, and what resources will be needed?

EXAMINE THE SYMPTOMS

The symptoms worth looking at include higher than normal frequency of workers calling in sick, arriving late, leaving early, and being unaccountably absent from their workstations; rises in overtime costs; drops in productivity; rises in incidents of poor decision making, wastage, and damage to equipment and materials; higher than normal use of medical benefits; rises in safety rule violations and accidents; rises in theft and insubordination incidents; and grumbling by workers. Other symptoms include visual evidences of on-the-job drug abuse, e.g., discarded containers of inhalants and paper bags used for glue sniffing, remainders of marijuana cigarettes, and glassine envelopes of a type used to package powdered cocaine, crack, and heroin.

The Anonymous Questionnaire

Digging beneath the symptoms can yield a gold mine of useful information. One method is the anonymous questionnaire. It is typically short, simple, not overly inquisitive, and non-threatening. The questions might include: Have you ever observed drug abuse at work? If yes, can you name the drug abused? When did the abuse occur? In the last month, last six months, or the last 12 months? Where did the abuse occur?

A questionnaire of this type can be revealing, especially when it is administered by a third party who assures absolute anonymity. The questionnaire is designed to uncover the nature and extent of abuse without naming names, and responding to it is purely voluntary. When honestly projected as a neutral information-gathering tool, a questionnaire can obtain high quality information at modest cost. And when interpreted as a whole, the information can serve as a guide to policy development, sanctions and penalties, the appropriateness of company-paid rehabilitation, supervisory training, and education of the workers.

Observe and Listen

The tried and true practice of engaging workers in constructive face-to-face dialogue is also informative. Workers who are aware of drug abuse violations and who have confidence in their supervisors will often volunteer information. Supervisors who supervise by "walking around" and talking to subordinates can learn a great deal, both by observing and listening. This method is useful to the extent that supervisors know what to say to subordinates to encourage feedback, know what to look for in the way of abuse indicators, and know how to report their findings so that proper use can be made of the information.

Diagnosis Through Drug Screening

Another option is to screen the entire workforce with the use of a "one time and fit for purpose" urine drug test. Individual consent and absolute anonymity must apply. If screening the entire workforce is impractical, a percentage of the workforce can be screened with a random selection approach. A side benefit to this option is the deterring message conveyed to employees.

The Undercover Route

Another information-gathering technique is the undercover route. Trained undercover professionals are placed into the workforce to look for violations. However, this option should only be considered when there are good reasons to believe that a serious problem does in fact exist and that it involves criminality (i.e., not merely personal consumption) such as selling drugs on-the-job or using company resources to facilitate drug trafficking.

ASSESS THE PROBLEM

Doing the Homework

Less direct methods of problem identification include learning from studies of occupational drug abuse. These can serve as rough guidelines forged through the experiences of companies in a similar line of business or geographical area.

The staff of the industry's professional association may be helpful. Chances are that research has been conducted and that useful materials are on the shelf waiting. A professional association may also be in a position to provide consultations, program recommendations, implementation assistance, and follow-up evaluations.

Another avenue are the agencies whose charters address drug abuse issues such as state agencies that deal with employment, workers' compensation, and labor grievances.

The character of drug abuse in the local communities that provide manpower can be examined. Health offices, social services agencies, and drug treatment facilities often have special insight.

Law enforcement officials are another good source concerning the extent of abuse in the local population, the age groups of abusers, the preferred drugs of abuse, and the methods of drug administration. A side issue to be explored are an organization's responsibilities to report drug trafficking by workers and how to seize and turn over to law enforcement illicit drugs discovered in the workplace.

PREPARE AN ACTION PLAN

After the problem has been defined, the logical question to ask is, "What do I do now?" This is the time to examine the components of a drug-free workplace program. For the same reason each company will have a different problem, each will be wise to select a different solution. The solution differences are not so much a matter of selecting certain program components and not others, but more a matter of using all of the components in various ways to various degrees. Think of program components as tools. The idea is not to rule out one tool

22

in favor of another, but to apply those that work best. The tools or components are as follows.

Policy Considerations

Management expresses in writing its business reasons for maintaining a workplace free of drug abuse; specifies prohibited activities, expected employee behaviors, and the consequences of non-compliance; assigns responsibilities for program execution; and identifies fairness guarantees and the availability of treatment benefits.

Employee Awareness

Management announces the policy and ensures it is fully understood. Through an ongoing process, management educates workers concerning the impact of drug abuse on productivity, safety, personal health, and other issues of concern.

Supervisory Involvement

Management taps into the special insights of supervisors and prepares them, through training and other means, to carry out their anti-drug responsibilities such as looking for the indicators of abuse, intervening when violations occur, documenting violations, making referrals to diagnosis and treatment, and making follow-up evaluations of employees recovering from abuse.

Employee Assistance

Management crafts and operates an employee assistance program (EAP) that balances employee needs against company goals.

ASSESS THE PROBLEM

Testing

Management selects and oversees a program of drug testing that includes state-of-the-art testing methodologies, professional review of positive tests results, and appeal procedures.

Program Evaluation

Management monitors the entire effort and makes adjustments as needed.

APPLY THE TOOLS

Here are a few examples of the different ways that tools are applied. In developing a policy, a company that operates chemical plants will emphasize safety as an important business necessity; a company engaged in advanced computer chip research will base its policy on a concern about the unauthorized disclosure of sensitive information. The awareness component for the safety-oriented company will stress accident reduction; the research and development company will stress employee duties in respect to trade secret protections. If a company's defined drug abuse problem is minor, a full menu of drug testing options may not be required. If the company is regulated (e.g., by the Department of Transportation) the drug testing component will be mandated. EAPs among companies will vary according to each company's ability to afford treatment benefits. An organization's unique set of circumstances will dictate the tools to apply and the methods of application.

A fundamental and powerful influence affecting a drug-free workplace program is the company's financial viability. If the money to fund the program is not there, neither can the program be there. It often happens, however, that a company will already possess resources that can be harnessed. For example:

- Expertise of key staff in the company's medical, industrial health, safety, human resources, and security departments.

- Office space, equipment, and clerical support staff.

- An existing EAP might be modified to address drug abuse issues.

- The company's group health insurance plan might already provide coverage of drug abuse treatment costs or be modified with an affordable increase to the premium.

Exploitable resources outside of the company include community health agencies, hospital drug clinics, detoxification centers, psychiatric treatment facilities, methadone maintenance programs, therapeutic communities, halfway houses, local drug abuse councils, safety associations, and self-help groups such as Narcotics Anonymous.

FORM A TASK FORCE

It is always a good idea in the early stages of program development to form a task force. A carefully comprised task force will bring to the effort a combination of skills, knowledge, and broad organizational buy-in. The effort should be headed up by the chief executive officer (CEO) or a direct report to that position such as the senior human resources executive. The task force should include representatives at the managerial level from human resources, safety, security, health, legal, operations, and public affairs. In a unionized company, union representation is well-advised.

An action plan will be the product of the task force. It will assign responsibilities, e.g., human resources can be tasked with writing the action plan and writing the final program document; safety can identify the safety-sensitive locations and jobs in the company; security can confer with security peers and local law enforcement officials concerning the nature of abuse in the industry and the surrounding community; health can network with treatment providers and acquire the bona fides of drug testing companies; legal can advise on liability issues; operations can provide guidance on how to administer the program with minimum disruption; and public affairs can provide insights on how to announce the program to the workforce and the public.

The action plan need not be formal. Style, appearance, and the like have no importance. The matters that count are assigning tasks to the members, setting and meeting completion deadlines, and ensuring that the effort stays within budget, both to the work of the task force and to the operation of the program when it is up and running. After becoming thoroughly informed of the drug abuse risks confronting the company and of the options and resources available to counter the risks, the CEO decides on the major components of the program. The central program component is policy. It determines every facet of every program component.

4

Write the Policy

A policy tends to either abound in tautology or linger in obscurity. Confused? Excellent; that was the intention. A policy that cloaks meaning by wordiness or by not enough words will do little good. A policy loses its effectiveness when it is overly detailed or overly vague. Each extreme suggests a particular authorial concern. The author of the detailed policy intends there be no wiggle room, i.e., "This is the way it is, folks, and there's no getting around it." Everyone has to be told everything and with absolute certainty. No person subject to the policy should later be able to say, "Gee, I didn't know." Every base plus every seat in the stadium is covered. All issues, important and otherwise, are explained a dozen times. Nothing is immune to repetition, thus sorely testing the reader's will to go on. An epidemic of legalese tends also to infect the detailed policy. When every other sentence contains a heretofore or a hereinafter, clarity goes right down the tube.

27

In the vague policy the author wants room to maneuver, almost to the point of admitting that management would like later to interpret the policy as it sees fit. Interpretation, of course, cuts two ways, so that enforcing an unclear policy can be like pushing a marshmallow into the slot of a piggy bank, a frustrating and sticky situation. A vague policy is akin to having no policy at all. Aim to produce a policy that lies between the two extremes.

ESSENTIAL POLICY ELEMENTS

Be sure to tell why the policy is necessary, define the terms that appear in it, identify the jobs affected, name the forbidden activities, describe the manner of enforcement, assign responsibilities, specify the sanctions, and describe treatment benefits.

Determine Organizational Necessity

The purpose of a policy must be compelling and reasonable. It is compelling when it describes drug abuse in terms of the damage it inflicts upon the organization. The reader of the policy should be able to understand why the policy is necessary. The policy's business necessity can be emphasized using insights as to the nature of the business. The organization's overall mission can be explicated along with an explanation of how illegal drug use detracts from its accomplishment. In putting the organizational necessity on paper, it may be helpful to think of examples of the adverse impact that abuse has had or could have on the attainment of the mission. Reports on file that document the damage caused by abuse, such as accident reports and workers' compensation records, may provide helpful background detail. Of particular value are case histories that support the policy's business necessity. Large numbers or particularly horrendous occurrences are neither necessary nor essential. A point worth considering is the principle that even one impaired employee presents an intolerable risk.

A policy is to a business organization what a constitution is to a government. It is the ultimate expression of how an organization

28

intends to carry out its affairs. A policy is never to be taken lightly, certainly not in the writing of it. A policy is brought into existence to meet a business purpose. When the purposes are many, as is often the case with a mature organization, the policies will be numerous. Purposes such as hiring without discrimination, operating ethically, protecting the environment, and protecting assets come immediately to mind as reasons for developing policies. The same applies to a policy aimed at maintaining a drug-free workplace, i.e., the policy must be based on an organizational necessity.

A number of necessities stand out: safety, productivity, reputation, information protection, loss prevention, and environmental protection. All are negatively impacted by abuse. For example, a company that manufactures toxic chemicals is concerned with safety; an assembly line company has a focus on productivity; an investment firm is concerned about reputation; an organization with major assets in sensitive data is likely to name information protection as a policy rationale and a company that handles gold and jewelry is likely to cite loss prevention as a reason for keeping drugs out of the workplace.

The policy for any of these organizations will explain the adverse impact of abuse on its operations. If drug testing is to be authorized by the policy, a very good reason must be spelled out as to why testing is appropriate and needed.

Define the Terms

Policy enforcement bogs down when meanings have not been made clear. For example, what does the policy mean when it says "drug abuse" or "illegal drug" or "detectable amount in the body system"? Terms like these can be interpreted in more than one way. In order to avoid confusion, the front end of the policy can include a section that defines all of the possibly confusing terms. After that has been done, the terms should be consistent throughout. For example, when drug abuse is meant, say "drug abuse" not "substance abuse" or "chemical abuse."

Following are examples of definitions that need to be nailed down in unambiguous language:

29

- Employee Assistance Program (EAP) means the Company-based counseling program that offers assessment, short-term counseling, and referral services to employees for drug problems, and monitors the progress of employees while in treatment.

- Employee Assistance Program Administrator means the individual responsible for ensuring the development, implementation, and review of the Company-based EAP.

- Employee Assistance Program Coordinator means the individual designated by the EAP Administrator to be responsible for implementing and operating the EAP by providing counseling, treatment, and education services to employees and supervisors regarding the EAP.

- Medical Review Officer means the individual responsible for receiving test results from the drug testing laboratory. The MRO is a licensed physician with knowledge of drug abuse disorders and the appropriate medical training to interpret and evaluate positive test results together with an individual's medical history and any other relevant biomedical information.

- Illegal Drugs means a controlled substance included in Schedule I or II, as defined by section 802(6) of Title 21 of the United States Code, the possession of which is unlawful under chapter 13 of that Title. The term "illegal drugs" does not mean the use of a controlled substance pursuant to a valid prescription or other uses authorized by law.

- Random Testing means a system of drug testing imposed without individualized suspicion that a particular individual is using illegal drugs, and may either be uniform, unannounced testing, or statistically random sampling based on a neutral criterion such as social security numbers.

- Supervisor means an employee having authority to hire, direct, assign, promote, reward, transfer, furlough, lay off, recall, suspend, discipline, or remove other employees, to adjust their grievances, or to effectively recommend such action, if the exercise of the authority is not merely routine or clerical in nature, but requires the consistent exercise of independent judgment.

- Verified Positive Test Result means a test result that was positive on an initial immunoassay test, confirmed by a gas chromatography/mass spectrometry assay, and reviewed and verified by the Medical Review Officer.

Identify the Affected Jobs

If the policy is based solely on a safety rationale and includes testing, it logically follows that testing will be done only of those persons holding safety-sensitive jobs. It does not make sense to drug test a file clerk when the policy is based on safety-sensitive work occurring at construction sites. Legal hassles inevitably arise when a policy is based on a business necessity that cannot be served by drug testing. A policy based on one reason but authorizing drug testing for a different reason will land an employer in hot water.

When a workplace includes contractors, subcontractors, and vendors the policy will need to specifically state that those job groups fall under the policy. The written agreements under which non-employees enter the workplace should also reference adherence to the drug-free policy.

In a company regulated by the U.S. Department of Transportation (DOT), drug testing will apply to certain employees, and a policy for those employees will need to be in place. In that same company; other employees not subject to DOT rules may also need to be tested but testing of them cannot be conducted under the authority of DOT rules. The best advice in such a case, is to write separate policies.

Any action affecting jobs in a unionized company will have to be very carefully scrutinized. The support of a labor organization is often proportional to the early participation of union leadership in planning and design. An employer would do well to include bargaining unit representatives every step of the way; certainly during program implementation when it is essential to build employee confidence and obtain their willing cooperation. Equally important is the assurance given to a union that the personal dignity and privacy of employees will be respected in every aspect of the program.

Describe the Prohibited Activities

The behaviors typically forbidden by a drug-free workplace policy include using, possessing, selling, or transferring illicit drugs, or being on the job with a detectable amount of an illicit drug in the body's system. Examples of unacceptable behaviors help get the message across.

A policy might also prohibit the possession at work of drug-related paraphernalia such as coke spoons, hash bongs, and other items that administer illicit drugs.

The policy should specify the drugs for which employees are to be tested. In the federal sector, the drugs looked for are alcohol, marijuana, cocaine, amphetamines, opiates, and phencyclidine (PCP). An organization not subject to the federal government's drug-free workplace rules, may want to name other drugs, e.g., drugs that were identified in the needs assessment conducted prior to policy development.

Name the Enforcement Actions

The controls that will be put in place to detect policy violations and the actions the company will take in response to violations need to be explained. Controls can include, for example, screening of employee-owned containers being carried in to the premises, unannounced inspections of the workplace, observations by supervisors of work in progress, and automatic investigation of accidents, near-miss accidents, and violations of safety rules. When testing is a component of the program, job applicants can be screened for drugs; employees can be tested on periodic, unannounced, random, and reasonable cause bases; and employees in drug rehabilitation can be tested to monitor abstinence.

Assign Responsibilities

A responsibility not assigned is a responsibility very likely to go unperformed. Clarity and specificity can help greatly when stating who is to do what. For example, the policy might state: "The Human Resources Manager, in consultation with the Employee Assistance Program Coordinator, is charged with overseeing drug testing" or "The Safety Manager will provide to the Human Resources Manager an up-to-date listing of all safety-sensitive positions so that persons performing in such positions will be subject to the testing program" or "The Security Manager will establish and maintain an inspection program at the entry points to company premises. The program will be designed to keep out of the premises all items proscribed by this policy, e.g., illicit drugs and drug paraphernalia." The details of performance need not be identified. They can be enumerated in the operating procedures of the departments charged with carrying out the policy.

Identify the Penalties for Violations

The range of penalties for each policy violation need to be stated unequivocally. A common, and often regrettable error, is to leave open to question the possibility that penalties will not apply in every case. Even when it is management's intention to judge every violation according to its unique circumstances, the policy should make abundantly clear that every violation has a range of adverse actions. It is wise to also stress, and live up to, the proposition that similar punishments will be routinely administered for similar violations.

The policy needs to discuss the consequences of a positive drug test and of a refusal to take or cooperate with the administration of tests. The other side of this coin is a discussion of the opportunities available to an employee for explaining why his or her test showed positive and how to file an appeal or grievance.

Very much of interest in the policy will be the return to duty of an employee who has been found to be a user of an illegal drug. If in a safety-sensitive position (i.e., a testing-designated position), the employee should be removed from that position immediately. If the employee enters or completes a treatment program, some discretion is possible in respect to allowing the employee to resume safety-sensitive work. The overriding question is: "Will the return to duty of this employee create a danger to himself or to any other person?" Only when the answer is a conclusive no, should the discretion be granted.

Identify Treatment and Rehabilitation Benefits

An employer may be making a wise investment when offering treatment and rehabilitation benefits to employees who wish to resolve their personal drug abuse problems. Retaining a productive employee may be reason enough to provide assistance in lieu of automatic termination. If your company's economic situation does not allow the provision of such benefits, the policy might provide for continued employment or return to employment of employees who at personal expense undergo successful therapy in company-approved programs.

An employee assistance program plays an important role when it demonstrates a firm commitment to eliminating drug abuse. The commitment is evident when an EAP:

- Provides employees with help to discontinue their drug use, e.g., counsel employees who self-refer for treatment or whose drug tests have been verified positive, and monitor progress through treatment and rehabilitation.

- Provides educational materials to supervisors and employees on drug use issues, e.g., instruct employees at all levels concerning drug addiction, the types and effects of drugs, symptoms of abuse, the impact of abuse on performance and conduct, relationship of the EAP to testing, and treatment, rehabilitation, and confidentiality issues.

- Assists supervisors in the handling of employees who have performance and/or conduct problems and making referrals to treatment and rehabilitative facilities.

- Tracks the progress of individuals during their rehabilitation period and encourages them toward successful completion.

- Ensures that test results and related information are maintained with strict confidentiality.

An EAP works best when it is administered separately from a testing program and is available to all employees without regard to a finding of abuse. An enhanced EAP will be open to the families of employees. Experience and common sense tell us that drug abuse is contagious. Family support is essential to the effective treatment and recovery of a drug-abusing employee, and a non-abusing employee who lives with a drug-abusing family member most likely will not be able carry out work duties to full potential.

In the final analysis, the drug-abusing employee is responsible for successful completion of treatment. Assertions that the EAP failed to deliver an efficacious service should not constitute either an excuse for continued abuse or a defense to disciplinary action if the employee does not complete treatment.

THE WORKING DRAFT

Carte blanche adoption of another company's already existing policy can be tempting but has to be resisted. There is no such a thing as a generic drug abuse policy. Another company's policy can serve as a model. It would need, however, to be revised to incorporate differentiating characteristics.

Your Unique Characteristics

Asking the following questions can help:

- Do you have an Employee Assistance Program?

- Do you have a program for referring employees to psychiatric and/or psychological counseling, or to medical resources?

- Will your medical benefits program cover medical treatment and counseling of drug abusers? If so, will the benefits be available only to employees who voluntarily seek assistance or will "detected employees" also be given the benefits?

- Will you want to make referrals for treatment or counseling? If so, will the costs be at your expense or the employee's full or partial expense?

- Do you want to encourage employees with drug-related health problems to voluntarily seek assistance through a confidential program? If so, who is going to pay?

- Do you want everyone to be tested? If so, on what grounds? Safety? Security? Company reputation? Other?

- If only certain employees are to be tested, do you have documentation to support your reasons for testing those certain employees?

- Will you always immediately terminate employees whose urine tests result in a positive reading? If no, will the persons be required to undergo rehabilitation? Who will pay for the rehabilitation?

- Would you like the option to immediately terminate even though you might not always exercise that option?

- What are the differences that mean one employee is terminated upon a positive test result, but another person is not? (It is extremely important that punishment be uniformly and routinely handed out for like offenses.)

- If immediate termination of employees whose urine tests result in positive findings is not to be effected, what other alternatives will be used? Termination after an administrative hearing? Demotion? Forced retirement? Forced resignation? Transfer to another position? Other?

- When will the first collection of urine samples be scheduled? (There should be at least 30 days between implementation of the policy and the first collection.)

- What will be the appeals process for an employee who tests positive?

- What will be the penalties for:

    - Possession of drugs on premises?

    - Storing of drugs on premises?

    - Swapping/trading/loaning of drugs on premises?

    - Selling of drugs on premises?

    - Using drugs on premises?

- Under what circumstances will law enforcement be notified?

- Do you want the policy to mention other options, such as searches of the workplace?

- Do you want to combine drug and alcohol abuse in the same policy?

- Are you subject to any state or federal laws that apply to a drug-free workplace? If so, your policy will need to be tailored to meet the requirements of those laws.

- Are you subject to any federal drug testing rules, such as those that apply to companies subject to regulation by the Department of Transportation, Department of Defense, and Department of Energy? If so, the policy will need to take these rules into consideration.

- Are any of your employees union workers? You may want to bring union representatives into the policy drafting process.

- In which of the following situations do you want the policy to include drug screening?

WRITE THE POLICY

- Pre-employment.

- Post-accident.

- Annual physicals.

- When behavior/performance suggests drug abuse.

- When employees are enrolled in drug rehabilitation.

- On a random basis.

- On a periodic basis.

- During or at the end of the probationary period.

- At time of reinstatement.

- If you plan to conduct random or periodic screening, how frequently will you do it? Quarterly? Semi-annually? What will be the technique for selecting employees for testing on a random basis?

- Will you retain a third party to perform any of the services related to the policy? For example:

  - Drafting the policy.

  - Reviewing the policy for legal sufficiency.

  - Announcing the policy to employees/public.

  - Making employees aware of the health and disciplinary consequences of drug abuse.

  - Preparing supervisors and managers to detect and properly respond to on-the-job drug abuse.

- Developing written procedures that set out responsibilities in clear and unambiguous detail.

- Collecting urine specimens.

- Testing urine specimens.

- Conducting blind performance testing to evaluate the drug testing laboratory's quality assurance program.

- Storing urine specimens.

- Maintaining files and preparing summaries of test results.

- Will urine collections be done by:

  - the direct observation method?

  - dry bathroom method?

  - modified dry bathroom method?

  - using supplemental checks such as

    - temperature measurement?

    - color evaluation?

    - specific gravity?

- What will be the consequences if an applicant/employee refuses to provide a specimen or to cooperate?

- What department in the company will be assigned responsibility for administering the policy?

- Will the company use its existing resources or obtain resources in support of the policy? For example:

- Provide training/education on an ongoing basis to maintain a continuing awareness by employees and supervisors of individual responsibilities.

- Counsel employees who are self-referred or referred by supervisors.

- Perform follow-up evaluations of rehabilitated employees.

A Right and an Obligation

An employer has both a right and an obligation to maintain a safe and healthy workplace. A potential for disagreement, however, will always occur when unreasonable methods are applied in exercising the right and obligation. Simply put, a goal of orderliness in the workplace can't be challenged, but the tactics taken in achieving that goal are very much subject to challenge.

Here are some policy hints that can help avoid challenges:

- A positive test result is not evidence of a crime. It is not illegal to have a drug in the body's system. Make a distinction between employees who test positive and those who are caught using, possessing, distributing, or selling illicit drugs.

- Treat drug test results as confidential information. Collect and keep only what you have to keep. Segment confidential information and keep it under lock and key.

- Do not force employees to consent to a drug test. Employees who refuse can be made subject to disciplinary action, including discharge, provided that the policy allows it.

- If employees are selected for testing on a random basis, care must be taken to avoid the appearance of discrimination. A selection technique that appears to focus on race, sex, or lifestyle can lead to discrimination complaints.

- If certain job positions are selected for testing, document a relationship between the performance of the jobs and the effect of drug abuse.

- If the company is unionized, develop the policy with union input and modify the union contract as needed.

- Use a qualified laboratory to make tests, and ensure that test methods are state-of-the-art. For example, select an immunoassay method for preliminary screening, and confirm positives using the gas chromatography/mass spectrometry method.

- Obtain a consent from each tested employee at the point of collection. Don't rely on a "timeless" consent given by the employee at an earlier time, e.g., when the policy was first announced.

- Take precautions in the collecting of specimens to prevent contamination, switching, and mislabeling. Initiate chain of custody documentation at the time of collection.

- Avoid charges that the drug testing program is "rigged." When specimens are collected and/or tested by company employees, the door is opened to claims that the program is being used to generate false accusations against certain employees or groups such as minorities. A third party vendor can be used to make witnessed collections of specimens, analyze specimens, maintain drug test records, and provide storage of positive specimens that may be needed for future litigation.

- Notify employees who test positive and allow them to confer with a supervisor or manager. Recognize that a positive test result does not automatically mean illicit drug abuse. For example, an employee may have neglected to declare that he had been taking prescribed medication immediately prior to the test. An opportunity to explain and a re-examination of the specimen would verify the employee's claim.

- Enforce the policy consistently and uniformly. Don't allow the policy to merely exist on paper. Apply fairness when administering discipline. Inform affected employees of the appeals process.

The Centrality of Testing

You have surely noticed by now the centrality of testing in drug abuse prevention. Testing clearly works, and works best when combined with an employee assistance component. It will not alone be the full answer. In the hands of an enlightened employer, testing can be an invaluable tool for uncovering the source of work-related problems and for indicating needed management intervention. And, yes, testing does present a risk but one that can be worth taking when committed to doing it right.

Let's look at some ideas for reducing risk in a prevention program that features testing:

- Examine rates of absenteeism, turnover, accidents, theft, compensation and medical claims, problems in supervision, product waste/loss, morale, and other factors that indicate abuse. Do not merely be satisfied with a finding that abuse exists; attempt to find out what drugs are being abused, by what groups of employees, at what locations, when, and under what circumstances. Consider this information when formulating your policy.

- Anticipate the impact that a drug abuse program is likely to have on your non-abusing employees, the union, the public, and your stockholders.

- If unionized, inform the union representative of the policy/program and include him or her, if practical, in the development process. Bargain as may be necessary, and keep the union representative aware of any upcoming changes to and application of policy to union employees.

- Anticipate the possibility of grievances and legal claims. Consult with counsel and be prepared to deal with those situations.

- Consider interfacing the drug abuse program with medical, EAP, and employee self-help programs. Identify the costs and alternatives. The alternatives may include readily available tax-funded services in the community.

- Decide what actions you will take in response to policy violations. Establish a range of responses that are appropriate to violations. Administer the responses uniformly and fairly. When termination is the appropriate response, set up an administrative mechanism designed to ensure that any termination action is reviewed by a senior manager, a human resources specialist, and legal counsel.

- Announce the program in every conceivable way. At a minimum publish it for appearance in employee manuals, on bulletin boards, in memos, and make it a major topic at employee meetings.

- Provide an amnesty period of 30 to 60 days before conducting drug testing. This will allow drug-abusing employees time to rid their systems of drugs.

- During the amnesty period inform workers as to the reasons for the program, the disciplinary consequences of violations, and the health and safety risks of drug abuse.

- Following the amnesty period, continue to communicate your concerns to the employees.

- Emphasize to employees that consenting to take a drug test is a condition of employment. Require newly hired employees to sign a form stating they agree to be tested when asked and that they understand that a refusal to be tested or a positive test finding will subject them to disciplinary action.

- Require job applicants to acknowledge in writing that being hired is dependent upon passing the drug test.

- Develop procedures for dealing with employees whose legitimate use of prescribed drugs may conflict with safety or other requirements.

- Prepare supervisors, preferably prior to or during the amnesty period, in how to identify the drugs of abuse and related paraphernalia, and how to intervene in on-the-job situations that indicate drug abuse.

- Develop a capability for collecting urine specimens from the job applicants/employees who are subject to testing. Create an in-house resource or engage a third party vendor. In either option, ensure that the collecting procedures include strict chain of custody documentation, and guard against switching, contamination, mislabeling, improper packaging, handling by unauthorized persons, administrative error, and other circumstances that can lead to grievances and legal challenge.

- Engage a qualified, competent laboratory to conduct the tests. A federally-certified laboratory should be selected.

- Never threaten or coerce someone to take a drug test.

- Maintain strict confidentiality of test results.

- Be careful in deciding who is to be tested. Avoid even the appearance of discrimination. A reasonable, articulable justification must exist for each person tested. The reasons may vary, but in every instance there should be a justification based on a reasonable business necessity.

- Establish documentation of:

  - Why the program was necessary.

  - Why certain employees were selected for testing.

  - How the program was announced.

  - Training provided to supervisors.

- The types of tests conducted.

- Discipline that was administered.

Blueprint Your Policy With a Worksheet

Drafting a policy with the aid of a worksheet can help ensure that key points have been addressed.

Following is a worksheet that may be helpful:

Section One: General Issues

A Policy Based on DOT Rules

Policy provisions that are based on the authority of DOT rules must exactly correspond to those rules. However, a policy can include provisions based on the authority of management. These provisions can set rules for the employees who are not DOT-regulated, and they can set rules for all employees, including the DOT-regulated employees.

If this policy is being prepared pursuant to DOT drug testing rules, which rules apply?

- Trucking?

- Railroad?

- Pipeline?

- Marine?

- Urban Mass Transit?

- Aviation?

Will the policy cover:

- Only the DOT-regulated employees? If you select this option, are you sure you want to exclude the non-DOT employees from rules that regulate activities such as being at work in a drug-impaired condition or distributing drugs at work? Explain:

  _____

  _____

- The DOT-regulated employees plus certain classes or groups of other non-DOT employees but not all employees (such as secretaries)? If you select this option, identify the classes or groups of employees to be covered. Instead of naming all such jobs, use a single term like "safety-sensitive positions" or "persons holding designated jobs." Provide a term and define it. The term will appear in the definitions section of the policy.

  _____

  _____

- The DOT-regulated employees plus all other employees? If you selected either of the options above, the policy will have a main section that covers the DOT-regulated employees and another main section that addresses non-DOT employees. It will be helpful to include a third main section which relates to all employees, regardless of DOT status. In the absence of such a section, the policy is likely to provide disparate (and potentially discriminatory) treatment of employees; for example, the DOT employees might not be subject to testing for alcohol or for certain drug classes while the non-DOT employees would be. A third section covering all employees would provide uniform provisions for everyone. The net result would be to administer the policy to all affected employees, by authority of management's prerogative to set work rules, and at the same time administer the policy to the DOT-regulated employees by authority of DOT regulations.

Testing Pursuant to Other Requirements

Is this policy being prepared to meet requirements of the Drug-Free Workplace Act?

- Yes

- No

If yes, do you want the policy to additionally include drug testing or any other policy provisions that are not mandated by the Act? Provide a general explanation below and use other sections of this worksheet to provide the specifics of such provisions.

_____

_____

Is this policy being prepared pursuant to the drug-free workplace requirements of a state workers' compensation law?

- Yes

- No

If yes, do you want the policy to additionally include drug testing or any other policy provisions that are not mandated? Provide a general explanation below and use other sections of this worksheet to provide the specifics of such provisions, e.g., testing, rehabilitation, etc.

_____

_____

If there is this some other reason why this policy is being prepared, explain below.

_____

_____

WRITE THE POLICY

Name of the Policy

What name do you want to give to the policy?

_____

_____

On-Site Drug Screening

In work organizations where safety issues demand the most rapid turnaround time, there may be justification for conducting initial (unconfirmed) tests. Such programs are not easily nor inexpensively developed and maintained. Further, they carry risks to an employer who takes actions based on drug tests that have not been confirmed.

If you plan to conduct on-site, initial screening, describe the testing technique and describe the safeguards for accuracy, e.g., chain of custody, specimen splitting, open and blind proficiency sampling, cut-off concentrations, confirmation by a DHHS-certified laboratory, and medical review of test results.

_____

_____

_____

_____

_____

_____

Section Two: Policy Issues That Apply in Non-DOT Testing

Reasonable Business Necessity

The reasonable business necessity for drug testing will often rely on management's obligation to provide a safe working environment. Safety is also the rationale for the DOT drug testing rules. If your policy is to include testing under the DOT rules, it is appropriate for the overall rationale to be safety.

Is safety your rationale for drug testing?

- Yes

- No

Do you want to cite any of these other reasonable business necessities?

- National security

- Productivity

- Assets protection/loss prevention

- Preservation of company image or reputation

- Health of the employees

- Protection of proprietary information

- Contractual obligations

Drug Testing or Drug and Alcohol Testing

The policy will provide for:

- Drug testing only.

- Drug and alcohol testing.

Activities That Will Be Prohibited

The following activities are typically prohibited. They are also offenses for which termination is appropriate.

Circle the activities and discipline if you agree, or enter your choices on the Comment line.

- Use on the job or on the premises of (illegal drugs) (alcohol)

- Disciplinary action: (May) (Will) Discharge

- Comment: _____

- Possession of (illegal drugs) (drug paraphernalia) (alcohol)

  - Disciplinary Action: (May) (Will) Discharge

  - Comment: _____

- Sale of (illegal drugs) (drug paraphernalia) (alcohol)

  - Disciplinary Action: (May) (Will) Discharge

  - Comment: _____

- Transfer/distribution of (illegal drugs) (drug paraphernalia) (alcohol)

  - Disciplinary Action: (May) (Will) Discharge

  - Comment: _____

- Possession in the body system of any detectable amount of illegal drugs.

  - Disciplinary Action: (May) (Will) Discharge

  - Comment: _____

- Possession in the body system of alcohol at a level of (.05) (.10) as measured by a standard blood alcohol concentration test.

  - Disciplinary Action: (May) (Will) Discharge

  - Comment: _____

- Refusal to take a drug test or refusal to cooperate in a drug test.

  - Disciplinary Action: (May) (Will) Discharge

  - Comment: _____

Circumstances in Which Testing Will Be Required

Circle the situations in which testing will be conducted:

- Pre-employment (Drugs) (Alcohol)

- Following an accident (Drugs) (Alcohol)

- Following a near accident (Drugs) (Alcohol)

- As part of a routine health evaluation (Drugs) (Alcohol)

- Reasonable cause (Drugs) (Alcohol)

- (During) (Following) rehabilitation (Drugs) (Alcohol)

- Random selection basis (Drugs) (Alcohol)

- Periodically for (all) (selected) employees (Drugs) (Alcohol)

- (During) (at the end of) a probationary period (Drugs) (Alcohol)

- At time of return from prolonged absence (Drugs) (Alcohol)

- Other: _____

Appeal of a Positive Drug Test Result

An employee whose drug test is reported positive will have the opportunity:

- To obtain the remaining portion of the urine specimen so that it can be independently tested at

  - (the employee's expense) or

  - (the Company's expense).

- To a review of the test findings by a licensed physician with knowledge of drug abuse disorders at

  - (the employee's expense) or

  - (the Company's expense).

- To a private meeting with designated Company officials.

- Other: _____

If an employee's challenge or explanation of a positive drug test merits further inquiry, the employee for the duration of the inquiry will be:

- Suspended

  - (with) or

  - (without) pay.

- Returned to work in a non-safety sensitive position.

- Other: _____

Rehabilitation

You may not find it appropriate in every case to discharge the offending employee. For example, rather than discharge an employee for testing positive in a random test, you may want to give the employee an opportunity to retain employment status or be re-hired contingent upon completing a program of rehabilitation.

Rehabilitation in lieu of discharge may be offered:

- When the employee has requested rehabilitation and the request is unrelated to an identification of the employee as a violator of the policy.

- When the violation does not involve selling or distributing drugs or serious misconduct.

- When the employee agrees to undergo rehabilitation

  - (in a rehabilitation program that has been pre-approved by the Company)

  - (in a rehabilitation program)

The costs of rehabilitation will be:

- At no expense to the Company.

- Paid for by the Company only within the limits of the medical benefits provided in the employee's sick pay plan.

- Other: _____

During the period of rehabilitation, the employee will be:

- Discharged but eligible for re-hire

  - (at the end of successful rehabilitation)

  - (not sooner than _____ months following successful rehabilitation.)

- Suspended

  - (with pay) or

  - (without pay)

- Other: _____

WRITE THE POLICY

Education and Training

A drug testing policy will typically call for an education/awareness component designed to inform all employees of the health and disciplinary consequences of drug and/or alcohol abuse, and a component for training supervisors in how to recognize the indicators of drug and/or alcohol and how to intervene effectively.

Do you want the policy to call for

- Drug and/or alcohol abuse education/awareness?

- Training for supervisors?

Section Three: Optional Issues

In previous sections you indicated your preferences concerning issues that are typically addressed in a balanced, reasonable policy. Following are some pertinent issues that you may want to include as well. If they are not addressed in the policy, they at least deserve to be spelled out in implementing procedures or other written documents that control the organization's drug-free workplace program. Consider these issues for inclusion in the policy and indicate your desires.

Notification to Applicants/Employees of Test Results

Drug test results, including the identity of any drugs that may have been discovered, can be made known to job applicants, if they request such notice within 60 days of being tested. This option is (accepted) (rejected).

Drug test results of all positive tests pertaining to employees can be made known to the employees, including the identity of the drugs discovered. This option is (accepted) (rejected).

Announcement of the Policy

Do you want to specify in the policy how the policy will be made known to the affected employees?

- Yes. The methods for notifying employees of the policy will include:

- Giving to each employee a copy of the policy.

- Obtaining a written acknowledgement from each employee that the policy has been received and read.

- Other: _____

- No.

Searches

A search in this context could be an unannounced search conducted of some or all employees at some or all work locations for the purpose of enforcing the policy. A search could also be conducted of a particular employee or group of employees based on reasonable cause information.

Do you want the policy to authorize:

- unannounced searches?

- reasonable cause searches?

Amnesty

Amnesty is appropriate when a testing program first starts or is significantly changed. An amnesty period allows employees who may be using drugs to discontinue use before a drug testing program is first put into effect. A 30 or 60 day period is standard. Amnesty does not apply to job applicants or employees who are to be tested following an accident or near accident, or for reasonable cause.

An amnesty period is (desired) (not desired). The amnesty period desired is (30) (60) days.

Selection of a Laboratory

Selection of a laboratory certified by the U.S. Department of Health and Human Services is critical to the reliability and accuracy of test results and to the legal defensibility of a drug and/or alcohol testing program. DOT rules require use of a DHHS-certified laboratory. If you have a mix of DOT and non-DOT employees, it would be practical to have all testing done by the same DHHS-certified laboratory.

Do you want the policy to prescribe selection of a DHHS-certified laboratory?

- Yes

- No

Drugs of Interest

The DOT rules call for tests that seek to identify five classes of drugs: opiates, cocaine, marijuana, amphetamines, and phencyclidine (PCP). Nearly all drug testing conducted outside of the DOT rules involve tests for other drugs of abuse as well, e.g., benzodiazepines, barbiturates, methadone, methaqualone and propoxyphene.

Do you want to test the non-DOT employees:

- Only for the five drugs specified by DOT?

- For the five drugs specified by DOT plus other drugs?

Remember you have the option of testing the DOT employees under the authority of the DOT rules and testing them separately under the authority of company rules.

Methods of Testing

DOT rules require strict adherence to federal drug testing standards. These standards assure the highest level of accuracy and are the best defense against legal challenges. Methods of testing that do not conform to the standards are generally viewed as inferior, and therefore open to challenge.

If your testing program is not required to conform to the standards and you wish to select non-conforming methods of testing, name the methods for both initial screening and confirmatory testing.

If your testing program follows the federal standards in some cases (when testing employees, for example) but uses non-federal testing in other cases (when testing job applicants, for example), so indicate.

_____

_____

Medical Review of Test Results

Medical review is a procedure to determine if a positive drug test could have resulted from something other than illegal drug use. Many organizations use medical review because they believe it enhances their programs and provides a safeguard against the possibility of false-positive test results.

Medical review is mandatory in DOT testing. If some of your employees are subject to DOT testing, it may be practical for you to select medical review for all employees.

Do you want the policy to prescribe medical review?

- Yes

- No

Section Four: Follow-Up Issues

Development of a written policy is only a first step in establishing a drug-free workplace. Plan to take these action steps after the policy has been developed:

- Write detailed procedures that support the policy.

- Announce the policy.

- Educate employees and train supervisors.

- Contract with a vendor to collect specimens.

- Contract with a drug testing laboratory.

- Set up a medical review procedure for positive results.

- Establish a linkage with EAP and treatment professionals.

- Keep records and prepare summaries of progress.

A Sample Policy

A good way to close out this chapter is to present a sample policy. The policy presented happens to be one that a DOT-regulated pipeline company would use.

Drug and Alcohol Abuse Policy

I. Purpose

A. The chief purpose of this policy is to reduce accidents, fatalities, injuries, and property damage that result from use of illegal drugs and alcohol by employees who work at pipeline facilities involved in the transportation of natural gas, LPG, and/or hazardous liquids and at liquefied natural gas facilities.

B. This policy is also intended to promote overall a safe, healthful, and efficient working environment for all employees. Being under the influence of an illegal drug or alcohol on the job poses serious safety and health risks to the user and to all those who work with the user. The use, sale, purchase, transfer, or possession of an illegal drug in the workplace, and the use, possession, or being under the influence of alcohol also poses unacceptable risks for safe, healthful, and efficient operations.

C. The Company recognizes its contractual obligations to its clients for the provision of services that are free of the influence of illegal drugs and alcohol, and will endeavor through this policy to provide such drug-free services.

D. Furthermore, the Company takes note of requirements to comply with Research and Special Programs Administration (RSPA) and Department of Transportation (DOT) regulations relating to illegal drug use and will endeavor through this policy to maintain compliance.

II. Definitions

As used in this policy:

"Accident" means an incident reportable under Part 191 of Title 49 of the Code of Federal Regulations involving gas pipeline facilities or LNG facilities, or an accident reportable under Part 195 of the Code of Federal Regulations involving hazardous liquid facilities, to include vehicle accidents in the course and scope of business as required by Company management, or any incident or accident required by Company management to be investigated.

"Alcohol" means any beverage that contains ethyl alcohol (ethanol), including but not limited to beer, wine, and distilled spirits.

"Biological testing" or "chemical testing" or "drug testing" or "testing" means the scientific analysis of urine, blood, breath, saliva, hair, tissue, and other specimens of the human body for the purpose of detecting a drug or alcohol.

"Collection site" means a place where individuals present themselves for the purpose of providing body fluid or tissue specimens. A collection site will have all necessary personnel, materials, equipment, facilities, and supervision to provide for the collection, security, temporary storage, and transportation or shipment of the samples to a laboratory.

"Company premises or Company facilities" means all property of the Company, including but not limited to buildings and surrounding areas on Company-owned or leased property, parking lots, and storage areas. The term also includes Company-owned or leased vehicles and equipment wherever located. It also includes premises where the Company performs contract services.

"Contraband" means any article, the possession of which on Company premises or while on Company business, causes an employee to be in violation of a Company work rule. Contraband includes illegal drugs and alcoholic beverages, and drug paraphernalia.

"Controlled substances" has the meaning assigned by 21 USC 802 and includes all substances listed on Schedules I through V as they may be revised from time to time.

"DOT Procedures" means those procedures published by the Office of the Secretary of Transportation.

"Drug" means any substance (other than alcohol) that is a controlled substance as defined in this policy.

"Illegal drug" means any drug which is not legally obtainable; any drug which is legally obtainable but has not been legally obtained; any prescribed drug not legally obtained; any prescribed drug not being used for the prescribed purpose; any over-the-counter drug being used at a dosage level different than recommended by the manufacturer or being used for a purpose other than intended by the manufacturer; and any drug being used for a purpose not in accordance with bona fide medical therapy. Examples of illegal drugs are Cannabis substances, such as marijuana and hashish, cocaine, heroin, phencyclidine (PCP), and so-called designer drugs and look-alike drugs.

"Legal drug" means any prescribed drug or over-the-counter drug which has been legally obtained and is being used for the purpose for which prescribed or manufactured.

"Medical practitioner" means a licensed doctor of medicine (MD) or osteopathy (DO) or a doctor of dental surgery (DDS) authorized to practice by the state in which the person practices.

"Medical review officer" means a licensed doctor of medicine or osteopathy with knowledge of drug abuse disorders. The MRO has the knowledge and medical training to interpret and evaluate an individual's positive test result together with his/her medical history and any other relevant biomedical information.

"Operator" means a person who owns or operates pipeline facilities subject to Part 192, 193, or 195 of Title 49 of the Code of Federal

Regulations. Not included for coverage in this policy are operators of "master meter systems" as defined in Part 191, Title 49 of the Code of Federal Regulations.

"Possession" is meant to also include the presence in the body system of any detectable amount of drug.

"Random testing" means a testing process in which selection for testing is made by a method employing objective, neutral criteria which ensures that every person subject to testing has a substantially equal statistical chance of being selected. The method does not permit subjective factors to play a role in selection, i.e., no person may be selected as the result of discretion.

"Rehabilitation committee" means the individuals who develop and determine an employee's rehabilitation plan and a schedule for the employee's return to work.

"Reasonable cause" means a belief that the actions or appearance or conduct of a person are indicative of the use of an illegal drug or alcohol. Such a belief is based on objective, articulable facts. A reasonable cause or "for cause" situation is any situation in which an employee's job performance is in conflict with established job standards relating to safety and efficiency. The term includes accidents, near accidents, erratic conduct suggestive of drug or alcohol use, any unsafe performance behaviors, and unexplained deviations from productivity.

"RSPA" means the Research and Special Programs Administration of the U.S. Department of Transportation.

"Under the influence" means a condition in which a person is affected by a drug or alcohol in any detectable manner. The symptoms of influence are not confined to those consistent with misbehavior, nor to obvious impairment of physical or mental ability, such as slurred speech or difficulty in maintaining balance. A determination of being under the influence can be established by a professional opinion, a scientifically valid test, such as urinalysis or blood analysis, and in some cases by the opinion of a layperson.

WRITE THE POLICY

III. Affected Persons

A. Compliance by all employees is mandatory, except when compliance would violate the domestic laws of another country while in the other country.

B. This policy applies to contractors and persons employed by contractors. The Company will require by contract that contractors provide to their employees drug testing, education, and training that conform to this policy, and allow the Company reasonable access to inspection of property and records for the purpose of monitoring compliance.

D. This policy establishes two drug testing plans: (1) testing subject to DOT requirements (called the DOT Plan), and (2) testing subject to the Company's requirements (called the Company's Plan).

IV. Testing in Accordance with the Company's Plan

A. General

1. Testing under the provisions of the Company's Plan will be performed separate and independent of testing conducted pursuant to DOT requirements and RSPA rules.

B. Testing of Job Applicants

1. If the applicant refuses to take a test, the employment process will be suspended.

2. If an applicant attempts to substitute or contaminate his or her specimen to be tested, the employment process will be suspended.

3. If an applicant fails to pass the test, the employment process will be suspended.

C. Testing of Current Employees

1. The Company may, in addition to testing employees in every manner as prescribed by DOT regulations, test said employees for any reason at the discretion of the Company.

2. An employee's consent to submit to testing is required as a condition of employment and the employee's refusal to consent may result in disciplinary action, including discharge, for a first refusal or any subsequent refusal.

3. An employee who is tested for any reason other than for random testing may be suspended without pay pending completion of whatever inquiries may be required.

V. Testing in Accordance with the DOT Plan

A. General

1. The provisions of the DOT Plan apply only to DOT designated employees. DOT designated employees, when drug tested for purposes of conforming with DOT regulations, shall be tested with precise conformance with DOT drug testing regulations and RSPA rules. DOT designated employees, however, may at any time and for any reason be subject to drug testing conducted by the Company in accordance with the Company's Plan.

2. DOT designated employees will be instructed as to whether their test is conducted pursuant to the DOT Plan or the Company's Plan.

3. An employee subject to DOT Testing is a person who performs on a pipeline or LNG facility an operating, maintenance, or emergency-response function. This includes clerical, truck driving, accounting, or other functions that may from time to time be subject to regulation by Parts 192, 193, or 195 of Title 49 of the Code of Federal Regulations.

4. An employee subject to the provisions of the DOT Plan may be a person employed by the operator, a contractor engaged by the operator or an employee of such contractor.

B. Program and Procedures

1. Any program or procedures resulting from the DOT Plan will conform to this policy, the DOT Procedures, and RSPA rules. In the event of conflict, the RSPA rules will prevail.

2. The Company will maintain and follow a program and procedures containing:

a. Methods and actions for complying with all the requirements of this policy, DOT Procedures and RSPA rules, including requirements with respect to the employee assistance program;

b. The name and address of each laboratory that analyzes the specimens collected for drug testing; and

c. The name and address of the medical review officer employed in the administration of drug testing under this section of the policy.

C. Drug Testing

1. Pre-employment Testing

a. The Company will not hire or contract for the use of any person as an employee whose functions are subject to DOT Procedures or RSPA rules unless that person passes a drug test or is covered by an anti-drug program that conforms to the requirements of the DOT Plan.

b. The Company will require, as a prequalification condition, drug testing of any applicant who the Company intends to hire or use, and any applicant will submit to testing as a prequalification condition.

c. Prior to collection of a urine sample, an applicant will be notified that the sample will be tested for the presence of certain controlled substances.

d. The provisions contained in the Company's Plan as relates to Testing of Job Applicants will apply to the DOT Plan as well.

2. Post-accident Testing

a. Each employee involved in an accident will, when directed, provide a urine specimen as soon as possible after an accident but in no case later than 32 hours after the accident. An employee involved in an accident is, in the discretion of the Company, any employee whose performance either contributed to the accident or cannot be completely discounted as a contributing factor.

b. An employee who is seriously injured and cannot provide a specimen at the time of the accident will provide the necessary authorization for obtaining hospital reports and other documents that would indicate whether there were any controlled substances in his/her system.

c. The specimens to be collected will be urine specimens.

d. The Company will ensure through its trained supervisors that the collected specimens are forwarded and processed by a laboratory in accordance with DOT Procedures and RSPA rules.

3. Random Testing

a. During the first 12 months following implementation of random drug testing, the Company will ensure that:

-The random drug testing is spread reasonably through the 12-month period;

-The last test collection during the year is conducted at an annualized rate of 50 percent; and

-The total number of tests conducted during the 12 months is equal to at least 25 percent of the employees subject to testing.

b. Starting in the 13th month following implementation of random drug testing, the Company will ensure that random drug testing is conducted on a monthly basis and that the number of employees tested each month will assure attainment of an annualized rate of 50 percent.

c. The Company will use a random selection process to select employees to be tested. The random selection process will utilize a random number table or a computer-based random number generator that is matched with a selected employee's social security number, payroll identification number, or other appropriate identification number.

d. An employee will submit to testing when selected by a random selection process.

4. Reasonable Cause Testing

a. The Company will require an employee to be tested, upon reasonable cause. The decision to test will be based on a reasonable and articulable belief that the employee is using a prohibited drug on the basis of specific, contemporaneous physical, behavioral, or performance indicators of probable drug use.

b. An employee will submit to testing, upon reasonable cause, when requested to do so by the Company.

c. The conduct which forms the basis for reasonable cause should be witnessed by at least two supervisors, if at all practicable. If only one supervisor is available, only one supervisor need witness the conduct. The witnesses must have received training in the detection of probable drug use.

d. The documentation of the employee's conduct will be prepared and signed by the witnesses within 24 hours of the observed behavior or before the results of the tests are released, whichever is earlier.

e. The Company will ensure that the employee is transported immediately to a collection site for the collection of a urine sample.

5. Testing After Rehabilitation

a. A person who returns to duty as an employee subject to DOT Procedures or RSPA rules will be subject to a reasonable program of follow-up drug testing without prior notice for not more than 60 months after return to duty.

D. Record Keeping

1. The Company will keep the following records for the periods specified and permit access to the records as provided by paragraph 2 of this section:

a. Records that demonstrate the collection process will be kept for 3 years.

b. Records of employee drug test results that show employees failed a drug test, and the type of test failed, and records that demonstrate rehabilitation, if any, will be kept for 5 years, and will include the following information pertaining to each employee who failed a drug test:

-The functions performed by the employee.

-The drugs which were used by the employee.

-The administrative or disciplinary action taken.

-The age of the employee.

c. Records of employee drug test results that show employees passed a drug test will be kept for 1 year.

d. A record of the number of employees tested, by type of test, will be kept for 5 years.

e. Records confirming that supervisors and employees have been trained as required by this policy will be kept for 3 years.

2. Information regarding an individual's drug testing results or rehabilitation may be released only upon the written consent of the individual, except that such information must be released regardless of consent to the RSPA or a state agency upon request as part of an accident investigation. Statistical data related to drug testing and rehabilitation that is not name-specific and training records must be made available to the RSPA or the appropriate state agency upon request.

VI. Matters Affecting All Employees

The following provisions apply to all employees irrespective of status relative to DOT Procedures and RSPA rules.

A. Prohibited Activities

1. The undisclosed use of any legal drug by any employee while performing Company business or while on Company premises is prohibited. However, an employee may continue to work, even though using a legal drug if Company management has determined, after consulting with appropriate health and/or human resources representatives, that such use does not pose a threat to safety and that the using employee's job performance will not be significantly affected. Otherwise, the employee may be required to take leave of absence or comply with other appropriate action as determined by Company management.

2. An employee whose medical therapy requires the use of a legal drug must report such use to his or her supervisor prior to the performance of Company business. The supervisor who is so informed will contact the appropriate health and/or human resources representative for guidance.

3. The Company at all times reserves the right to judge the effect that a legal drug may have upon work performance and to restrict the using employee's work activity or presence at the workplace accordingly.

4. The use, sale, offer to sell, purchase, offer to purchase, transfer, distribution, or possession in any detectable manner of an illegal drug or alcohol by any employee while on Company premises or while performing Company business is prohibited.

5. No employee shall be on duty if the employee uses any illegal drugs or alcohol or tests positive for the use of such substances, except as provided in the section titled Prescribed Drugs.

6. A person who tests positive for the use of an illegal drug or alcohol will be considered medically unqualified to work.

7. A person who refuses to be tested will not be permitted to work. Such refusal will be treated as a positive test and cause the employee to be considered medically unqualified to work.

B. Prescribed Drugs

1. Any employee who is alleged to have violated the section of this policy titled Drug Use Prohibitions will have available as an affirmative defense, to be proven by the employee through clear and convincing evidence, that his/her use of a controlled substance (except for methadone) was prescribed by a licensed medical practitioner who is familiar with the employee's medical history and assigned duties. The MRO may provide an opportunity for an employee to discuss a positive test result and clarify if a prescribed medication was involved.

2. This section does not release an employee from the requirement to notify the Company of therapeutic drug use.

C. Responsibilities

1. Each individual required to submit to drug testing shall, as soon as practicable, provide the required biological specimens for testing. Failure to meet this responsibility is an offense punishable by termination.

2. Individuals in supervisory positions shall, as soon as practicable following an incident which requires drug testing, collect the required biological specimens for testing and arrange for their prompt delivery or transfer to the drug testing laboratory. Failure to meet this responsibility is an offense punishable by termination.

D. Failure to Pass or Refusal to Take a Drug Test

1. The Company will not use as an employee any person:

    a. Whose drug test upon medical review has been determined to be positive; or

    b. Who refuses to take a drug test.

2. Paragraph 1, however, will not apply to an employee who:

    a. Has successfully completed a rehabilitation program and passed a drug test under DOT Procedures;

    b. Has been recommended by the medical review officer for return to duty as a result of the rehabilitation program; and

    c. Has not failed a drug test after the successful completion of a rehabilitation program.

E. Discipline

1. Disciplinary action consisting of discharge without benefit of rehabilitation may be applied to any employee who:

    a. Uses, possesses, distributes, transfers, conceals, sells, offers to sell, purchases, or offers to purchase illegal drugs on Company premises or on Company business.

    b. Substitutes or contaminates or makes attempts to substitute or contaminate a specimen to be presented for testing.

2. Disciplinary action up to and including discharge may be applied to any employee who:

a. Shows positive for an illegal drug or alcohol in a test conducted under the provisions of this policy. For this violation, the Company may allow the offending employee to return to work following a 30-day suspension, contingent upon passing a drug or alcohol test.

b. Refuses to take a test when asked to do so.

c. Is found to be in possession of contraband.

d. Fails to cooperate with the Medical Review Officer during the investigation of a positive test result.

3. Suspension without pay for the duration of investigation may be applied to an employee who is the subject of a drug-related inquiry by the Company or a law enforcement agency.

4. Disbarment from the Company's work or workplace may be applied to any contractor or contractor employee who violates this policy.

F. Notification of Test Results

1. The Company will notify each applicant of the results of a pre-employment test provided the applicant requests such results within 60 days of being notified of the disposition of the employment application.

2. The Company will notify each employee of the results of tests when the test results are positive. The employee will also be advised what drug was discovered.

G. Appeals

1. An employee whose test is reported positive for drug or alcohol will be asked in a confidential meeting or telephone conference to offer an explanation. The purpose of the meeting or telephone conference will be to determine if there is any reason that a positive test could have resulted from some cause other than drug or alcohol use that is in violation of this policy. If the employee is desirous of a second

opinion, he may request a retest by an alternate laboratory, approved by the Company, of the same specimen at the employee's expense.

2. An appeal that merits further inquiry may require that the employee be suspended until the inquiry and the appeals process are completed. The suspension will be without pay but will not suspend provision of fringe benefits.

3. An employee whose appeal is successful will be made whole, i.e., compensated for lost pay and reimbursed for expenses related to specimen retesting.

H. Confidentiality

1. All employee information relating to testing will be protected by the Company as confidential unless otherwise required by law, overriding public health and safety concerns, or authorized in writing by the employee.

2. The Company will ensure that no person will obtain the individual test results retained by the MRO, and the MRO will not release the individual test results of any employee to any person, without first obtaining written authorization from the tested employee. Nothing in this paragraph will prohibit the MRO from releasing to the Company the information delineated in the sections dealing with Notification of Test Results and Record Keeping.

3. The Company will maintain confidentiality of drug testing information that is entered into an employee's qualification file and will not release such information without first obtaining written authorization from the tested employee.

I. Employee Assistance Program (EAP)

1. The Company will maintain an EAP program. The EAP program will, as a minimum, include:

  a. An education and training component of not less than 60 minutes for employees which addresses the effects and consequences of drug and alcohol use on personal health, safety, and the work environment.

b. A training component of not less than 120 minutes duration for supervisory personnel. The component will address the specific, contemporaneous, physical, behavioral, and performance indicators of probable drug use; intervention tactics; reasonable cause, including the two supervisor rule; post-accident testing procedures; and supervisory responsibilities for the execution of this policy.

c. A written statement which outlines the EAP. The statement will be kept on file and available for inspection at the Company's principal place of business.

J. Rehabilitation

1. Rehabilitation in lieu of termination may be offered to an employee who has been found to be in violation of this policy when:

a. The violation does not involve selling or distributing illegal drugs, or serious misconduct; and

b. The employee agrees to undergo rehabilitation in a rehabilitation program approved by the Company.

2. The costs of rehabilitation will be paid for by the Company only within the limits of the medical benefits provided in the employee's medical benefits plan. Time spent away from the job for rehabilitative reasons will be counted as leave without pay, and will in no event exceed 90 days.

3. The Company will establish a rehabilitation committee that will develop and determine an employee's rehabilitation plan and a schedule for the employee's return to work. The committee will consist of a Company representative, the medical review officer, and the individual in charge of the employee's personal rehabilitation program.

4. After returning to work, the employee must continue in an after-care program and be subject to follow-up testing for not longer than 60 months following return to work.

K. Inspections and Searches at the Workplace

1. The Company may conduct unannounced general inspections and searches for drugs or alcohol on Company premises or in Company

vehicles or equipment wherever located. Employees are expected to cooperate.

2. Search of an employee and his or her personal property may be made when there is reasonable cause to believe that the employee is in violation of this policy.

3. An employee's consent to a search is required as a condition of employment and the employee's refusal to consent may result in disciplinary action, including discharge, even for a first refusal.

4. Illegal drugs, drugs believed to be illegal, and drug paraphernalia found on Company property may be turned over to the appropriate law enforcement agency and full cooperation given to any subsequent investigation. Substances which cannot be identified as an illegal drug by a layman's examination will be turned over to a drug testing vendor for scientific analysis.

5. Other forms of contraband, such as firearms, explosives, and lethal weapons, will be subject to seizure during an inspection or search. An employee who is found to possess contraband on Company property or while on Company business will be subject to discipline up to and including discharge.

VII. Laboratory Analysis and Medical Review

A. Testing Laboratory

1. The Company will engage a laboratory certified by the Department of Health and Human Services in accordance with DOT Procedures. The testing laboratory will be required to permit:

      a. Inspections by the Company before the laboratory is selected to perform testing; and

      b. Unannounced inspections, including the examination of records, at any time, by the Company, the RSPA, or a state agency if the laboratory is subject to state agency jurisdiction.

B. Medical Review of Testing Results

WRITE THE POLICY

1. The Company will designate or appoint a medical review officer (MRO) who will be a licensed physician with knowledge of drug abuse disorders. The MRO will:

a. Review the results of drug testing before they are reported to the Company.

b. Review and interpret each confirmed positive test result as follows to determine if there is an alternative medical explanation for the confirmed positive test result:

-Conduct a medical interview with the individual tested.

-Review the individual's medical history and any relevant biomedical factors.

-Review all medical records made available by the individual tested to determine if a confirmed positive test resulted from legal prescribed medication.

-If necessary, require that the original specimen be reanalyzed to determine the accuracy of the reported test result.

-Verify that the laboratory report and assessment are correct.

c. Determine whether and when an employee involved in a rehabilitation program may be returned to duty.

d. Set a schedule of unannounced testing, in consultation with the rehabilitation committee, for an employee who has returned to duty after rehabilitation.

e. Ensure that an employee has been drug tested in accordance with the DOT Procedures before the employee returns to duty after rehabilitation.

2. The following rules will govern MRO determinations:

a. If the MRO determines, after appropriate review, that there is a legitimate medical explanation for the confirmed positive test result, the MRO is not required to take further action.

b. If the MRO determines, after appropriate review, that there is no legitimate explanation for the confirmed positive test result, the MRO will refer the individual to the employee assistance program.

c. Based on a review of laboratory inspection reports, quality assurance and quality control data, and other drug test results, the MRO may conclude that a particular drug test result is scientifically insufficient for further action. Under these circumstances, the MRO will conclude that the test is negative.

C. Retention of Samples and Retesting

1. Specimens that yield positive results on confirmation will be retained by the laboratory in frozen storage for at least 365 days, during which the Company, the RSPA, or a state agency may request retention for an additional period.

2. If the MRO determines there is no legitimate medical explanation for a confirmed positive test result, the original specimen will be retested if the employee makes a written request for retesting within 60 days of receipt of the final test result from the MRO. The Company will require the employee to pay in advance the cost of shipment, if any, and reanalysis, but the Company will reimburse the employee for such expense if the retest is negative.

3. If the employee specifies retesting by a second laboratory, the original laboratory must follow approved chain-of-custody procedures in transferring a portion of the specimen.

4. Since some analytes may deteriorate during storage, detected levels of the drug below the detection limits established in the DOT Procedures, but equal to or greater than the established sensitivity of the assay, must, as technically appropriate, be reported and considered corroborative of the original positive results.

VIII. Amnesty

A. The Company will provide an amnesty period that will start on the effective date of this policy and conclude not sooner than 30 days nor later than 60 days.

5

Communicate the Policy

A newly developed policy needs to be communicated to the affected persons. The usual avenues of communication are memoranda, letters, newsletters, and the like, both in hard copy and electronic formats, plus bulletin board notices. The most effective communication methods can be of the face-to-face variety in which managers and supervisors brief the employees at meetings of all sizes. One-on-one and small group tutorials can be extremely effective. To attain long-term understanding, the policy can be published in orientation packets for new hires and in handbooks for employees.

The communication methods that initially announce the new policy should include opportunities for feedback. Employees will have questions that if left unanswered can impede smooth implementation.

Ultimately, the most effective method of making the policy known and obtaining acceptance will be word-of-mouth communication. A sensible way of helping the informal networks operate to everyone's advantage is to provide each employee with his or her own copy of the policy. The distribution technique can include downloading the policy on personal computers, sending it desk-to-desk in hard copy, and mailing it with a formal letter to the employees' homes. The last option provides an opportunity for the families to be informed and has added value in that drug abuse is frequently a family problem as well as a problem for the individual employee.

NOTICES AND ACKNOWLEDGMENTS

A general notice, such as an all-staff memo from the senior executive, given to employees 60 days prior to the implementation date, can be of enormous help in relieving employee anxieties. As appropriate, the notice can include:

The purpose and necessity of the policy.

- A description of the testing scheme, e.g., the accuracy and reliability of tests and medical officer review of positive findings.

- The circumstances under which testing may occur, e.g., pre-employment, random, and reasonable cause.

- Appeals procedures, e.g., how to contest positive test findings or disciplinary actions.

- Identification of jobs that will be subject to testing.

- The availability of treatment benefits.

- Confidentiality protections.

In addition to information provided in the general notice, individual notices can be distributed to those employees directly affected by the policy. The matters of individual interest might be:

- The employee's position has been designated as a position subject to random testing.

- The employee will be granted a "safe harbor" provision, e.g., the opportunity to voluntarily admit to being an abuser and to receive counseling or rehabilitation without exposure to disciplinary action.

Because there will always be a small percentage of employees who fail to receive or heed the message, no matter how extensive the communication, the employer may want to have each worker return a signed form acknowledging receipt and understanding of the policy.

Special notice should be given to and written acknowledgments obtained from workers who hold testing-designated positions. Two key points of acknowledgment are:

- That the worker has received and read the policy and/or notice which states that the worker's position has been designated for random testing.

- That refusal to submit to testing can result in disciplinary action up to and including dismissal.

If the worker refuses to sign the acknowledgement, the supervisor should make a note to that effect on the acknowledgement form. A refusal or failure would not, however, exempt the employee from testing.

Following are sample acknowledgments.

ACKNOWLEDGMENT

I have received and I have read the Company's drug-free workplace policy. I understand that the Company randomly tests employees who hold safety-sensitive jobs. I also understand that the job I hold is a safety-sensitive job and that I am subject to random testing.

I understand that I have the right to refuse to undergo testing, and that the consequences of refusal to undergo testing or a refusal to cooperate in testing by me will result in disciplinary action up to and including discharge.

_____   _____

(Signature)   (Date Signed)

If searching or testing are authorized by the policy, you may want also to obtain written consents in advance. Keep in mind, however, that a consent can be withdrawn at any time; and the only consent that counts is the one given at the moment in time the search or test is conducted. Nonetheless, a pre-obtained consent has value, if only to underscore management's serious determination to confront the drug abuse problem head-on.

EMPLOYEE'S CONSENT TO BE TESTED

I have been made aware of and I understand my employer's policy concerning drug and/or alcohol abuse. I understand that the policy authorizes testing to ensure compliance.

I understand that I cannot be compelled to give specimens, but that giving specimens and cooperating in the testing is a condition of my continued employment. I understand that if I refuse to provide specimens I will be subject to disciplinary action up to and including discharge.

I understand that if I give specimens, such as urine, breath, or blood specimens, they will be analyzed for the presence of drugs and/or alcohol, and that a positive test will subject me to disciplinary action up to and including discharge.

I understand I am now being asked to give one or more specimens, and I understand the reason for the testing is related to:

[ ] A reasonable cause determination that I may be impaired by a drug and/or alcohol.

[ ] The investigation of a work-related accident or incident.

[ ] Random testing conducted on an unannounced basis to assure safe operations.

[ ] Periodic testing conducted incident to health or fitness for duty evaluations.

[ ] Testing conducted following release from a program of rehabilitation.

[ ] My assignment to a position that requires testing as a pre-assignment condition.

[ ] Other:_____

I understand the testing is being done pursuant to:

[ ] DOT regulations

[ ] My employer's authority

I authorize the officers, employees and agents of my employer, the specimen collecting agency, the drug testing laboratory, the medical review officer, and other officially interested parties to communicate among themselves for official purposes my drug and/or alcohol test results, both orally and in writing, and to communicate such test results at any official, administrative, or judicial proceeding.

I also authorize the above named parties to have continued access to my test specimens for the purpose of conducting any further analyses or studies that may be necessary.

At this time I consent to provide the specimen(s) for testing.

_____   _____

(Signature of Employee)   (Date Signed)

Following is an example of a fact sheet for explaining a newly developed policy. It can be distributed in ways similar to notices of the

COMMUNICATE THE POLICY

policy and it can be used by managers and supervisors when they brief employees.

A FACT SHEET ON DRUG TESTING

1. The policy mentions periodic testing. What does this mean?

On an unannounced basis, the Company will test at a given location some, but not all, employees. The contractor chosen to provide the testing service will use a random number system to identify a percentage of employees. The identified employees are likely to work at all levels, not just as part of a particular grouping. The Company will not play a part in the identification of employees, other than to specify the percentage of the total employees to be tested.

2. Will testing cover just drugs or drugs and alcohol?

Routine periodic tests will be for drugs only. Depending on the circumstances, "for cause" testing could include drugs, alcohol, or both.

3. Exactly what types of samples are involved?

Drug tests will involve urine samples; alcohol testing may involve breath, saliva, and/or blood.

4. How will the tests be made and how accurate are they?

For drug detection, a fully certified laboratory will do a two-step urinalysis. The first step is to examine the urine specimen using a radioimmunoassay technique. A positive result on the first test will lead to a second test using the gas chromatography/mass spectrometry procedure. Quality control at the laboratory will be monitored with blind samples. The overall testing system is state-of-the-art and extremely accurate. Alcohol detection will be done through local clinics or hospitals, using state-of-the-art techniques.

5. What drugs will be looked for in the urinalysis?

Marijuana, cocaine, opiates, amphetamines, barbiturates, and other commonly-abused substances.

6. Will a test show positive for a person who is passively exposed to marijuana smoke?

No. The analytical procedure ignores findings of marijuana at the "passive level."

7. What about drugs that are prescribed by a physician?

At the time you give a specimen, you will be asked to identify any over-the-counter or prescription medicines recently taken. The analytical procedure will take this information into account.

8. What does "for cause" really mean?

The Company has defined three situations in which an employee might be requested to take a drug test. These are:

When an employee's behavior affects safety, is destructive to Company property, equipment or work environment, or is an immediate threat to the Company's reputation.

When an employee is involved in a responsible vehicular accident while driving a company unit, or involved in an on-the-job accident or near miss in which the circumstances surrounding the accident would lead a reasonable person to suspect that drug abuse is possible.

When an employee demonstrates recurring behavior/performance problems and drug abuse is believed a probable factor.

9. Will an individual be fired for refusing to be tested?

Failure to cooperate with a properly authorized request for testing will be considered insubordination and grounds for termination. The actual disciplinary action taken in a specific instance will depend on the circumstances and the seriousness of the situation that triggered the need for the test.

10. What happens to an employee who tests positive?

The employee will be subject to disciplinary action, up to and including discharge.

11. Is there an appeals procedure for a person who shows positive?

Yes. Before any action is taken after a positive test result is reported, the employee will be given an opportunity in private to explain why the test was positive. If a plausible explanation is offered, an investigation will be conducted. Discipline will be withheld pending completion of the investigation.

12. How often will periodic testing occur?

Periodic testing may occur on an unannounced basis between 3 and 5 times per year or more if needed.

13. Will the extent of employee testing be expanded in the future?

Prior to developing this program, management carefully considered national statistics on drug use, the experience of other companies that have testing programs, and our experience with incidents of drug use. We don't think we have an abnormal problem, but we are part of a society in which drug abuse is becoming more commonplace. We feel our program as presently constituted is sound and reasonable. If over time the level of drug abuse proves to be greater than first thought, consideration will be given to other options, including a more aggressive testing effort involving increased periodic sampling.

14. Why is there an amnesty period?

The amnesty period will allow time for a drug-abusing employee to rid his or her body system of drugs prior to any testing the Company may choose to conduct.

15. Why are medical benefits limited to the amnesty period?

To obtain drug abuse rehabilitation benefits, the employee must apply for them within the amnesty period. The benefits, however, can continue beyond the amnesty period provided the rehabilitation process is unbroken and connected to the original application. Because drug abuse is a self-induced and treatable illness, the

Company believes the individual is responsible for making the primary effort at rehabilitation. An individual who comes forward during the amnesty period will not be subject to discipline or adverse action, and will be entitled to receive Company assistance for a single effort at rehabilitation in a Company-approved rehabilitation program.

16. What will be an employee's status during rehabilitation?

The employee will be placed on leave without pay, but will be allowed to use sick leave and vacation days to offset time lost from the job. Reinstatement will be made upon medical certification that the employee has successfully completed a rehabilitation program approved by the Company. Prior to reinstatement and during rehabilitation, the Company reserves the right to administer urine tests to evaluate the effectiveness of therapy.

17. Can rehabilitation be conducted on a part-time basis or during the employee's personal time?

Not as part of the Company's program. The purpose of this procedure is to remove from the workplace persons who pose a potential threat to human safety and the efficiency of operations.

18. Does the testing program include all levels and all locations?

The program is being implemented across the board at all locations. Testing will apply to job applicants, probationary employees being considered for regular employee status, employees being considered for promotion or transfer to sensitive or safety-critical positions, employees being considered for reinstatement, and employees who are required to undergo routine periodic health examinations. The program also includes periodic unannounced testing and "for cause" testing.

19. Who will have access to drug test records and results?

Drug test results will be treated as confidential information and will be maintained by the Company's Personnel Department.

20. If a job applicant fails a test, can he or she be re-tested?

No. However, if an applicant who has been rejected for failing the test can show, not sooner than 90 days later, that he or she subsequently completed a rehabilitation program recognized by the Company, a new application may be accepted. The applicant will, of course, be subject to another pre-employment urine test.

21. If a job applicant fails a test, can he or she be hired on a probationary basis?

No.

22. Could this policy be used to harass or discriminate against employees?

We don't believe so. Employees tested on an unannounced basis will be selected by a third party using a random number system. Before an employee can be tested in a "for cause" situation, three persons must agree that the test is appropriate. These persons are the employee's immediate supervisor, the immediate supervisor's manager, and the Company's employee relations representative.

OBTAIN BUY-IN

An employee's willingness to attain a goal set by management tends to increase relative to the amount of input the employee has given in determining the methods for reaching the goal. The motivation of employees to attain a drug-free work environment will be enhanced when employees are asked to participate in preparing and implementing the action steps of the program aimed at preventing drug abuse.

Participation often consists of supervisors asking their people for suggestions. Employees who offer ideas (especially ideas that are adopted) will be more likely to make a personal commitment to the program than employees who were not brought into the picture.

Employees who are informed about what is being planned and how they fit into the plan will have a higher level of motivation. On the other hand, employees will be turned off when kept in the dark. Open communications coupled with an opportunity to provide input will convey the idea that employees are trusted team members. A supervisor who talks straight and pays attention to employee concerns will build an interest among employees to make the organization's drug abuse prevention program a success.

Most of the important work activity takes place within sight of or in close proximity to supervisors. Although management may make the decision to establish a drug-free environment, the critical program activities are carried out where workers work and supervisors supervise. The action takes place not in the corporate boardroom, but at places where employees provide the services or make the products.

Supervisors carry the main burden for explaining and gaining acceptance of management decisions; they are also the management's agent for triggering program activities such as intervening when abuse is present, referring drug abusers for discipline and/or treatment, and ordering drug testing in accident and reasonable cause situations.

Resistance to a drug abuse prevention program can be high for at least three reasons. First, the program itself represents a change and people tend to resist change. Next, different people hold different views about drug abuse and what to do about it. Third, the drug-abusing minority of employees will resist a prevention program because of the threat it poses to them personally.

Do not expect wild enthusiasm from workers when announcing the policy. There is simply no way to sugarcoat the penalty aspects. Being up front and honest about the consequences of policy violations is the best way to go. Any lesser effort can lead employees to believe that management is being deceptive or that the policy will not be enforced. Positive information can be a counterbalance such as showing a caring attitude about the health of the worker and the well-being of the worker's family. Another is to demonstrate the impact of abuse on health and safety. When the policy is explained along these lines, management conveys a concern for the employee as a person. The policy is presented not as a mechanism for administering sanctions but as a sensible and rational means for safeguarding health and avoiding accidents.

Obtaining approval of the policy by employees is easier said than done. Resistance will appear among a minority of employees who will oppose the policy on principle, such as the principle of personal privacy or the notion that an employer has no business trying to regulate off-work behavior. The drug-abusing employees will oppose

COMMUNICATE THE POLICY

the policy because it represents a direct threat to their jobs. In a general sense, a majority of employees will be less than enthusiastic simply because they, like all humans, tend to resist change.

What can be done to overcome resistance? Why not do the same things that are done when implementing any other major change? For example, tell employees what is being planned, ask for their input, and show them what you have in mind before it is set in stone. It will help also to recognize that informal groups inside the organization can be friends or foes, and enlist their support. Change that is anticipated is change that can be managed.

6

Develop Awareness

Announcing a policy and obtaining buy-in to it are types of awareness endeavors. With those tasks behind you, you are ready to carry awareness to an entirely new level. The effort has two objectives: help employees understand the nature of drug abuse, and help them understand why drug abuse in the workplace cannot be tolerated.

INFLUENCING EMPLOYEE BEHAVIORS

The well-being of an organization rests squarely on the practices of employees. Management can design the finest drug-free workplace program and support it with the finest equipment and staff. The program, however, will surely be less than effective if the employees fail to meet their individual responsibilities. A drug-free program, no matter how perfectly conceived and abundantly funded, is incapable

DEVELOP AWARENESS

of overcoming the apathy of employees. Like the analogy of the weak link in the chain, an organization's drug-free program cannot be stronger than the weakest day-to-day behaviors of employees.

This reality leads to a serious question: How can management influence employee behaviors? The answer is through education, or stated another way, by making employees aware of the consequences of their conduct. In this sense, awareness has three dimensions:

- The employees are made to understand their individual responsibilities to maintain a drug-free environment,

- They are taught how to carry out those responsibilities, and

- They are engaged in the first two dimensions willingly.

INFLUENCING EMPLOYEE ATTITUDES

The first two dimensions require the employee to gain knowledge. The third dimension is distinctly different and difficult to attain because it calls for an attitudinal shift. To illustrate the point, imagine that Tommy Smith, forklift operator, is at a friend's home on an evening before going to work. Tommy's friend lights up a marijuana cigarette and offers to share it. Tommy has used marijuana in the past and has recently been informed of the company's new rule that prohibits being at work with a detectable amount of an illegal drug in the body system. Will Tommy take a drag from the cigarette or will he abstain? His attitude will be the determining factor.

You can teach Tommy your anti-drug rules but you cannot directly shape his attitude toward them, especially if Tommy has already formed a pro-drug mindset. What you can hope to achieve, however, is the exercising of an indirect influence upon Tommy that comes from his drug-free co-workers. The strength of peer influence upon Tommy will be proportional to the strength of the message from management which says "drugs don't work here."

DRUG ABUSE AWARENESS

An effective awareness effort:

- Will be an important element in the drug-free workplace program. The awareness element will be a formal entity administered by one or more responsible employees with skills in vocational education and training. The element will be subject to the routine processes of the business, such as planning, budgeting, and evaluation.

- Will be an ongoing effort, not a one-time effort. Although awareness may be initiated with great fanfare and periodically reinvigorated, it will be a continuously operating enterprise. Don't make the mistake of engaging in a blitzkrieg of education at the front end of the program and then allow whatever awareness has been developed to fade off into oblivion. The initial awareness activities serve as a foundation for follow-on education.

- Will be a local affair that addresses the needs of the business. The effort will be principally dedicated to making the employees aware of the do's and don'ts pertinent to the goals of the business.

- Will exploit all available forums that influence employee behaviors.

- Will send awareness messages to all levels of the organization. Message style and mode of message delivery will vary according to the audience.

FORMULATING THE MESSAGE

When selecting a topic for inclusion in the awareness program, ask yourself: Is the topic important and does it need to be presented? If the

91

answer is yes, then ask: Is the content of the topic doctrinally correct? Is it consistent with policy?

If a topic is long or complicated, break it down into comprehensible parts. Arrange the parts in a logical series with each part building on the other.

Package the topic imaginatively. Go outside the envelope of traditional methods. Be innovative. Emulate the techniques of professional idea marketers.

PRESENTING THE MESSAGE

The avenues for raising awareness include:

- Making presentations at meetings and conferences in which various employee groups view films, slides, and other audiovisuals. Having a subject matter expert on hand to answer questions adds to the credibility of the presentation. At a single, large meeting for all employees, the CEO can deliver the message personally.

- Bringing in outside experts to address topics of concern; for example, having a law enforcement officer display paraphernalia used to administer commonly abused drugs, or having a medical practitioner explain the health consequences of abuse.

- Sending periodic bulletins to employees at work or to their homes. A monthly bulletin, for example, could feature a different drug-related topic. Several advantages are inherent:

  - Management's concern is highlighted over an extended period.

  - Knowledge retention is enhanced when information is presented in discrete, digestible portions.

- Hard copy materials that reach the home may help promote family involvement in preventing or resolving drug abuse problems.

- Conducting tutorials that meet special needs; for example, teaching family members how to support an employee who is recovering from drug abuse.

- Placing awareness materials on static and electronic bulletin boards, on the security Web site of the organization's intranet, on placards in public hallways, and on signage at safety-sensitive locations. Other materials might be a company-prepared handbook, posters in hallways, and flyers placed inside paycheck envelopes.

- Conducting an on-site health fair that features display booths, awareness literature, video presentations, and talks by local celebrities.

A drug-free program simply has to include an awareness component. Other program components, such as supervisory intervention, drug testing, and employee assistance, rely on an informed workforce. A supervisor cannot step in to correct an on-the-job abuse situation if the supervisor has no understanding of abuse; drug testing will not be fully accepted if the why and how of drug testing are not thoroughly explained; and employees will shy away from assistance if they are unsure of the associated implications.

7

Involve Supervisors

THE SUPERVISOR'S CENTRAL ROLE

The supervisor plays a central role in a company's program for attaining a drug-free workplace. What a supervisor believes and knows will strongly influence his or her willingness to accept that central role. A supervisor who has accepted the premise that workplace drug abuse is unacceptable is ready to assume the important duties of dealing with it.

A supervisor who has an understanding of drug abuse will be aware of the adverse consequences that drug use can have on safety, productivity, and business costs. With that understanding comes an awareness of the specific responsibilities assigned to the supervisor for preventing on-the-job drug use, identifying it when it occurs, and taking action to correct it.

Why is the supervisor a central figure in making the workplace free of drug abuse? The answer is simple - the supervisor is the person most likely to first detect changes in the performance and behavior patterns of abusing employees, and is also the person responsible for initiating corrective actions. The nature of an employee's conduct will dictate the type of action that is appropriate.

A corrective action can range from admonishment to discharge. It can also combine discipline with assistance, such as referral of the employee for diagnosis, counseling, or treatment. In addition to being positioned to influence what will be done, the supervisor is in the best position to determine if the corrective action has succeeded.

A supervisor will understand that all drugs when consumed in sufficient amounts produce abnormal signs which may be detected by visual observation. Many of these signs are generic in that they are similar regardless of which type of drug has been taken. Because such signs are apparent, it is possible to make an initial evaluation of possible abuse.

While indicators of drug use are always valid reasons for supervisory action, the purpose of the action is not to punish or accuse. The purpose of taking action is to direct the employee's attention to the unsatisfactory performance or behavior and the detrimental effects of it. The idea is not to confront the employee with an opinion about drug abuse, but to bring an end to the employee's unacceptable work conduct. For example, if the indicator is carelessness, the employee should be counseled, not in terms of possible drug abuse, but in terms of the effect that the carelessness is having upon safety and productivity.

LEADERSHIP

Obtaining employee support of the organization's drug abuse program requires the application of many skills. Following are some leadership ideas that help build support for a drug-free workplace.

Inspire Respect

A supervisor does not accept favors from subordinates and does not grant favors in order to be liked. A popular decision can be outstanding when correct, but an absolute disaster when wrong - particularly if it involves drugs. Discipline should be applied when needed, and done so fairly and evenly across the board.

Interact With Subordinates

People tend to accept responsibility for the solution of a problem when they are invited to participate in defining and dealing with it. Drug abuse within the work group is the kind of problem that subordinates can relate and respond to in a positive fashion. A supervisor may find a solution by asking for advice and help, and following through on employee ideas.

Criticize Positively

When something goes wrong, the best course of action is to control emotions, remain calm, and get all the facts before taking action, especially disciplinary action. Criticism should be voiced not as a punishment but as a learning experience to prevent recurrence. When it is appropriate, the supervisor should combine criticism with praise and always avoid offending a subordinate's personal dignity.

Be Up Front With People

A good supervisor will tell employees what to expect, and tell them as early as possible of any changes that may affect them. A new drug abuse policy, for example, is the type of change that can be a major source of worry for employees. A drug abuse policy must be thoroughly communicated so that everyone will know what is expected of them and what will happen when violations of policy occur.

EARLY INVOLVEMENT

Supervisors need to brought into the picture at the earliest possible stages, e.g., when defining the nature of the abuse problem affecting the organization and when developing a policy for eradicating the problem. Supervisors, particularly those at the line level, are better positioned than upper middle and senior management to know the nitty-gritty details of life in the trenches. Supervisors have, or should have, a feel for what is really on the minds of the rank and file. This insider perspective will often be at odds with management's idealized expectations. Almost without exception, line supervisors have risen through the ranks; they know the true nature of work being performed in the operational venues; and they often keep and nurture shoulder-to-shoulder relationships with their subordinates. Supervisors are the natural conduits for moving relevant information upward.

Insights possessed by supervisors can be enormously valuable in the development of a drug-free program. When key supervisors are active members of the program's task force, they bring a unique richness to the planning and design process. The same holds true at a later time when implementing procedures are under development. The contributions of supervisors are often accompanied by practical comments: "This will work; this will not work; and this will work better if ...."

In the same way that supervisors are able to reach down into the organization and pull up useful information and ideas, they are able to carry the drug-free message downward. They can also lend tweaks and nuances to the message when they anticipate or sense resistance from subordinates. Supervisors play a facilitative role by helping define the abuse problem, by helping formulate a solution; by helping deliver the drug-free message; and helping their subordinates understand and accept the program.

The previous chapter presents ideas for raising the employees' awareness of drug abuse. Supervisors are included, along with staff and management. But supervisors need to be more than aware; they need to be taught how to look, what to look for, and what to do when they see it.

HOW TO LOOK

Just observing is an excellent method for keeping drugs off the job. Observing is a natural supervisory activity for spotting drug use and in showing the intent to enforce rules.

The act of observing is natural, but so is the common human tendency to not always understand what we see. In familiar surroundings, such as where we work, we tend to overlook the obvious. The indicators of drug abuse will not be found when a supervisor does not consciously look for them. And even when there is a conscious intent, the discovery is difficult because the indicators are often carefully masked and easily mistaken for other things. Observing works best when planned and deliberately carried out.

A planned approach to observing will help:

- Ensure that looking actually occurs.

- Demonstrate management's concern.

- Provide feedback to management.

- Identify new abuse patterns and trends.

- Measure employee cooperation.

Preparation for observing includes determining where and when to look, knowing what to look for, and making a record of the findings. The detection process will be enhanced when the supervisor pre-determines the area to be looked at, and considers the operations performed in the area selected for inspection.

Knowing where to look is not enough. It is not sufficient to plan to look for drug use, but to look for the evidences and symptoms of use. Planning a walk-through would involve an itinerary for inspecting rest rooms, employee break and changing rooms, trash receptacles, and parking lots. Why? Because these are the places where a supervisor may find discarded items such as glassine envelopes that once contained marijuana or cocaine, plastic vials that contained crack, empty adhesive tubes and paper bags that were used for glue sniffing, butt tips of marijuana cigarettes, and soiled paper towels that were used to clean drug residues from pipes and bongs.

WHAT TO LOOK FOR

The indicators of drug abuse fall into three categories: performance, behavior, and general.

Performance Indicators

- Frequent no-shows and lateness. Examples include not showing up for work on Fridays and Mondays, and repeated lateness in arriving at work.

- Unexplained absences from the assigned workstation. This may suggest the employee is leaving work to meet with his drug supplier or to take a drug.

- Frequent telephone calls, perhaps for the purpose of arranging to meet with a supplier.

- Frequent and long visits to the rest room or locker room, perhaps to take a drug.

- Visits to the employee by strangers or other employees for matters unrelated to the job.

Behavior Indicators

- An unexplained change in disposition in a short period of time. The employee may go from being uncooperative to cooperative, from quiet to talkative, from sad to happy. The reason may be that between the "down" mood and the "up" mood, the employee took a drug. If the mood swings in the opposite direction, it may indicate that a drug is wearing off.

- Weight loss and loss of appetite.

- Nervousness that might appear in the form of starting to smoke or increasing a smoking habit.

- Reluctance to show the arms or legs. If an employee is taking drugs intravenously, he or she will try to hide the injection marks by wearing long-sleeve garments and wearing slacks in place of skirts and dresses. Blood spots on pant legs and sleeves may appear.

- Withdrawal symptoms. The employee may show the physiological effects of a drug as it is wearing off. The common symptoms are runny nose, sniffling, red eyes, trembling of hands or mouth, unsteady gait, and a general tiredness.

- Active symptoms. The employee may show signs of being under the influence. Generally, a drug will either relax or excite. A person who has taken a relaxant (depressant) tends to be "mellowed out," slow moving, dreamily happy, and likely to talk with slurring of words. The person who has taken a stimulant tends to be energetic, twitchy, fast moving, and likely to talk in a rapid and non-stop manner.

General Indicators

- An admission. A drug-abusing employee may admit to use, possibly to seek help or to explain unacceptable performance.

- Possession of a drug without medical reason. Drugs can be in the form of prescription drugs or illegally manufactured drugs. They might appear as pills, tablets, capsules, powders, pastes, leafy materials, gum-like substances, and liquids. They can also be converted to innocent-appearing objects. For example, an opiate in a liquid form can be soaked into a handkerchief and allowed to dry. When water is later added, the handkerchief is wrung out into a small dish, drawn into a hypodermic syringe, and injected.

- Concealment. An employee may hide a drug on the body or in some place that is accessible to the user. A user will sometimes favor concealment in an area also used by other employees. If the concealed drug is found, the user can avoid being singled out.

- Paraphernalia. An employee may possess or conceal drug paraphernalia, such as a syringe, needle, cooker spoon, roach clip, or glass pipe.

- Injection marks. An employee may show needle marks, boil-like abscesses, scabs and scars, especially on the arms, legs and backs of the hands.

- Drowsiness. An employee may show unusual sleepiness or general lethargy. This can be indicative of a slight overdose of an opiate, especially when it is accompanied by scratching of the body.

- Changes in the size of eye pupils. The pupils will greatly constrict immediately after taking an opiate. The pupils of an amphetamine user will dilate after use.

- Unusual behavior. The opiate user may vacantly stare and be generally unaware of surroundings; the stimulant user may be excited, euphoric and talkative; the user of marijuana, inhalants, and depressants may be sleepy or appear to be drunk; and the user of hallucinogens, like PCP and LSD, may engage in bizarre and possibly violent conduct.

- Change in eating habits. The abuser of stimulants will go for long periods of time without eating. The narcotics user may have a loss of appetite or consume candy, cookies, soda pop, and sweet-tasting food items.

- Illness symptoms. Users will display a variety of illness symptoms. For example, the opiate user in withdrawal may have the sniffles, flushed skin, muscular twitching, and nausea; the user of hallucinogens may experience an increase in blood pressure, heart rate, and blood sugar, irregular breathing, sweating, trembling, dizziness, and nausea; the cocaine user may have inflamed nasal membranes.

- Drug jargon. The use of drug jargon, awareness of how drugs are administered and their effects, and an attitude that excuses or defends drug use. The possession of magazines or literature that are marketed for persons interested in drug abuse is another indicator.

- Drug refuse. Trash receptacles in rest rooms and public areas may contain items that suggest drug use. Discarded paper and plastic bags, paint cans and aerosol cans may have been left behind by someone who has sniffed glue or gasoline. The small vial that contained crack or the glassine envelope that contained heroin might be discarded, as well as metal bottle caps, eye droppers, syringes and burnt matches that are used for cooking heroin preparatory to injection.

- Frequent absences. Absence from the job for 15-30 minutes every 4 or 5 hours, especially in cases where the individual isolates himself in absolute privacy is a tell-tale sign. This is the time when an addict "shoots up" or "snorts."

- Nothing to show for money. An addict will experience a discrepancy between income and expenditures for necessities, spending most of what is earned (or stolen) on drugs.

- Borrowing. A constant need for money that may appear as borrowing from fellow workers, stealing, writing bad checks, and working as a prostitute.

WHAT TO DO WHEN ABUSE IS INDICATED

To see an indicator of drug abuse and to do nothing about it is a waste of everyone's time. The supervisor has to make a personal commitment to take action when he observes the indicators.

A note of caution needs to be made at this point. The supervisor should not assume that every observed indicator is proof positive of drug abuse. All of the facts present in an individual case will have to be carefully weighed before reaching an opinion, and even then it is still an opinion, at least until proven such as by a urine test or an admission by the employee. One thing not to do, is to accuse an employee based on observation alone.

The central point is that the indicators may be valid reasons for a supervisor to intervene. The intervention is not to accuse the employee of drug abuse, but to direct the employee's attention to the effect his conduct is having upon the organization. For example, if an employee is frequently absent from his workstation, the supervisor should discuss this with the employee, not in terms of possible drug abuse, but in terms of the effect that the employee's absence is having upon productivity.

The supervisor has to move carefully in the area of drug abuse. The actions to avoid are:

- Accusing an employee of drug abuse.

- Raising the subject of abuse directly. The focus should be on the unacceptable performance or behavior.

- Avoid harsh disciplinary action because drug abuse is believed to be involved. The disciplinary action should be based on the unacceptable performance or behavior, not on the possible causes.

- Being drawn into a protective or confidential relationship with a drug-abusing employee. An employee's drug-related work problems are really beyond the solving capacity of a supervisor. Also, some employees are very skillful at manipulating their superiors into compromising situations.

- Discussing actual or suspected drug-abusing employees with other workers. Findings or suspicions need to be reported upward but with confidentiality.

Actions To Take

- Confront the offending employee in a non-accusing way. Describe the unacceptable conduct, explain why it cannot be tolerated, and try to get the employee to tell the reason for it. There may be a simple explanation, or the employee may admit to drug abuse.

- If an indicator is most probably drug-related, suggest to the employee that he or she seek medical assistance. Remind the employee that a failure to correct the basic problem will lead to discipline, including termination.

- Keep detailed records of what was observed and what was done in the way of intervention. Clear and factual documents will be needed if it becomes necessary to discipline.

- Report observations and intervention actions to the next higher level of management. It may be that other supervisors will have similar observations and that what you are dealing with is one part of a larger pattern.

- If an employee has agreed to seek medical help or has been referred to a company-sponsored assistance program, follow up to ensure that the help is being given and that the employee is making positive use of it.

- If an employee admits a drug abuse problem, go beyond just recommending medical help. Insist that the help be obtained immediately, even to the extent of making continued employment contingent on successful therapy.

In a case where drug abuse has damaged or poses a danger to safety, production, or property, you must remove the offending employee. Even if the employee comes forward voluntarily, admits abuse, and asks for medical help, he or she cannot be allowed to continue working in a job that involves high risk.

MAKING REFERRALS

The referral of an employee for assistance concerning a drug-related problem is often done through what is called an employee assistance program, or EAP.

An EAP is a structured program designed to provide problem identification and treatment. Many of the common problems that affect worker productivity can be addressed by an EAP. These include performance problems rooted in financial, domestic, and legal difficulties, as well as drug and alcohol abuse. In some organizations the EAP may be conducted by in-house resources. In others it may be contracted to an outside agency or may be a combination of in-house and outside resources.

The introduction of an employee to an EAP can be through self-referral or referral by a second party, such as the employee's supervisor. Because self-referral has the advantage of commitment by the employee, it is the preferred method for bringing the employee into contact with professional help. Some supervisors are skillful in helping needy employees make the decision to contact the EAP. In the absence of a self-referral, an employee with a continuing problem will need to be told to obtain help.

The first step is problem identification or diagnosis of the problem that appears to be affecting the worker's performance or behavior. The employee discusses the problem with a professional counselor who makes a preliminary determination as to the type of treatment that is needed. In many cases, the appropriate treatment will be further counseling; and in a few cases the worker will be referred to another individual or agency for special attention.

A worker with a manageable drug-related problem is usually placed in an outpatient treatment program consisting of counseling, therapy, and support motivation in one-on-one and group sessions. The length of treatment and the extent of follow-up care is typically influenced by the worker's need and progress in overcoming the problem.

Someone with a profound problem, such as addiction or dependency, may require hospitalization or residential treatment, followed by long-term maintenance care.

THE DRUG-DEPENDENT EMPLOYEE

We tend to think of a drug-dependent person as someone who can't get by without drugs, who is frequently under the influence, and is a poor excuse for a human being. The truth is that many people who are drug dependent are able to conceal their craving and impairment; they find ways to use drugs without detection; and while their conduct is unacceptable, they are not necessarily bad people.

Recent research tells us that genetic factors contribute to a person's chances of becoming dependent and eventually addicted. Some of us have genes which make us more vulnerable to dependency than others. The best defense for those of us who are predisposed to dependency is to not use illegal drugs at all - to not even experiment once. A person's first use is a voluntary act, but after that the person's willpower alone may not be enough to keep from sliding into dependency.

The supervisor may actually see dependency and not know it. The signs might be out in the open but not so clear that they can be easily interpreted. Dependent persons are usually skilled at camouflaging the problem with excuses and lies. The urge for the drug and the impairment may be there, but the individual presents an appearance that is totally deceiving.

People who are hooked on drugs often do stupid things while under the influence. They may act in ways that are against work rules such as engaging in horseplay, using profanity, being offensive to co-workers, disregarding safety practices, or sleeping on the job.

Impaired workers endanger their own lives and the lives of others. The innocent persons nearby - both at home and at work - are exposed to injury and death. Stories are constantly reported in the news media about drug-intoxicated people who killed others in traffic accidents and house fires, and we hear about loved ones who die from AIDS because a sexual partner shared an infected needle or engaged in unsafe sex while under the influence.

The first step in escaping from dependency is to face up to it. A supervisor can help by calling the dependent employee's attention to the unacceptable performance that results from abuse. While care should be taken to avoid diagnosing the employee's dependency, the supervisor can guide the employee toward serious self-examination and soul searching.

THE ADDICTED EMPLOYEE

Addiction is a physical and mental dependence that usually begins by taking or doing something to feel "good." The feeling often helps the individual escape physical or mental pain. After a while the person needs to take or do more of the something in order to maintain the same level of feeling good. The person also finds it impossible to stop.

Addiction and dependency are often used in the context of drug abuse. Although both mean pretty much the same thing, addiction is generally understood to involve a much higher level of craving, to be much more debilitating to the mind and body, and much more resistant to abstinence.

Addiction Is Not Uncommon

Addiction is not limited to drugs. People get addicted to all sorts of things, such as alcohol, tobacco, caffeine, sex, food, work, exercise, television, gambling, and hobbies. All addictions are undesirable, and some are more undesirable than others. Addiction to drugs is especially undesirable because of the enormous negative impact these addictions have at work, at home, and in society generally.

Everyone Is Vulnerable

Scientific studies point to evidence that some people seem to have a greater tendency toward addiction, and heredity is believed to be a major factor. Each of us, however, is a potential addict; no one is invulnerable.

The indicators of addiction are numerous. They include performance signals such as chronic absenteeism and low productivity; behavioral signals such as bizarre and embarrassing conduct; and physical appearance signals such as needle marks and hangovers.

Prevention of Accidents

A supervisor who has an understanding of addiction is in a position to spot and interpret the signals when they appear. A main objective of looking for the signals is not to label and punish addicted employees, but to direct them into medical channels. Another main objective is to prevent accidents and the many other negative outcomes of addiction.

IMPEDIMENTS TO ACTION

While the supervisor is not expected to be a drug treatment professional or even a counselor trained to help employees overcome drug-related problems, it is the proper role of the supervisor to look for the problems and refer employees for help.

Far too many supervisors do not understand or accept this role as a job responsibility. Even when they observe the indicators of employee drug abuse some supervisors will ignore them, hoping they will go away. Most people would agree that the job of finding and dealing with drug-related problems at work is not an easy one. They would also agree that the job is too important not to be done.

Rationalizing

This obstacle occurs when the supervisor becomes aware of a drug-related problem but regards it as something that will eventually correct itself. The indicators may be present but the supervisor finds it easier to believe that they point to something else or are so minor as to not require action.

Blocking

In this case the supervisor refuses to admit the problem exists. He or she will simply "block it out" because to accept its existence will require some action. Blocking can be the product of not knowing the required action, not agreeing with the required action, not agreeing in general with the idea of drug abuse intervention, or just not wanting to get involved.

Enabling

Here the supervisor identifies the problem; discusses it with the employee; and the employee agrees to correct the problem. The supervisor breathes a sigh of relief and then takes no further action, even when it is apparent that the employee's performance has not changed. Enabling is a cycle of repeated meetings, repeated promises, and repeated failure of both the employee and the supervisor to end the problem.

Uncorrected drug-related work problems usually conclude with an intolerable incident that forces the supervisor or a higher level manager to take decisive action. Such incidents often result in personal injury, equipment damage, or a significant loss in productivity.

Denial

It should come as no surprise that an employee dependent on a drug is likely to deny use altogether or deny even having a problem. Denial and dependence go hand-in-hand. Denial is a defensive mechanism that humans naturally and understandably put up when they feel threatened. A supervisor should expect it and be prepared to deal with it.

Denial of dependence is rooted in fear, and fear can come in many forms. They include the fear of having a serious problem; undergoing treatment; being humiliated; losing one's job; and being unable to get by without continued use of drugs. Fear can overwhelm all considerations of truth and of fairness to others, including loved ones.

Denial is usually accompanied by self-delusion. Dependent persons convince themselves that they are not hooked and can quit whenever they want. To them it's nothing more than a habit that can be dropped by simply making the decision to do so. They will also believe that the habit is a personal matter that is no one else's business.

Employees dependent on illegal drugs will go to great lengths to escape detection. They will contrive elaborate stories, get friends and family to lie for them, and will do almost anything to avoid taking a drug test. And even when the evidence removes all doubts about illegal drug use, they will persist in denials. Why? Because denial is a refuge, a place where a person can hide from reality.

A dependent employee is hurt rather than helped when a supervisor ignores the indicators of dependency. A supervisor who chooses to look the other way because the worker is a long-time employee and possesses many positive qualities is doing the wrong thing. The supervisor's motive may be right, but the action is wrong.

In addition to being concerned about the personal welfare of dependent employees, supervisors have to be concerned about the interests of the non-abusing employees. Employees who are impaired by drugs pose definite safety risks, and work not performed by the abusing employees places a heavier load on others who must pick up the slack.

The overall result of impairment is to drive up the cost of doing business and drive down productivity. Lower profit also means that the employer is unable to raise wages or grant bonuses.

SUPPORTING KNOWLEDGE

Supervisors need to have:

- Full understanding of the company's policy.

- Visual familiarity with the preferred drugs of abuse, the methods of administration, and the associated paraphernalia.

- Knowledge of the impairment indicators associated with drug abuse.

- Full understanding of the actions to take and to not take when responding to on-the-job situations indicative of drug abuse.

Supervisors need to understand the loss factors associated with accidents that result from abuse. In addition to the productive time lost by injured employees, the loss factors include:

- Time lost by co-workers.

- Assisting the injured at the scene.

- Assisting the post-accident investigation and testifying at hearings.

- Discussing the accident with other employees, collecting donations or expressions of sympathy from workers, and similar time-consuming activities.

- Cleaning up the accident, conducting a formal investigation, preparing a report of investigation, and preparing recommendations intended to prevent recurrence.

THE BOTTOM LINE CONNECTION

The linkage between drug abuse and accidents is well-understood. What we sometimes don't understand is the associated dollar loss. Loss can strongly and negatively influence a company's bottom line, and efforts that successfully control loss can have an opposite positive influence. For every dollar lost, the company must generate a higher level of sales just to stay even; and for every dollar saved through loss control, the company improves its profit. For example, if a company's annual loss due to drug abuse is $100,000 (and this is not an unrealistic figure when all relevant costs are factored in) and the company's profit margin is five percent, the company would need to make an additional $2 million in sales in order to keep pace. When the profit margin is smaller, the impact is greater. The same loss of $100,000 would require an increase of $3.3 million in sales if the profit margin is at the 3 percent level.

When costs continue and sales remain flat, a company will eventually get into serious financial difficulty and might even go out of business. It is not an overstatement to say that the supervisor is the linchpin in maintaining a company's financial viability.

Absenteeism

Absenteeism is a major cost and is often linked to an involvement with drugs, and is almost always accompanied by other indicators, especially indicators relating to how the employee looks and acts.

People who use drugs tend to leave work early and arrive late, not show up for work on Fridays and Mondays, be away from their workstations for unexcused reasons, and spend more time being treated for medical problems - problems that often stem from drug abuse.

Absenteeism impacts business by reducing output and putting a strain on workers who have to pick up the slack created by absent workers. Several options exist for dealing with absenteeism.

Insist on Notification

Insist on prompt notification every time an employee is absent unexpectedly. Require subordinates to call in without fail and without delay when they must be gone from the job without prior approval. Insist on prior discussions about necessary absences for personal reasons, rather than after-the-fact explanations. Don't routinely accept vague stories and weak excuses.

Keep a Record

Keep a running record of absences. Pay particular attention to absences that occur on Monday or the first day after a holiday. Also look at absences that occur on the day following payday. The strong linkage between drug dependency and the need for money may account for an employee being on or recovering from a using spree immediately following a payday. It won't hurt either to let your subordinates know that you routinely maintain a record of absences and that you have identified those employees who are absence-prone.

Make a Statement

Educate your employees concerning absenteeism. Make it a point to privately counsel each absence-prone employee. Obtain from the employee a commitment to take steps to correct the problem. Discuss absenteeism at departmental meetings, and explain its seriousness in terms of higher costs, lost profits, lower productivity, and morale.

Take Corrective Action

The perspective should be upon absenteeism as a performance problem. Although the source of the problem may result from drug abuse, your focus will be upon how to supervise your subordinates so that absenteeism can be reduced. In cases where drug use is indicated, the supervisory action may be to impose discipline and/or refer the employee to a treatment professional. When employees fail to meet the established standards of work, whether for drug-related or other reasons, the supervisor's responsibility is to take corrective action.

A FRAMEWORK FOR GUIDANCE

A supervisor is expected to cooperate with efforts to achieve and maintain a safe working environment. The best opportunities for doing this occur while directing and evaluating the work performance of subordinates. When safety or productivity become unsatisfactory, the supervisor intervenes.

The organization's policy, along with implementing procedures, provide the framework of guidance and the imperative to act. When a supervisor has reason to believe that an employee is in violation of rules concerning drug abuse, the supervisor is expected to take the required action.

Following is a sample memorandum that reminds supervisors of their responsibilities in administering the organization's drug-free program.

MEMORANDUM

TO: All Supervisors

SUBJECT: Drug-Free Program Responsibilities

It is the express intention of management that supervisors will carry out the responsibilities assigned to them in the Company's Drug-Free Program.

Those responsibilities are expected to be carried out through supervisory practices which ensure that:

Each subordinate is given a thorough briefing of the rules concerning drug use when initially assigned, and a review of the rules on at least an annual basis.

Any observed or reported violation of the drug rules by a subordinate is investigated and documented, and disciplinary/corrective action administered, if substantiated.

A formal inspection is conducted by the supervisor of the physical area under his/her supervision at least once every two months for the specific purpose of looking for the indications of drug use.

The subject of drug use is included on the agenda of employee meetings organized by the supervisor.

Every accident that is required to be investigated is promptly and efficiently investigated; that a report of all details - even if only preliminary in nature - is prepared within 24 hours; and that urine specimens are obtained without delay from all subordinates whose actions contributed or may have contributed to the accident.

The personal attitude and conduct of the supervisor with respect to drug use are exemplary and a model for subordinates to follow.

The supervisor is the person most likely to first detect changes in the performance and behavior pattern of a drug-abusing employee. The supervisor will also be the person responsible for initiating action to correct the problem, and if the organization has referral or treatment programs, the supervisor is in the best position to follow up and determine if an employee's basic drug problem has indeed been corrected.

Problems of loss and productivity can appear to result from innocent causes, but when a supervisor looks closely at them he or she may discover that the causes are rooted in drug abuse.

Avoid Labels

Labels like drug abusers and pot heads are counter productive because they draw attention away from the central issue, i.e., the maintenance of a productive and safe working place for all employees.

Document the Intervention

Every significant action taken with respect to an employee, whether positive or negative, requires creating a record of some type. This fact of life is called documentation.

Documentation is important because oftentimes a seemingly simple employee problem turns out to be highly resistant to correction and is eventually found to be rooted in drug use. The record would be valuable as a source of information helpful to concerned persons, e.g., the supervisor, the supervisor's superior, the personnel manager, and treatment professionals.

The demand for documentation is always present in cases involving drug use. Documentation will include facts that are complete and accurate. These characteristics provide a basis for making informed decisions, and one of the decision makers might very well be the employee himself. A record which shows the performance picture over a period of time will convey the seriousness of the situation and may trigger in the employee a decision to turn things around.

Good documentation will provide a true record of all interactions with the employee. It will also reflect the involvement of other persons, such as witnesses to incidents and specialists who have been consulted. The record will set forth all pertinent facts discussed at meetings about the employee; for example, purpose of discussion, persons present, when, and conclusions reached. It will summarize comments by all involved persons, and will outline any plan or action steps determined to be appropriate in resolving the problem.

Documentation is called for when the supervisor:

- Intervenes to correct a serious performance problem, such as a violation of a safety rule or unexcused absence from the job.

- Admonishes or meets with an employee.

- Develops with the employee any actions for improving the employee's performance.

- Observes any indicator of possible drug use.

117

Full documentation should accompany every instance of intervention. Information provided by the supervisor's report can aid in the diagnosis of a treatment provider and, if the employee's unacceptable performance continues, the information can aid in taking disciplinary action.

Following is a sample report for documenting an intervention.

REPORT OF REASONABLE CAUSE INCIDENT

Time, Date of Incident: _____

Name of Individual: _____

INSTRUCTIONS

Use this form to document the decision to conduct drug testing of a person who is reasonably believed to be impaired by a drug.

This form is to be filled out and signed by at least one supervisor who has received training in how to make reasonable cause determinations. When possible, two supervisors trained in making reasonable cause determinations should sign.

Fill out this form as soon as possible and in no case later than 24 hours following the reasonable cause incident.

Describe the conduct or appearances that indicated impairment:

_____

_____

_____

_____

_____

_____

Provide the names of persons, other than the witnessing supervisors, who have pertinent information:

_____   _____

_____   _____

MARK THE ITEMS THAT APPLY

The individual's appearance was:

    [ ] Normal

    [ ] Sleepy

    [ ] Hyperactive

    [ ] Tremors

    [ ] Bloodshot Eyes

    [ ] Runny Nose

    [ ] Pale

    [ ] Flushed

    [ ] Nervous

    [ ] Confused

    [ ] Sweating

    [ ] Unkempt

    [ ] Staggering

    [ ] Uncoordinated

    [ ] Glazed Eyes

    [ ] Dreamy

    [ ] Other   _____

Provide specific details concerning the employee's appearance, including any unusual odors.

_____

_____

_____

_____

_____

The individual's conduct was:

[ ] Normal

[ ] Loud

[ ] Abusive

[ ] Disruptive

[ ] Erratic

[ ] Violent

[ ] Giggling

[ ] Rapid Talking

[ ] Mood Swings

[ ] Wandering

[ ] Argumentative

[ ] Sleeping

[ ] Destructive

[ ] Belligerent

[ ] Irritable

INVOLVE SUPERVISORS

Provide specific details about what the employee did or said.

_____

_____

_____

Overall, the individual seemed:

[ ] Normal

[ ] Intoxicated

[ ] Not usual self

[ ] Impaired

[ ] Unable to function normally

[ ] Unsafe to be around

[ ] Under the influence

As a result of the determination made by the supervisor(s) whose signature(s) appears below, the individual suspected of impairment:

[ ] Provided a urine specimen

[ ] Refused to provide a specimen

COMMENTS

_____

_____

The specimen was:

Collected by: _____

Collected at: Time _____   Date _____

Forwarded to the lab: Time _____   Date _____

SIGNATURE(S) OF SUPERVISOR(S) MAKING THE DETERMINATION

_____   _____

(Signature)   (Signature)

_____   _____

(Date)   (Date)

Meeting With the Troubled Employee

Correcting a performance problem that appears related to drug abuse often starts with a meeting between the supervisor and the employee.

The major purpose of a meeting is to clearly advise the employee that corrective steps must be taken by the employee to eliminate the unacceptable work behavior, and that if performance does not improve within a reasonable time some further action, including discipline, will be necessary. Although no-nonsense in tone, the conversation should be non-accusatory, and if the subject of drug abuse is raised, it should be raised by the employee.

It is important to be specific about the behavior that is unacceptable, and refer only to the aspects of job performance. There should be no references to what may be the underlying cause of the unacceptable performance. For example, no mention should be made of drug use even though there may be strong suspicions along this line.

If the employee mentions drug use or some other reason as the cause of the unacceptable performance, it would be appropriate to allow the employee to fully explain. It must be kept in mind, however, that the purpose of the meeting is to discuss the employee's performance - not to engage in drug abuse counseling, which is a function of treatment professionals.

The supervisor has to be firm and clear about the nature and extent of improvement the employee will be expected to make. Lecturing and moralizing should be left out, and comments should be confined to job performance issues. The focus should be upon formal actions designed to present the employee with a firmly expressed intention to resolve the problem. Discussions might include performance targets and timetables, which if met, will restore the employee's performance to the expected standards.

The supervisor can anticipate that the employee will try sympathy-evoking tactics. Heartrending stories may come out, but these can't be allowed to detract from an insistence on improved performance. Misguided kindness can be fatal to a drug abusing employee's chances for eventual recovery. Giving a second chance will only prolong the unacceptable performance, and delay needed help.

CONCEPTS IMPORTANT TO SUPERVISION

An impediment to a uniformly consistent drug-free program can be the lack of a common understanding of basic concepts. Supervisors will be on the same sheet of music when each has a solid grasp of the following concepts.

Reasonable Cause

The terms reasonable belief, just cause, proper cause, and for cause generally mean the same thing. The term probable cause is a law enforcement or legal term similar to reasonable cause but much more precise and demanding in its application.

The term reasonable is often used in the context of searching. A search is said to be reasonable when it is based on a good faith belief, amounting to more than mere suspicion, that evidence of a certain violation can be found on a particular person or at a particular place.

The term unreasonable is often used to describe a search conducted when there are no facts which would lead a prudent person to believe that evidence of a violation will be found somewhere. An example would be a search of an employee's locker for the purpose of finding anything that could be used against the employee. This type of search is unreasonable because it is a kind of fishing expedition.

In the context of drug testing, a reasonable cause situation involves observed actions which indicate the use of a drug by an employee. The observed actions are subjected to a decision making model that helps the intervening supervisor make the correct decision. The decision making model takes the supervisor through a process of analysis that poses critical questions:

- Are the observed actions capable of explanation and substantiation?

- Are they specific, contemporaneous, and tangible?

- Are they associated with probable drug use?

When all the answers are clearly yes, drug testing is the appropriate course of action.

Two Supervisors Rule

The purpose of this rule is to increase the level of confidence in a decision to test in a reasonable cause situation. The rule calls for two supervisors who have knowledge of the facts of the situation to jointly make the determination to refer the employee for testing. Both or at least one of the supervisors will have been trained in how to make a reasonable cause determination.

A reasonable cause situation is a situation in which a supervisor is required to decide whether or not to order a drug or alcohol test of an employee whose on-duty conduct indicates intoxication or impairment. Any decision to test must be based on a reasonable belief that the employee is impaired as the result of drug use. The Two

Supervisors Rule requires certain critical questions to be asked and answered:

Is Impairment Present?

Testing cannot be authorized unless there are facts that point to impairment resulting from the possible use of drugs.

Are the Facts Reliable?

The supervisor can consider the facts of a situation to be wholly reliable when he personally has witnessed the situation. Reliability is also established when the facts of a situation are reported directly to the supervisor from another person who is considered believable and who claims to have been a direct witness. Reliability would not be present in a case where the credibility of the reporting person is questionable or when the reporting person does not have first-hand information.

Are the Facts Explainable?

A decision to conduct reasonable cause testing must be supported by specific details that can be explained. For example, it would not be sufficient to say only that an employee appeared to be under the influence of a drug. An explanation would need to include details of the observed impairment such as "the employee was staggering and his speech was slurred."

Is the Impairment Present Now?

The supervisor making a reasonable cause testing decision has to be sure that the suspected impairment exists at the moment the decision is being made. There are two good reasons for this: first, the test will most likely be negative if there is no impairment, and second, it would be unreasonable to require a person to take a test based on suspected past impairment.

Consent to Test

Under this concept, which carries the force of law, no person may be compelled to provide specimens. An employer, however, has the right to terminate an employee who refuses to provide a specimen when requested to do so. The employer's right must be supported by prior notice to the employee that a consent to test is a condition of employment.

Search With Implied Consent

A search with implied consent is a search conducted as a condition of employment or as part of an employment contract. Conditions of employment and employment contracts frequently express or imply consent to search employees and their belongings.

The rationale for implied consent searching is based on preventing an injurious outcome that can be reasonably expected to occur in the absence of a regularly conducted search program. An injurious outcome could be an explosion or fire in the workplace. The search program would be justified because of the need to ensure that ignition devices are excluded from the workplace. The same can be said for excluding impaired workers whose judgment or lack of motor skills might contribute to an explosion or fire or might detract from the proper emergency response.

The performance of an implied consent search is more like an inspection than anything else. It does not rely on reasonable belief; there need not be an accident, an incident, or a set of suspicious facts for the implied consent search.

Contraband

In the strict legal context, contraband is any item which by itself is a crime to have. Untaxed whiskey, illegal drugs, stolen property, pornographic materials, military explosives, and counterfeit money are contraband. All of these are prohibited from the workplace because possession of them places the possessor in violation of the law. An employer will sometimes include in its definition of contraband other prohibited items such as firearms and knives.

Amnesty

An amnesty provision usually accompanies the announcement of a drug abuse policy. The period of amnesty is typically not less than 30 and not longer than 60 days. Essentially, management pledges to forego drug testing for a period of time sufficient for drug-abusing employees to get "clean."

Amnesty does not usually apply in cases where the policy offense is other than merely having drugs in one's body system. Selling, possessing, and distributing drugs or drug paraphernalia would not be forgiven on grounds of amnesty.

Detectable Amount

This term relates to scientific studies which show lingering effects of drug impairment in persons who consumed drugs several days previously. While such studies may not be totally conclusive, especially on a person-by-person basis, the employer elects to act on the side of caution when adopting the detectable amount rule. The rule makes the statement that any employee found through drug testing to have in his or her body system a detectable amount of an illegal drug is in violation of the company's policy and is subject to discipline.

Chain of Custody

A very important concept relates to the procedures that are followed to document how and by whom a specimen is handled from the time it is taken from the individual, processed through the laboratory, and placed into protective storage. This record is referred to as the chain of custody.

A failure to properly monitor the collection of a urine specimen can result in actions by the donor to substitute a false specimen, contaminate his or her fresh specimen, or switch specimens with another donor. Other problems related to chain of custody include mislabeling and cross-contamination of specimens due to carelessness at the time of collection and poor packaging.

TRAINING OUTCOMES FOR SUPERVISORS

The intent of supervisory training is to develop in the supervisor new or enhanced skills that support on-the-job performance. Performance in this case is of certain responsibilities necessary to the administration of the organization's drug-free workplace program. Let's look at a few examples of training outcomes that bear on this aspect of supervisory performance.

As a result of training, the supervisor will be able to:

- Explain the business necessity that drives the company's drug abuse policy.

- Recognize by physical appearance marijuana, cocaine, heroin, phencyclidine, amphetamines, benzodiazepines, and alcohol.

- Recognize by physical appearance the common drug-related devices such as coke and heroin spoons, bongs, roach clips, and cigarette rolling paper.

- Identify the physiological indicators of impairment such as gait ataxia, nystagmus and strabismus, pupil dilation and contraction, and slurred speech.

- Identify the behavioral indicators of impairment such as mood swings, uncharacteristic arguing, violence, and bizarre acts.

- Explain the correct intervention responses when the indicators of impairment appear.

- Explain drug testing procedures to be followed in accidents and near-miss situations.

- Define illegal drugs, under the influence, detectable amount, consent required, reasonable cause, and the two supervisors rule.

Note that the outcomes are unambiguous and amenable to objective evaluation. Mystery does not surround what is expected, and the expected responses are easily assessed. In most cases, the evaluation verdict is a simple yes or no. The supervisor, for example, did or did not correctly define reasonable cause. Note also that the outcomes provide a degree of latitude as to methods of training. For some outcomes, the lecture method may be suitable. Others lend themselves to role playing, practical exercises based on hypothetical situations, and videotapes that require learners to react to short scenarios involving drug abuse at work.

No supervisor should be exempt from training. A supervisor who has not completed the training should not be allowed to carry out important provisions of the policy such as sending an employee to testing in a reasonable cause situation or referring an employee to an employee assistance program.

The training can be delivered as a stand-alone module or as a component of a larger program such as the training given to persons incidental to their moving into supervisory positions. Supervisor training should initially consist of one block of basic instruction, followed by periodic refresher or advanced blocks.

CONCLUSION

Areas related to drug testing in which the supervisor is likely to be involved include:

- Helping identify the drug abusers.

- Intervening when abuse is present.

- Administering discipline.

- Referring drug abusers to treatment.

- Evaluating rehabilitated abusers.

- Educating employees about drug dangers.

- Assisting in the collection of specimens.

A drug testing program will usually require supervisors to take specific actions designed to achieve the program's objectives. An important and sometimes complex supervisory action is to administer discipline. The program may, for example, call for removal of an employee who has tested positive. Removal could mean discharge, suspension pending rehabilitation, or transfer to another job such as a job having no safety duties.

In many organizations the drug testing program will treat some employees differently than others. Management may decide, for example, that only persons holding safety-sensitive positions need to be tested. Another common example is in the area of government regulation. An organization may be subject to rules that require certain categories of employees to be tested in certain ways, while the non-regulated employees are tested in other ways. The supervisor has to know these important differences and act accordingly.

Although drug testing programs are generally similar in purpose and practice, some organizations choose to include options that are important to the management's philosophy. These options are also important to supervisors because implementation of them requires active supervisory involvement.

When supervisors are brought into policy development and program planning and design, they tend naturally to acquire a commitment to the organization's drug-free goal. But the involvement of supervisors does not end there. They become the major practitioners of the program, and for this effort they require training to acquire the appropriate knowledge and skill.

8

Drug Testing

STARTING A DRUG TESTING PROGRAM

The start-up of a drug testing program can mean a great deal of change to an organization and the people in it. Employers know from experience how difficult it can be to get workers to accept change. It doesn't seem to matter whether the change is large or small, good or bad. People just naturally don't like change.

Fear is usually just beneath the surface of resistance to change. Not understanding the nature of the change feeds upon the fear. The greater the misunderstanding, the greater the fear; the greater the fear, the greater the resistance. Workers who don't understand drug testing will see it as a threat to their jobs or how they stand in the organization, and they will resist. Resistance in this case springs from very human and very natural emotions.

Lack of understanding leads to uncertainty. An employee may not be against the change itself, but will resist it because of the uncertainty about what the change may bring. A worker's concern may not be with testing but with the possibility that testing will negatively impact the worker personally.

What can be done? First, management should anticipate resistance and be prepared to deal with it in a positive way. Next should be the recognition that most employees are drug-free and can be won over to the idea of testing because they know that a drug-free working environment is to everyone's best interest. Third is a consideration that the drug-abusing minority will strongly resist because they will see testing as a definite threat.

The best weapons against resistance are truth and openness. The concept of drug testing and the effect of it on employees should be extensively publicized throughout the organization. Many of the concerns that employees will have about drug testing can be addressed by their supervisors before they get blown out of proportion. A supervisor who meets one-on-one and in small groups with employees will make it possible for concerns to be aired, considered, and carefully answered.

Communicating the drug testing program is also a good way to overcome the counterproductive information that tends to flow through an organization's grapevine. When plans are kept under wraps people become suspicious and eventually resistive. The best approach is to be completely open about plans for drug testing and to use every opportunity to explain what is going on.

THE FUNDAMENTALS

Drug testing seeks to identify in a person's body the evidence of illegal drug use. The most common method of drug testing is the analysis of urine. The individual to be tested is asked (not compelled) to provide a urine specimen. A consent form signed by the individual demonstrates the willingness to be tested.

The specimen is collected in a manner that prevents cheating and error. The integrity of the specimen has to be unquestionably reliable. Any indication of contamination, switching, or mislabeling will render a test result invalid. A chain of custody form initiated by the collector is filled out by every person who handles the specimen from collection until final destruction.

A specimen is carefully packaged and quickly transported to a testing lab where it is analyzed for the presence of drugs. Federal drug testing programs currently test for five drugs: cocaine, marijuana, opiates, amphetamines, and PCP. Non-federal testing programs usually test for these same five drugs and others as well, usually barbiturates, benzodiazepines, and methaqualone.

Most testing programs follow a two-step approach. If no drugs are found in the first step, the specimen is not further tested and is declared negative. If a drug is found, the specimen is tested a second time using a different technique.

If the second test fails to confirm the first test, the specimen is declared negative; if the second test confirms the first test, the specimen is declared positive.

In some programs a positive report is forwarded to a physician who evaluates the report in light of information about the individual. The information may come from what the individual says and what a medical examination reveals. If there is any reliable indication that the positive test resulted from something other than illegal drug use, such as the proper use of a prescription drug, the test is declared negative.

Almost all testing programs provide opportunities for challenging positive test reports, including the right to obtain a re-test by the lab or an equally competent lab of the individual's choosing. Some programs have treatment and return to duty provisions, and almost all organizations that conduct drug testing assist employees by identifying treatment resources in the local community.

DRUG TESTING

Applicant Testing

Pre-employment screening for drug abuse is used widely to screen job applicants. Urine analysis is solidly entrenched in the pre-employment screening processes of employers large and small and in all sectors. Many employers make it clear up front that they will not hire individuals who present urine specimens that indicate current use of illegal drugs.

Reasonableness

Issues of privacy rights and equal employment argue strongly for a well thought-out policy that carefully considers the need for unbiased, accurate, and legally defensible actions, particularly in the area of testing. An employer concerned about legal challenges will craft a reasonable policy, inform employees of the policy and the consequences of policy violations, and make employees aware that testing is a job condition.

Company policy regarding the circumstances of testing is usually determined with consideration of risk factors associated with safety, security, and health. The least intrusive is an incident-driven policy wherein screening occurs only after an accident, an incident (e.g., a fight), or other "probable cause" event. High-risk or safety-sensitive occupations where safety is of special concern may require routine scheduled screening. In these cases, screening is often tied to evaluation of fitness for duty or to annual physical examinations. In extremely hazardous and high-risk occupations, unannounced or random testing may be warranted.

How best to deal with the problems associated with employee drug use is a complex issue. Principles of safety, performance, and productivity must be balanced against reasonable expectations of privacy and confidentiality. Job situations where there is a substantial risk to safety justify greater permissible intrusions than would be acceptable where risks are perceived as minimal. On the one hand, an employer has the right to demand a workplace free of drug abuse; on the other, workers have reasonable rights to privacy and confidentiality. Since drug abuse is generally accepted as diagnosable and treatable, policy and procedures should ensure the confidentiality of employee medical records, as in any other medical or health-related condition. Test results, which could be part of such a diagnosis, should be treated with the same degree of care.

An early priority for the employer is to determine the need for testing. Is drug abuse present in the workplace and, if so, is it significant? Can abuse be deterred by means other than testing? If adopted, what will be the purpose of testing? If the answer to the last question is to rid the workplace of drug abusers, the employer needs to go back to the drawing board and rethink the whole matter. The purpose of testing must center on a reasonable business necessity, such as health and safety, and the testing must be carried out with the highest regard for the personal privacy and dignity of workers.

Impairment

Although urinalysis is extremely effective in determining previous drug use, the positive results of a test cannot be used to prove intoxication or impaired performance. Inert drug metabolites may appear in urine for several days (or weeks depending upon the drug) without related impairment. However, positive urine tests do provide evidence of prior drug use and evidence to support disciplinary action under the "detectable amount" rule.

Accuracy and Reliability

A variety of methods are available to laboratories for identifying drugs through urinalysis. Most of these are suitable for determining the presence or absence of a drug in a urine sample. Accuracy and reliability of these methods must be assessed in the context of the total laboratory system. If the laboratory uses well-trained and certified personnel who follow the correct scientific procedures, high accuracy and reliability will result. An assurance of accuracy and reliability is the U.S. Department of Health and Human Services drug testing laboratory certification. The DHHS certificate is not easily obtained, is held by a relatively small number of laboratories, and is the best indicator of quality.

Quality Assurance

Quality assurance procedures are documented protocols that a laboratory follows to ensure accuracy and reliability. QA protocols include controlling the way samples for analysis are handled, instruments checked and calibrated to be sure they are functioning correctly, and minimizing human error. Self assessment through analysis of standard samples and blank samples along with unknown samples is a method for ensuring that the total laboratory system is producing the expected results.

TESTING METHODS

Urine testing follows a two-step process consisting of a screen and a second test to confirm any positive findings of the screen. When a specimen shows negative in the screen, testing stops for that sample; when the screen is positive, the specimen is subjected to a confirmation test.

Screening is done with immunoassay techniques. If a screening assay shows a sample as being positive, a second assay, using a different detecting principle, is employed to confirm the initial result. Two different assays operating on different principles, both having given positive results, greatly decreases the possibility of error.

The confirmation assay is made by a method which is more specific (or selective) than a screening assay. The commonly used confirmation methods include gas chromatography (GC), gas chromatography/mass spectrometry (GC/MS), and high performance liquid chromatography (HPLC). These are sophisticated instrumental methods requiring highly trained technicians. Such tests cost more than screening tests, but they provide a greater margin of certainty

Sensitivity and Cutoff

The ability of an assay to detect low levels of drugs has an inherent limit. The concentration of a drug in the urine sample below which the assay can no longer be considered reliable is the "sensitivity" limit. Manufacturers of commercial urine screening systems set cutoff limits to their assays well above the sensitivity limits to minimize the possibility of a sample which is truly negative giving a positive result. For example, although immunoassays that detect marijuana are sufficiently sensitive at levels below 20 nanograms per milliliter, the assays are usually used at cutoff levels of 50 or 100 nanograms. This not only decreases the possibility of a false positive resulting from operating the assay too close to its level of sensitivity, but also significantly decreases the possibility of a positive test resulting from an outside influence, e.g., passive inhalation of marijuana.

False Positive

A false positive occurs when a drug is reported to be present in a urine specimen, when in fact it is not there at all. False positives can be put into three categories:

- A chemical false positive. This may occur if another substance in the specimen is mistakenly identified as the drug being analyzed. A chemical false positive may also occur if the specimen is contaminated or adulterated during handling or analysis.

- An administrative false positive. This may occur if the wrong specimen is tested. It can result from improper labeling or recording and transcription errors. Another type of administrative error is to report a negative as a positive; for example, a clerk at the laboratory may make an incorrect entry on a report form. Administrative errors are human errors and almost all false positives fall into this category.

- Operator error. This may occur during a testing procedure at the laboratory, particularly if quality assurance precautions are not carefully followed.

A few foods and medications with chemical structures very similar to drugs may sometimes produce positive results. An example are poppy seeds, such as can be found on a hamburger bun. Poppy seeds come from the poppy plant, as does opium. It is technically possible for a person to consume poppy seeds and very shortly thereafter test positive for an opiate. However, the laboratory would conduct further testing to resolve questions about whether the opiate is related to poppy seeds or to heroin, morphine, codeine and other forms of opium.

The two most frequent reasons for false positives are poor quality assurance procedures in the laboratory, and the failure to conduct confirmation tests. A good laboratory will maintain a quality assurance program and insist that the client authorize confirmation of all positive tests. The best confirmation technique is GC/MS.

By contrast, a false negative occurs when a test fails to identify a drug that really was present in the specimen. False negatives occur all the time and, in fact, they are designed to occur. Why? Because the testing laboratories set up their testing systems so that a positive result is reported only when the amount of the drug is above a certain level.

The Need to Use Quality Testing

The need to use assay systems that are based on state-of-the-art methods and rigorously controlled procedures is inherent in situations where the consequences of a positive result to the individual are great. Where reputation, livelihood, incarceration, or the right to employment is an issue, maximum accuracy and reliability of the entire detection or deterrent system is indicated. In a case where the consequences are less severe, such as a counseling situation, it might be acceptable to use less rigorous systems. For instance, pediatricians sometimes use portable screening systems in their practices to assist in the diagnosis and treatment of drug problems in adolescents. Deterrence screening programs might employ screening assays alone when warnings are the only consequence.

Passive Inhalation

Inadvertent exposure to marijuana is frequently claimed as the basis for a positive urine sample. Passive inhalation of marijuana smoke does occur and can result in detectable body fluid levels of THC (tetrahydrocannabinol, the primary pharmacological component of marijuana) in blood and of its metabolites in urine. Clinical studies have shown, however, that it is highly unlikely that a nonsmoking individual could inhale sufficient smoke by passive inhalation to result in a high enough drug concentration in urine for detection at the cutoff level.

Time of Previous Drug Use

Urine specimens that show positive for cannabinoids signify that a person has consumed marijuana or marijuana derivatives from within 1 hour to as much as 3 weeks or more before the specimen was collected. Generally, a single smoking session by a casual user of marijuana will result in subsequently collected urine samples being positive for 2 to 5 days, depending on the screening method employed and on physiological factors which cause the drug concentration to vary. Detection time increases significantly following a period of chronic use. Determination of a particular time of use is thus difficult. The same issues would hold for other drugs, although the time after use during which a positive analysis would be expected might be reduced to a few days rather than a week or more.

Can a Pattern of Abuse Be Determined?

Impairment, intoxication, or time of last use cannot be predicted from a single urine test. In the case of marijuana, a true-positive urine test indicates only that the person used marijuana in the recent past, which could be hours, days, or weeks depending on the specific use pattern. Repeated analyses over time will, however, allow a better understanding of the past and current use patterns. An infrequent user should be completely negative in a few days. Repeated positive analyses over a period of more than 2 weeks probably indicate either continuing use or previous heavy chronic use.

Detection Times for Hard Drugs

Detection times are dependent on the sensitivity of the assay. The more sensitive the assay, the longer the drug can be detected. Drug concentrations are initially highest hours after drug use and decrease to undetectable levels over time. The time it takes to reach the point of nondetectability depends on the particular drug and other factors such as an individual's metabolism. The sensitivity of urine assay methods generally available today allows detection of cocaine use for a period of 1-3 days and heroin or phencyclidine (PCP) use for 2-4 days. These detection times would be somewhat lengthened in cases of previous chronic drug use but probably to no more than double these times.

Detection Time for Marijuana

Metabolites of the active ingredients of marijuana may be detectable in urine for up to 10 days after a single smoking session. However, most individuals cease to excrete detectable drug concentrations in 2 to 5 days. Metabolites can sometimes be detected several weeks after a heavy chronic smoker (several smoking sessions a day) has ceased smoking.

Liquid Intake

The actual concentration of drug in urine can change considerably depending on the individual's liquid intake. The more an individual drinks, the more the drug is diluted in the urine. A negative result on a sample taken a few hours after drinking significant amounts of liquid

140

is quite possible, even though a clearly positive sample might have been evident before the liquid intake. For this reason, a negative result does not mean that the person has not used the drug recently. For example, the excretion of marijuana metabolites reaches the approximate limit of detection by a given assay, repeated samples collected over several days may alternate between positive and negative before becoming all negative.

Test Reports

Frequently the results of an assay are reported by the laboratory simply as positive or negative. If a sample is reported as positive, this means that the laboratory detected the drug in an amount exceeding the cutoff level set for that drug. Different laboratories using different procedures and methods may have different cutoff levels. For this reason, one laboratory could determine a sample to be positive and another determine the same sample to be negative if the actual amount of the drug in the sample fell between the cutoff levels used by the two laboratories.

Nanograms and Micrograms

Analyses may also be reported quantitatively. The actual concentration of the drug is expressed as a certain amount per volume of urine. Depending on the drug or the drug metabolite that is being analyzed, urine concentrations may be expressed either as nanograms per milliliter (ng/ml) or as micrograms per milliliter (ug/ml). (There are 28,000,000 micrograms in an ounce, and 1,000 nanograms in a microgram.) Cocaine metabolites may be detected in amounts as high as several micrograms in a heavy user, but the levels of metabolites from marijuana use rarely reach one microgram per milliliter and are usually expressed in nanograms per milliliter.

DRUG TESTING

LEGAL ISSUES IN DRUG TESTING

Court decisions have consistently held that employers have the right to conduct drug testing. Many of the civil suits that challenge an employer's drug testing program do so on grounds that testing was done in a manner that violated an individual's right. The challenge is not whether drug testing is legal, but whether it is being done in a fair and reasonable way.

Civil suits have also been brought against employers who have not taken reasonable steps to maintain a safe working environment. A complaint may allege that the employer was negligent by not conducting drug testing as a means for preventing accidents caused by impaired workers.

Many employers who have looked at the legal pros and cons have concluded that safety, health, and productivity outweigh other considerations. The need to protect workers and the public from injury or death is of greater importance than individual desires.

Legal issues strongly influence the way in which an employer conducts a drug testing program. Following are some principles:

- Testing is founded on a written policy and is communicated to employees and job applicants.

- Pre-employment testing is applied to all applicants, not just some.

- Random testing is conducted for safety or other important reasons.

- Reasonable cause testing is authorized only when specific, objective facts clearly point to drug abuse.

- Specimens are collected carefully and documented accurately.

- Testing methods are highly accurate and reliable.

- Policy violations are disciplined fairly and consistently.

- Drug testing results are treated as confidential information.

A drug testing program will reflect a complex arrangement of its own policy choices, labor contracts, regulations, laws, and court rulings.

CONCLUSION

The evaluation of employees to determine fitness for duty has long been performed in industry. Job-related health programs traditionally include physical examinations intended to ensure the selection of personnel free of medical conditions that could interfere with safety and efficiency. In recent years, an additional purpose of the medical evaluation has evolved; that is, to address risk factors that may impair employee health (e.g., poor nutrition, substance abuse, and hypertension).

As drug abuse in the United States has risen, many companies have developed pre-employment and in-service drug abuse testing programs. A primary purpose of these programs is to protect the health and safety of employees through the early identification of drug problems, followed by referral to treatment. The integration of testing with programs of prevention and treatment is proving to be effective.

9

Employee Assistance Program (EAP)

BACKGROUND

Attention to employee alcohol and other drug problems first emerged in the 1970s and expanded rapidly into the 1980s with the spread of employee assistance programs (EAPs) created to help employees overcome problems that interfere with their work, including drug use and other health issues, as well as personal, marital, family, legal, and financial problems. Usually based on a written policy statement, EAPs provide a means to access appropriate expertise and consultation and help with employees experiencing such problems. EAPs also provide

145

EMPLOYEE ASSISTANCE PROGRAM (EAP)

for employee self-referral, and in many instances, provide services to dependents of employees.

An important characteristic of EAPs is an emphasis upon constructive rather than punitive treatment of employees experiencing drug problems. The underlying assumption of EAPs is that help for employees will reduce turnover and enable them to resume effective work performance.

Employees who work for larger companies are more likely to have access to the services of an EAP. One study found that 52 percent of workplaces with 750 or more employees have EAPs, compared with 15 percent for workplaces with 50 to 99 employees. In total, over 80 percent of large U.S. firms have EAPs and over 31 percent of all American workers are employed by companies with EAPs.

An EAP is a worksite-based program designed to assist in the identification and resolution of safety and productivity problems associated with employees whose performance and/or conduct is adversely affected by personal concerns including health, marital, family, financial, alcohol, drug, legal, emotional, stress, or other personal concerns.

Core activities of the typical EAP include:

- Expert consultation and training of designated persons in the identification and resolution of job-performance issues related to the personal concerns of employees.

- Confidential, appropriate, and timely problem-assessment.

- Referrals for appropriate diagnosis, treatment, and assistance.

- Formation of linkages between workplace and community resources that provide such services.

- Follow-up services.

The services that EAPs offer include crisis intervention, assessment and referral, short-term problem resolution, monitoring and follow-up, supervisor training and consultation, organizational consultation, program promotion, and education. The common EAP models are as follows.

- The internal program is company-staffed by an employee who accepts both supervisor- and self-referrals, conducts initial assessments, and refers employees to community resources for counseling or treatment.

- The external program is for companies that want to contract with outside agencies to provide most services of the EAP, including assessment.

- The labor union model is staffed by qualified union representatives and serves union members. The primary service offered is referral.

- The professional association program includes the possibility of license withdrawal as an inducement for members to obtain assistance.

- The consortia model is often used by small or medium-sized companies. It enables these businesses to combine resources and efforts for the provision of EAP services. By joining several work populations into a single group, small businesses are able to contract with an EAP provider to deliver services at a quantity discount.

The Employee Assistance Professionals Association (EAPA) and the Employee Assistance Society of North America (EASNA) are national organizations whose professional membership includes EAP directors and counselors, behavioral specialists, organizational development specialists, workplace researchers, and labor leaders.

EAPs are often part of a larger employer effort to promote the health and fitness of employees. Programs to promote wellness are becoming more and more common in the workplace. Wellness programs are generally described as efforts to maintain good health by changing destructive habits and having people take greater responsibility for the state of their health. Employers have come to realize the importance of educating people about the health effects of drug use, stress, poor

EMPLOYEE ASSISTANCE PROGRAM (EAP)

eating habits, and other controllable aspects of their lifestyles. The idea behind corporate wellness programs is to prevent problems from occurring and not having to treat problems after they have occurred.

EAP Staffing

In large organizations, the duties associated with administering an employee assistance program (EAP) tend to be distributed among several key persons. A key person may perform program duties only or include program duties with other job duties. In medium and small organizations, the full range of program duties tend to be carried out by one or two persons who may or may not wear another hat. The following descriptions give an idea of the duties involved:

Drug Program Coordinator

- Serves as the principal contact with the testing laboratory.

- Assesses the reliability and accuracy of test results by conducting or arranging for periodic inspections of the testing laboratory.

- Supervises specimen collection activities.

- Ensures that employees subject to random testing receive individual notice that they are subject to random testing.

- In concert with the EAP Administrator, prepares and disseminates awareness and training materials, and monitors awareness and training sessions.

- Coordinates the above-described duties as they are performed by others at separate work locations.

EMPLOYEE ASSISTANCE PROGRAM (EAP)

Employee Assistance Program Administrator

- Receives verified positive test results from the Medical Review Officer.

- Assumes the lead role in the development, implementation, and evaluation of the EAP.

- Acts as the principal point of contact with treatment diagnosticians and counselors.

Employee Assistance Program Coordinator

- Provides counseling and treatment services to employees referred to the EAP.

- Coordinates EAP activities with the Medical Review Officer and supervisors.

- Collaborates with the Drug Program Coordinator in providing awareness and training materials.

- Assists supervisors in the handling of performance and/or personnel problems that may be related to drug abuse.

- Monitors the progress of referred employees during and after the rehabilitation period, and provides relevant feedback to supervisors.

- Assists supervisors in making reasonable cause determinations.

- Networks with rehabilitation or treatment organizations that provide counseling and rehabilitative programs. Assesses the experience, certification, and educational level of treatment staff.

EMPLOYEE ASSISTANCE PROGRAM (EAP)

Employee Assistance Counselor

- Serves as the initial point of contact for employees who ask for or are referred for counseling.

- Counsels employees who have drug abuse problems.

- Ensures that the EAP operates in accord with applicable laws and regulations.

- Ensures the appropriateness of treatment plans prescribed for employees referred for treatment.

- Makes referrals with consideration of the nature and severity of the problem, location of the treatment site, cost of the treatment, intensity of the treatment environment, availability of inpatient and outpatient care, and the preferences of the employee.

Medical Review Officer

- Receives laboratory test results and assures that an individual who has tested positive has been afforded an opportunity to discuss the test result.

- Consistent with confidentiality requirements, refers written determinations regarding verified positive test results to the EAP Administrator.

- Coordinates Medical Review Officer duties at separate work locations.

EAP DEVELOPMENT

The development of an EAP that includes treatment services may take one of several forms. A program may be designed to deal specifically and exclusively with drugs, or it may focus on drugs and alcohol together. Such programs are sometimes said to address "substance abuse" or "chemical dependency" problems. An even broader approach would be to include drug-abusing employees within the "troubled employee" concept.

There is a general trend away from explicit references to problems, such as drug abuse, toward a more general concept embodied in the employee assistance program approach. The reasons are several. The broader troubled employee concept implies assistance for an employee, no matter what the problem may be - drugs, alcohol, financial, legal, emotional, family, and so forth.

The troubled employee approach offers two distinct advantages when the problem stems from drug abuse:

- Employees are more likely to seek help when the assistance program is not identified as a drug abuse program. This is because people do not want to be labeled as drug abusers.

- Drug-abusing employees may seek help in dealing with secondary problems, e.g., problems that result from abuse such as family strain or financial difficulty. It may become evident during counseling that the "presented" problem is in reality a symptom of the larger problem of drug abuse.

Regardless of approach, a program that includes treatment usually includes five components:

- A means for identifying drug-abusing employees. This can be done in several ways. Supervisors and managers can be trained to spot the indicators of drug abuse, and to report or refer suspected abusers to the appropriate person or department. The company can strive to establish a climate of concern and trust that will encourage employees to seek help on their own. Urinalysis can also be very effective.

- A mechanism for referring employees to the appropriate counseling or treatment resource. This might be a trained or designated staff member who is capable of evaluating the nature of the employee's problem and is knowledgeable concerning company and community resources.

EMPLOYEE ASSISTANCE PROGRAM (EAP)

- Provisions for treatment, which in most cases will include counseling of some type. Treatment, depending on company resources, can be provided in-house or from the community.

- Monitoring during and after treatment. The purposes of follow-up are to determine if therapy was successful, to identify relapse, and to provide to the employee further treatment services that may be needed to ensure lasting recovery.

- Complete and accurate records that provide individual case histories, from identification to follow-up. Utmost confidentiality is required. The documentation system can also serve as a basis for evaluating the effectiveness of the program.

Decision Factors

The design of a drug abuse treatment component will be conditioned by the answers to these questions:

- Does management want to exercise a high degree of program control by providing treatment services from in-house resources? Keep in mind that some forms of counseling and treatment are well beyond the expertise and facilities of even the best staffed and equipped companies.

- Is management prepared to commit the financial and staff resources required? Some companies may be too small or too fragile economically to permit expenditures of any amount. When this is the case, the company should at least encourage needy employees to obtain treatment even though the company is not in a position to assist financially.

- Does the local community have good treatment resources? Are the resources affordable and conveniently accessible? If so, an alternative might be to channel needy employees to outside agencies.

- Is it possible to set up a pooling arrangement in which the company and one or more other companies form a consortium? The consortium would share among its members the financial and staff burdens of a fully developed program. Arrangements of this type tend to work best when the consortium, though jointly funded, operates with some degree of independence.

Drug abuse programs that include treatment generally take one of two configurations: the Community Model or the In-house Model.

The Community Model

Companies with limited resources or companies that operate in areas having appropriate quality treatment services are logically attracted to the use of community resources.

The company's staff is likely to consist of a single coordinator and clerical support. The coordinator typically possesses a combination of interactive and administrative skills, and has a strong knowledge of available treatment resources. While not necessarily a trained counselor, the coordinator is sufficiently skillful in evaluating the gross dimensions of an employee's problems so that a correct referral can be made.

There are three major channels through which employees with drug abuse problems come into contact with the coordinator.

- Identification by supervisors and managers who have been trained to observe and document unsatisfactory job performance.

- Self-initiated action by employees seeking assistance.

- Identification through the administration of drug testing.

After consultation with an employee, the coordinator proposes to the employee a rehabilitation strategy, obtains the employee's agreement, and then makes arrangements for the employee to receive the proposed treatment through a facility located in the community.

The coordinator monitors an employee's progress during and after treatment. The criteria for successful therapy might be the elimination of the unsatisfactory performance indicators that channeled the employee into the program initially. Also, a return to unsatisfactory job performance after treatment might indicate a relapse.

The major advantage of the community resources model is the minimal commitment of company staff. A disadvantage is that community resources are not usually designed for resolving drug abuse problems as they relate to a work environment generally or to a particular company's work environment.

In-House Model

This approach is almost always reserved for companies able and willing to commit substantial in-house resources.

Counseling services are provided by staff members, with some forms of treatment provided in the community.

The program staff typically consists of a coordinator and clerical support staff. The coordinator is a trained counselor who interfaces with a medical director or medical complement (doctors, nurses, technicians) which may also provide relevant services or guidance.

The major advantage of the in-house model is that it allows counseling to be more attuned to the employee's unique work situation. The counselor is better positioned to monitor improvement or deterioration of the employee's job performance, and to intercede where necessary to keep the employee on track with the prescribed rehabilitation strategy. The chief disadvantage of this model is cost.

EMPLOYEE ASSISTANCE PROGRAM (EAP)

EAP POLICY

Like other programs impacting employees, an EAP rests on a sound policy. An EAP policy, unlike a drug testing policy, is rewarding in nature and has few, if any, negative implications. For that reason, it can be relatively short.

Following is an example of an EAP policy:

EMPLOYEE ASSISTANCE PROGRAM POLICY

I. Statement of Policy

The goals of the Company employee assistance program (EAP) are to motivate employees to seek help with personal problems, and to improve, maintain, or restore employee productivity through early identification and assistance with these problems.

Currently, the Company has a contract with an EAP provider for comprehensive employee assistance services to employees and their immediate family members. The EAP provider offers confidential evaluation, short-term counseling, and referral service assistance to employees experiencing problems that may affect job, family, or community life.

II. Using the Employee Assistance Program

A. Full-time and part-time regular employees and their dependents are eligible to make use of the employee assistance program.

B. Employees may contact the EAP provider directly for assistance. In addition to self referrals, an employee may utilize the program through a management referral.

C. All contacts with the employee assistance program are confidential. No information specific to any employee will be released without the employee's written consent.

D. When an employee's job performance or attendance becomes unsatisfactory, and the employee has been unable to correct the job problems with normal supervisory assistance, the supervisor, in consultation with the Company personnel department, may formally recommend that the employee utilize the employee assistance program.

E. Use of the employee assistance program is voluntary. Acceptable job performance and attendance remain the employee's responsibility whether or not he or she chooses to seek assistance from the employee assistance program.

F. Leave procedures will apply to treatment for psychological or alcohol and drug problems on the same basis as they apply to other illnesses and health problems.

G. Employees may contact the benefits section of the Company personnel department for more specific information related to the employee assistance program.

SELECTING AN EMPLOYEE ASSISTANCE VENDOR

A starting point in evaluating and choosing an EAP vendor is to first define what is needed. Begin by asking these questions:

- What clinical services do I need?

- What supervisory training do I need?

- How much do I want to involve my company in the operation of the program?

- How should the program be promoted?

EMPLOYEE ASSISTANCE PROGRAM (EAP)

Clinical Services

Clinical services are the assessment, diagnostic, and treatment services provided by trained and experienced professionals. The individuals providing these services should have at least a master's degree in their respective disciplines and three years of clinical experience.

Assessment and diagnosis typically occur together; treatment takes place later. The client (e.g., a drug-abusing employee) would meet with a diagnostician in one or a series of sessions. A provisional or working evaluation of the client's problem and a treatment plan would be prepared. The diagnostician would additionally identify treatment providers who are qualified in the problem area.

Some EAP vendors offer only assessment and diagnosis, while others also offer treatment services. An employer will need to weigh the pros and cons of working with two vendors or of using a "one-stop, full-service" vendor. Another consideration is whether or not the employer wants treatment to be held at the worksite or at the vendor's location.

It is important that the client have the right to choose the treatment provider. When treatment is offered by the same EAP vendor that provided the assessment, and the client opts to stay with the vendor, the client should sign an affidavit showing that other choices were offered.

Simple problems, such as coping with a temporary financial crisis, can be treated in 1 to 3 brief counseling sessions that are often educational in nature and include practical, problem-solving guidance. Difficult problems, such as drug dependency, require a more intense approach delivered in 6 or more sessions. In a 6-session program dealing with drug abuse, a realistic goal may be to overcome the employee's denial of the problem. Full rehabilitation will often require longer-term therapy through a community-based agency.

The EAP can be no better than the resources it draws upon. A well-constructed network of resources will consist of social agencies, private practitioners, community-based programs, educational services, and self-help groups. If a company employs people at remote locations where resources are scarce or unknown, an option is to establish a toll-free number. A caller can be given a brief diagnostic

157

interview by a clinician who can refer the caller to the nearest available treatment provider or a network affiliate.

There are distinct advantages to the company when the EAP vendor (or affiliate) is in close proximity to the workplace. First, the employee or supervisor can deal with a person, as opposed to a voice on the telephone. Second, the response time to calls for services will be prompt. Third, a nearby EAP vendor will have first-hand knowledge of local resources.

A Phased Approach

Let's assume that an employer has assessed EAP needs and examined the wide range of issues associated with clinical services, training, involvement, and promotion. At this point the matter of costs begin to intrude. Unless the company is large and profitable, the employer will rule out starting a fully comprehensive EAP. Instead, the employer will want to start modestly and move by degrees to an optimum level. A growing or expanding approach that moves through three phases might be the answer.

Phase 1.

- The company's human resources department handles all referrals.

- A referred employee is availed of 1 to 3 assessment/diagnostic sessions that end with the provision of a treatment plan and a referral to a treatment provider, or a referral to treatment provided by a tax-supported community agency.

- The company conducts or hires a vendor to conduct supervisor training consisting of at least one 60-minute session.

- The company promotes the EAP internally, e.g., by an introductory letter to employees, bulletin board notices, etc.

EMPLOYEE ASSISTANCE PROGRAM (EAP)

Phase 2.

- The company's supervisors, with overview by the human resources department, makes referrals.

- A referred employee is availed of 3 to 6 assessment/diagnostic sessions that end with the provision of treatment provided by paid and/or tax-supported professionals, as recommended by an EAP vendor and approved by the employee.

- The company conducts or hires a vendor to conduct supervisor training consisting of at least one 60-minute session, and provides one 90-minute small-group workshop.

- The company promotes the EAP internally, plus one 60-minute awareness presentation for employees.

Phase 3.

- The company's supervisors, with overview by the human resources department, makes referrals.

- A referred employee is availed of 6 to 9 assessment/diagnostic sessions that end with the provision of treatment provided by paid professionals, as recommended by an EAP vendor and approved by the employee.

- The company provides a toll-free number for employees seeking assistance.

- The company conducts or hires a vendor to conduct supervisor training consisting of at least one 60-minute session, one 90-minute small-group workshop, and one 60-minute refresher session conducted semiannually.

- The company establishes a Board of Advisors.

EMPLOYEE ASSISTANCE PROGRAM (EAP)

- The company promotes the EAP internally, provides one 60-minute awareness presentation for employees, sponsors quarterly brown-bag meetings, and an annual wellness event.

Evaluating an EAP Vendor

Following is a checklist for evaluating an EAP vendor.

A CHECKLIST FOR EVALUATING AN EAP VENDOR

Credentials

- Determine the education, training and experience of staff.

- Determine the ratio of clinical to administrative staff.

- Determine the turnover of staff.

- Is staff familiar with workplace issues, such as drug testing?

- Who are the principals? What role do they play?

- How long has the vendor been in business?

- Does the vendor have liability insurance that meets state requirements? Have liability claims been placed against the vendor? Has the vendor been sued? Disposition of cases?

- Is vendor independent, or affiliated with a treatment agency or insurance carrier?

- Is the vendor a for profit or nonprofit agency?

- Who are the vendor's clients?

- What is the vendor's reputation in the EAP field?

- Is the vendor local, regional, or national?

- Who are the vendor's subcontractors and affiliates?

- Is the vendor familiar with your company and the nature of your work and industry?

Program Issues

- What kinds of information will the vendor share with your EAP coordinator?

- What reports will the vendor routinely or specially provide?

- In what fashion does the vendor evaluate program effectiveness?

- What audit opportunities does the vendor grant to its clients?

- Determine the vendor's capabilities for data processing and communications.

- Does the vendor have and follow written procedures?

- Does the vendor comply with confidentiality rules and laws?

- What are the vendor's practices with respect to releasing information to third parties, such as regulatory agencies and law enforcement? To your EAP coordinator?

- Are the vendor's services narrowly focused (such as on substance abuse problems) or broadly focused?

- What services does the vendor offer in promoting a client's EAP?

EMPLOYEE ASSISTANCE PROGRAM (EAP)

Accessibility

- Is the vendor's location such that visits to it will not harm confidentiality?

- Is the initial phone intake accompanied by a phone assessment or immediate follow-up face-to-face session?

- What is the average time between phone intake and first session?

- During a crisis intervention, will the vendor go to the employee? Transport the employee to a meeting or treatment site?

- What services can be offered on-site? Off-site?

- Does the vendor have a hot line service?

Education and Training

- Does the vendor offer employee education? Supervisory training?

- Does the vendor offer refresher education and training?

- Do the learning objectives correspond to your needs?

- What are the qualifications of the instructors?

- Are handouts included? Are they job-related?

Fees

- What is the basis for the pricing structure? Headcounts?

- Are fees for services or per diem, or both?

- Is the vendor subsidized by public monies? Donations?

Miscellaneous

- If the vendor is affiliated with a treatment provider, will referrals be made to that provider?

- Does the vendor's record reflect an ability to work with collective bargaining units?

- Does the vendor's client list include any of your major competitors?

- Does the vendor have a Preferred Provider network?

- Is the vendor aware of conflict of interest issues and how they can be avoided?

Support and Involvement

Without the support and involvement of the management and supervisory staff, the EAP cannot fully succeed. The organization's supervisors are best positioned to see the problem indicators, to intervene as necessary, and to channel employees to the EAP services. Hand-in-hand with these functions are special and careful attention to documenting instances of unacceptable performance, conferring with problem employees and EAP professionals, and conducting follow-up evaluations of employees who have returned to work after completing a rehabilitation program.

Confidentiality and the voluntary nature of the EAP demand a central focus. Without confidentiality and voluntariness, the EAP runs the risk of being perceived as punitive, thereby negating its intent and value.

Involving supervisors is also a mechanism for obtaining supervisory buy-in to the EAP philosophy and rationale. Supervisors need to understand the benefits of the program to the company, to the employees and their families, and how the EAP can be applied as a supervisory tool for improving morale, meeting production goals, and enforcing workplace rules. A seriously committed approach will place EAP as a topic on the agenda of every supervisory meeting.

Management determines the extent of the organization's direct participation in the operation of the EAP. For example, management may decide that all supervisory referrals to EAP services are to pass through the personnel department. Those referrals that can be handled in-house are assigned to personnel specialists holding qualifications in EAP disciplines. Alternatively, the decision may be to give to supervisors the responsibility of making referrals directly to an EAP vendor. Involvement in the first instance is somewhat limited because only one or a few human resource specialists will be EAP professionals, while involvement in the second instance potentially brings the entire supervisory workforce into the picture.

Greater involvement requires greater commitment of company time, energy, and resources, and while commitment does not guarantee success, it is a positive force in that direction. Greater involvement also means greater control of the program, not in an authoritarian sense, but in keeping the EAP focus on organizational goals and needs.

A highly-committed option is to develop a Board of Advisors comprised of representatives from all levels of the company. The Board would control or monitor the EAP budget, evaluate program effectiveness, assess current and future needs, and establish a partner relationship with the vendor. The Board could also serve as a barometer for measuring employee attitudes toward the EAP.

Program Promotion

A purpose of promotion is to build employee trust in the EAP. If a company has a history of good relations between workers and management, building trust in the EAP won't be difficult. Promoting can vary from simple things, like an introductory letter from the chief executive officer, to more complicated efforts, like health and wellness fairs that educate employees on drug abuse, as well as alcohol and smoking cessation, parenting strategies, and stress management. Other techniques include an EAP newsletter, bulletin board posters and notices, mail-outs, envelope stuffers, etc. Surely, the strongest promotion occurs when the senior management demonstrates support for the program.

Program promotion is always an ongoing process. It requires a combination of creativity and continuity. While the initial effort must be large in order to capture attention, the day-to-day effort must be long in order to keep the program viable.

THE SUBSTANCE ABUSE PROFESSIONAL

The designation Substance Abuse Professional (SAP), at least in the current context, grew out of rules put into place by the Department of Transportation rules to prevent alcohol- and drug-afflicted employees from performing transportation safety-sensitive functions.

DOT defines a SAP as a licensed physician (i.e., a medical Doctor or Doctor of Osteopathy), a licensed or certified psychologist, a licensed or certified social worker, or a licensed or certified employee assistance professional. Also included in DOT's definition are alcohol and drug abuse counselors who meet certification requirements of the National Association of Alcoholism and Drug Abuse Counselors (NAADAC), an organization that sets qualification standards for treatment of alcohol-related disorders. Degrees and certificates alone, however, do not earn the designation. A SAP is expected to be knowledgeable of and have clinical experience in the diagnosis and treatment of substance abuse-related disorders.

Interestingly, DOT does not certify, license, or approve individual SAPs. A SAP candidate must be able to demonstrate to the employer qualifications necessary to meet DOT rules. The employers, i.e., the entities regulated by DOT, bear the burden of proving the qualifications of the SAPs they engage.

In a situation where an employer fires an individual for violating DOT drug or alcohol rules, the employer provides the individual with a list of resources for evaluation and treatment. The list includes locally available SAPs. The employer's obligation ends at this point. It is entirely up to the individual to contact or not contact a resource for assistance.

A discharged individual who wishes to return to his job will be motivated to contact a SAP for the simple reason that DOT forbids the employer to allow the employee to return to safety-sensitive work until evaluated. If the SAP's evaluation reveals that assistance is needed, the employee must, prior to returning to work, receive the assistance, be later evaluated by the SAP, and be judged through that follow-up evaluation to have demonstrated successful compliance with the SAP's recommendations. Granting of the return-to-work privilege must also be preceded by a drug test.

The SAP evaluation is done face-to-face with the individual. When the evaluation indicates a need for treatment, the SAP recommends a course of treatment and education appropriate for the individual. The individual must successfully meet the recommendations before returning to DOT safety-sensitive duties. Recommendations can include in-patient treatment, partial in-patient treatment, out-patient treatment, education programs, and aftercare.

Self-help groups and community lectures qualify as education but do not qualify as treatment. While self-help groups such as Alcoholics Anonymous (AA) and Narcotics Anonymous (NA) are crucial to many employees' recovery processes, these efforts are not considered to be treatment programs in and of themselves. However, they can serve as vital adjuncts in support of treatment program efforts. DOT's exclusion of AA and NA programs as acceptable treatment modalities has to do with the anonymity aspects of those programs. DOT's position is that anonymity makes reporting client progress and prognosis for recovery very difficult, if not impossible.

When the client permits, AA and NA sponsors can provide attendance status reports to the SAP. Therefore, if a client is referred by the SAP to one of these groups, the employee's attendance, when it can be independently validated, can satisfy a SAP recommendation for education, but not for treatment.

To be effective, the SAP has to possess a working knowledge of EAP programs, health insurance benefit plans, and like matters dealing with diagnosis and treatment of alcohol- and drug-related disorders. Also implied is an understanding of the employer's policies and procedures such as those relating to administrative leave, entitlement to benefits, etc.

After the employee has partially or fully completed the prescribed course of treatment, but prior to his or her return to safety-sensitive duties, the SAP consults with the employer to obtain assurance of the employer's satisfaction that the employee has made treatment progress sufficient to satisfy the safety demands of the job.

The SAP also directs a follow-up testing plan for the employee returning to work following treatment. The number and frequency of unannounced follow-up tests is directed by the SAP. As mandated by DOT rules, follow-up testing consists of at least six tests in the first year following the employee's return to safety-sensitive duties. If the SAP previously determined that the employee's personal pattern of abuse involved a combination of alcohol and drugs, the follow-up testing plan may include testing for both.

Follow-up testing can last up to five years but can be terminated by the SAP following completion of the first six tests that are spread throughout the initial one-year period. This follow-up testing requirement is in addition to tests routinely administered to all employees through the employer's random testing program.

Because testing rules vary among the DOT regulatory agencies, a SAP tends to specialize in one or a few of those six transportation industries (i.e., highway, railroad, urban transit, aviation, maritime, and pipeline).

The Face-to-Face Evaluation

Central to the realm of SAP duties is the face-to-face clinical evaluation of the "client." The SAP looks for the non-verbal physical cues to the client's internal feelings and thoughts. Body language and appearance offer important physical cues vital to the evaluation process. Tremors, needle marks, dilated pupils, exaggerated movements, yellow eyes, glazed or bloodshot eyes, lack of eye contact, physical slowdown or hyperactivity, appearance, posture, carriage, and an unexplained ability to communicate are indicators of importance to the SAP. A strong focus is also placed upon the rule violation that brought the employee to the attention of the SAP. Of concern to the SAP, to the employer, and to DOT is the risk that the client poses to himself or herself or others.

The evaluation includes a standard psychosocial history and an in-depth drug and alcohol use history. The SAP captures details regarding onset, duration, frequency, and amount of drug and alcohol use, the emotional and physical characteristics of use, and resultant health, work, family, personal, and interpersonal problems. The SAP also evaluates the client's current mental status.

The process results in a clinical assessment that includes a treatment plan. The client exercises a choice. Either remain removed from safety-sensitive duties or comply with the treatment plan. When the SAP determines that the client has complied with the plan, the employer is consulted. The employer has the final say-so as to whether or not the client will be returned to safety-sensitive duties.

All of the SAP's work is documented and made a part of the formal record. This is the case even when the SAP makes a finding that a client does not need treatment.

The work of a SAP is not black and white, cut and dried. Decisions arrived at include consideration of many variables, e.g., the SAP's referral of the client to a particular treatment provider or program is conditioned by the client's needs, the client's ability to pay, the employer's health insurance benefits, the employer's leave provisions, and the availability of treatment programs that correspond to the client's treatment needs. To effectively make such decisions, the SAP has to be networked with treatment providers in the local area and, in respect to DOT rules, the SAP is prohibited from making referrals to the SAP's private practice or to a person or organization from which the SAP receives remuneration or to a person or organization in which the SAP has a financial interest.

The SAP's determination that a client is ready to resume safety-sensitive duties is not an easy decision and one that can be vital in protecting human life and property. The facts of the client's cause for removal from safety-sensitive work has been established, thus bringing into question the client's reliability in performing life- and property-threatening duties. The SAP's judgment in recommending the return of the individual to such work can have far-reaching consequences.

Of particular note along this line is the SAP's latitude in conducting a follow-up evaluation prior to the individual's completion of the full range of recommended treatment. The SAP essentially goes out on a limb when he or she decides to consider allowing the individual to return to work before the treatment program is over. The only back-up and assurance the SAP has when making the determination are the written reports from and personal communication with the treatment program professionals, plus a follow-up face-to-face interview with the individual. The written reports are often routinely prepared documents such as progress reports and summaries; the personal communication with treatment professionals is often telephonic. A natural concern of the SAP has to be the possibility that a treatment professional, whose future referrals may depend on how the SAP views the professional's efficacy of treatment, will fudge on a report or in a conversation by stating that the individual has progressed well when such is not the case.

When the treatment professional reports that the individual has not made sufficient progress, the SAP is prevented by DOT rules from proceeding with a follow-up interview. Insufficient progress is often the result of an individual's failure to participate in the treatment program, even when attendance has been perfect. A SAP who concludes that an individual has not demonstrated successful compliance with the treatment plan is obligated to postpone re-evaluation until attainment of satisfactory compliance.

Follow-up Testing

Follow-up testing serves as more than an employer's additional assurance that an employee is drug- or alcohol-free. Testing is an adjunct to the ongoing rehabilitation effort. Even when treatment is short term, the rehabilitation process is long term. Because most relapses occur during the first 12 months following treatment, rehabilitation can be enhanced by follow-up testing. Other enhancements include participation in aftercare programs and self-help groups.

The SAP's plan for follow-up testing has an important dimension. The SAP is at liberty to re-evaluate the testing plan at any time and terminate it following completion of six mandatory tests conducted during the first year following release from treatment. Testing works best when it is unannounced and spread throughout the year. The follow-up testing program can last up to five years, depending on the judgment of the SAP. The SAP recommends to the employer the number of tests and their approximate frequency, e.g., 4 tests in the first 6 months with 2 in the final six months of the first year.

Random testing is independent of rule violations. Random testing and follow-up testing are separate activities. One cannot be substituted for the other or be conducted in lieu of the other.

Neither can follow-up testing be conducted in a random way. Random testing by its nature cannot ensure that the individual will be tested the number of times and with the frequency determined by the SAP to be appropriate.

Referrals

As stated earlier, DOT rules prohibit the SAP from making referrals that work to the SAP's financial interest. The rules, however, do not prohibit the SAP from referring an employee for assistance by:

- An agency of the government, such as a state, county, or municipal health agency.

- The employer or a person under contract to provide treatment for alcohol or drug problems on behalf of the employer.

- The sole source of therapeutically appropriate treatment under the employee's health insurance program.

- The sole source of therapeutically appropriate treatment reasonably accessible to the employee.

Confidentiality

Essential to the work of a SAP is the ability to receive, process, and communicate information regarding the employee's evaluation and treatment progress. Because much of the information is confidential in nature, the SAP needs to obtain from the employee specific releases authorizing disclosure of information. These specific releases permit the SAP to:

- Give the synopsis of the employee's treatment plan to the employer.

- Provide the assessment evaluation and treatment plan to counseling or treatment organizations or practices.

- Receive diagnostic information, treatment progress reports, and program completion information, as well as program involvement dates from counseling or treatment organizations or practices.

- Provide a follow-up evaluation synopsis to the employer.

The privileged client-counselor relationship is generally supported by federal and state laws and rules, codes of ethical standards, and certification and licensing boards. Exceptions to confidentiality primarily occur when the client poses a clear and imminent danger to self or others, when there is known or suspected child abuse or neglect, when medical records are court ordered by a judge compelling disclosure, or when the counselor seeks medical or legal consultation. Client record information can also be released for audit and review purposes in accordance with disclosure rules.

EMPLOYEE ASSISTANCE PROGRAM (EAP)

A Complicating Factor

The SAP process can be very complicated when the employer decides not to retain the individual. This is because the SAP will likely not have a connection with the employer nor have immediate access to the exact nature of the rule violation. The SAP may have no choice except to hold the evaluation and treatment files until asked by the individual to forward them to another employer interested in returning the individual to safety-sensitive duties. If the gaining employer has a designated SAP, that SAP may be asked by the employer to conduct a follow-up evaluation despite the fact that the employee's SAP has already done so.

A penalty can be applied to an employer who returns a worker to safety-sensitive duties when the worker has not complied with the SAP's recommendations. On the other hand, DOT rules do not obligate an employer to return the worker to a safety-sensitive job. Meeting the SAP's recommendations and passing a drug or alcohol test are not guarantees of employment or of return to work in a safety-sensitive position. These are preconditions the employee must meet in order to be considered eligible for hiring or reinstatement.

SAP Record Keeping

Records pertaining to a determination by a SAP concerning an employee's need for assistance and records concerning an employee's ability to demonstrate successful compliance with recommendations of the SAP are maintained for a period of five years. Records are required to be kept in limited access areas that deny unauthorized entry.

Payment for SAP Services

The DOT rules do not address responsibility for payment for SAP services. Payment is often determined by employer policies and labor-management agreements. Some employers obtain SAP services from in-house staff; others acquire the services from contract staff. In some cases, it is the discharged worker who assumes payment responsibility. Whatever the case, the SAP has to be suitable to the employer. It is the employer, after all has been said and done, who chooses to return the worker to the job.

THE EAP-AMENABLE ORGANIZATION

Organizations that adopt and take advantage of EAPs tend to share certain characteristics, for example:

- An organizational climate that supports the concept of change, creativity, and innovation through open communication among personnel, with all levels participating in the making of decisions; collegial endorsement of help-seeking and problem-solving; and available time for consideration of innovation.

- Organizational size and structure with some emphasis on self-monitoring and assessment to detect troubles, without being too big or too complex for rapid assimilation of change or too bureaucratic, complacent, or conforming to tradition.

- Organizational affluence and capacity sufficient to take chances with innovation and implement change.

Leaders in the organization who are attuned to change, politically astute, and respectful of different professional disciplines.

- Professionalism, age, and security of staff members who look forward to innovations; are not threatened by change; and are willing to entertain, discuss, and attempt new procedures or technologies.

- Relationship to the community and the consumer constituency with a demonstrated ability to lead and a capacity for autonomy rather than vulnerability and immediate capitulation to outmoded traditions.

10

Treatment

DIMENSIONS OF DRUG TREATMENT

Costs to Society

A study prepared for the National Institute on Drug Abuse and the National Institute on Alcohol Abuse and Alcoholism estimated the total economic cost of alcohol and drug abuse to be $245.7 billion for 1992. Of this cost, $97.7 billion was due to drug abuse. This estimate includes substance abuse treatment and prevention costs as well as other healthcare costs, costs associated with reduced job productivity or lost earnings, and other costs to society such as crime and social welfare. The study also determined that these costs are borne primarily by governments (46 percent), followed by those who abuse drugs and members of their households (44 percent).

The 1992 cost estimate increased 50 percent over the cost estimate from 1985 data. The four primary contributors to this increase were

- The epidemic of heavy cocaine use.

- The HIV epidemic.

- An eightfold increase in state and federal incarcerations for drug offenses.

- A threefold increase in crimes attributed to drugs.

More than half of the estimated costs of drug abuse were associated with drug-related crime. These costs included lost productivity of victims and incarcerated perpetrators of drug-related crime (20.4 percent); lost legitimate production due to drug-related crime careers (19.7 percent); and other costs of drug-related crime, including federal drug traffic control, property damage, and police, legal, and corrections services (18.4 percent). Most of the remaining costs resulted from premature deaths (14.9 percent), lost productivity due to drug-related illness (14.5 percent), and healthcare expenditures (10.2 percent).

The White House Office of National Drug Control Policy (ONDCP) conducted a study to determine how much money is spent on illegal drugs that otherwise would support legitimate spending or savings by the user in the overall economy. ONDCP found that, between 1988 and 1995, Americans spent $57.3 billion on drugs, broken down as follows: $38 billion on cocaine, $9.6 billion on heroin, $7 billion on marijuana, and $2.7 billion on other illegal drugs and on the misuse of legal drugs.

Hospital Visits and Deaths

Since 1990, estimates of drug-related visits to hospital emergency rooms have increased. In 1995, 531,800 drug-related visits occurred, up slightly from 1994. More than half of these visits were due to drug overdoses. Nearly 143,000 cocaine-related visits occurred, with increases noted in people age 35 and older. Heroin-related visits increased by 19 percent from 1994, and marijuana-related visits increased by 17 percent. Methamphetamine-related visits decreased by 34 percent from the first to second half of 1995.

Crack cocaine continues to dominate the Nation's illicit drug problem. The overall number of cocaine users did not change significantly between 1995 and 1996 (1.45 million in 1995 and 1.75 million in 1996). This is down from a peak of 5.7 million in 1985. Nevertheless, there were still an estimated 652,000 Americans who used cocaine for the first time in 1995. Supplies remain abundant in nearly every city. Data indicate a leveling off in many urban areas: cocaine-related deaths were stable or up slightly in 9 of the 10 areas where such information was reported.

The percentage of treatment admissions for primary cocaine problems declined slightly or remained stable in 12 of the 14 areas where data were available; and prices of cocaine remained stable in most areas. Although demographic data continue to show most cocaine users as older, inner-city crack addicts, isolated field reports indicate new groups of users: teenagers smoking crack with marijuana in blunts (cigars emptied of tobacco and refilled with marijuana, often in combination with another drug), Hispanic crack users in Texas, and in the Atlanta area, middle-class suburban users of cocaine hydrochloride and female crack users in their thirties with no prior drug history.

Treatment Trends

In 1995, there were nearly 1.9 million admissions to publicly funded substance abuse treatment. About 54 percent were alcohol treatment admissions; and nearly 46 percent were for illicit drug abuse treatment. Men made up about 70 percent of individuals in treatment; and women 30 percent. Fifty-six percent were White, followed in number by African Americans (26 percent), Hispanics (7.7 percent), Native Americans (2.2 percent), and Asians and Pacific Islanders (0.6 percent). The largest number of illicit drug treatment admissions were for cocaine (38.3 percent), followed by heroin (25.5 percent), and

177

marijuana (19.1 percent). Fifty-nine percent of admissions were to treatment in an ambulatory environment.

Treatment Methods

Drug addiction is a treatable disorder. Through treatment that is tailored to individual needs, patients can learn to control their condition and live normal, productive lives. Like people with diabetes or heart disease, people in treatment for drug addiction learn behavioral changes and often take medications as part of their treatment regimen.

Behavioral therapies can include counseling, psychotherapy, support groups, or family therapy. Treatment medications offer help in suppressing the withdrawal syndrome and drug craving and in blocking the effects of drugs. In addition, studies show that treatment for heroin addiction using methadone at an adequate dosage level, combined with behavioral therapy, reduces death rates and many health problems associated with heroin abuse.

In general, the more treatment given, the better the results. Many patients require other services as well, such as medical and mental health services and HIV prevention services. Patients who stay in treatment longer than 3 months usually have better outcomes than those who stay less time. Patients who go through medically assisted withdrawal to minimize discomfort but do not receive any further treatment, perform about the same in terms of their drug use as those who were never treated. Over the last 25 years, studies have shown that treatment works to reduce drug intake and crime. Researchers also have found that drug abusers who have been through treatment are more likely to have jobs.

TYPES OF TREATMENT PROGRAMS

The ultimate goal of all drug abuse treatment is to enable the patient to achieve lasting abstinence, but the immediate goals are to reduce drug use, improve the patient's ability to function, and minimize the medical and social complications of drug abuse.

There are several types of drug abuse treatment programs. Short-term methods last less than 6 months and include residential therapy, medication therapy, and drug-free outpatient therapy. Longer term treatment may include, for example, methadone maintenance outpatient treatment for opiate addicts and residential therapeutic community treatment.

Maintenance Treatment

In maintenance treatment for heroin addicts, people in treatment are given an oral dose of a synthetic opiate, usually methadone hydrochloride or levo-alpha-acetyl methadol (LAAM), administered at a dosage sufficient to block the effects of heroin and yield a stable, noneuphoric state free from physiological craving for opiates. In this stable state, the patient is able to disengage from drug-seeking and related criminal behavior and, with appropriate counseling and social services, become a productive member of the community.

Methadone maintenance programs are usually more successful at retaining clients with opiate dependence than are therapeutic communities, which in turn are more successful than outpatient programs that provide psychotherapy and counseling. Within various methadone programs, those that provide higher doses of methadone (usually a minimum of 60 mg.) have better retention rates. Also, those that provide other services, such as counseling, therapy, and medical care along with methadone, generally get better results than the programs that provide minimal services.

Outpatient Treatment

Outpatient drug-free treatment does not include medications and encompasses a wide variety of programs for patients who visit a clinic at regular intervals. Most of the programs involve individual or group counseling. Patients entering these programs are abusers of drugs other than opiates or are opiate abusers for whom maintenance therapy is not recommended, such as those who have stable, well-integrated lives and only brief histories of drug dependence.

Therapeutic Communities

Therapeutic communities (TCs) are highly structured programs in which patients stay at a residence, typically for 6 to 12 months. Patients in TCs include those with relatively long histories of drug dependence, involvement in serious criminal activities, and seriously impaired social functioning. The focus of the TC is on the resocialization of the patient to a drug-free, crime-free lifestyle.

Short-Term Residential Programs

Short-term residential programs, often referred to as chemical dependency units, are often based on the Minnesota Model of treatment for alcoholism. These programs involve a 3- to 6-week inpatient treatment phase followed by extended outpatient therapy or participation in 12-step self-help groups, such as Narcotics Anonymous or Cocaine Anonymous. Chemical dependency programs for drug abuse arose in the private sector in the mid-1980s with insured cocaine abusers as their primary patients. Today, as private provider benefits decline, more services are being extended to publicly funded patients.

Prison Programs

Drug treatment programs in prisons can succeed in preventing patients' return to criminal behavior, particularly if they are linked to community-based programs that continue treatment when the client leaves prison. Some of the more successful programs have reduced the rearrest rate by one-fourth to one-half. For example, the Delaware Model, an ongoing study of comprehensive treatment of drug-addicted prison inmates, shows that prison-based treatment including a therapeutic community setting, a work release therapeutic community, and community-based aftercare reduces the probability of rearrest by

57 percent and reduces the likelihood of returning to drug use by 37 percent.

TREATMENT MEDICATIONS

Treatment for people who abuse drugs but are not yet addicted to them most often consists of behavioral therapies, such as psychotherapy, counseling, support groups, or family therapy. But treatment for drug-addicted people often involves a combination of behavioral therapies and medications. Medications, such as methadone and LAAM, are effective in suppressing the withdrawal symptoms and drug craving associated with narcotic addiction, thus reducing illicit drug use and improving the chances of the individual remaining in treatment.

The primary medically assisted withdrawal method for narcotic addiction is to switch the patient to a comparable drug that produces milder withdrawal symptoms, and then gradually taper off the substitute medication. The medication used most often is methadone, taken by mouth once a day. Patients are started on the lowest dose that prevents the more severe signs of withdrawal and then the dose is gradually reduced. Substitutes can be used also for withdrawal from sedatives. Patients can be switched to long-acting sedatives, such as diazepam or phenobarbital, which are then gradually reduced.

Once a patient goes through withdrawal, there is still considerable risk of relapse. Patients may return to taking drugs even though they no longer have physical withdrawal symptoms. A great deal of research is being done to find medications that can block drug craving and treat other factors that cause a return to drugs.

Patients who cannot continue abstaining from opiates are given maintenance therapy, usually with methadone. The maintenance dose of methadone, usually higher than that used for medically assisted withdrawal, prevents both withdrawal symptoms and heroin craving. It also prevents addicts from getting a high from heroin and, as a result, they stop using it. Research has shown that maintenance therapy reduces the spread of AIDS in the treated population. The overall death rate is also significantly reduced.

TREATMENT

Within various methadone programs, those that provide higher doses of methadone (usually a minimum of 60 milligrams) have better retention rates. Also, those that provide other services, such as counseling, therapy, and medical care, along with methadone generally get better results than the programs that provide minimal services.

Another drug recently approved for use in maintenance treatment is LAAM, which is administered three times a week rather than daily, as is the case with methadone. The drug naltrexone is also used to prevent relapse. Like methadone, LAAM and naltrexone prevent addicts from getting high from heroin. However, naltrexone does not eliminate the drug craving, so it has not been popular among addicts. Naltrexone works best with highly motivated patients.

There are currently no medications approved by the Food and Drug Administration (FDA) for treating addiction to cocaine, LSD, PCP, marijuana, methamphetamine and other stimulants, inhalants, or anabolic steroids. There are medications, however, for treating the adverse health effects of these drugs, such as seizures or psychotic reactions, and for overdoses from opiates. Currently, NIDA's top research priority is the development of a medication useful in treating cocaine addiction.

BEHAVIORAL CHANGE THROUGH TREATMENT

Recovery from the disease of drug addiction is often a long-term process, involving multiple relapses before a patient achieves prolonged abstinence. Many behavioral therapies have been shown to help patients achieve initial abstinence and maintain prolonged abstinence. One frequently used therapy is cognitive behavioral relapse prevention in which patients are taught new ways of acting and thinking. For example, patients are urged to avoid situations that lead to drug use and to practice drug refusal skills. They also are taught to think of the occasional relapse as a slip rather than a failure. Cognitive behavioral relapse prevention has proven to be a useful and lasting therapy for many drug addicted individuals.

One of the more well-developed behavioral techniques in drug abuse treatment is contingency management, a system of rewards and punishments to make abstinence attractive and drug use unattractive. Ultimately, the aim of contingency management programs is to make a drug-free, pro-social lifestyle more rewarding than a drug-using lifestyle. The community reinforcement approach is a comprehensive contingency management approach that has proven to be extremely helpful in promoting initial abstinence in cocaine addicts.

Once drug use is under control, education and job rehabilitation become crucial. Rewarding lifestyle options must be found for people in drug recovery to prevent their return to the old environment and way of life.

OPIATES: ABUSE AND ADDICTION

In 1997, the National Institutes of Health (NIH) convened a panel of national experts to look at opiate addictions. The panel concluded that opiate drug addictions are diseases of the brain and medical disorders that can be treated effectively. The panel strongly recommended:

- Broader access to methadone maintenance treatment programs for people who are addicted to heroin or other opiate drugs.

- Federal and state regulations and other barriers impeding this access be eliminated.

- The provision of counseling, psychosocial therapies, and other supportive services to enhance retention and successful outcomes in methadone maintenance treatment programs.

Heroin is both the most abused and the most rapidly acting of the opiates. Heroin is processed from morphine, a naturally occurring substance extracted from the seed pod of certain varieties of poppy plants. It is typically sold as a white or brownish powder or as the black sticky substance known on the streets as black tar heroin. Although purer heroin is becoming more common, most street heroin is cut with other drugs or with substances such as sugar, starch, powdered milk, or quinine. Street heroin can also be cut with strychnine or other poisons. Because heroin abusers do not know the actual strength of the drug or its true contents, they are at risk of overdose or death. Heroin also poses special problems because of the transmission of HIV and other diseases that can occur from sharing needles or other injection equipment.

Administration

Heroin is usually injected, sniffed/snorted, or smoked. Typically, a heroin abuser may inject up to four times a day. Intravenous injection provides the greatest intensity and most rapid onset of euphoria (7 to 8 seconds), while intramuscular injection produces a relatively slow onset of euphoria (5 to 8 minutes). When heroin is sniffed or smoked, peak effects are usually felt within 10 to 15 minutes. Although smoking and sniffing heroin do not produce a rush as quickly or as intensely as intravenous injection, researchers have confirmed that all three forms of heroin administration are addictive.

Injection continues to be the predominant method of heroin use among addicted users seeking treatment; however, researchers have observed a shift in heroin use patterns, from injection to sniffing and smoking. With the shift in heroin abuse patterns comes an even more diverse group of users. Older users (over 30) continue to be one of the largest user groups in most national data. However, several sources indicate an increase in new, young users across the country who are being lured by inexpensive, high-purity heroin that can be sniffed or smoked instead of injected. Heroin has also been appearing in more affluent communities.

Rush

Soon after injection (or inhalation), heroin crosses the blood-brain barrier. In the brain, heroin is converted to morphine and binds rapidly to opioid receptors. Abusers typically report feeling a surge of pleasurable sensation, called a rush. The intensity of the rush is a function of how much drug is taken and how rapidly the drug enters the brain and binds to the natural opioid receptors. Heroin is particularly addictive because it enters the brain so rapidly. With heroin, the rush is usually accompanied by a warm flushing of the skin, dry mouth, and a heavy feeling in the extremities, which may be accompanied by nausea, vomiting, and severe itching.

After the initial effects, abusers usually will be drowsy for several hours. Mental function is clouded by heroin's effect on the central nervous system. Cardiac functions slow. Breathing is also severely slowed, sometimes to the point of death. Heroin overdose is a particular risk on the street, where the amount and purity of the drug cannot be accurately known.

Addiction and Dependence

One of the most detrimental long-term effects of heroin is addiction itself. Addiction is a chronic, relapsing disease, characterized by compulsive drug seeking and use, and by neurochemical and molecular changes in the brain. Heroin also produces profound degrees of tolerance and physical dependence, which are also powerful motivating factors for compulsive use and abuse. As with abusers of any addictive drug, heroin abusers gradually spend more and more time and energy obtaining and using the drug. Once they are addicted, the heroin abusers' primary purpose in life becomes seeking and using drugs. The drugs literally change their brains.

Physical dependence develops with higher doses of the drug. With physical dependence, the body adapts to the presence of the drug and withdrawal symptoms occur if use is reduced abruptly. Withdrawal may occur within a few hours after the last time the drug is taken. Symptoms of withdrawal include restlessness, muscle and bone pain, insomnia, diarrhea, vomiting, cold flashes with goose bumps (called cold turkey), and leg movements. Major withdrawal symptoms peak between 24 and 48 hours after the last dose of heroin and subside after about a week. However, some people have shown persistent withdrawal signs for many months. Heroin withdrawal is never fatal to otherwise healthy adults, but it can cause death to the fetus of a pregnant addict.

At some point during continuous heroin use, a person can become addicted to the drug. Sometimes addicted individuals will endure many of the withdrawal symptoms to reduce their tolerance for the drug so that they can again experience the rush.

Physical dependence and the emergence of withdrawal symptoms were once believed to be the key features of heroin addiction. It is now known this may not be the case entirely, since craving and relapse can occur weeks and months after withdrawal symptoms are long gone. It is also known that patients with chronic pain who need opiates to function (sometimes over extended periods) have few if any problems leaving opiates after their pain is resolved by other means. This may be because the patient in pain is simply seeking relief of pain and not the rush sought by the addict.

Health Damage

Medical consequences of chronic heroin abuse include scarred and/or collapsed veins, bacterial infections of the blood vessels and heart valves, abscesses (boils) and other soft-tissue infections, and liver or kidney disease. Lung complications (including various types of pneumonia and tuberculosis) may result from the poor health condition of the abuser as well as from heroin's depressing effects on respiration. Many of the additives in street heroin may include substances that do not readily dissolve and result in clogging the blood vessels that lead to the lungs, liver, kidneys, or brain. This can cause infection or even death of small patches of cells in vital organs. Immune reactions to these or other contaminants can cause arthritis or other rheumatologic problems.

Sharing of injection equipment or fluids can lead to some of the most severe consequences of heroin abuse, i.e., infections with hepatitis B and C, HIV, and a host of other blood-borne viruses, which drug abusers can then pass on to their sexual partners and children.

Heroin abuse can cause serious complications during pregnancy, including miscarriage and premature delivery. Children born to addicted mothers are at greater risk of SIDS (sudden infant death syndrome), as well. Pregnant women are not detoxified from opiates because of the increased risk of spontaneous abortion or premature delivery; rather, treatment with methadone is strongly advised. Although infants born to mothers taking prescribed methadone may show signs of physical dependence, they can be treated easily and safely in the nursery. Research has demonstrated also that the effects of in utero exposure to methadone are relatively benign.

HIV/AIDS

Because many heroin addicts often share needles and other injection equipment, they are at special risk of contracting HIV and other infectious diseases. Infection of injection drug users with HIV is spread primarily through reuse of contaminated syringes and needles or other paraphernalia by more than one person, as well as through unprotected sexual intercourse with HIV-infected individuals. For nearly one-third of Americans infected with HIV, injection drug use is a risk factor. In fact, drug abuse is the fastest growing vector for the spread of HIV. Research has found that drug abusers can change the behaviors that put them at risk for contracting HIV, through treatment, prevention, and community-based outreach programs. They can eliminate drug use, drug-related risk behaviors such as needle sharing, unsafe sexual practices, and, in turn, the risk of exposure to HIV/AIDS and other infectious diseases. Drug abuse prevention and treatment are highly effective in preventing the spread of HIV.

Heroin Treatment

A variety of effective treatments are available for heroin addiction. Treatment tends to be more effective when heroin abuse is identified early. The treatments that follow vary depending on the individual, but methadone, a synthetic opiate that blocks the effects of heroin and eliminates withdrawal symptoms, has a proven record of success for people addicted to heroin. Other pharmaceutical approaches, like LAAM, and many behavioral therapies also are used for treating heroin addiction.

TREATMENT

Detoxification

The primary objective of detoxification is to relieve withdrawal symptoms while patients adjust to a drug-free state. Not in itself a treatment for addiction, detoxification is a useful step only when it leads into long-term treatment that is either drug-free (residential or outpatient) or uses medications as part of the treatment. The best documented drug-free treatments are the therapeutic community residential programs lasting at least 3 to 6 months.

Methadone Treatment

Methadone treatment has been used effectively and safely to treat opioid addiction for more than 30 years. The programs use methadone as a substitute for heroin. Properly prescribed methadone is not intoxicating or sedating, and its effects do not interfere with ordinary activities such as driving a car. The medication is taken orally and it suppresses narcotic withdrawal for 24 to 36 hours. Patients are able to perceive pain and have emotional reactions. Most important, methadone relieves the craving associated with heroin addiction; craving is a major reason for relapse. Among methadone patients, it has been found that normal street doses of heroin are ineffective at producing euphoria, thus making the use of heroin more easily extinguishable.

Methadone's effects last for about 24 hours - four to six times as long as those of heroin - so people in treatment need to take it only once a day. Also, methadone is medically safe even when used continuously for 10 years or more. Combined with behavioral therapies or counseling and other supportive services, methadone enables patients to stop using heroin (and other opiates) and return to more stable and productive lives.

LAAM and Other Medications

LAAM, like methadone, is a synthetic opiate that can be used to treat heroin addiction. LAAM can block the effects of heroin for up to 72

188

hours with minimal side effects when taken orally. In 1993, the Food and Drug Administration approved the use of LAAM for treating patients addicted to heroin. Its long duration of action permits dosing just three times per week, thereby eliminating the need for daily dosing and take-home doses for weekends. LAAM is increasingly available in clinics that already dispense methadone.

Naloxone and naltrexone are medications that also block the effects of morphine, heroin, and other opiates. As antagonists, they are especially useful as antidotes. Naltrexone has long-lasting effects, ranging from 1 to 3 days, depending on the dose. Naltrexone blocks the pleasurable effects of heroin and is useful in treating some highly motivated individuals. Naltrexone has also been found to be successful in preventing relapse by former opiate addicts released from prison on probation.

Although not yet approved for the treatment of opioid addiction, buprenorphine is another medication being studied by NIDA as a treatment for heroin addiction. Buprenorphine is a particularly attractive treatment because it does not produce the same level of physical dependence as other opiate medications, such as methadone. Discontinuing buprenorphine is easier than stopping methadone treatment because there are fewer withdrawal symptoms. Several other medications with potential for treating heroin overdose or addiction are currently under investigation by NIDA.

Behavioral Therapies for Heroin Addiction

Although behavioral and pharmacologic treatments can be extremely useful when employed alone, science has taught us that integrating both types of treatments will ultimately be the most effective approach. There are many effective behavioral treatments available for heroin addiction. These can include residential and outpatient approaches. An important task is to match the best treatment approach to meet the particular needs of the patient. Moreover, several new behavioral therapies, such as contingency management therapy and cognitive-behavioral interventions, show particular promise as treatments for heroin addiction. Contingency management therapy uses a voucher-based system, where patients earn points based on negative drug tests, which they can exchange for items that encourage healthy living.

TREATMENT

Cognitive-behavioral interventions are designed to help modify the patient's thinking, expectancies, and behaviors and to increase skills in coping with many and various life stressors. Both behavioral and pharmacological treatments help to restore a degree of normalcy to brain function and behavior.

Drug analogs are chemical compounds that are similar to other drugs in their effects but differ slightly in their chemical structure. Some analogs are produced by pharmaceutical companies for legitimate medical reasons. Other analogs, sometimes referred to as designer drugs, can be produced in illegal laboratories and are often more dangerous and potent than the original drug. Two of the most commonly known opioid analogs are fentanyl and meperidine (marketed under the brand name Demerol, for example).

Fentanyl was introduced in 1968 by a Belgian pharmaceutical company as a synthetic narcotic to be used as an analgesic in surgical procedures because of its minimal effects on the heart. Fentanyl is particularly dangerous because it is 50 times more potent than heroin and can rapidly stop respiration. This is not a problem during surgical procedures because machines are used to help patients breathe. On the street, however, users have been found dead with the needle used to inject the drug still in their arms.

METHAMPHETAMINE ABUSE AND ADDICTION

Methamphetamine is a powerfully addictive stimulant that dramatically affects the central nervous system. The drug is made easily in clandestine laboratories with relatively inexpensive over-the-counter ingredients. These factors combine to produce a high potential for widespread abuse.

Methamphetamine is a white, odorless, bitter-tasting crystalline powder that easily dissolves in water or alcohol. The drug was developed early in this century from its parent drug, amphetamine, and was used originally in nasal decongestants and bronchial inhalers. The drug's chemical structure is similar to that of amphetamine, but it has more pronounced effects on the central nervous system. Like amphetamine, it causes increased activity, decreased appetite, and a general sense of well-being. The effects can last 6 to 8 hours. After the initial rush, there is typically a state of high agitation that in some individuals can lead to violent behavior.

Methamphetamine is a Schedule II stimulant, which means it has a high potential for abuse and is available only through a prescription that cannot be refilled. There are a few accepted medical reasons for its use, such as the treatment of narcolepsy, attention deficit disorder, and obesity.

Administration

Methamphetamine comes in many forms and can be smoked, snorted, orally ingested, or injected. The drug alters moods in different ways, depending on how it is taken. Immediately after smoking the drug or injecting it intravenously, the user experiences an intense rush or flash that lasts only a few minutes and is described as extremely pleasurable. Snorting produces effects within 3 to 5 minutes, and oral ingestion produces effects within 15 to 20 minutes.

As with similar stimulants, methamphetamine most often is used in a "binge and crash" pattern. Because tolerance occurs within minutes, meaning that the pleasurable effects disappear even before the drug concentration in the blood falls significantly, users try to maintain the high by repeated administration.

In the 1980's, a smokable form of methamphetamine, called ice, came into use. Ice is a large, usually clear crystal of high purity that is smoked in a glass pipe like crack cocaine. The smoke is odorless, leaves a residue that can be resmoked, and produces effects that may continue for 12 hours or more.

As a powerful stimulant, even in small doses, methamphetamine can increase wakefulness and physical activity and decrease appetite. A brief, intense sensation, or rush, is reported by those who smoke or inject the drug. Oral ingestion or snorting produces a long-lasting high instead of a rush, which reportedly can continue for as long as half a day. Both the rush and the high are believed to result from the release of very high levels of the neurotransmitter dopamine into areas of the brain that regulate feelings of pleasure.

TREATMENT

Health Consequences

Methamphetamine has toxic effects. In animals, a single high dose of the drug has been shown to damage nerve terminals in the dopamine-containing regions of the brain. The large release of dopamine is thought to contribute to the drug's toxic effects on nerve terminals in the brain. High doses can elevate body temperature to dangerous, sometimes lethal, levels, as well as cause convulsions.

Long-term methamphetamine abuse results in many damaging effects, including addiction accompanied by functional and molecular changes in the brain. Chronic abusers exhibit symptoms that can include violent behavior, anxiety, confusion, and insomnia. They also can display a number of psychotic features, including paranoia, auditory hallucinations, mood disturbances, and delusions (for example, the sensation of insects creeping on the skin, called formication). The paranoia can result in homicidal as well as suicidal thoughts.

With chronic use, tolerance for methamphetamine can develop. In an effort to intensify the desired effects, users may take higher doses of the drug, take it more frequently, or change their method of drug intake. In some cases, abusers forego food and sleep while indulging in a binge, injecting as much as a gram of the drug every 2 to 3 hours over several days until the user runs out of the drug or is too disorganized to continue. Chronic abuse can lead to psychotic behavior, characterized by intense paranoia, visual and auditory hallucinations, and out-of-control rages that can be coupled with extremely violent behavior.

Although there are no physical manifestations of a withdrawal syndrome when methamphetamine use is stopped, there are several symptoms that occur when a chronic user stops taking the drug. These include depression, anxiety, fatigue, paranoia, aggression, and an intense craving for the drug.

In scientific studies examining the consequences of long-term exposure in animals, concern has arisen over the drug's toxic effects on the brain. Researchers have reported that as much as 50 percent of the dopamine-producing cells in the brain can be damaged after prolonged exposure to relatively low levels of methamphetamine. Researchers also have found that serotonin-containing nerve cells may be damaged even more extensively. Whether this toxicity is related to the psychosis seen in some long-term abusers is still an open question.

Methamphetamine is classified as a psychostimulant as are such other drugs of abuse as amphetamine and cocaine. It is structurally similar to amphetamine and the neurotransmitter dopamine, but it is quite different from cocaine. Although these stimulants have similar behavioral and physiological effects, there are some major differences in the basic mechanisms of how they work at the level of the nerve cell. However, the bottom line is that methamphetamine, like cocaine, results in an accumulation of the neurotransmitter dopamine, and this excessive dopamine concentration appears to produce the stimulation and feelings of euphoria experienced by the user. In contrast to cocaine, which is quickly removed and almost completely metabolized in the body, methamphetamine has a much longer duration of action and a larger percentage of the drug remains unchanged in the body. This results in the drug being present in the brain longer, which ultimately leads to prolonged stimulant effects.

Methamphetamine can cause a variety of cardiovascular problems. These include rapid heart rate, irregular heartbeat, increased blood pressure, and irreversible, stroke-producing damage to small blood vessels in the brain. Hyperthermia (elevated body temperature) and convulsions occur with overdoses, and if not treated immediately, can result in death.

Chronic abuse can result in inflammation of the heart lining, and among users who inject the drug, damaged blood vessels and skin abscesses. Abusers also can have episodes of violent behavior, paranoia, anxiety, confusion, and insomnia. Heavy users also show progressive social and occupational deterioration. Psychotic symptoms can sometimes persist for months or years after use has ceased.

Acute lead poisoning is another potential risk. A common method of illegal production uses lead acetate as a reagent. Production errors may therefore result in methamphetamine contaminated with lead. There have been documented cases of acute lead poisoning in intravenous abusers.

Fetal exposure also is a significant problem. At present, research indicates that methamphetamine abuse during pregnancy may result in prenatal complications, increased rates of premature delivery, and altered neonatal behavioral patterns, such as abnormal reflexes and extreme irritability. Abuse during pregnancy may be linked also to congenital deformities.

Research indicates that methamphetamine and related psychomotor stimulants can increase the libido in users, in contrast to opiates which actually decrease the libido. However, long-term use may be associated with decreased sexual functioning, at least in men. Additionally, methamphetamine seems to be associated with rougher sex which may lead to bleeding and abrasions. The combination of injection and sexual risks may result in HIV becoming a greater problem among methamphetamine abusers than among opiate and other drug abusers.

Treatment for Methamphetamine Abuse

At this time the most effective treatments for methamphetamine addiction are cognitive behavioral interventions. These approaches are designed to help modify the patient's thinking, expectancies, and behaviors and to increase skills in coping with various life stressors. Methamphetamine recovery support groups also appear to be effective adjuncts to behavioral interventions that can lead to long-term drug-free recovery.

There are currently no particular pharmacological treatments for dependence on amphetamine or amphetamine-like drugs. The current pharmacological approach is based on experience with treatment of cocaine dependence. Unfortunately, this approach has not met with much success since no single agent has proven efficacious in controlled clinical studies. Antidepressant medications are helpful in combating the depressive symptoms frequently seen in methamphetamine users who recently have become abstinent.

Protocols for treating overdose victims are routine at emergency rooms. Because hyperthermia and convulsions are common and often fatal complications of overdoses, emergency room treatment focuses on the immediate physical symptoms. Overdose patients are cooled off in ice baths, and anticonvulsant drugs may be administered also.

Acute methamphetamine intoxication can often be handled by observation in a safe, quiet environment. In cases of extreme excitement or panic, treatment with antianxiety agents such as benzodiazepines has been helpful, and in cases of methamphetamine-induced psychoses, short-term use of neuroleptics has proven successful.

LESSONS FROM PREVENTION RESEARCH

Prevention programs currently in use are typically designed to enhance "protective factors" and move toward reversing or reducing known "risk factors." Protective factors are those associated with reduced potential for drug use. Risk factors are those that make the potential for drug use more likely:

Protective factors include:

- Strong and positive bonds within a prosocial family.

- Parental monitoring.

- Clear rules of conduct that are consistently enforced within the family.

- Involvement of parents in the lives of their children.

- Success in school performance.

- Strong bonds with prosocial institutions, such as professional and religious organizations.

- Adoption of conventional norms about drug use.

Risk factors include:

- Chaotic home environments, particularly in which family members abuse substances or suffer from mental illnesses.

- Ineffective parenting, especially with children with difficult temperaments or conduct disorders.

- Lack of mutual attachments and nurturing.

- Inappropriately shy or aggressive behavior.

- Failure in performance.

- Poor social coping skills.

- Affiliations with deviant peers or peers displaying deviant behaviors.

- Perceptions of approval of drug-using behaviors.

Prevention programs often include general life skills training and training in skills to resist drugs when offered; strengthen personal attitudes and commitments against drug use; and increase social competency (e.g., in communications, efficacy, and assertiveness).

Prevention programs are necessarily of long duration, with relapse and repeat interventions. For example, work-based efforts directed at drug-abusing employees often include follow-up evaluation, refresher counseling, and drug testing that extend over a period of years.

Work-based prevention programs can be especially effective when augmented by family interventions. Combining the two helps develop employee skills for better family communication, discipline, consistent rulemaking, and resistance to the temptations of abuse. To the extent that drug abuse is diminished in the family, it is diminished in the workplace.

Community-based prevention programs that strengthen norms against drug use in all settings can be linked to work-based programs. Prevention programs at the community level are often operated by civic, religious, law enforcement, and governmental organizations. These programs enhance antidrug norms and prosocial behavior through changes in policy or regulation, mass media efforts, and community-wide awareness programs. Community-based programs might include new laws and enforcement, advertising restrictions, and drug-free school zones, all of which contribute to drug-free work environments.

Prevention programming can be adapted to address the specific nature of the drug abuse problem in the work environment. The higher the level of risk of the target population, the more intensive the prevention effort must be and the earlier it must begin. Prevention programs should be age-specific, developmentally appropriate, and culturally sensitive. Well-operated prevention programs are cost-effective. For every $1 spent on drug use prevention, an employer can save $4 to $5 in costs for drug abuse treatment and counseling.

MYTHS HINDER TREATMENT

Many people view drug abuse and addiction as strictly a social problem. Parents, teens, older adults, and other members of the community tend to characterize people who take drugs as morally weak or as having criminal tendencies. They believe that drug abusers and addicts should be able to stop taking drugs if they are willing to change their behavior.

These myths have not only stereotyped those with drug-related problems, but also their families, their communities, and the health-care professionals who work with them. Drug abuse and addiction comprise a public health problem that affects many people and has wide-ranging social consequences. Employers can help the public replace its myths and long-held mistaken beliefs about drug abuse and addiction.

While it is true that addiction begins when an individual makes a conscious choice to use drugs, it is not simply a matter of continued use or out-of-control use. Recent scientific research provides overwhelming evidence that not only do drugs interfere with normal brain functioning creating powerful feelings of pleasure, but they also have long-term effects on brain metabolism and activity. At some point, changes occur in the brain that can turn drug abuse into addiction, a chronic, relapsing illness. Those addicted to drugs suffer from a compulsive drug craving and usage and cannot quit by themselves. Treatment is necessary to end this compulsive behavior.

A variety of approaches are used in treatment programs to help patients deal with these cravings and possibly avoid drug relapse. Research shows that addiction is clearly treatable. Through treatment that is tailored to individual needs, patients can learn to control their condition and live relatively normal lives.

Treatment can have a profound effect not only on drug abusers, but on society as a whole, including work organizations. By returning people to useful lives, treatment significantly improves social functioning, decreases drug-related criminality and violence, and reduces the spread of AIDS. It also dramatically reduces the high costs to society of drug abuse.

Demythologizing drug abuse also helps in preventing use in the first place. Comprehensive prevention programs that involve the family, schools, communities, and the media are effective in sending the message that it is far better to not fool with drugs at all than to get trapped by addiction and have to enter rehabilitation. Overcoming misconceptions and replacing myths with scientific knowledge is the best hope for bridging the gap between public perception of drug abuse and the scientific facts.

THE AIDS CONNECTION

Behavior associated with drug abuse is now the single largest factor in the spread of HIV infection in the United States. HIV is the Human Immunodeficiency Virus, which causes Acquired Immunodeficiency Syndrome, or AIDS. AIDS is a condition characterized by a defect in the body's natural immunity to diseases, and individuals who suffer from it are at risk for severe illnesses that are usually not a threat to anyone whose immune system is working properly. Although many individuals who have AIDS or carry HIV may live for many years with treatment, there is no known cure or vaccine.

Using or sharing unsterile needles, cotton swabs, rinse water, and cookers, such as when injecting heroin, cocaine, or other drugs, leaves a drug abuser vulnerable to contracting or transmitting HIV. Another way people may be at risk for contracting HIV is by using drugs of abuse, regardless of whether a needle and syringe are involved. Research has shown that drug and alcohol use interferes with judgment about sexual (and other) behavior, making it more likely that users have unplanned and unprotected sex. This places them at increased risk for contracting HIV from infected sex partners.

Infection Rates

Half of all new infections with HIV now occur among injecting drug users (IDUs). According to data gathered from the Nation's 96 largest cities, where HIV infection rates are the highest, an average of 27 percent of all IDUs are HIV-infected. The areas surveyed have an estimated 1.5 million IDUs, 1.7 million gay and bisexual men, and 2.1 million at-risk heterosexuals (men and women who have sex with IDUs or gay and bisexual men). Among these three risk groups, there are currently an estimated 565,000 HIV infections, with 38,000 new infections occurring each year. Using these data to make nationwide projections, the review concludes that there are about 700,000 current HIV infections, with 41,000 new HIV infections occurring each year in the U.S.

An estimated 19,000 IDUs are infected each year in these areas, indicating an HIV incidence rate of about 1.5 infections per 100 IDUs per year. Infection rates are lower for the other two high-risk groups. Although gay and bisexual men still represent the group with the greatest number of current HIV infections, the rate of infection - except in young and ethnic/minority gay men - is much lower now than it was a decade ago. For gay and bisexual men, the HIV infection rate per 100 persons per year is 0.7; for at-risk heterosexuals, the rate is 0.5 infections per 100 persons per year. At-risk heterosexual women outnumber at-risk heterosexual men about 4 to 1.

HIV Among IDUs

It is clear from research that drug abuse treatment is a proven means of preventing the spread of HIV and AIDS, especially when combined with prevention and community-based outreach programs for at-risk people. These efforts can reduce or eliminate drug use and drug-related HIV risk behaviors such as needle sharing and unsafe sex practices. One study comparing HIV infection rates among drug abusers enrolled in methadone treatment programs to rates among

TREATMENT

those not in treatment found that those not in treatment were nearly seven times more likely to have become infected with HIV during the first 18 months. The study also found that the longer drug abusers remained in treatment, the less likely they were to become infected.

In addition, drug treatment programs help reduce the spread of other blood-borne infections, including hepatitis B and C viruses. Adequate medical care for HIV or AIDS and any related illnesses is also critical to reducing spread.

Appendix A

Executive Order 12564

Executive Order 12564: Drug-Free Federal Workplace

I, RONALD REAGAN, President of the United States of America, find that:

APPENDIX A

Drug use is having serious adverse effects upon a significant proportion of the national workforce and results in billions of dollars of lost productivity each year;

The federal government, as an employer, is concerned with the well-being of its employees, the successful accomplishment of agency missions, and the need to maintain employee productivity;

The federal government, as the largest employer in the Nation, can and should show the way towards achieving drug-free workplaces through a program designed to offer drug users a helping hand and, at the same time, demonstrating to drug users and potential drug users that drugs will not be tolerated in the federal workplace;

The profits from illegal drugs provide the single greatest source of income for organized crime, fuel violent street crime, and otherwise contribute to the breakdown of our society;

The use of illegal drugs, on or off duty, by federal employees is inconsistent not only with the law-abiding behavior expected of all citizens, but also with the special trust placed in such employees as servants of the public;

federal employees who use illegal drugs, on or off duty, tend to be less productive, less reliable, and prone to greater absenteeism than their fellow employees who do not use illegal drugs;

The use of illegal drugs, on or off duty, by federal employees impairs the efficiency of federal departments and agencies, undermines public confidence in them, and makes it more difficult for other employees who do not use illegal drugs to perform their jobs effectively. The use of illegal drugs, on or off duty, by federal employees also can pose a serious health and safety threat to members of the public and to other federal employees;

The use of illegal drugs, on or off duty, by federal employees in certain positions evidences less than the complete reliability, stability, and good judgment that is consistent with access to sensitive information and creates the possibility of coercion, influence, and irresponsible action under pressure that may pose a serious risk to national security, the public safety, and the effective enforcement of the law; and

Federal employees who use illegal drugs must themselves be primarily responsible for changing their behavior and, if necessary, begin the process of rehabilitating themselves. By the authority vested in me as President by the Constitution and laws of the United States of America, including section 3301(2) of Title 5 of the United States Code, section 7301 of Title 5 of the United States Code, section 290ee-1 of Title 42 of the United States Code, deeming such action in the best interests of national security, public health and safety, law enforcement and the efficiency of the federal service, and in order to establish standards and procedures to ensure fairness in achieving a drug-free federal workplace and to protect the privacy of federal employees, it is hereby ordered as follows:

SECTION 1. DRUG-FREE WORKPLACE.

(a)   Federal employees are required to refrain from the use of illegal drugs.

(b)   The use of illegal drugs by federal employees, whether on duty or off duty, is contrary to the efficiency of the service.

(c)   Persons who use illegal drugs are not suitable for federal employment.

SEC. 2. AGENCY RESPONSIBILITIES.

(a)   The head of each Executive agency shall develop a plan for achieving the objective of a drug-free workplace with due consideration of the rights of the government, the employee, and the general public.

(b)   Each agency plan shall include:

(1)   A statement of policy setting forth the agency's expectations regarding drug use and the action to be anticipated in response to identified drug use;

(2)   Employee Assistance Programs emphasizing high level direction, education, counseling, referral to rehabilitation, and coordination with available community resources;

(3)   Supervisory training to assist in identifying and addressing illegal drug use by agency employees;

(4)   Provision for self-referrals as well as supervisory referrals to treatment with maximum respect for individual confidentiality consistent with safety and security issues; and

(5)   Provision for identifying illegal drug users, including testing on a controlled and carefully monitored basis in accordance with this Order.

SEC. 3. DRUG TESTING PROGRAMS.

(a)   The head of each Executive agency shall establish a program to test for the use of illegal drugs by employees in sensitive positions. The extent to which such employees are tested and the criteria for such testing shall be determined by the head of each agency, based upon the nature of the agency's mission and its employees' duties, the efficient use of agency resources, and the danger to the public health and safety or national security that could result from the failure of an employee adequately to discharge his or her position.

(b)   The head of each Executive agency shall establish a program for voluntary employee drug testing.

(c)   In addition to the testing authorized in subsections (a) and (b) of this section, the head of each Executive agency is authorized to test an employee for illegal drug use under the following circumstances:

(1)   When there is a reasonable suspicion that any employee uses illegal drugs;

(2)   In an examination authorized by the agency regarding an accident or unsafe practice; or

(3)   As part of or as a follow-up to counseling or rehabilitation for illegal drug use through an Employee Assistance Program.

(d)   The head of each Executive agency is authorized to test any applicant for illegal drug use.

SEC. 4. DRUG TESTING PROCEDURES.

(a)   Sixty days prior to the implementation of a drug testing program pursuant to this Order, agencies shall notify employees that testing for use of illegal drugs is to be conducted and that they may seek counseling and rehabilitation and inform them of the procedures for obtaining such assistance through the agency's Employee Assistance Program. Agency drug testing programs already ongoing are exempted from the 60-day notice requirement. Agencies may take action under section 3(c) of this Order without reference to the 60-day notice period.

(b)   Before conducting a drug test, the agency shall inform the employee to be tested of the opportunity to submit medical documentation that may support a legitimate use for a specific drug.

(c)   Drug testing programs shall contain procedures for timely submission of requests for retention of records and specimens; procedures for retesting; and procedures, consistent with applicable law, to protect the confidentiality of test results and related medical and rehabilitation records. Procedures for providing urine specimens must allow individual privacy, unless the agency has reason to believe that a particular individual may alter or substitute the specimen to be provided.

(d) The Secretary of Health and Human Services is authorized to promulgate scientific and technical guidelines for drug testing programs, and agencies shall conduct their drug testing programs in accordance with these guidelines once promulgated.

APPENDIX A

SEC. 5. PERSONNEL ACTIONS.

(a)   Agencies shall, in addition to any appropriate personnel actions, refer any employee who is found to use illegal drugs to an Employee Assistance Program for assessment, counseling, and referral for treatment or rehabilitation as appropriate.

(b)   Agencies shall initiate action to discipline any employee who is found to use illegal drugs, provided that such action is not required for an employee who:

(1)   Voluntarily identifies himself as a user of illegal drugs or who volunteers for drug testing pursuant to section 3(b) of this Order, prior to being identified through other means;

(2)   Obtains counseling or rehabilitation through an Employee Assistance Program: and

(3)   Thereafter refrains from using illegal drugs.

(c)   Agencies shall not allow any employee to remain on duty in a sensitive position who is found to use illegal drugs, prior to successful completion of rehabilitation through an Employee Assistance Program. However, as part of a rehabilitation or counseling program, the head of an Executive agency may, in his or her discretion, allow an employee to return to duty in a sensitive position if it is determined that this action would not pose a danger to public health or safety or the national security.

(d)   Agencies shall initiate action to remove from the service any employee who is found to use illegal drugs and:

(1)   Refuses to obtain counseling or rehabilitation through an Employee Assistance Program; or

(2)   Does not thereafter refrain from using illegal drugs.

(e)   The results of a drug test and information developed by the agency in the course of the drug testing of the employee may be considered in processing any adverse action against the employee or for other administrative purposes. Preliminary test results may not be used in an administrative proceeding unless they are confirmed by a second analysis of the same sample or unless the employee confirms the accuracy of the initial test by admitting the use of illegal drugs.

(f)   The determination of an agency that an employee uses illegal drugs can be made on the basis of any appropriate evidence, including direct observation, a criminal conviction, administrative inquiry, or the results of an authorized testing program. Positive drug test results may be rebutted by other evidence that an employee has not used illegal drugs.

(g)   Any action to discipline an employee who is using illegal drugs (including removal from the service, if appropriate) shall be taken in compliance with otherwise applicable procedures, including the Civil Service Reform Act.

(h)   Drug testing shall not be conducted pursuant to this Order for the purpose of gathering evidence for use in criminal proceedings. Agencies are not required to report to the Attorney General for investigation or prosecution any information, allegation, or evidence relating to violations of Title 21 of the United States Code received as a result of the operation of drug testing programs established pursuant to this Order.

SEC. 6. COORDINATION OF AGENCY PROGRAMS.

(a)   The Director of the Office of Personnel Management shall:

(1)   Issue government-wide guidance to agencies on the implementation of the terms of this Order;

(2)   Ensure that appropriate coverage for drug abuse is maintained for employees and their families under the Federal Employees Health Benefits Program;

(3)   Develop a model Employee Assistance Program for federal agencies and assist the agencies in putting programs in place;

(4)   In consultation with the Secretary of Health and Human Services, develop and improve training programs for federal supervisors and managers on illegal drug use: and

(5)   In cooperation with the Secretary of Health and Human Services and heads of Executive agencies, mount an intensive drug awareness campaign throughout the federal workforce.

(b)   The Attorney General shall render legal advice regarding the implementation of this Order and shall be consulted with regard to all guidelines, regulations, and policies proposed to be adopted pursuant to this Order.

(c)   Nothing in this Order shall be deemed to limit the authorities of the Director of Central Intelligence under the National Security Act of 1947, as amended, or the statutory authorities of the National Security Agency or the Defense Intelligence Agency. Implementation of this Order within the Intelligence Community, as defined in Executive Order No. 12333, shall be subject to the approval of the head of the affected agency.

SEC. 7. DEFINITIONS.

(a)   This Order applies to all agencies of the Executive Branch.

(b)   For purposes of this Order, the term "agency" means an Executive agency, as defined in 5 U.S.C. 105; the Uniformed Services, as defined in 5 U.S.C. 2101 (3) (but excluding the armed forces as defined by 5 U.S.C. 2101(2)); or any other employing unit or authority of the federal government, except the United States Postal Service, the Postal Rate Commission, and employing units or authorities in the Judicial and Legislative Branches.

(c)   For purposes of this Order, the term "illegal drugs" means a controlled substance included in Schedule I or II, as defined by section 802(6) of Title 21 of the United States Code, the possession of which is unlawful under chapter 13 of that Title. The term "illegal drugs" does not mean the use of a controlled substance pursuant to a valid prescription or other uses authorized by law.

(d)   For purposes of this Order, the term "employee in a sensitive position" refers to:

(1)   An employee in a position that an agency head designates Special-Sensitive, Critical-Sensitive, or Noncritical-Sensitive under Chapter 731 of the Federal Personnel Manual or an employee in a position that an agency head designates as sensitive in accordance with Executive Order No. 10450, as amended;

(2)   An employee who has been granted access to classified information or may be granted access to classified information pursuant to a determination of trustworthiness by an agency head under Section 4 of Executive Order No. 12356;

(3)   Individuals serving under Presidential appointments;

(4)   Law enforcement officers as defined in 5 U.S.C. 8331(20); and

(5)   Other positions that the agency head determines involve law enforcement, national security, the protection of life and property, public health or safety, or other functions requiring a high degree of trust and confidence.

(e)   For purposes of this Order, the term "employee" means all persons appointed in the Civil Service as described in 5 U.S.C. 2105 (but excluding persons appointed in the armed services as defined in 5 U.S.C. 2102(2)).

(f)   For purposes of this Order, the term "Employee Assistance Program" means agency-based counseling programs that offer assessment, short-term counseling, and referral services to employees for a wide range of drug, alcohol, and mental health programs that affect employee job performance. Employee Assistance Programs are responsible for referring drug-using employees for rehabilitation and for monitoring employees' progress while in treatment.

SEC. 8. EFFECTIVE DATE.

This Order is effective immediately.

Ronald Reagan

THE WHITE HOUSE, September 15, 1986.

Appendix B

Resources

Hotlines, Helplines, and Web Sites

Alcohol Hotline
1-800-ALCOHOL
The alcohol hotline is a nationwide help and referral hotline for alcohol and drug problems. The phones are answered by individuals trained to assist callers 24 hours a day, seven days a week.

RESOURCES

American Council for Drug Education (ACDE)
1-800-488-DRUG (3784)
ACDE is an independent non-profit organization that
produces print and video information materials for sale. The
Council has various programs, including a workplace
education program dealing with alcohol and illegal drug use.

American Council on Alcoholism Helpline (ACA)
1-800-527-5344
ACA discusses alcohol problems with callers and refers callers
to treatment centers. ACA also publishes a newsletter and
various pamphlets, and conducts a Driver Alcohol Training
and Evaluation School (DATES).

Center for Substance Abuse Treatment (CSAT)
1-800-662-HELP (4357)
The CSAT helpline provides advice and referrals about the
availability of drug and alcohol services. It also serves as an
information clearinghouse on drugs, particularly cocaine.

Cocaine Hotline
1-800-COCAINE
The Cocaine Hotline provides 24-hour referrals and phone
numbers of treatment centers to individuals with cocaine
problems.

Cocaine Hotline (Spanish)
1-800-662-9832
This is the Cocaine Hotline's number for Spanish-speaking
individuals.

Drug-Free Workplace Helpline
1-800-WORKPLACE
This is a toll-free service which provides information and
consultation to business owners, managers, and union leaders
regarding the development and implementation of workplace
substance abuse programs. The helpline distributes a variety
of information on workplace substance abuse policies,

regulations, and drug testing programs. Counselors also refer callers to local contacts. The Center for Substance Abuse Prevention (CSAP) operates this helpline.

National Clearinghouse for Alcohol and Drug Information (NCADI)
1-800-729-6686
NCADI distributes information on alcohol and drugs, and provides prevention materials to teachers, community organizations, businesses, and individuals. NCADI supports the Regional Alcohol and Drug Awareness Resource Network (RADAR), a network of state substance abuse information centers and clearinghouses. (See state section, or call NCADI, for each local RADAR contact.)

National Council on Alcoholism and Drug Dependence, Inc. (NCADD)
(800) NCA-CALL (24 Hour Affiliate Referral)
NCADD provides education, information, help and hope in the fight against alcoholism and other drug addictions. NCADD has more than 100 councils around the country, and is able to provide a local perspective on alcoholism and other drug addictions. Affiliates of NCADD provide information and referrals to local services, including counseling and treatment. They also conduct community prevention and education programs.

National Intervention Network
1-800-654-HOPE
This network is operated by certified affiliates of the National Council on Alcoholism and Drug Dependence (NCADD). The affiliates guide family, friends, and co-workers of people with drug or alcohol problems through the intervention process. Located throughout the nation, NCADD affiliates provide education and help clients plan, rehearse, and conduct interventions for the greatest chance of success.

National Resources

American Council for Drug Education (ACDE)
1 (800) 488-DRUG
The American Council for Drug Education is an independent non-profit organization that produces print and video information and offers services for sale. The Council has various programs, including a workplace education program dealing with alcohol and illegal drug use.

Business Against Drunk Drivers, Inc. (BADD)
(414) 273-BADD
This 180-member organization focuses on workplace education and is dedicated to reducing the human and financial costs of drunk driving. BADD is not opposed to consumption of alcohol but is opposed to drunk driving. BADD sponsors safety events, issues policy statements, develops educational materials, and conducts training seminars. BADD provides access to information, literature, and promotional materials to employers and employees on such topics as policy guidelines, designated driver/cab fare reimbursement programs, and drunk driving laws and penalties.

Center for Substance Abuse Prevention (CSAP)
(301) 443-6780   (800) WORKPLACE
CSAP was established in 1986 to steer the federal government's alcohol, tobacco, and other drug prevention and intervention programs. CSAP administers prevention programs including, "Community Partnership," "High-Risk Youth," National Clearinghouse for Alcohol and Drug Information (NCADI), and the Drug-Free Workplace Helpline.

Centers for Disease Control and Prevention (CDC)
(404) 639-3824
Charged with protecting the nation's public health, the CDC works with state and local health departments and community members to organize local intervention programs. The CDC provides materials and technical assistance on substance abuse programs.

Drugs Don't Work Partnership (DDW)
(703) 706-0578
The National Drugs Don't Work Partnership (DDW) was launched in January 1993 by the President's Drug Advisory Council and the Partnership for a Drug-Free America. Its purpose was to engage the business community in our nation's efforts to reduce the devastating effects of drug and alcohol abuse in the workplace, as well as the communities in which we live and work. In May 1995, DDW merged with Community Anti-Drug Coalitions of American (CADCA) to encourage the business community to link with CADCA's more than 4,300 member coalitions.

Employee Assistance Professionals Association (EAPA)
(703) 522-6272
EAPA represents over 7,000 employee assistance program (EAP) professionals including labor representatives, consultants, and internal and external providers. EAPA provides information on how to select EAPs, the value they can provide, the theory behind them, and how they operate, as well as contact information for those who wish to get in touch with local EAPs. EAPA publishes in the areas of prevention, treatment, and education.

Employee Assistance Society of North America (EASNA)
(313) 545-3888
EASNA is an extensive networking association for those working in the employee assistance field. EASNA publishes THE SOURCE, a quarterly newsletter, and the EMPLOYEE ASSISTANCE QUARTERLY, its official journal.

Join Together

(617) 437-1500

Join Together is a resource center created by a grant to the Boston University School of Public Health from the Robert Wood Johnson Foundation. The resource center is a clearinghouse for information on drug abuse, and maintains an international database of citizens, organizations, and government groups that work on substance abuse issues. Join Together's mission is to help these groups overcome barriers they face in the prevention of substance abuse through technical assistance, public policy panels, National Leadership Fellows, communications, and a national computer network. Join Together's computer network is part of HandsNet, a national network linking over 3,000 organizations.

National Association of State Alcohol and Drug Abuse Directors (NASADAD)

(202) 783-6868

NASADAD assists state governments and agencies to develop drug policies through each state's drug abuse director. It fosters the development of alcohol and drug abuse programs and facilitates the exchange of related information.

National Clearinghouse for Alcohol and Drug Information (NCADI)

(301) 468-2600

NCADI distributes information on alcohol and drugs, and provides prevention materials to teachers, community organizations, businesses, and individuals. Most National Institute for Drug Abuse (NIDA) materials are available at NCADI. Materials can be ordered by calling NCADI at 1-800-729-6686.

National Council on Alcoholism and Drug Dependence, Inc. (NCADD)

(212) 206-6770

NCADD provides education, information, help and hope in the fight against the chronic, often fatal disease of alcoholism and other drug addictions. Founded in 1944, NCADD is a voluntary health organization with a nationwide network of affiliates. NCADD is a strong advocate of prevention, intervention, research, and treatment and is dedicated to ridding the disease of its stigma and its sufferers from their patterns of denial and shame.

National Highway Traffic Safety Administration (NHTSA)
(202) 366-2721
A major focus of NHTSA is the prevention of impaired driving. NHTSA provides resources to state and community law enforcement agencies, as well as impaired driving programs and a range of prevention publications.

National Inhalant Prevention Coalition (NIPC)
(800) 269-4237
NIPC is a public-private effort to promote awareness and recognition of the under-publicized problem of inhalant use throughout the country. NIPC serves as an inhalant referral and information clearinghouse to educate and devise multi-faceted awareness and prevention campaigns designed to educate youth and adults about the debilitating effects of these dangerous gateway drugs. NIPC also provides in-service training for educators. NIPC can be reached at:

> National Inhalant Prevention Coalition
> 1201 W. Sixth Street, Suite C-200
> Austin, TX 78703

National Institute on Alcohol Abuse and Alcoholism (NIAAA)
(301) 443-1677
NIAAA is the federal research organization that focuses on alcohol-related problems. NIAAA disseminates scientific and educational information to the public stating the risks and

consequences associated with alcohol abuse and alcohol dependence.

National Institute on Drug Abuse (NIDA)
(301) 443-6014
NIDA is the federal research organization that focuses on drug-related problems. NIDA disseminates scientific and educational information to the public stating the risks and consequences associated with drug abuse through the media. NIDA is part of the U.S. Department of Health and Human Services (HHS).

State Alcohol and Drug Abuse Agency Directory
(301) 443-8956
The State Alcohol and Drug Abuse Agency Directory contains contact information for all state Alcohol and Drug Abuse Agencies, and provides a link to the Agency's Web site, if one exists. It is provided via the Center for Substance Abuse Treatment's (CSAT) Treatment Improvement Exchange (TIE) Web site.

Substance Abuse Program Administrators' Association (SAPAA)
(800) 672-7229
SAPAA is a membership organization founded to establish and promote standards of quality, integrity, and profession-alism for providers of products and services related to the administration of substance abuse and drug testing programs in the workplace. Its membership includes, and is a source for, names of providers of all services necessary to set-up and manage workplace drug and alcohol testing programs. SAPAA monitors state and federal legislation, legal developments and regulatory issues and keeps its members informed.

U.S. Department of Transportation (DOT)
(202) 366-3784 (Drug Enforcement and Program Compliance)
DOT mandates and regulates drug and alcohol testing for safety-sensitive transportation industries. In addition to DOT's

common rules, each of DOT's modes issues regulations.
Following are the different modes and their contact
information.

Maritime
UNITED STATES COAST GUARD (USCG)
Investigations Division
2100 2nd Street, SW
Room 2406
Washington, DC 20593-0001
(202) 267-1430

Aviation
FEDERAL AVIATION ADMINISTRATION (FAA)
Drug Abatement Division
(AAM-800)
800 Independence Ave., SW
Washington, DC 20591
(202) 267-8442

Commercial Motor Vehicles
FEDERAL HIGHWAY ADMINISTRATION (FHWA)
Office of Motor Carrier Standards
400 7th Street, SW
Room 3107
Washington, DC 20590
(202) 366-4009
(800) 832-5660

Railroad
FEDERAL RAILROAD ADMINISTRATION (FRA)
Operating Practices Division
(RRS-11)
400 7th Street, SW
Washington, DC 20590
(202) 632-3378

Transit
FEDERAL TRANSIT ADMINISTRATION (FTA)

Office of Safety and Security, Room 9301
400 7th Street, SW
Washington, DC 20590
(202) 366-2896

Pipeline
RESEARCH AND SPECIAL PROGRAMS
ADMINISTRATION (RSPA)
Office of Pipeline Safety
400 7th Street, SW
Room 2335
Washington, DC 20590
(202) 366-6199

U.S. Drug Enforcement Administration (DEA)

(202) 307-7936
DEA is responsible for the enforcement of federal drug laws and regulations. It conducts prevention programs in concert with numerous national organizations through its Demand Reduction Program. The DEA also develops and distributes a variety of publications and videos on prevention.

State and Territory Resources

ALABAMA

ALABAMA NATIONAL GUARD
COUNTERDRUG PROGRAM
Drug Demand Reduction Administrator
1750 Cong. W.L. Dickinson Drive
P.O. Box 3711 Montgomery, AL 36109-0711
(334) 213-7724 Fax: (334) 213-7754

CSAP RADAR NETWORK STATE CENTER
Crystal Jackson
Division of Substance Abuse Services
Alabama Department of Mental Health/Mental Retardation
RSA Union Building
P.O. Box 301410 Montgomery, AL 36130-1410
(334) 242-3417

MORGAN COUNTY SUBSTANCE ABUSE NETWORK
Sue Brantly
Phone: (205) 353-1160

U.S. DRUG ENFORCEMENT ADMINISTRATION
DEMAND REDUCTION FIELD OFFICE
New Orleans Field Division
Special Agent Michael Streicher
Drug Enforcement Administration
3838 North Causeway Blvd.
Suite 1800
Metairie, LA 70002
Phone: (504) 840-1032
Fax: (504) 840-1052

ALASKA

ALASKA NATIONAL GUARD
COUNTERDRUG PROGRAM
Drug Demand Reduction Administrator
Bldg. 49000 P.O. Box 5800
Fort Richardson, AK 99505
Phone: (907) 428-6204
Fax: (907) 428-6238

CSAP RADAR NETWORK STATE CENTER
Pam Truax
Alaska Council on Prevention of Alcohol and

Drug Abuse
3333 Denali Street, Suite 201
Anchorage, AK 99503
Phone: (907) 258-6021

STATE OF ALASKA
The Division of Alcohol and Drug Abuse, in the Alaska
Department of Health & Social Services, provides alcohol and
other drug abuse prevention, treatment and outreach services
through its grant-in-aid program. Substance abuse programs
are available in every region of the state. The outreach
services of these regional centers extend to private sector
employers and trade associations, as well as schools and
youth groups. The centers provide information, education,
outpatient counseling, detoxification, residential treatment,
emergency care, and relapse prevention services. This office
distributes a free employer's guide to assist firms wishing to
address workplace substance abuse. The guide highlights the
problems associated with alcohol and other drug abuse,
explains the Employee Assistance Program process, and
includes sample written policies as well as lists of resources
available. The guide and other information relating to alcohol
and other drug abuse issues are available through the
Division of Alcoholism and Drug Abuse and through three
non-profit prevention organizations which serve as information clearinghouses.
Joseph DiMatteo
Alaska Council on Prevention of
Alcohol and Drug Abuse
3333 Denali Street, Suite 201
Anchorage, AK 99503
Phone: (907) 258-6021

Karen Elliott
National Council on Alcoholism - Juneau
P.O. Box 020568
Juneau, AK 99801
Phone: (907) 463-3755

Mr. Loren Jones
Division of Alcoholism & Drug Abuse
State of Alaska
Department of Health & Social Services
P.O. Box 110607
Juneau, AK 99811
Phone: (907) 465-2071

U.S. DRUG ENFORCEMENT ADMINISTRATION AGENT
DEMAND REDUCTION FIELD OFFICE
Seattle Field Division
Special Agent Juliana Parra-West
Drug Enforcement Administration
220 West Mercer, Suite 300
Seattle, WA 98119
Phone: (206) 553-5443
Fax: (206) 533-1069

AMERICAN SAMOA

CSAP RADAR NETWORK STATE CENTER
Julia Foifua
Department of Human and Social Services
Alcohol and Drug Program
Government of America Samoa
Pago Pago, AS 96799
Phone: (684) 633-2696

ARIZONA

ARIZONA NATIONAL GUARD
JOINT COUNTER-NARCOTICS TASK FORCE
Drug Demand Reduction Administrator
5636 E. McDowell Rd

Phoenix, AZ 85008
Phone: (602) 267-2341
Fax: (602) 267-2474
E-mail: jentf@primenet.com

CSAP RADAR NETWORK STATE CENTER
Patty Hibbler
Arizona Prevention Resource Center
Arizona State University
College of Extended Education
641 East VanBuren, Suite B2
Phoenix, AZ 85004
Phone: (602) 727-2772
Fax: (602) 965-8198

DRUGS DON'T WORK IN ARIZONA!
A non-profit public-private partnership facilitating the establishment of comprehensive workplace substance abuse programs for Arizona employers. Grants will be awarded to chambers of commerce or business coalitions which will receive free training and technical assistance on how to provide workplace substance abuse services to businesses, particularly small businesses. DRUGS DON'T WORK IN ARIZONA! will also provide group rates for drug testing and employee assistance programs.
Susan Jones
3010 N. 2nd St., Suite 301
Phoenix, AZ 85012
Phone: (602) 248-845
(800) 380-3392 (intrastate)

MARICOPA COUNTY DEMAND REDUCTION PROGRAM
Through its PUT DRUGS OUT OF WORK campaign, the Maricopa County Demand Reduction Program conducts workplace substance abuse seminars and provides technical assistance to businesses that wish to establish a substance abuse policy. The Maricopa County Demand Reduction Program is involved in a public-private partnership that is

working closely with the National DRUGS DON'T WORK
Partnership on developing a statewide comprehensive
workplace substance abuse program called DRUGS DON'T
WORK IN ARIZONA.
Rebecca Jahn
Maricopa County Demand Reduction Program
Maricopa County Attorney's Office
301 West Jefferson, 8th Floor
Phoenix, AZ 85003
Phone: (602) 506-7799

STATE OF ARIZONA
The Governor's Office of Drug Policy utilizes the expertise of
Arizonans For A Drug-Free Workplace, a private, non-profit
organization that provides training and technical assistance in
the establishment of workplace substance abuse programs, to
assist small businesses who request assistance. "Arizonans"
has assisted over 450 small businesses throughout the state to
develop workplace substance abuse policies and programs.
Arizonans for a Drug-Free Workplace is a member of the
Institute for a Drug-Free Workplace.
Elizabeth Edwards
Arizonans For A Drug-Free Workplace
P.O. Box 13223
Tucson, AZ 85732-3223
(520) 740-5063
Outside Tucson: (800) 592-3339 (intrastate)
The Office of Drug Policy has organized an ad hoc working
group composed of representatives from various state
agencies, federal, state and regional law enforcement
agencies, private industry, and Arizonans for a Drug-Free
Workplace, to develop a statewide Workplace Substance
Abuse Program system.
Peggy Eggmeyer
State of Arizona
Governor's Office of Drug Policy
1700 West Washington Phoenix, AZ 85007
(602) 542-3456

RESOURCES

U.S. DRUG ENFORCEMENT ADMINISTRATION
DEMAND REDUCTION FIELD OFFICE
Special Agent Roger Taylor
Drug Enforcement
3010 North Second Street Suite 301
Phoenix, AZ 85012
(602) 664-5844 Fax: (602) 664-5627

ARKANSAS

ARKANSAS NATIONAL GUARD
COUNTERDRUG PROGRAM
Drug Demand Reduction Administrator
Camp Joseph T. Robinson
North Little Rock, AR 72199-9600
(510) 212-5484 Fax: (510) 212-5479

BUREAU OF ALCOHOL AND DRUG ABUSE PREVENTION
Janice Cheat
(501) 280-4508

CSAP RADAR NETWORK STATE CENTER
Percy Brown
Office on Alcohol and Drug Abuse Prevention
5800 West 10th Street, Suite 901
Little Rock, AR 72203-1437
(501) 280-4500

DRUGS DON'T WORK
The Arkansas Department of Human Services, Division of
Alcohol and Drug Abuse Prevention, was awarded a Block
Grant from the Office of Alcohol, Drug Abuse and Mental
Health Services. These funds were provided to the Office of
the Governor to conduct a DRUGS DON'T WORK project,
modeled after the campaign of the same name developed by
the President's Drug Advisory Council and the Partnership for
a Drug-Free America. Through a sub-grant to the Arkansas

226

State Chamber of Commerce, DRUGS DON'T WORK targets small to medium sized private sector businesses, assisting them with informational and educational material and program opportunities, the development of workplace substance abuse policies, and other activities.
Olan Reeves
Office of the Governor
Arkansas State Capitol Room 011
Little Rock, AR 72201
(501) 682-8040

Ron Russell
Arkansas Chamber of Commerce
410 S. Cross St.
Little Rock, AR 72201
(501) 374-9225

U.S. DRUG ENFORCEMENT ADMINISTRATION
DEMAND REDUCTION FIELD OFFICE
Special Agent Michael Streicher
Drug Enforcement Administration
3838 North Causeway Blvd. Suite 1800
Metairie, LA 70002
(504) 840-1032 Fax: (504) 840-1052

CALIFORNIA

CALIFORNIA NATIONAL GUARD
COUNTERDRUG TASK FORCE
Through numerous community-based, leadership, educational and informational programs, the National Guard Counterdrug Program supports individuals and organizations dedicated to drug intervention and prevention, anti-legalization efforts, and the positive development of youth.
Drug Demand Reduction Administrator
9800 Goethe Road,
Box G Sacramento, CA 95826-9101

227

RESOURCES

(916) 854-3309 Fax: (916) 854-3834
E-mail: d.banowetz@cacdhq.org

CSAP RADAR NETWORK STATE CENTER
Gwen Aldridge
Department of Alcohol and Drug Programs
1700 K Street Sacramento, CA 95814-4022
(916) 323-4675

STATE OF CALIFORNIA
The California Department of Alcohol and Drug Programs
(ADP) established a Drug-Free Workplace section within its
Office of Prevention in April 1991. The Office's charter is to
help businesses throughout California learn about the impact
of inappropriate or illegal use of alcohol and other drugs.
Alcohol, illegal drugs, and misused pharmaceuticals are all
given equal billing. There are over 500,000 employers in the
state of California, and 90 percent of them have fewer than 20
employees. It is the philosophy of the Drug-Free Workplace
section that establishing a workplace substance abuse program is an economic issue related to many other management
considerations. Components of the substance abuse program
(DFWP) include: 1. DFWP Recognition Program, designed to
give visibility to DFWP by having employers apply to the
state for recognition as a DFWP. To receive recognition,
employers must have a DFWP program in place which is
scaled to needs of their employees, setting, and objectives.
Employers are awarded a distinctive California DFWP decal
and document for public display. The common logo is
intended to result in immediate recognition of DFWP throughout the state. 2. Distribution of information on the California
DFWP Act of 1990 and federal DFWP Act of 1988, to assist
employers in understanding the various mandated DFWP
requirements -- the California Act is much like the Federal
Act. 3. Demonstration DFWP Recognition Program Five of
California's 58 counties were awarded start-up funds for three
years to organize local DFWP teams within their respective
counties. The state developed detailed curriculum and

228

provided technical training to the teams. 4. Resource Center - The Resource Center offers videos that may be borrowed and a limited amount of commercial and federal printed material. The pamphlet, A Serious Problem Facing Business -- The Abuse of Alcohol and Other Drugs, produced by the state, is available by calling 1-800-879- 2772. The Resource Center also utilizes the Department of Labor's Substance Abuse Information Database (SAID). 5. The California National Guard supports DFWP by training reservists who can then take DFWP concepts back to their respective civilian workplaces. This multiplier will help the Office of Alcohol and Drug Programs (ADP) staff influence sites which might be missed by other outreach efforts. 6. Associations and other formal organizations are sought by ADP to provide an efficient method of expanding DFWP awareness. Examples include the California Veterinary Medical Association, the League of Cities, and the County Supervisors Association.
Antonia Taylor
Office of Prevention DFWP
California Department of Alcohol and Drug Programs
1700 K Street Sacramento, CA 95814-4037
(916) 445-7771

THE WORKPLACE FOUNDATION
Iola Gold
The Workplace Foundation
1367 8th Ave. #B
Sacramento, CA 95818
(916) 447-9471

U.S. DRUG ENFORCEMENT ADMINISTRATION
DEMAND REDUCTION FIELD OFFICE
Special Agent Rodney Adams
Drug Enforcement Administration
4560 Viewridge Ave.
National City, CA 92123
(619) 616-4166 Fax: (619) 616-4084

RESOURCES

Special Agent Joycelyn Barnes
Drug Enforcement Administration
450 Golden Gate Avenue Room 12215
San Francisco, CA 94102
(415) 436-7851 Fax: (415) 436-7810

COLORADO

COLORADO NATIONAL GUARD
JOINT SUPPORT OPERATIONS COUNTERDRUG OFFICE
Through numerous community-based, leadership, educational
and informational programs, the National Guard Counterdrug
Program supports individuals and organizations dedicated to
drug intervention and prevention, anti-legalization efforts, and
the positive development of youth. The National Guard also
supports the National Red Ribbon Celebration--a week-long
celebration of drug-free lifestyles held annually in late
October. Booths, displays, and demonstrations often are used
along with the distribution of ribbons and literature to spread
the drug awareness theme among communities.
Drug Demand Reduction Administrator
6868 South Revere Parkway
Englewood, CO 80112-6703
(303) 397-3091/3204 Fax: (303) 397-3029

CSAP RADAR NETWORK STATE CENTER
Linda Garrett
Colorado Alcohol & Drug Abuse Division
Resource Department
4300 Cherry Creek Drive
South Denver, CO 80222-1530
(303) 692-2930 (303) 692-2956 Fax: (303) 782-4883

STATE OF COLORADO
An information packet, initially developed for public sector
employers, is available to Colorado businesses from the State
Personnel Department. The packet has been enhanced to

include sample workplace substance abuse policies and a list of local EAP providers and drug testing facilities. The Department offers technical assistance on policy development and implementation on a limited basis. If extended assistance is required, the department can help refer the business to appropriate private sector service providers.
Ann Kelly
State of Colorado Department of Personnel
1313 Sherman, Room 115
Denver, CO 80203
(303) 866-4316

U.S. DRUG ENFORCEMENT ADMINISTRATION
DEMAND REDUCTION FIELD OFFICE
Special Agents Ron Hollingshead and/or Dennis Follett
Drug Enforcement Administration
115 Inverness Drive
East Englewood, CO 80112-5116
(303) 705-7317 Fax: (303) 705-7414

CONNECTICUT

CONNECTICUT NATIONAL GUARD
COUNTERDRUG PROGRAM
Drug Demand Reduction Administrator
National Guard Armory
360 Broad Street
Hartford, CT 06105-3795
(860) 493-2724 Fax: (860) 493-2784
E-mail: captain_master@msn.com

CSAP RADAR NETWORK STATE CENTER
Amy Powell
Connecticut Clearinghouse
334 Farmington Avenue
Plainville, CT 06062
(860) 793-9791 Fax: (860) 793-9813

DRUGS DON'T WORK!

Connecticut's DRUGS DON'T WORK! is a public/private partnership jointly funded by the State of Connecticut and private industry. Working through local Chambers of Commerce, industry groups and associations, DRUGS DON'T WORK! provides consultation and technical assistance to small-to-medium sized businesses. The initiative boasts nearly two thousand member companies. Members receive a comprehensive resource package covering drug-free workplace policies, federal and state regulations, training, treatment, and drug testing facilities. Business seminars are staffed by experts in the fields of labor law, policy writing, employee assistance programming, and prevention and treatment. A 1-800 Business Advisory Line is available to businesses during daytime working hours for answering questions concerning drug-free workplace issues.

Orlene Weyland

DRUGS DON'T WORK!

The Governor's Partnership

30 Arbor Street Hartford, CT 06106

(860) 232-0381

U.S. DRUG ENFORCEMENT ADMINISTRATION

DEMAND REDUCTION FIELD OFFICE

Special Agent Tina Murphy

Drug Enforcement Administration

1441 Main Street - 10th Floor

Springfield, MA 01103

(413) 785-0284 ext. 206 Fax: (413) 785-0483

DELAWARE

CSAP RADAR NETWORK STATE CENTER

Laurie Tutor

Division of Children, Youth, and Their Families

Office of Prevention Resource Clearinghouse

1825 Faulkand Road
Wilmington, DE 19805-1195
(302) 892-4513 Fax: (302) 892-4512

DELAWARE NATIONAL GUARD
COUNTERDRUG PROGRAM
Drug Demand Reduction Administrator
First Regiment Road
Wilmington, DE 19808-2191
(302) 326-7079 Fax: (302) 326-7074

STATE OF DELAWARE
The Delaware Division of Alcoholism, Drug Abuse & Mental
Health is the single state agency for drug, alcohol and mental
health issues. The Division operates a continuous training
program for treatment personnel serving Delaware comm-
unities and businesses, and workplace issues are addressed.
Together with the Addictions Coalition of Delaware, the
Division provides consultation to small business, and offers
referral if more extensive consultation is needed. The state
has a network of providers.
Paul Poplawski
Division of Alcoholism
Drug Abuse & Mental Health Training Office
1901 North Dupont Highway - Springer Building
New Castle, DE 19720
(302) 577-4980

U.S. DRUG ENFORCEMENT ADMINISTRATION
DEMAND REDUCTION FIELD OFFICE
Special Agent Donna Wilson
Drug Enforcement Administration
600 Arch Street, Suite 10224
Philadelphia, PA 19106
(215) 597-7866 Fax: (215) 597-6063

DISTRICT OF COLUMBIA

CSAP RADAR NETWORK STATE CENTER
Regina Knox Woods
Office of Health Planning and Development
800 9th St. SW Third Floor
Washington, D.C. 20024
(202) 645-5525 Fax: (202) 645-4112

DISTRICT OF COLUMBIA NATIONAL GUARD
COUNTERDRUG PROGRAM
Drug Demand Reduction Administrator
2001 East Capitol Street, SE
Washington, DC 20003-1719
(202) 433-5221 Fax: (202) 433-3040

D.C. EMPLOYEE CONSULTATION AND COUNSELING
SERVICES
The District of Columbia offers all private employers
operating within the District of Columbia access to the D.C.
Employee Consultation and Counseling Service. The fundamental goal of the Service is to help employed persons deal
with job-related problems caused by alcohol abuse. The
Service's program has three components. Outreach efforts
promote the implementation of occupational health services
focusing on the "troubled employee" through educational
literature, workshops, seminars, orientation sessions, and
training programs. Counseling services are available for
persons with problems which affect their job performance.
Finally, comprehensive, family-oriented treatment services are
offered to those employees whose diagnoses indicate that
their job performances are affected by their abuse of alcohol.
The Service welcomes formal referrals from employers and
also accepts clients on an informal, walk-in basis. There are
no fees for services at this time.
Silas L. Parrish
Employee Counseling and Consultation Service
Department of Human Services

Government of the District of Columbia
33 N. St. NE 2nd Floor
Washington, DC 20002
(202) 494-2851

U.S. DRUG ENFORCEMENT ADMINISTRATION
DEMAND REDUCTION FIELD OFFICE
Special Agent Mark Warpness
Drug Enforcement Administration
801 I Street N.W. Room 514
Washington, D.C. 20024
(202) 305-8639 Fax: (202) 307-5823

FLORIDA

BAND (BUSINESS AGAINST NARCOTICS AND DRUGS)
Developed by the Greater Miami Chamber of Commerce,
BAND has developed two booklets; the "Step-by-Step Guide
to Develop Your Drug-Free Workplace Program" which is
supplemented by "Drug-Free Workplace Program and
Supporting Policies." The booklets are part of a kit which
includes lists of numerous resources for recommended drug
testing laboratories, substance abuse information publishers,
crime and prevention groups, the chamber's partners, and a
list of available education materials. BAND serves as a
support service for Metropolitan Dade county companies in
developing workplace substance abuse programs. The
organization also offers seminars, a resource library and a
variety of material to assist companies.
Mary Ann Blom
BAND (Business Against Narcotics and Drugs)
Greater Miami Chamber of Commerce Omni International
Complex
1601 Biscayne Blvd.
Miami, FL 33132
(305) 350-7700 (305) 374-6902

RESOURCES

CSAP RADAR NETWORK STATE CENTER
Margaret Clark
Florida Alcohol and Drug Abuse Association
1030 E. Lafayette Suite 100
Tallahassee, FL 32301-4559
(904) 878-6922 (904) 878-2196 Fax: (904) 878-6584

DRUGS DON'T WORK - A PARTNERSHIP FOR A DRUG-FREE
WORKFORCE
As a member of the Partnership for a Drug-Free Workforce,
members receive an employer's handbook, a briefing on how
to set up workplace substance abuse programs, educational
sessions and package, workplace substance abuse workshops,
use of the Chamber's materials library, and group rates for
drug-testing and EAPs. The Partnership was formed by the
Pensacola Chamber of Commerce to help local businesses
establish and maintain workplace substance abuse programs.
Carol J. Law, Ph.D.
DRUGS DON'T WORK
Partnership for a Drug-Free Workforce
Pensacola Area Chamber of Commerce
P.O. Box 550
Pensacola, FL 32593
(904) 438-4081

FLORIDA ALCOHOL AND DRUG ABUSE ASSOCIATION
The Florida Alcohol and Drug Abuse Association offers a
folder containing handouts about workplace substance abuse,
including types of drugs, case studies, signs and symptoms,
glossary of terms, employee rights, work performance
problems, and an alcoholism progression and recovery chart.
The folder also features a list of substance-abuse-related
programs for children and families. The Association is
sponsored by the Florida Department of Children and
Families and the Department of Community Affairs.
Jennifer Monroe
Resource Center Coordinator
1030 East Lafayette St., Suite 100

236

Tallahassee, FL 32301-4559
(850) 878-2196
www.fadaa.org

FLORIDA CHAMBER OF COMMERCE
At the state level, the Florida Chamber serves as a resource
clearinghouse, providing a wealth of workplace substance
abuse information. A report, describing the scope and
consequences of the substance abuse problem in the Florida
workplace and outlining techniques for establishing workplace substance abuse programs, is available through the
Chamber. Local chapters of Chambers of Commerce are active
throughout the state in assisting employers in developing
workplace substance abuse programs. These chambers often
sponsor workplace substance abuse initiatives that provide
information kits, workshops and discounted EAP membership
and drug-testing services to make drug-free workplace
programs feasible for even the smallest employer.
Jenny Tompkins
Florida Chamber of Commerce
136 S. Bronough St. P.O. Box 11309
Tallahassee, FL 32302-3309
(904) 425-1200

FLORIDA DRUG TESTING CONTACTS
Florida was the first state to enact a frequently-lauded statute
dealing with drug testing. It allows any public or private
sector employer that establishes a program to receive
workers' compensation insurance premium discounts and to
deny benefits after an accident if the employee tests positive
for drug use. Participants are required to utilize a state-
licensed laboratory for all drug testing under the program.
Regarding the Florida workers' compensation rules for testing:
Contact: Florida Department of Labor (Willie Ellis)
Division of Workers' Compensation
Forrest Building, Suite 103
2728 Center View Drive
Tallahassee, FL 32399

237

RESOURCES

(904) 488-7700 or (800) 342-5860
For information regarding state laboratory licensing and testing procedures:
Contact: The Agency for Health Care Administration (Patricia James)
Laboratory Licensure Section
2727 Mahan Drive
Tallahassee, FL 32308
(904) 487-3063
For general information on Florida's care providers for substance abuse:
Contact: Kenneth DeCerchio
Department of Children and Families
1317 Winewood Blvd.
Tallahassee, FL 32399-0700
(904) 487-2920

FLORIDA NATIONAL GUARD
COUNTERDRUG PROGRAM
Drug Demand Reduction Administrator
2305 State Road #207
St. Augustine, FL 32086
(904) 823-0167 Fax: (904) 823-0173

MANATEE CHAMBER OF COMMERCE
Joni Korzen
(941) 748-4842

PENSACOLA PARTNERSHIP FOR A DRUG-FREE
WORKFORCE
Carol Law
(850) 434-3782
E-mail: dfwclaw@aol.com

TAMPA CHAMBER OF COMMERCE
Ron Kramer
(813) 228-7777

U.S. DRUG ENFORCEMENT ADMINISTRATION
DEMAND REDUCTION FIELD OFFICE
Special Agent Omar Aleman
Drug Enforcement Administration
8400 N.W. 53rd Street
Miami, FL 33166
(305) 590-4604 Fax: (305) 590-4437

GEORGIA

ATLANTA CHAMBER OF COMMERCE
Jacqui Derrick
(404) 586-8522

CSAP RADAR NETWORK STATE CENTER
John Watson
Division of Mental Health, Mental Retardation & Substance
Abuse
2 Peachtree St., 4th Floor, Suite 550
Atlanta, GA 30303
(404) 657-2296 Fax: (404) 657-6426

DRUGS DON'T WORK
The Georgia Chamber of Commerce has instituted DRUGS
DON'T WORK, a program launched by the President's Drug
Advisory Board and designed specifically to assist small and
medium sized businesses in creating their own workplace
substance abuse programs. DRUGS DON'T WORK is implemented through local chambers, which provide policies and
technical assistance to members and negotiate discount
pricing on drug testing and EAP services based on consortium
model volume. The chambers also organize workshops and
sponsor a speakers bureau of professionals for employee
education and supervisor training, and form grassroots
support for the legislative agenda set by DRUGS DON'T
WORK at the Georgia Chamber. The Georgia Chamber and
local chambers worked with the State Legislature to pass a 5%

premium credit for Workers' Compensation based on a certified workplace substance abuse program. The certifying agency is the State Board of Workers' Compensation. In a private/public partnership, the Georgia State Board of Workers' Compensation and the DRUGS DON'T WORK program worked with small to medium sized employers, labor attorneys, and other professionals to ensure that the certification requirements are straightforward and easy to implement. The Georgia program is structured to promote the flow of resources from the national DRUGS DON'T WORK program to the state level, and then to the local level. At the local level, the program relies on public grants and corporate contributions in the initial stages, while statewide corporate sponsorship and the fee structures of individual chambers are expected to make the programs self-sustaining in the future. Efforts to institute workplaces free of substance abuse throughout Georgia are spearheaded by the Georgia Chamber and funded by Drug-Free Schools and Communities Grant money distributed through the State Department of Human Resources, Program Resource Center.

Chuck Wade
DRUGS DON'T WORK in Georgia
Georgia Chamber of Commerce
233 Peachtree Street, Suite 200
Atlanta, GA 30303
(404) 223-2262

Jackie Ogden
Savannah Area Chamber of Commerce
P.O. Box 1628
Savannah, GA 31402
(912) 944-0444

John Watson
Department of Human Resources Prevention Resource Center
2 Peachtree Street, N.W. Suite 160
Atlanta, GA 30303-3171
(404) 657-2295 Fax: (404) 657-2160

GEORGIA CHAMBER OF COMMERCE
Chuck Wade
(404) 223-2277

GEORGIA NATIONAL GUARD
COUNTERDRUG PROGRAM
Drug Demand Reduction Administrator
1651 Perry Street, Bldg 826
Dobbins AFB, GA 30069-4812
(770) 919-3477 Fax: (770) 919-3482
E-mail: wradcliffe@gawrband.af.mil

U.S. DRUG ENFORCEMENT ADMINISTRATION
DEMAND REDUCTION FIELD OFFICE
Special Agent Steve Starling
Task Force Officer
75 Spring Street, S.W. Room 740
Atlanta, GA 30303
(404) 730-9515 (404) 730-3198 Fax: (404) 331-0166

Leslie Pair
Task Force Officer
75 Spring Street, S.W. Room 740
Atlanta, GA 30303
(404) 730-9515 (404) 730-3198 Fax: (404) 331-0166

Harry Thornton
Drug Enforcement Administration
75 Spring Street, S.W. Room 740
Atlanta, GA 30303
(404) 730-9515 (404) 730-3198 Fax: (404) 331-0166

GUAM

CSAP RADAR NETWORK STATE CENTER
Richard Colamba

RESOURCES

Department of Mental Health and Substance Abuse
P.O. Box 9400
Tamuning, GU 96931
(671) 647-5438 Fax: (671) 649-6948

GUAM NATIONAL GUARD
COUNTERDRUG PROGRAM
Drug Demand Reduction Administrator
622 East Harmon Industrial Park Road
Fort Juan Muna,
Tamuning, Guam 96911-4421
(671) 647-2752 Fax: (671) 647-6037

TERRITORY OF GUAM
In the Territory of Guam, the Department of Mental Health
and Substance Abuse offers comprehensive inpatient and
outpatient treatment and education programs to combat
alcohol and other drug abuse.
Dr. Nory Santz
Department of Mental Health and Substance Abuse
P.O. Box 9400
Tamuning, GU 96931
(671) 647-5438

HAWAII

COALITION FOR A DRUG-FREE HAWAII
Programs addressing workplace substance abuse problems in
Hawaii's private sector are spearheaded by the Coalition for a
Drug-Free Hawaii. The Coalition provides technical assistance
and resource information for Hawaii businesses interested in
addressing workplace substance abuse. The group recently
published the first edition of "Creating a Drug-Free Workplace: Business & Industry Resource Guide." The guide
includes sections on training and education resources,
employee assistance programs, drug testing, and on national
workplace substance abuse programs. The Hawaii Depart-

242

ment of Health and Human Services provides funding
assistance to the Coalition's efforts.
Coalition for a Drug-Free Hawaii
1130 Nimitz Highway (A259)
Honolulu, HI 96817
(808) 545-3228 Fax: (808) 545-2686

CSAP RADAR NETWORK STATE CENTER
Lisa Minato
Drug-Free Hawaii Prevention Resource Center
1130 Nimitz Highway (A259)
Honolulu, HI 96817
(808) 545-3228 Fax: (808) 545-2686

HAWAII NATIONAL GUARD
COUNTERDRUG PROGRAM
3949 Diamond Head Road
Honolulu, HI 96816
(808) 733-4229 Fax: (808) 733-4227
E-mail: tnakamoto@hihik.ang.af.mil or
abergeson@hihik.ang.af.mil

U.S. DRUG ENFORCEMENT ADMINISTRATION
DEMAND REDUCTION FIELD OFFICE
Special Agent Roland Talton
Drug Demand Reduction Administrator
255 East Temple Street 20th Floor
Los Angeles, CA 90012
(213) 894-5632

IDAHO

CSAP RADAR NETWORK STATE CENTER
Phylis Sawyer
Boise State University
Idaho Radar Network Center
1910 University Drive

Boise, ID 83725
(208) 385-3471 Fax: (208) 385-3334

IDAHO NATIONAL GUARD
COUNTERDRUG PROGRAM
Drug Demand Reduction Administrator
4736 Kennedy Street, Gowen Field
Boise, ID 83705-8135
(208) 422-6080 Fax: (208) 422-6299

U.S. DRUG ENFORCEMENT ADMINISTRATION
DEMAND REDUCTION FIELD OFFICE
Special Agent Juliana Parra-West
Drug Enforcement Administration
220 West Mercer, Suite 300
Seattle, WA 98119
(206) 553-5443 Fax: (206) 533-1069

ILLINOIS

CHICAGOLAND CHAMBER OF COMMERCE
Laura Durkalski
(312) 983-7113

CSAP RADAR NETWORK STATE CENTER
Prevention Resource Center Library
2800 Montvale Drive
Springfield, IL 62704
(217) 525-7353

ILLINOIS CHAMBER OF COMMERCE
John Mulcare
(312) 983-7113

ILLINOIS NATIONAL GUARD
COUNTERDRUG PROGRAM
Drug Demand Reduction Administrator

1301 North MacArthur Blvd.
Springfield, IL 62702-2399
(217) 761-3763 Fax: (217) 761-2636

STATE OF ILLINOIS
The Illinois Department of Alcoholism and Substance Abuse
has developed a document to address issues regarding
workplace substance abuse policies, drug testing policies and
procedures, legal considerations, and employee assistance
referrals. This document is available free to Illinois businesses.
Ron Vlasaty
Illinois Department of Alcoholism & Substance Abuse
James R. Thompson Center
100 West Randolph, Suite 5-600
Chicago, IL 60601
(312) 814-3840

The Department of Alcoholism and Substance Abuse has also
compiled informational material for use in training entitled
"Drug Testing - Elements" and "Drug Use in the Workforce -
Legal Requirements and Legal Protections."
Nancy Bennett
Illinois Department of Alcoholism and Substance Abuse
James R. Thompson Center
100 West Randolph, Suite 5-600
Chicago, IL 60601
(312) 814-3840

The Illinois Criminal Justice Information Authority has
prepared a booklet giving an overview of the Illinois Drug-
Free Workplace Act. Copies are available free of charge from
the Authority by calling (312) 793-8550. A manual, "Creating a
Drug-Free Workplace," posters, and other printed materials
are available from the Office of the Illinois Attorney General.
Pat Kosar
Office of the Illinois Attorney General
Public Affairs Bureau
100 West Randolph, Suite 12-000

245

RESOURCES

Chicago, IL 60601
(312) 814-2699

The state also funds the Prevention Resource Center which maintains a library of written and video materials available to the public regarding workplace substance abuse issues.
Prevention Resource Center Library
2800 Montvale Drive
Springfield, IL 62704
(217) 793-7353

U.S. DRUG ENFORCEMENT ADMINISTRATION
DEMAND REDUCTION FIELD OFFICE
Special Agent Michael Zawadzki
Drug Enforcement Administration
230 South Dearborn St., 12th Floor
Chicago, IL 60604
(312) 353-1427 Fax: (312) 353-1476

Special Agent Shirley A. Armstead
Drug Enforcement Administration
7911 Forsyth Blvd, Suite 500
St. Louis, MO 63105
(314) 538-4752 Fax: (314) 538-4758

INDIANA

BALDWIN AND LYONS, INC.
Robert Osha
(317) 983-7113

CSAP RADAR NETWORK STATE CENTER
Barbara Seitz
Indiana University
Indiana Prevention Resource Center
Creative Arts Building, Room 110
840 State Road, 46 Bypass

Bloomington, IN 47405
(812) 855-1237 (812) 855-4940

INDIANA NATIONAL GUARD
COUNTERDRUG OPERATIONS
Drug Demand Reduction Administrator
2002 S. Holt Road
Indianapolis, IN 46241
(317) 247-3179 Fax: (317) 487-1901

STATE OF INDIANA
Indiana businesses that maintain or begin employee
assistance programs are eligible for a one-time state tax credit.
Norma Bradway
Division of Mental Health
State of Indiana Family and Social Services Administration
402 West Washington Street, W353
Indianapolis, IN 46204
(317) 232-7866

The state also distributes a manual targeting small businesses,
entitled Putting Drugs Out of Work - Suggestions for Creating
a Drug-Free Workplace Program. The manual contains sample
policies and helpful information on employee education,
supervisor training, employee assistance programs, drug
testing, state and federal regulations, and a resource directory.
This manual is available free to Indiana businesses.
Lilian Henegar
Governor's Commission for a Drug-Free Indiana
150 West Market Street, Suite 320
Indianapolis, IN 46204
(317) 232-4219

U.S. DRUG ENFORCEMENT ADMINISTRATION
DEMAND REDUCTION FIELD OFFICE
Special Agent Michael Zawadzki
Drug Enforcement Administration
230 South Dearborn St, 12th Floor

Chicago, IL 60604
(312) 353-1427 Fax: (312) 353-1476

IOWA

CSAP RADAR NETWORK STATE CENTER
Tressa Youngbear
Iowa Substance Abuse Information Center
Cedar Rapids Public Library
500 1st Street, S.E.
Cedar Rapids, IA 52401
(319) 398-5133 Fax: (319) 398-0408

GOVERNOR'S ALLIANCE ON SUBSTANCE ABUSE
The Governor's Alliance on Substance Abuse is planning to
launch a statewide workplace initiative in 1995, presumably in
conjunction with the National Drugs Don't Work Partnership
in New York City. This workplace program would be
implemented as a joint venture with the Iowa Association of
Business and Industry, and the Partnership for a Drug-Free
Iowa. While the program is not developed in its entirety, it is
likely to envision four major areas of concern: (1) writing,
adopting and promulgating an alcohol and drug-free
workplace policy; (2) providing skill-based training for middle
managers; (3) providing general information on a continuous
basis to all employees; and (4) establishing employee
assistance programs.
David Woolery and Charles Larson
Governor's Alliance on Substance Abuse
Lucas State Office Building
Des Moines, IA 50319
(515) 281-3788

IOWA NATIONAL GUARD
COUNTERDRUG PROGRAM
Drug Demand Reduction Administrator
7700 NW Beaver Drive

Johnston, IA 50131
(515) 252-4643 Fax: (515) 252-4738

U.S DRUG ENFORCEMENT ADMINISTRATION
DEMAND REDUCTION FIELD OFFICE
Special Agent Shirley A. Armstead
Drug Enforcement Administration
7911 Forsyth Blvd, Suite 500
St. Louis, MO 63105
(314) 538-4752 Fax: (314) 538-4758

KANSAS

CSAP RADAR NETWORK STATE CENTER
Judy Donovan
Kansas Alcohol and Drug Abuse Services
Department of Social and Rehabilitation Services
Biddle Building, Second Floor
Topeka, KS 66606
(913) 296-3925 Fax: (913) 296-0511

KANSAS NATIONAL GUARD
COUNTERDRUG PROGRAM
Drug Demand Reduction Administrator
2722 SW Topeka Blvd
Topeka, KS 66611-1298
(913) 274-1380 Fax: (913) 274-4382
E-mail: jwilliam@kssthq.ang.af.mil

REGIONAL PREVENTION CENTER
This center serves Johnson, Leavenworth and Miami counties
and is funded through the Kansas Social Rehabilitation
Service, Division of Alcohol and Drug Abuse Services. The
Center organizes and participates in the Kansas City
metropolitan area's Drug-Free Workplace Committee. The
Committee, composed of representatives from the FBI Drug
Demand Reduction Program, the Lenexa Police Department, a

local Chamber of Commerce, business owners, and the Wyandotte County Regional Prevention Center, provides small to medium sized businesses with information on substance abuse and resources to increase awareness of workplace substance abuse issues. It is the Committee's goal to provide: (1) alcohol and other drug awareness and education to businesses in the form of information, resources, and referral services for testing and treatment; (2) technical assistance in developing business-site policies; and (3) workplace substance abuse workshops targeting the small to medium sized business owner in the Kansas City metropolitan area. At least twice a year, the Committee offers workshops at a nominal cost and publishes a newsletter which is distributed by two Regional Prevention Centers, the Chambers of Commerce in the metropolitan area, and the National Council on Alcoholism and Drug Dependence.
Nancy Keller
Regional Prevention Center
6000 Lamar, Suite 130
Mission, KS 66202
(913) 362-1990

U.S. DRUG ENFORCEMENT ADMINISTRATION
DEMAND REDUCTION FIELD OFFICE
Special Agent Shirley A. Armstead
Drug Enforcement Administration
7911 Forsyth Blvd. Suite 500
St. Louis, MO 63105
(314) 538-4752 Fax: (314) 538-4758

KENTUCKY

CSAP RADAR NETWORK STATE CENTER
Dianne D. Shuntich
Drug Information Services for Kentucky
Division of Substance Abuse
275 E. Main Street

Frankfurt, KY 40621
(502) 564-2880

DRUG INFORMATION SERVICES FOR KENTUCKY (DISK)
Drug Information Services for Kentucky (DISK) serves as a
clearinghouse for substance abuse information in the
Commonwealth of Kentucky. DISK provides businesses with
regional information including a directory and current listing
of alcohol and drug abuse consultants, EAP providers, and
drug screening laboratories in the state. DISK also distributes
a selection of federal publications regarding workplace
substance abuse programs as well as specific information
packets on EAPs and workplaces free of substance abuse.
Sharon Bell
Drug Information Services for Kentucky (DISK)
Division of Substance Abuse
275 East Main Street
Frankfort, KY 40621
(502) 564-2880

KENTUCKY NATIONAL GUARD
COUNTERDRUG PROGRAM
Drug Demand Reduction Administrator
100 Minuteman Parkway
Boone National Guard Center
Frankfort, KY 40601-6168
(502) 564-6278 Fax: (502) 564-6230

U.S. DRUG ENFORCEMENT ADMINISTRATION
DEMAND REDUCTION FIELD OFFICE
Special Agent Mary Neville
Drug Enforcement Administration
431 Howard St.
Detroit, MI 48226
(313) 234-4310 Fax: (313) 234-4057

RESOURCES

LOUISIANA

COMMUNITY PARTNERSHIP COALITION
Robert Gaston
(504) 389-7871

CSAP RADAR NETWORK STATE CENTER
Sanford W. Hawkins Sr.
Division of Alcohol and Drug Abuse
P.O. Box 3868 1201, Capitol Access Road
Baton Rouge, LA 70821-3868
(504) 342-9352 Fax: (504) 342-1384

LOUISIANA NATIONAL GUARD
COUNTERDRUG PROGRAM
Drug Demand Reduction Administrator
Jackson Barracks Bldg 35, Room 251
New Orleans, LA 70146-0330
(504) 278-8555 Fax: (504) 278-8552
E-mail: wellsj@la-arng.ngb.army.mil

OFFICE OF ALCOHOL AND DRUG ABUSE
The Office of Alcohol and Drug Abuse (OADA) in the State of
Louisiana Department of Health and Hospitals conducted a
Drug-Free Workplace Survey and a Drug-Free Workplace
Conference in 1990. As a result, OADA developed a Resource
Book, designed specifically for small business. The Resource
Book is a comprehensive guide for employers to help them
recognize the problems of substance abuse in the workforce.
The Book includes a checklist of questions to consider when
developing a written policy; an analysis of the pros and cons
of drug testing; and a thorough explanation of the costs,
services and benefits of an EAP. The Book also lists and
discusses federal and state laws and regulations regarding
employer-based substance abuse prevention and intervention.
The Resource Book is available to Louisiana businesses upon
request.
Alton E. Hadley

Office of Alcohol and Drug Abuse
P.O. Box 2790, Bin 18
Baton Rouge, LA 70802
(504) 342-6717

U.S. DRUG ENFORCEMENT ADMINISTRATION
DEMAND REDUCTION FIELD OFFICE
Special Agent Michael Streicher
Drug Enforcement Administration
3838 North Causeway Blvd. Suite 1800
Metairie, LA 70002
(504) 840-1032 Fax: (504) 840-1052

MAINE

CSAP RADAR NETWORK STATE CENTER
Earle Simpson, Jr.
Office of Substance Abuse Clearinghouse
State House Station #159
24 Stone Street Augusta, ME 04333
(207) 287-2962

MAINE NATIONAL GUARD
COUNTERDRUG PROGRAM
Drug Demand Reduction Administrator
Camp Keyes
Augusta, ME 04333-0033
(207) 626-4334 Fax: (207) 626-4531
E-mail: cox@me-ngnet.army.mil

STATE OF MAINE
At least three units of the government of the State of Maine
work in collaboration to address the problem of workplace
substance abuse. Maine legislation requires that any employer
who wants to have employee drug testing must develop an
employee assistance program (EAP). The proposed EAP is
reviewed and approved by the Maine Department of Human

Services using standards established by that Department in collaboration with the Maine Department of Labor and the Office of Substance Abuse in the State Executive Department.

Maine Department of Labor

The Maine Department of Labor has developed regulations and sends out applications which include guidelines for the development of acceptable policies and procedures for employee drug testing. The Department also offers technical assistance to employers wishing to develop written policies and institute drug testing.

Maine Department of Human Services

The Maine Department of Human Services has a Public Health Unit which establishes guidelines and offers technical assistance regarding actual drug testing procedures, regulations on chain of custody and laboratory analysis, and a listing of approved drug testing laboratories.

Office of Substance Abuse

The Office of Substance Abuse (OSA) maintains a clearinghouse of information and literature regarding the merits and philosophy of EAPs, and a staff member participates in the regular quarterly meetings of the Maine State Employee Assistance Program Association. As part of the New England Institute, and in cooperation with other New England state agencies, OSA plans a conference for EAP professionals which is cosponsored by the New England regional EAP associations.

Alan Hinsey
Maine Department of Labor
Bureau of Labor Standards
45 State House Station
Augusta, ME 04333-0045
(207) 624-6400

Lynn Duby
Director, Maine Executive Department
Office of Substance Abuse
AMHI Complex Marquardt Bldg., Third Floor State House Station #159

Augusta, ME 04333-0159
(207) 287-2595

Michael C. Sodano
Certification Officer Maine Department of Human Services
Public Health Laboratory
221 State St. Station #12
Augusta, ME 04333
(207) 287-2727

U.S. DRUG ENFORCEMENT ADMINISTRATION
DEMAND REDUCTION FIELD OFFICE
Special Agent Tina Murphy
Drug Enforcement Administration
1441 Main Street, 10th Floor
Springfield, MA 01103
(413) 785-0284 ext. 206 Fax: (413) 785-0483

MARYLAND

CENTER FOR WORKPLACE HEALTH AND SAFETY
Judith Greene-Slaughter
(410) 239-8033

CSAP RADAR NETWORK STATE CENTER
Fran Jones
Alcohol and Drug Abuse Administration
Department of Health and Mental Hygiene, 4th Floor
201 W. Preston Street
Baltimore, MD 21201
(410) 767-6916 Fax: (410) 333-7206

MARYLAND DRUG-FREE WORKPLACE INITIATIVE
Maryland's Drug-Free Workplace Initiative provides consultation and technical assistance to the small and medium-sized
business community through free seminars on policy and
program development. The Initiative maintains a network of

255

over 60 volunteers (labor and management attorneys, employee assistance professionals, prevention and treatment experts) who provide assistance to companies on a pro-bono basis. As part of its public education component, the Initiative develops training and educational programs in conjunction with local Chambers of Commerce and community colleges throughout Maryland. It operates an Infoline which business can access during daytime working hours for immediate answers to questions regarding workplaces free of substance abuse. Together with Baltimore City Community College, the Initiative operates the Maryland Center for Drug-Free Workplace Services. The Center provides a series of non-credit courses on various issues surrounding workplace substance abuse program development, as well as business roundtables for the business community. An information package for Maryland employers is available from the Initiative free of charge.
Judy Green
Maryland's Drug-Free Workplace Initiative
300 E. Joppa Road, Suite 1105
Towson, MD 21286
(301) 321-3484

MARYLAND NATIONAL GUARD
COUNTERDRUG PROGRAM
Drug Demand Reduction Administrator
Fifth Regiment Armory
Baltimore, MD 21201-2288
(410) 576-6137 Fax: (410) 576-6122

U.S. DRUG ENFORCEMENT ADMINISTRATION
DEMAND REDUCTION FIELD OFFICE
Special Agent Mark Warpness
Drug Enforcement Administration
801 I Street N.W. Room 514
Washington, DC 20024
(202) 305-8639 Fax: (202) 307-5823

MASSACHUSETTS

CSAP RADAR NETWORK STATE CENTER
Tom McKenna
The Psychological Center's Prevention Network
1 South Union St.
Lawrence, MA 01843
(508) 688-2323 Fax: (508) 681-1281

FRAMINGHAM COALITION FOR THE PREVENTION OF
ALCOHOL AND DRUG ABUSE
The Framingham Coalition for the Prevention of Alcohol and
Drug Abuse is set in involving small businesses in AOD
prevention in the workplace. The Coalition's specific aims are:
to reach small businesses through a community-wide public
information and education campaign; to help small businesses
develop a substance abuse prevention program and train any
businesses' workforce; and to help in the distribution of
information and prevention materials to employees.
Framingham Coalition for the Prevention of Alcohol and Drug
Abuse
68 Henry Street
Framingham, MA 01701
(508) 879-6874

MASSACHUSETTS NATIONAL GUARD
COUNTERDRUG SUPPORT OFFICE
Drug Demand Reduction Administrator
25 Haverhill Street
Reading, MA 01867-1999
(617) 944-0500 ext. 2404 Fax: (617) 944-0500 ext. 2449

STATE OF MASSACHUSETTS
The Bureau of Substance Abuse Services, Massachusetts
Department of Public Health, sponsors approximately 100
events annually ranging from half-day seminars to multi-day
conferences on substance abuse and related issues. The
majority of these events are open to businesses, although that

is not often the primary focus of the events. Conferences are organized through AdCare Educational Institute, Inc., a non-profit organization, with funding from the Massachusetts Department of Health.
James J. Gorske
AdCare Educational Institute, Inc.
5 Northampton Street
Worcester, MA 01605
(508) 752-7313

THE BOSTON COALITION
Randi Donnis
(617) 451-1441

U.S DRUG ENFORCEMENT ADMINISTRATION
DEMAND REDUCTION FIELD OFFICE
Special Agent Tina Murphy
Drug Enforcement Administration
1441 Main Street, 10th Floor
Springfield, MA 01103
(413) 785-0284 ext. 206 Fax: (413) 785-0483

MICHIGAN

CSAP RADAR NETWORK STATE CENTER
Gail Johnson
Michigan Resource Center
111 West Edgewood Blvd., Suite 11
Lansing, MI 48911
(517) 882-9955

DRUGS DON'T WORK
A program of the Michigan Chamber Foundation, Drugs Don't Work is designed to assist small and medium-sized businesses in setting up a comprehensive drug-free workplace, including: implementing a drug-free workplace policy, starting pre-employment or other employee drug testing, and working

with an employee assistance program (EAP) for employee education, referrals, and supervisory training. Evaluation studies are being conducted to measure the program's effectiveness. The DRUGS DON'T WORK program began as a local-level initiative in 1994 at the Kalamazoo County and Battle Creek Area chambers of commerce. The Michigan Chamber of Commerce elected to bring the program to the state level, introducing DRUGS DON'T WORK to local chambers throughout Michigan. Since 1996, eight chambers began their own programs and are setting the pace for other organizations to follow. As the state-wide program moves into its third year, DRUGS DON'T WORK will be working directly with businesses throughout Michigan to assist in developing drug-free workplaces in areas where local programs are not available. For a complete listing of local Michigan programs, see the contact list below.

Susan Combs, Executive Director, and Bob Thomas, Projects Coordinator
DRUGS DON'T WORK
600 S. Walnut St.
Lansing, MI 48933
(517) 371-2100 Fax: (517) 371-7275

Andy Browne
Association of Commerce & Industry
(616) 842-4910

Drugs Don't Work Coordinator
Greenville Chamber of Commerce
(616) 754-5697

Christine Greve
Midland Area Chamber of Commerce
(517) 839-9901

Bill Slawnik
Ypsilanti Chamber of Commerce
(313) 482-4920

RESOURCES

Ron Weber
Cornerstone Alliance
(616) 925-6100

Chris Byrnes
Holland Area Chamber of Commerce
(616) 392-2389

Marty Berghorst
Kalamazoo County Chamber of Commerce
(616) 381-4000

MICHIGAN NATIONAL GUARD
COUNTERDRUG PROGRAM
Drug Demand Reduction Administrator
2500 S. Washington Ave.
Lansing, MI 48913
(517) 483-5567 Fax: (517) 483-5822

MODEL DRUG-FREE WORKPLACE
The development of a model "Drug-Free Workplace" program
is a private-public initiative supported by Governor John
Engler and former Kellogg CEO William LaMothe, and
spearheaded by the Battle Creek Area Chamber of Commerce
and the Kalamazoo County Chamber. The purpose of the
initiative is to build a strong business community free of
substance abuse, with services available to even the smallest
companies. Those businesses will provide an example that
can be replicated in other Michigan communities. Cost-
effective consortiums will assist companies in establishing a
workplace substance abuse philosophy and program,
accessing EAP services, and obtaining drug testing services.
Darnell Jackson
Director, Michigan Office of Drug Control Policy
Michigan National Tower Bldg., Suite. 1200
124 W. Allegan Street
Lansing, MI 48913
(517) 373-4700

REGIONAL STATE CENTERS
The substance abuse prevention network in Michigan centers around 18 regional coordinating agencies -- each representing one or more counties. Three of these coordinating agencies provide training and technical assistance to private businesses interested in workplace substance abuse initiatives and are actively involved with EAP and other workplace programs.
Dave Olin
Macomb County Community Mental Health Services
10 North Main St., 6th floor
Mt. Clemens, MI 48043
(313) 469-5278

Randy O'Brien
Executive Director, Mid-South Substance Abuse Commission
2875 Northwind Dr., Suite 105
East Lansing, MI 48823

Kim Piepkow
Asst. Assoc. Director, Mid-South Substance Abuse Commission
120 West Michigan, Suite 900
Jackson, MI 49201
(517) 788-4400

Mark Halkola
Coordinator, Western Upper Peninsula Substance Abuse Services
323 Quincy
Hancock, MI 49930
(906) 482-7710

Many of the other 15 coordinating agencies are involved in other activities including providing technical assistance and training programs, planning employee assistance conferences, and promoting worksite wellness programs.

RESOURCES

U.S. DRUG ENFORCEMENT ADMINISTRATION
DEMAND REDUCTION FIELD OFFICE
Special Agent Mary Neville
Drug Enforcement Administration
431 Howard St.
Detroit, MI 48226
(313) 234-4310 Fax: (313) 234-4057

MINNESOTA

MINNESOTA NATIONAL GUARD DEPARTMENT OF
MILITARY AFFAIRS COUNTERDRUG PROGRAM
Drug Demand Reduction Administrator
20 West 12th Street
St. Paul, MN 55155-2098

U.S. DRUG ENFORCEMENT ADMINISTRATION
DEMAND REDUCTION FIELD OFFICE
Special Agent Michael Zawadzki
Drug Enforcement Administration
230 South Dearborn Street, 12th Floor
Chicago, IL 60604
(312) 353-1427 Fax: (312) 353-1476

MISSISSIPPI

CSAP RADAR NETWORK STATE CENTER
Stephanie Foster
Mississippi Department of Mental Health
Division of Alcoholism and Drug Abuse
1101 Robert E. Lee Building, 9th Floor
239 N. Lamar Street
Jackson, MS 39207
(601) 359-1288

MISSISSIPPI NATIONAL GUARD
COUNTERDRUG SUPPORT OFFICE
550 Keyway Drive
Jackson, MS 39208-8860
(601) 936-7670 Fax: (601) 936-7673
E-mail: ngmsdes1@ngms.state.msvs

STATE OF MISSISSIPPI
The Division Employee Assistance Programs, established by
the Department of Mental Health of the State of Mississippi,
provides consultation, technical assistance, and limited
training to help state agencies and small businesses develop
employee assistance programs. The Division also works with
employee assistance service providers in an attempt to assure
that resources, including substance abuse prevention and
treatment services, are available to the state agencies and
businesses.
Herbert Loving
Mississippi Department of Mental Health
Employee Assistance Programs
1101 Robert E. Lee Building
239 North Lamar Street
Jackson, MS 39201
(601) 359-1288

U.S. DRUG ENFORCEMENT ADMINISTRATION
DEMAND REDUCTION FIELD OFFICE
Special Agent Michael Streicher
3838 North Causeway Blvd, Suite 1800
Metairie, LA 70002
(504) 840-1032

MISSOURI

CSAP RADAR NETWORK STATE CENTER
Randy Smith
Missouri Division of Alcohol and Drug Abuse

RESOURCES

1706 E. Elm Street
Jefferson City, MO 65102
(573) 751-4942 Fax: (573) 751-7814

DRUGS DON'T WORK!
The Greater Kansas City Chamber of Commerce has launched
a DRUGS DON'T WORK! program. Its mission is to assist
small and medium-sized businesses in developing and
implementing workplace substance abuse policies and
procedures. It has put together service providers, resources
and support to ensure the smooth and successful implementation of a workplace free of substance abuse. The
program will offer five main components: a model substance
abuse workplace policy, supervisor training, employee
education, employee assistance program, and NIDA certified
drug testing. A subscriber may select any or all of the
components in creating their workplace substance abuse
programs. A group of attorneys, who offer pro bono
assistance, will help subscribers modify their policy and
medical review officers are also available for those who use
drug testing. Subscriber workshops are held to further assist
the businessperson in understanding both the problem and
the solution. Kansas City's DRUGS DON'T WORK! is available
to both Chamber and non-Chamber members and will initially
be piloted in Jackson County, Missouri. Eventually, the goal is
to offer the program to the ten-county metropolitan area,
which would include Kansas businesses as well.
Beverly Livingston
DRUGS DON'T WORK!
Greater Kansas City Chamber of Commerce
911 Main, Suite 2600, Commerce Tower Building
Kansas City, MO 64105
(816) 221-2424

KANSAS CITY CHAMBER OF COMMERCE
Beth Livingston
(816) 374-5469

MISSOURI NATIONAL GUARD
COUNTERDRUG PROGRAM
Drug Demand Reduction Administrator
2302 Militia Drive
Jefferson City, MO 65101-1203
(573) 526-9307 Fax: (573) 526-4546

STATE OF MISSOURI
The Division of Alcohol and Drug Abuse, in the Missouri
Department of Mental Health, provides workplace substance
abuse programs through a network of local agencies and area
offices. The Division sponsors seminars (in cooperation with
appropriate chambers of commerce) in major population
centers. These seminars target small-to-medium sized
businesses. In addition, the Division provides basic information, materials, and technical assistance to interested
employers. Contact persons for the State of Missouri are the
area administrators for the Division of Alcohol and Drug
Abuse.
Dr. Andrew Homer
Division of Alcohol and Drug Abuse
1306 Business 63 South, Suite C
Columbia, MO 65201
(573) 882-9920

Barbara Keehn
Division of Alcohol and Drug Abuse
5400 Arsenal, Building N
St. Louis, MO 63139
(314) 644-7975

Sheryl Cleaver
Division of Alcohol and Drug Abuse
600 East 22nd St.
Kansas City, MO 64108
(816) 889-6735

RESOURCES

Patricia Drennen
Division of Alochol and Drug Abuse
901 Pine St., Suite 101
P.O. Box 884
Rolla, MO 65402
(573) 368-2297

U.S. DRUG ENFORCEMENT ADMINISTRATION
DEMAND REDUCTION FIELD OFFICE
Special Agent Shirley A. Armstead
Drug Enforcement Administration
7911 Forsyth Blvd, Suite 500
St. Louis, MO 63105
(314) 538-4752 Fax: (314) 538-4758

Special Agent Michael Harrington
Midwest HIDTA
10220 Executive Hills Blvd, Suite 620
Kansas City, MO 64153
(816) 746-4911 ext. 228 Fax: (816) 746-9712

MONTANA

CSAP RADAR NETWORK STATE CENTER
Ken Mordan
Alcohol and Drug Abuse Division
Montana Department of Public Health and Human Services
P.O. Box 202951
1400 Broadway, Rm C118
Helena, MT 59620-2951
(406) 444-4928

MONTANA NATIONAL GUARD
COUNTERDRUG PROGRAM
Drug Demand Reduction Administrator
P.O. Box 4789
1100 N. Main

Helena, MT 59604-4789
(406) 444-6909 Fax: (406) 449-7689

STATE OF MONTANA
Montana is a very large and sparsely populated state, and the
majority of businesses are small and lack formal employee
assistance programs. Therefore, most businesses rely on the
community-based programs for providing education, early
intervention, and treatment when needed. All 56 counties in
Montana have some level of community-based, publicly-
funded chemical dependency services available. Several of
the programs in larger communities are available to provide
employee assistance to local business. Services generally
provided include screening, assessment and referral,
outpatient counseling and intensive outpatient services.
Ken Mordan
Alcohol and Drug Abuse Division
PO Box 202951
1400 Broadway, Rm C118
Helena, MT 59620-2951
(406) 444-4928

U.S. DRUG ENFORCEMENT ADMINISTRATION
DEMAND REDUCTION FIELD OFFICE
Special Agent Juliana Parra-West
220 West Mercer, Suite 300
Seattle, WA 98119
(206) 553-5443 Fax: (206) 553-1069

NEBRASKA

CSAP RADAR NETWORK STATE CENTER
Nancy Boelts
To Prevent Alcoholism and Drug Abuse Council of Nebraska
650 J Street, Suite 215
Lincoln, NE 68508
(402) 474-0930 (402) 474-0323

RESOURCES

NEBRASKA NATIONAL GUARD
PLANS, OPERATIONS AND MILITARY SUPPORT OFFICE
1300 Military Road
Lincoln, NE 68508-1090
(402) 458-1129 Fax: (402) 458-1128

STATE OF NEBRASKA
Businesses having contracts with the State of Nebraska are
required to have a workplace substance abuse program. Four
regional councils serve as information clearinghouses and
offer assistance on policy development and employee
awareness training. These councils are private, non-profit
organizations funded by federal and state dollars administered
by the Division of Alcohol and Drug Abuse in the Nebraska
Department of Public Institutions, which funds more than
seventy-five community treatment centers to assist troubled
individuals.
Robin Donahue
Lincoln Council on Alcoholism and Drugs, Inc.
914 "L" Street Lincoln, NE 68508
(402) 475-2694

Barbara Jolliffe
Panhandle Substance Abuse Council
1517 Broadway, Suite 124
Scottsbluff, NE 69361
(308) 632-3044

National Council on Alcoholism
5010 Dodge Street
Omaha, NE 68132
(402) 553-8000

Jeanette Sulzman
Central Nebraska Council on Alcoholism
219 West 2nd Street
Grand Island, NE 68801
(308) 384-7365

U.S. DRUG ENFORCEMENT ADMINISTRATION
DEMAND REDUCTION FIELD OFFICE
Special Agent Shirley A. Armstead
Drug Enforcement Administration
7911 Forsyth Blvd, Suite 500
St. Louis, MO 63105
(314) 538-4752 Fax: (314) 538-4758

NEVADA

CSAP RADAR NETWORK STATE CENTER
Trenna E. Smith
Montes Department of Employment Training and
Rehabilitation, Bureau of Alcohol and Drug Abuse
505 E. King Street, Rm. 500
Carson City, NV 89701
(775) 684-4095 Fax: (775) 684-4185
E-mail: tsmith@govmail.state.nv.us

NEVADA NATIONAL GUARD
COUNTERDRUG PROGRAM
Drug Demand Reduction Administrator
4600 Alpha Avenue, Bldg. 8212
Reno, NV 89506
(702) 677-5221 Fax: (702) 677-5222

STATE OF NEVADA
The Nevada Bureau of Alcohol and Drug Abuse operates in
cooperation with the Rotary and funds the Small Business
Training Consortium. The consortium provides free training to
small businesses, including policy development, supervisory
training and awareness, employee education, employee
assistance programs, and drug testing. A directory of regional
EAP and drug testing providers is also available. The
Consortium offers free quarterly training series of half-day
programs covering four key areas: policy development; drug
and alcohol testing; employee assistance programs and

supervisory training; and legal issues and benefits programs. In order to reach as much of the small business community as possible, the Consortium engages in an extensive outreach program, contacting local chambers, rotaries, trade associations, professional groups and public education institutions.
Rob Johnston
Bureau Chief, Department of Employment, Training and Rehabilitation
505 E. King St., Rm. 500
Carson City, NV 89701
(775) 684-4190 Fax: (775) 684-4185
E-mail: robjohn@govmail.state.nv.us

U.S. DRUG ENFORCEMENT ADMINISTRATION
DEMAND REDUCTION FIELD OFFICE
Special Agent Roland Talton
Drug Enforcement Administration
255 East Temple Street 20th Floor
Los Angeles, CA 90012
(213) 894-5632 Fax: (213) 894-0157

NEW HAMPSHIRE

CSAP RADAR NETWORK STATE CENTER
Mary Dube
Bureau of Substance Abuse
State Office Park South
105 Pleasant Street
Concord, NH 03301
(603) 271-6100 Fax: (603) 271-5051

NEW HAMPSHIRE NATIONAL GUARD
COUNTERDRUG PROGRAM
Drug Demand Reduction Administrator
State Military Reservation
4 Pembroke Road

Concord, NH 03301-5652
(603) 228-3364 Fax: (603) 225-1208

STATE OF NEW HAMPSHIRE
The Office of Alcohol and Drug Abuse Prevention serves as a clearinghouse for publications on establishing a workplace free of substance abuse. The Office also provides a resource guide of state-funded treatment centers and a partial listing of private treatment providers.
Rosemary Shannon
Bureau of Substance Abuse
State of New Hampshire
State Office Park South
105 Pleasant St.
Concord, NH 03301
(603) 271-6100

U.S. DRUG ENFORCEMENT ADMINISTRATION AGENT
DEMAND REDUCTION FIELD OFFICE
Special Agent Tina Murphy
Drug Enforcement Administration
1441 Main Street, 10th Floor
Springfield, MA 01103
(413) 785-0284 ext. 206 Fax: (413) 785-0483

NEW JERSEY

CSAP RADAR NETWORK STATE CENTER
Barry Hantman
New Jersey State Department of Health
Division of Addiction Services
129 E. Hanover Street
Trenton, NJ 08625-0362
(609) 984-6961 Fax: (609) 292-3816

GOVERNOR'S COUNCIL FOR A DRUG-FREE
WORKPLACE/DRUGS DON'T WORK
The Governor's Council for a Drug-Free Workplace is a
public/private sector initiative funded by the New Jersey
Department of Health and matching funds from the private
sector. The Council has instituted a DRUGS DON'T WORK IN
NEW JERSEY program. The program objectives are to: (1)
Determine the need for workplace substance abuse assistance
among small businesses; (2) Encourage New Jersey's larger
firms to share their experiences, policies, programs, and other
resources with smaller businesses; and to (3) Encourage
EVERY New Jersey business to adopt a comprehensive
workplace substance abuse program, including written policy,
employee education and awareness, managerial and
supervisory training, an employee assistance program, and
drug testing. The program is housed in the State Chamber of
Commerce, and takes advantage of local chambers as a
distribution network. A survey of 6500 New Jersey businesses
was conducted to determine the extent of workplace
substance abuse and the incidence of drug-free workplace
programs. An overwhelming number of respondents made it
clear that they want help in combating the problem.
Businesses find it difficult to find the time to devote to
developing a workplace free of substance a abuse. Therefore,
the Council has developed a kit with the theme: "Give us
three hours and we'll give you a drug-free workplace
program." The kit provides step-by-step instruction on the
processes and issues involved in establishing a program. The
kit is available to small businesses in return for membership
in the Council. Cost was identified as a major factor in
employers' reluctance to establish comprehensive programs.
In order to address this concern, the Council is working to
form consortia so that even the smallest New Jersey business
can benefit from low-priced employee assistance programs
and drug testing that is presently available only to larger
firms. The Council's next project is to approach banks, real
estate companies, auto dealers, and other firms offering
services to businesses, and suggest that they offer discounts to

those New Jersey firms showing certification of a workplace substance abuse program.
Joseph T. Vitale
Governor's Council for a Drug-Free Workplace
Drugs Don't Work in New Jersey
33 Washington St., Tenth Floor
Newark, NJ 07102
(201) 565-9199

Riley Regan
Governor's Council on Drug Abuse and Alcoholism
33 Washington St., Tenth Floor
Newark, NJ 07102
(201) 777-0526

NEW JERSEY COUNCIL ON ALCOHOLISM AND DRUG ABUSE, INC.
As a private, non-profit, public health agency, the New Jersey Council on Alcoholism and Drug Abuse provides public education and information about alcohol, drugs, alcoholism, drug addictions, and related problems. The council also provides consultation and assistance to professionals. The council can be contacted for a listing of affiliate county councils throughout the state.
NCADD - New Jersey
206 West State St.
Trenton, NJ 08608
(609) 392-0644

NEW JERSEY NATIONAL GUARD
COUNTERDRUG PROGRAM
Drug Demand Reduction Administrator
3650 Saylors Pond Road
Fort Dix, NJ 08640-7600
(609) 562-0667/0669 Fax: (609) 562-0655

RESOURCES

U.S. DRUG ENFORCEMENT ADMINISTRATION
DEMAND REDUCTION FIELD OFFICE
Special Agent Earl Fielder
Drug Enforcement Administration
80 Mulberry Street
Newark, NJ 07102
(973) 273-5095 Fax: (973) 645-2317

NEW MEXICO

CSAP RADAR NETWORK STATE CENTER
Elaine Benavidez
Department of Health/BHSDDSA
1190 St. Francis Drive, Room N3200
Santa Fe, NM 87502-6110
(505) 827-2601

NEW MEXICO NATIONAL GUARD
COUNTERDRUG TASK FORCE
Drug Demand Reduction Administrator
1951 1st Street, Bldg 20140
Kirtland AFB, NM 87117
(505) 846-7234 Fax: (505) 846-4879

SANTA FE COMMUNITY PARTNERSHIP
Ester Kovari
(505) 982-8899

STATE OF NEW MEXICO
The New Mexico Department of Health, Division of Substance
Abuse (DSA) contracts with forty-one (41) community-based
programs to provide adult substance abuse prevention and
treatment services. Employee assistance programming will
soon be included among the services available. Before
embarking on a large-scale outreach effort throughout the
state, DSA staffers underwent a comprehensive EAP training
program. While efforts are currently focused on local city and

county governments, the DSA is planning specialized EAP training which will address the provision of services to the private sector.
Lynn Brady
BHS/Division of Substance Abuse
New Mexico Department of Health
1190 St. Francis Drive, Room N3200
Santa Fe, NM 87502
(505) 827-2601

U.S. Drug Enforcement Administration
Special Agent Ron Hollingshead
115 Inverness Drive
East Englewood, CO 80112-5116
(303) 705-7317 Fax: (303) 705-7414

Special Agent David Monette
Drug Enforcement Administration
660 N. Mesa Hills, Suite 2000
El Paso, TX 79912
(915) 832-6000 ext. 6095 Fax: (915) 832-6001

NEW YORK

CSAP RADAR NETWORK STATE CENTER
Wendy Gibson
New York Division of Alcoholism and Alcohol Abuse
1450 Western Ave.
Albany, NY 12203-3526
(518) 473-3460 Fax: (518) 485-6014

National Development and Research Institute Inc.
2 World Trade Center 16th Floor
New York, NY 10048
(212) 845-4400 Fax: (212) 845-4698

DRUGS DON'T WORK
The state's DRUG'S DON'T WORK organization is very active in the area of workplace substance abuse. DRUG'S DON'T WORK puts out an extensive kit to guide businesses with their workplace substance abuse program needs. The group also publishes annually a survey entitled "Survey on Problems Arising for Drug Abuse." DRUGS DON'T WORK provides assistance in the areas of policy development, training & education, EAPs, drug testing and treatment resources.
Sharon Wulforst
Director of Member Services
Drugs Don't Work - New York Business Alliance
c/o Phoenix House Foundation
164 West 74th St.
New York, NY 10023
(800) 883-DRUG Fax: (212) 721-2164

NEW YORK NATIONAL GUARD
COUNTERDRUG PROGRAM
Stratton Air National Guard Base
1 Air National Guard Road
Scotia, NY 12302
(518) 344-2064 Fax: (518) 344-2067

STATE OF NEW YORK
The Governor's Statewide Anti-Drug Abuse Council has designated the workplace as one of the major areas on which to focus prevention and intervention activities. Efforts in the state are spearheaded by the Office of Alcoholism and Substance Abuse Services (OASAS). Employee assistance programs (EAPs) are regarded by the state as the cornerstone in promoting workplace substance abuse programs. The state's program for small business includes the EAP Consortia Initiative an EAP media campaign, and the sponsorship of a state workplace substance abuse workshop. OASAS' EAP Consortia Initiative, established by a state law passed in 1988, provides EAP access to more than 21,000 workers and 157 businesses. Outreach efforts focus on under-served establish-

276

ments, such as those with less than 750 employees or those located in economically distressed regions. OASAS maintains a 1-800 information line for New York small businesses and others interested in obtaining information or assistance on workplace initiatives. The Office also distributes workplace substance abuse materials, including several documents developed in-house: "Guidelines for the Development of Workplace Intervention/Employee Assistance Programs," "EAP: Selecting Your EAP Service," and "Extending the Alcohol and Drug-Free Workplace to Smaller Work Organizations: A Report on the Inventory of EAPs in NYS."
Elizabeth Hession
Office of Alcoholism and Substance Abuse Services
1450 Western Ave.
Albany, NY 12203
(518) 473-3460 Fax: (518) 485-6014
Treatment Referrals Hotline: (800) 522-5353

U.S. DRUG ENFORCEMENT ADMINISTRATION
DEMAND REDUCTION FIELD OFFICE
Special Agent Chris Browning
99 Tenth Avenue Eighth Floor
New York, NY 10011
(212) 337-1266 Fax: (212) 337-2916

NORTH CAROLINA

CENTER FOR A DRUG-FREE WORKPLACE
The Center was created by the Greater Winston-Salem Chamber of Commerce. It is designed to help businesses with implementing a workplace substance abuse program through resource guides, in-house education programs and drug-testing assistance. The Center also provides assistance in customized substance abuse programs for supervisors and employees - educating both groups in recognition of signs of abuse, appropriate action to take, facts on dependency and

the impact of substance abuse on the workplace and family. Employee assistance program guidance is also available.
Center for Drug-Free Workplace
601 West 4th St.
Winston-Salem, NC 27102
(910) 725-2361

CSAP RADAR NETWORK STATE CENTER
Betty Lane
North Carolina Alcohol and Drug Resource Center
3109A University Drive
Durham, NC 27707-3703
(919) 493-2881

DRUG-FREE WORKPLACE ALLIANCE
The Drug-Free Workplace Alliance maintains information and assistance on workplaces substance abuse and related issues.
Terri Hill
P.O. Box 32785
Charlotte, NC 28232
(704) 382-0370

NORTH CAROLINA NATIONAL GUARD
JOINT COUNTERDRUG TASK FORCE
Drug Demand Reduction Administrator
4105 Reedy Creek Road
Raleigh, NC 27607-6410
(919) 664-6552 Fax: (919) 664-6050
E-mail: nc-cd@cdmail.ngb.army.mil

U.S. DRUG ENFORCEMENT ADMINISTRATION
DEMAND REDUCTION FIELD OFFICE
Special Agent Steve Starling
Drug Enforcement Administration
75 Spring Street, S.W. Room 740
Atlanta, GA 30303
(404) 730-9515 (404) 730-3198 Fax: (404) 331-0166

Task Force Officer Leslie Pair
Drug Enforcement Administration
75 Spring Street, S.W. Room 740
Atlanta, GA 30303
(404) 730-9515 (404) 730-3198 Fax: (404) 331-0166

Task Force Officer Harry Thornton
Drug Enforcement Administration
75 Spring Street, S.W. Room 740
Atlanta, GA 30303
(404) 730-9515 (404) 730-3198 Fax: (404) 331-0166

NORTH DAKOTA

CSAP RADAR NETWORK STATE CENTER
Don Wright
North Dakota Prevention Resource Center
600 S. 2nd St. Suite 1E
Bismarck, ND 58504-5729
(701) 328-8919

NORTH DAKOTA NATIONAL GUARD
COUNTERDRUG PROGRAM
Drug Demand Reduction Administrator
P.O. Box 5511
Building 040
Fraine Barracks Road
Bismarck, ND 58506-5511
(701) 224-5271 Fax: (701) 224-5149

STATE OF NORTH DAKOTA
The Division of Mental Health and Substance Abuse Services
of the North Dakota Department of Human Services provides
posters, pamphlets, and loaned videotapes on workplace
substance abuse to any North Dakota business requesting
such information. In addition, the Division will provide

assistance in the area of workplace substance abuse and provides referrals to existing EAP providers in the state.
Karen Larson
Division of Mental Health and Substance Abuse Services
State of North Dakota
600 South 2nd St. Suite 1E
Bismarck, ND 58504-5729
(701) 328-8920

U.S. DRUG ENFORCEMENT ADMINISTRATION
DEMAND REDUCTION FIELD OFFICE
Special Agent Michael Zawadzki
Drug Enforcement Administration
230 South Dearborn Street, 12th Floor
Chicago, IL 60604
(312) 353-1427 Fax: (312) 353-1476

OHIO

CSAP RADAR NETWORK STATE CENTER
Deborah Chambers
Ohio Department of Alcohol and Drug Addiction Services
280 N. High Street, 12th Floor
Columbus, OH 43215
(614) 466-6379

OHIO NATIONAL GUARD
COUNTERDRUG PROGRAM
Drug Demand Reduction Administrator
2825 West Dublin Granville Road
Columbus, OH 43235
(614) 889-7000 Fax: (614) 766-3820
E-mail: paooh@oh-ngnet.army.mil

STATE OF OHIO
The Ohio Department of Alcohol and Drug Addiction Services
(ODADAS) has developed a comprehensive workplace

substance abuse training system for small businesses. The program, initially implemented through the four largest area chambers of commerce and local alcohol and drug addiction service boards, provides businesses with information on drug testing, employee assistance programs, supervisory training, substance abuse policy development, federal and state workplace substance abuse contract requirements, and employee education. A training manual, prepared by the Battelle Memorial Institute as a pro bono contribution to ODADAS, contains information for employers on guidelines, standards, decisions, and actions needed to implement a successful workplace substance abuse program. The manual contains model policy statements and lists important reference and training materials, as well as checklists for small business employers. This manual is free of charge to employers within the four pilot areas, and for a small fee to other interested parties. The Drugs Don't Work in Ohio program enlists corporate sponsors to provide resources and leadership to develop local workplace substance abuse consortia. Services provided by the consortia include assistance in policy development, management training, drug screening, and employee assistance. The Drugs Don't Work in Ohio program uses the Department of Labor's Substance Abuse Information Database (SAID) at each point of contact within the four chosen pilot sites, as well as at the state level.

Scott D. Brown
Department of Alcohol & Drug Addiction Services
State of Ohio
Two Nationwide Plaza
280 N. High Street, 12th Floor
Columbus, OH 43215-2537
(614) 466-3445

U.S. DRUG ENFORCEMENT ADMINISTRATION
DEMAND REDUCTION FIELD OFFICE
Special Agent Mary Neville
Drug Enforcement Administration
431 Howard Street

Detroit, MI 48226
(313) 234-4310 Fax: (313) 234-4057

OKLAHOMA

A CHANCE TO CHANGE
Kyle McGraw
(405) 840-9000

CSAP RADAR NETWORK STATE CENTER
Jane Hardwick
Oklahoma State Department of Mental Health
1200 NE 13th St., 2nd Floor
P.O. Box 53277
Oklahoma City, OK 73117
(405) 522-3908

DRUGS DON'T WORK
The workplace substance abuse initiative in central Oklahoma
is called DRUGS DON'T WORK - A Program for Drug-Free
Workplace in Central Oklahoma. The program is sponsored
by and operated through a consortium of fourteen Chambers
of Commerce, the Association of Central Oklahoma
Governments, and "Starting RIGHT!" a community anti-drug
coalition composed of 150 local organizations. Upon request,
any employer can receive a free comprehensive packet of
technical, educational, and local resource materials to assist
them in establishing a workplace program. The strategy of the
initiative is to blend a solid core of concerned and credible
business people to provide leadership, utilize the experience
and knowledge of Chamber membership, and focus on a
simple, straightforward, and cost effective approach.
Denise Hole
DRUGS DON'T WORK - A Chance to Change
5228 Classen Blvd.
Oklahoma City, OK 73118
(405) 840-9000

Dennis Doyle
Oklahoma Department of Mental Health and Substance Abuse
Services
1200 N.E. 13th
P.O. Box 53277
Oklahoma City, OK 73152-3277
(405) 522-3908

OKLAHOMA NATIONAL GUARD
COUNTERDRUG SECTION
Drug Demand Reduction Administrator
Oklahoma Military Department
3501 Military Circle
Oklahoma City, OK 73111-4398
(405) 425-8688 Fax: (405) 425-8610
E-mail: yoej@ok-tbird.ngb.army.mil

U.S. DRUG ENFORCEMENT ADMINISTRATION
DEMAND REDUCTION FIELD OFFICE
Special Agent Paul Villaescusa
Drug Enforcement Administration
1880 Regal Row
Dallas, TX 75235
(214) 640-08208 Fax: (214) 640-0895

OREGON

CSAP RADAR NETWORK STATE CENTER
Sue Ziglinski
Oregon Drug and Alcohol Information
2801 N. Gantenbein
Portland, OR 97227
(503) 280-3673 (800) 237-7808 Fax: (503) 280-4621

OREGON NATIONAL GUARD
COUNTERDRUG SUPPORT PROGRAM
Drug Demand Reduction Administrator

1921 Turner Road South
East Salem, OR 97302
(503) 945-3938 Fax: (503) 945-3238

OREGON PREVENTION RESOURCE CENTER
Oregon has designed a folder of information on workplace
substance abuse issues targeted especially at small business
owners. Included in the folder are model policies, resource
guides, information on EAPs in general and on the specific
services and goals of the Oregon Small Business EAP, and
two employer's guides. One guide was developed by the U.S.
Department of Labor and the second by a law firm that
specializes in labor and employment law. The guides provide
information on the steps and issues to be considered in
addressing the problem of workplace substance abuse. The
folder is available to Oregon businesses through the state's
drug and alcohol information clearinghouse.
Oregon Prevention Resource Center
555 24th Place, N.E.
Salem, OR 97310
(503) 378-8000

REGIONAL DRUG INITIATIVE
The Oregon Regional Drug Initiative puts out a detailed
workplace substance abuse kit which provides program
implementation assistance.
Carol Stone
522 S.W. 5th Street, Suite 1310
Portland, OR 97204
(503) 294-7074

STATE OF OREGON
The Office of Alcohol and Drug Abuse Programs in the
Oregon Department of Human Resources has primary
responsibility for monitoring workplace substance abuse
initiatives in the state. In an effort to target Oregon's smaller
businesses, the Office of Alcohol and Drug Abuse Programs

contracted the Oregon Small Business EAP to implement six specific strategies:

1. Establish and operate a state advisory board.
2. Survey small and medium sized businesses and report on the current levels of workplace policy existence, access of workers to employee assistance programs, and the extent to which these smaller businesses are working with their communities to establish workplace substance abuse norms.
3. Set off a state-wide media campaign based on the award-winning Drugs Don't Work program of Multnomah County, Oregon.
4. Develop and disseminate materials to small businesses.
5. Implement grant start-up funding for seven small business EAP consortiums to bring small businesses together to develop workplace policies, reinforce workplace substance abuse norms in the community, and form the critical mass necessary for smaller businesses to benefit from efficiencies of scale in EAP enrollment.
6. Repeat the survey to determine the impact of the program in helping small and medium sized businesses understand the challenges of workplace substance abuse.

Jeffrey Kushner
Oregon Office of Alcohol and Drug Abuse Programs
Human Resources Building
500 Summer Street, N.E.
Salem, OR 97310-1016
(503) 378-2163

Chris O'Neill
Oregon Small Business Employee Assistance Program
c/o Serenity Lane
616 E. 16th Avenue
Eugene, OR 97401
(503) 484-2156

U.S. DRUG ENFORCEMENT ADMINISTRATION
DEMAND REDUCTION FIELD OFFICE
Special Agent Juliana Parra-West

Drug Enforcement Administration
220 West Mercer, Suite 300
Seattle, WA 98119
(206) 553-5443 Fax: (206) 533-1069

PENNSYLVANIA

AFL-CIO APPALACHIAN COUNCIL
The Department of Labor and Industry contracts with the AFL-CIO Appalachian Council to provide employee assistance programs, endorsed by both labor and management, to individuals in the workforce. The goal of the Council is to make all workers aware of the wellness services available in their community to assist individuals experiencing any type of personal difficulties. Representatives visit worksites and conduct employee training sessions on the problems and symptoms of drug and alcohol abuse. Posters are placed throughout the worksite to reinforce worker awareness, and information is mailed out to all employees listing centers where troubled individuals can self-refer for confidential counseling or treatment. The state also provides funding to the Council for other workplace substance abuse initiatives, including technical assistance to firms wishing to establish workplaces free of substance abuse.
Frank Fantauzzo
AFL-CIO Appalachian Council Employee Assistance Program
111 Walnut Street, #4
Johnstown, PA 15901
(814) 536-2013

Frank C. Fantauzzo
AFL-CIO Appalachian Council, Inc.
501 Broad Street
Charleston, WV 25301
(304) 345-5811

CSAP RADAR NETWORK STATE CENTER
Chris Dubbs
PENNSAHIC
Columbus Square
652 W. 17th Street
Erie, PA 16502
(814) 459-0245 (800) 582-7746 Fax: (814) 453-4714

DRUG FREE PENNSYLVANIA, INC.
This organization is a non-profit corporation dedicated to being a primary resource for private sector anti-drug and alcohol abuse prevention efforts in the state. The coordination of private and public prevention efforts is a major goal of this organization. Efforts include promoting drug education, treatment, rehabilitation, research and law enforcement. Drug-Free Pennsylvania, Inc. also offers free regional workplace substance abuse seminars; participants learn about drugs in the workplace, drug testing, follow-up help, developing a policy, and setting up an employee assistance program (EAP). Seminars are presented by experts in the field, and each participant receives a Drug-Free Workplace kit.
Kathleen McGrath
Director, Drug-Free Pennsylvania, Inc.
200 N. 3rd St., Tenth Floor
Harrisburg, PA 17101
(717) 232-0300

PENNSYLVANIA NATIONAL GUARD
COUNTERDRUG PROGRAM
Drug Demand Reduction Administrator
Fort Indiantown Gap, BLDG 9-7
Annville, PA 17003-5002
(717) 861-8716 Fax: (717) 861-8225

STATE OF PENNSYLVANIA
Studies have consistently shown that job stability is a major factor in establishing long-term sobriety. In Philadelphia, four out of five of the approximately 18,000 persons who receive

287

treatment for alcohol and other drugs are unemployed. Employers who hire recovering workers find them to be hard-working, reliable, and honest. The Pennsylvania Department of Labor and Industry's Re-employment Assistance Program (RAP) is designed to help recovering people re-enter the workplace. RAP offers services to help employers hire re-covering workers, including job placement services, on-the-job training programs, apprenticeship programs, bonding services, employer seminars on a workplace substance abuse, tax credits, and other employer incentives. Pennsylvania's is the first state job service program in the country to address the placement of unemployed individuals after their treatment for substance abuse.
Richard Montgomery
Pennsylvania Department of Labor and Industry
Drug and Alcohol Intervention
444 N. 3rd Street, 3rd floor
Philadelphia, PA 19123
(215) 560-3205

U.S. DRUG ENFORCEMENT ADMINISTRATION
DEMAND REDUCTION FIELD OFFICE
Special Agent Donna Wilson
Drug Enforcement Administration
600 Arch Street, Suite 10224
Philadelphia, PA 19106
(215) 597-7866 Fax: (215) 597-6063

PUERTO RICO

CSAP RADAR NETWORK STATE CENTER
Priscilla Parrilla-Jacobs
RADAR Coordinator-ASSMCA
P.O. Box 21414
San Juan, PR 00928-1414
(787) 763-7575 ext. 2267 Fax: (787) 751-6915
E-mail: assmca@coqui.net

DEPARTMENT OF MENTAL HEALTH AND ANTI-ADDICTION
SERVICES
Puerto Rico offers private sector assistance in combating
substance abuse through the Division of Occupational
Assistance Programs in the Department of Anti-Addiction
Services. This Office provides information regarding local and
federal laws, drug testing procedures, and consultation on the
development of employee assistance programs. Additionally,
supervisory training and employee awareness programs are
available.
Rafael Monserrate
Private Sector Services
Puerto Rico Department of Anti-Addiction Services
Division of Occupational Assistance Programs
Apto 21414, Rio Piedras Station
Rio Piedras, PR 00928-1414
(787) 763-7575

PUERTO RICO NATIONAL GUARD
COUNTERDRUG PROGRAM
Drug Demand Reduction Administrator
General Esteves St. #100
Puerta Tierra, San Juan, PR 00901
(787) 289-1454/1455 Fax: (787) 723-6360

U.S. DRUG ENFORCEMENT ADMINISTRATION
DEMAND REDUCTION FIELD OFFICE
Special Agent Waldo P. Santiago
Drug Enforcement Administration
Casa Lee Building
2432 Loiza Street
San Turce, Puerto Rico 00913
(787) 253-4562 Fax: (787) 253-4255

RESOURCES

RHODE ISLAND

CSAP RADAR NETWORK STATE CENTER
Betty Ann McHugh
Department of Health Prevention Unit
Cannon Building #105
3 Capitol Hill
Providence, RI 02908-5097
(401) 277-4680 Fax: (401) 277-4688

RHODE ISLAND NATIONAL GUARD
COUNTERDRUG PROGRAM
Drug Demand Reduction Administrator
Command Readiness Center
645 New London Avenue
Cranston, RI 02920-3097
(401) 457-4139 Fax: (401) 457-4306

STATE OF RHODE ISLAND
In 1994, the Office of Substance Abuse in Rhode Island was
elevated to full Department status by a Legislative Act introduced and signed by the Governor. The new Department of
Health is working closely with providers and the business
coalition to encourage workplace initiatives. Several providers
in the mental health and substance abuse field offer EAP
services as well as some private corporations that offer only
EAP services. So the business community in Rhode Island has
an option of securing well-qualified firms to offer these
services. Additionally, the Rhode Island for a Drug-Free
Community, with funding from private industries, federal
block grants and the Department of Health, is presently in the
process of reviewing applications to form a consortium EAP
that would serve Chamber of Commerce members.
Dr. Sherry Knapp
Division of Substance Abuse
3 Capital Hill
Providence, RI 02908-5097
(401) 277-4680

Anna Prager
Rhode Island for a Drug-Free Community
30 Exchange Terrace
Providence, RI 02903
(401) 454-7210

U.S. DRUG ENFORCEMENT ADMINISTRATION
DEMAND REDUCTION FIELD OFFICE
Special Agent Tina Murphy
1441 Main Street, 10th Floor
Springfield, MA 01103
(413) 785-0284 ext. 206 Fax: (413) 785-0483

SOUTH CAROLINA

CAROLINA'S DRUG-FREE WORKPLACE
Terri Hill
(704) 382-0370

CSAP RADAR NETWORK STATE CENTER
Elizabeth Peters
South Carolina Commission on Alcohol & Drug Abuse
The Drug Store Information Clearinghouse
3700 Forest Drive Suite 300
Columbia, SC 29204
(803) 734-9559

SOUTH CAROLINA NATIONAL GUARD
COUNTERDRUG PROGRAM
Drug Demand Reduction Administrator
1 National Guard Road
Columbia, SC 29201-4766
(803) 806-4402 Fax: (803) 806-1556
E-mail: ctrdrug@sc-net.army.mil

RESOURCES

STATE OF SOUTH CAROLINA
The South Carolina Department of Alcohol and Other Drug Abuse Services (DAODAS) has been instrumental in establishing a Small Business Consortium through Palmetto Employee Assistance Programs, a state/county effort funded jointly by DAODAS and eight county commissions on alcohol and drug abuse. A special effort has been made to provide small businesses with a comprehensive employee assistance program. The EAP provides policy development, procedure development, supervisory training, a broad education program for all employees, periodic programmatic maintenance visits, evaluation assistance, assessments, and normal outpatient counseling. There is no limit to the number of counseling sessions available. The dependents of employees are also covered by the program. It is still too early to evaluate acceptance of the program, but it is hoped that the affordable rates offered through the consortium will attract even the smallest employers.
Beverly Hamilton
South Carolina Department of Alcohol & Other Drug Abuse Services
3700 Forest Drive, Suite 300
Columbia, SC 29204
(803) 734-9520

U.S. DRUG ENFORCEMENT ADMINISTRATION
DEMAND REDUCTION FIELD OFFICE
Special Agent Steve Starling
Drug Enforcement Administration
75 Spring Street, S.W. Room 740
Atlanta, GA 30303
(404) 730-9515 (404) 730-3198 Fax: (404) 331-0166

Task Force Officer Leslie Pair
Drug Enforcement Administration
75 Spring Street, S.W. Room 740
Atlanta, GA 30303
(404) 730-9515 (404) 730-3198 Fax: (404) 331-0166

Task Force Officer Harry Thornton
Drug Enforcement Administration
75 Spring Street, S.W. Room 740
Atlanta, GA 30303
(404) 730-9515 (404) 730-3198 Fax: (404) 331-0166

SOUTH DAKOTA

CSAP RADAR NETWORK STATE CENTER
Jeff McDorman
South Dakota Division of Alcohol and Substance Abuse
Hillsview Properties Plaza
c/o 500 E. Capitol
Pierre, SD 57501-5070
(605) 773-3123 Fax: (605) 773-5483

SOUTH DAKOTA NATIONAL GUARD
COUNTERDRUG PROGRAM
Drug Demand Reduction Administrator
2823 West Main Street
Rapid City, SD 57702-8186
(605) 399-6661 Fax: (605) 399-6556

STATE OF SOUTH DAKOTA
The Division of Alcohol and Drug Abuse of the South Dakota
Department of Human Services has several ongoing initiatives
on workplace substance abuse. Technical assistance is provided free to any business interested in developing or
maintaining an Employee Assistance Program. A Network
Center keeps abreast of all relevant information released
throughout the United States and Canada. The state funds
three Area Resource Centers to deliver educational
information and technical services. The Division's annual
Summer Institute focuses on substance abuse issues important
to all types of organizations.
Gilbert E. Sudbeck
Division of Alcohol and Drug Abuse

RESOURCES

South Dakota Department of Human Services
Hillsview Properties Plaza
c/o 500 East Capitol
Pierre, SD 57501-5070
(605) 773-3123

U.S. DRUG ENFORCEMENT ADMINISTRATION
DEMAND REDUCTION FIELD OFFICE
Special Agent Shirley A. Armstead
Drug Enforcement Administration
7911 Forsyth Blvd. Suite 500
St. Louis, MO 63105
(314) 538-4752 Fax: (314) 538-4758

TENNESSEE

CSAP RADAR NETWORK STATE CENTER
Department of Tennessee Alcohol and Drug Association
630 Hartlane
Nashville, TN 37216
(615) 532-3579

STATE OF TENNESSEE
The State of Tennessee has an EAP coordinator available to
consult with small and medium sized businesses that request
assistance. A conference on the Drug-Free Workplace Act,
jointly sponsored by the state and the National Association of
State Alcohol and Drug Abuse Directors (NASADAD), was
held in November of 1990. Regional follow-up conferences
have had impressive turnout -- in the Spring of 1991 over 180
businesses attended the sessions. An information clearinghouse is funded by the state to provide information regarding
substance abuse prevention to any Tennessee business upon
request.
Jackie Bruce
Bureau of Alcohol & Drug Abuse Services
Tennessee Department of Health

Cordell Hull Building, Third Floor
Nashville, TN 37247-4401
(615) 741-1921

TENNESSEE DRUG-FREE WORKPLACE PROGRAM
This state program offers businesses information about the
problem and costs associated with drugs in the workplace, as
well as solutions for implementing and maintaining a drug-
free workplace program. The program has available an
information kit that provides materials for helping companies
decide whether they would like to voluntarily participate in
the program.
Tennessee Drug-Free Workplace Program
Tennessee Department of Labor
Andrew Johnson Tower, Second Floor
710 James Robertson Parkway
Nashville, TN 37243
(615) 532-2403 Fax: (615) 532-1468
E-mail: lfrost@mail.state.tn.us
www.state.tn.us/labor/dfwp.html

TENNESSEE NATIONAL GUARD
COUNTERDRUG PROGRAM
Drug Demand Reduction Administrator
3041 Sidco Drive
Nashville, TN 37204
(615) 313-0889/0664 Fax: (615) 313-0749

U.S. DRUG ENFORCEMENT ADMINISTRATION
DEMAND REDUCTION FIELD OFFICE
Special Agent Steve Starling
75 Spring Street, S.W. Room 740
Atlanta, GA 30303
(404) 730-9515 (404) 730-3198 Fax: (404) 331-0166

Task Force Officer Leslie Pair
Drug Enforcement Administration
75 Spring Street, S.W. Room 740

Atlanta, GA 30303
(404) 730-9515 (404) 730-3198 Fax: (404) 331-0166

Task Force Officer Harry Thornton
Drug Enforcement Administration
75 Spring Street, S.W. Room 740
Atlanta, GA 30303
(404) 730-9515 (404) 730-3198 Fax: (404) 331-0166

TEXAS

CSAP RADAR NETWORK STATE CENTER
Laura Henemann
Texas Commission on Alcohol and Drug Abuse Resource
Center
9001 North IH 35 Suite 105
Austin, TX 78753
(512) 349-6642 Fax: (512) 837-4058

HOUSTON'S DRUG-FREE BUSINESS ALLIANCE
Houston's Drug-Free Business Alliance (HDFBA) is a non-
profit corporation formed by the Houston Chamber of
Commerce to promote business sector involvement in anti-
drug activities. HDFBA's members receive guidance on
carrying out a substance abuse program; access to a library
that includes employee education and awareness literature,
training materials, and sample drug abuse policies and
procedures; films and audiovisuals on loan; a newsletter that
reports events, trends, and seminars and workshops; and use
of a speaker's bureau. HDFBA's goal is to create a network
for its large and small member companies to contribute
insights and resources in support of the community's anti-
drug activities. The organization also produces a kit to assist
small business, and includes: a mission statement, newsletters,
membership information and handouts.
Becky B. Vance
Executive Director, Houston's Drug-Free Business Alliance

P.O. Box 3, Building MS-02, Rm. 105
Houston, TX 77001-0003
(713) 676-7275 Fax: (713) 676-7389
E-mail: hdfbi@flash.net drug-freeworkplace.org

TEXAS DRUG-FREE WORKPLACE INITIATIVE
Texas Workers Compensation regulations require all
employers who have fifteen or more employees and maintain
workers compensation insurance to have a written workplace
substance abuse policy, covering at least alcohol, illegal drugs
and inhalants. The Texas Commission on Alcohol and Drug
Abuse and the Workers Assistance Program, Inc. have formed
a partnership: the Texas Drug-Free Workplace Initiative. The
Initiative serves as the point of contact in the state for
workplace substance abuse information. Since its inception in
1988, the Initiative has assisted over 3,700 Texas
organizations. Services provided by the Initiative include:
1. Free Information Packets containing comprehensive,
concise information on governmental requirements, policy
development, drug testing, drug addiction, employee
assistance programs, and other topics. These packets provide
specific management options for satisfying legislative
requirements, improving employee morale, and assisting
employees whose performance is impaired by chemical
dependency or other problems.
2. Free Sample Workplace Substance Abuse Policies and
Procedures, which can serve as a starting point for any
organization. These samples cover a variety of workplace
environments. Policy review and technical support are
available at no cost.
3. An Information Clearinghouse continuously gathers and
reviews new information. The Clearinghouse specializes in
difficult topics such as legislative research, and stays abreast
of the latest changes in state and federal workplace substance
abuse laws.
4. Free Program Development Consultation offers employers
one-on-one sessions to clarify the goals, structure, and

benefits of new and existing programs. These sessions focus on putting paper programs into practice.

5. Free/Low Cost Educational and Training Workshops educate supervisors and employees on how to fully utilize the procedures and services of a workplace substance abuse program.

6. A Resource Network accessible through a 1-800 number enables employers to easily locate providers of workplace substance abuse services.

7. Networking with federal, state, City and Community Resources, such as the U.S. Small Business Administration, the Drug Enforcement Administration, the Texas Education Agency, the Texas Employment Commission, and local chambers of commerce, county judges, and police departments, enables the Initiative to spread the word about its services.

8. An EAP Consortium links workplaces to an EAP, and makes it affordable even to small organizations with limited resources. The rationale for the Consortium is that when one-hundred businesses with ten employees each are pulled together, they become an economic force comparable to one business with a thousand employees. Consequently, small businesses within the Consortium benefit from the same affordable, custom-tailored EAP services available to large businesses.

Rick Dielman
Texas Drug-Free Workplace Initiative
2525 Wallingwood Dr. Building 5
Austin, TX 78746
(512) 328-1144

TEXAS NATIONAL GUARD
COUNTERDRUG PROGRAM
Drug Demand Reduction Administrator
Attn: AGTX-CD-DDR
2200 W. 35th Street, Bldg. 10, Rm. 200
Austin, TX 78703
(512) 406-6975 Fax: (512) 465-5144

U.S. DRUG ENFORCEMENT ADMINISTRATION
DEMAND REDUCTION FIELD OFFICE
Special Agent Paul Villaescusa
Drug Enforcement Administration
1880 Regal Row
Dallas, TX 75235
(214) 640-0828 Fax: (214) 640-0895

Diversion Investigator Dawn Nunley
Drug Enforcement Administration
1433 West Loop South
Houston, TX 77027-9506
(713) 693-3152 Fax: (713) 693-3065

Special Agent David Monette
Drug Enforcement Administration
660 N. Mesa Hills, Suite 2000
El Paso, TX 79912
(915) 832-6000, ext. 6095 Fax: (915) 832-6001

UTAH

CSAP RADAR NETWORK STATE CENTER
Sherry Young
Utah State Division of Substance Abuse
Department of Human Services
4th Floor 120 N. 20 West
Salt Lake City, UT 84145-0500
(801) 538-3939

STATE OF UTAH
The Utah Division of Substance Abuse, Department of Human
Services, provides technical assistance on workplace
substance abuse policy and legislation, as well as referral
information on state and federal resources. Information about
EAP development and services for employees is available
from each of the state's thirteen planning districts. For a list of

these planning districts, contact the Division of Substance Abuse. The Utah Crime Prevention Council, with support from the Division of Substance Abuse and other federal, state, and private organizations, has prepared a manual containing guidelines for the development of workplace substance abuse policies. Utah employers interested in obtaining the manual may contact the Crime Prevention Council.
Hugh Craig Bunker
Utah Department of Human Services
Division of Substance Abuse
120 North 20 West, 4th Floor
P.O. Box 45500
Salt Lake City, UT 84145-0500
(801) 538-3939

Tibby Milne
Crime Prevention Council
66 East Cleveland Ave.
Salt Lake City, UT 84115
(801) 486-8691

STATE OF UTAH
The Utah Division of Substance Abuse, Department of Human Services, provides technical assistance on workplace substance abuse policy and legislation, as well as referral information on state and federal resources. Information about EAP development and services for employees is available from each of the state's thirteen planning districts. For a list of these planning districts, please contact the Division of Substance Abuse. The Utah Crime Prevention Council, with support from the Division of Substance Abuse and other federal, state, and private organizations, has prepared a manual containing guidelines for the development of workplace substance abuse policies. Utah employers interested in obtaining the manual may contact the Crime Prevention Council.

U.S. DRUG ENFORCEMENT ADMINISTRATION
DEMAND REDUCTION FIELD OFFICE
Special Agents Ron Hollingshead and/or Dennis Follett
Drug Enforcement Administration
115 Inverness Drive
East Englewood, CO 80112-5116
(303) 705-7317 Fax: (303) 705-7414

VERMONT

CSAP RADAR NETWORK STATE CENTER
Cathy Belleview
Department of Health
Office of Alcohol and Drug Abuse Programs
108 Jerry St.
P.O. Box 70
Burlington, VT 05402
(802) 651-1550

STATE OF VERMONT
Through the State Employee Assistance Program, the Office of
Alcohol and Drug Abuse Programs in the Vermont Agency of
Human Services assists small businesses in establishing a
workplace free of substance abuse and other substance abuse
prevention efforts. Examples of the services available to
businesses include:
1. Technical assistance on drug policy development,
interpretation of Vermont's drug testing law, employee
assistance policy development, employee education
programs, and referrals to potential providers.
2. Training on the nature of drug abuse, employee assistance
orientation for supervisors and employees, and other topics
on request.
3. Samples and suggestions of materials for use in continuing
employee education programs.
Peter Lee
Department of Health

RESOURCES

Office of Alcohol and Drug Abuse Programs
108 Jerry St.
P.O. Box 70
Burlington, VT 05402
(802) 651-1550

U.S. DRUG ENFORCEMENT ADMINISTRATION
DEMAND REDUCTION FIELD OFFICE
Special Agent Tina Murphy
Drug Enforcement Administration
1441 Main Street, 10th Floor
Springfield, MA 01103
(413) 785-0284 ext. 206 Fax: (413) 785-0483

VERMONT NATIONAL GUARD
COUNTERDRUG PROGRAM
Drug Demand Reduction Administrator
Green Mountain Armory, Camp Johnson
Colchester, VT 05446-3004
(802) 654-0440 Fax: (802) 655-6256
E-mail: tholmes@vt-ngnet.army.mil

VIRGINIA

CSAP RADAR NETWORK STATE CENTER
Bernice Morgan
Virginia Department of Mental Retardation and Substance
Abuse
Office of Prevention and Children Services
P.O. Box 1797
Richmond, VA 23218
(804) 371-7564 (804) 371-6179

METRO RICHMOND COALITION AGAINST DRUGS
Tim Bowring
(804) 649-3306

STATE OF VIRGINIA
The Office of Planning and Policy Analysis of the Virginia
Department of Labor and Industry publishes a brochure
giving employers an overview of the legalities, issues and
precautions involved in establishing a drug testing program.
The Virginia General Assembly directed the Department to
study the issue of workplace drug testing in the Commonwealth. The study gathered information on the prevalence of
drug testing in Virginia businesses by conducting an employer
survey and includes data on the characteristics of drug testing
in Virginia workplaces. Results of the study were published
and presented to the Governor and to the Virginia General
Assembly.
Office of Policy and Planning Analysis
Virginia Department of Labor and Industry
13 South 13th Street
Richmond, VA 23219
(804) 786-2377

Most of Virginia's other activities focus on the
Commonwealth's public sector treatment programs.
Gregory B. Stolcis
Commonwealth of Virginia
Department of Mental Health, Mental Retardation & Substance
Abuse Services
Post Office Box 1797
Richmond, VA 23218
(804) 786-1746

U.S. DRUG ENFORCEMENT ADMINISTRATION
DEMAND REDUCTION FIELD OFFICE
Special Agent Mark Warpness
Drug Enforcement Administration
801 I Street N.W. Room 514
Washington, D.C. 20024
(202) 305-8639 Fax: (202) 307-5823

RESOURCES

VIRGINIA NATIONAL GUARD
COUNTERDRUG PROGRAM
Drug Demand Reduction Administrator
600 East Broad Street
Richmond, VA 23219
(804) 775-9175 Fax: (804) 775-9315
E-mail: va@ngb-emh2.army.mil

VIRGIN ISLANDS

CSAP RADAR NETWORK STATE CENTER
Maren Roebuck
3500 Richmond Charles Harwood Complex
Division of Mental Health Prevention Unit
St. Croix, VI 00840-4370
(809) 773-1311 Fax: (809) 773-7900

TERRITORY OF THE VIRGIN ISLANDS
The Territory of the Virgin Islands has provided an employee
assistance service to the public and private sectors since 1984.
All agencies and businesses in the Virgin Islands requesting
services are encouraged to utilize the EAP package, which
consists of the following components:
1. Consultation with managers and union representatives;
2. Orientation to the EAP concept;
3. Education - alcohol and other drug awareness;
4. Supervisory training;
5. Referrals - development of a mechanism;
6. Treatment - or referrals to private practitioners;
7. Follow-up; and
8. Ongoing consultation for supervisors.
Carlos Ortiz
Division of Mental Health
Barbel Plaza
South Second Floor St.
Thomas, VI 00802
(340) 774-4888

U.S. DRUG ENFORCEMENT ADMINISTRATION
DEMAND REDUCTION FIELD OFFICE
Special Agent Waldo P. Santiago
Drug Enforcement Administration
Casa Lee Building
2432 Loiza Street
San Turce, Puerto Rico 00913
(787) 253-4562 Fax: (787) 253-4255

VIRGIN ISLANDS NATIONAL GUARD
COUNTERDRUG PROGRAM
Drug Demand Reduction Administrator
4031 LaGrande Princess Lot 1B
Christiansted, VI 00820-4353
(809) 774-5460/3066 Fax: (809) 776-3240
E-mail: vi@ngb-emh2.army.mil

WASHINGTON

CSAP RADAR NETWORK STATE CENTER
Jill Ferguson
Washington State Substance Abuse Coalition
12729 N.E. 20th Suite 18
Bellevue, WA 98005-1906
(425) 637-7011 Fax: (206) 637-7012

STATE OF WASHINGTON
Washington employs a Drug-Free Workplace Specialist to
provide technical assistance and consultation on workplace
substance abuse programs to employers and employer
groups. The Drug-Free Workplace Specialist also works with
and through drug prevention specialists in all 39 counties. A
number of county-wide prevention coalitions have been
developed. In one county, for example, an organization has
established criteria for a workplace substance abuse award;
the smallest recipient of the award thus far has only three
employees. In one rural county, the state funded a market

305

survey to test the feasibility of a county EAP consortium concept. When that survey demonstrated the potential to become self-sufficient, given some initial seed money, the consortium was awarded a $30,000 grant for a demonstration project.
Henry Govert
State of Washington Division of Alcohol and Substance Abuse
Post Office Box 45330
Olympia, WA 98504-5330
(360) 438-8200

U.S. DRUG ENFORCEMENT ADMINISTRATION
DEMAND REDUCTION FIELD OFFICE
Special Agent Juliana Parra-West
Drug Enforcement Administration
220 West Mercer, Suite 300
Seattle, WA 98119
(206) 553-5443 Fax: (206) 533-1069

WASHINGTON NATIONAL GUARD
COUNTERDRUG PROGRAM
Drug Demand Reduction Administrator
Building 1, Camp Murray
Tacoma, WA 98430-5018
(206) 512-8008 Fax: (206) 512-8592

WASHINGTON STATE DRUG-FREE BUSINESS INITIATIVE
Washington also contracts with Washington State Drug-Free Business Initiative to provide technical assistance to employers on various aspects of workplace substance abuse programming. Special emphasis is placed on both small business and women-and-minority-owned businesses. Technical assistance includes a series of half-day or one-day business seminars on the essential elements of a drug-free workplace program, local resources for program implementation, site visits and assistance, and supervisory training. An EAP consortium and a drug testing consortium

are available. Certificates are awarded to businesses who meet certain criteria for a workplace substance abuse program.
Tom Pool
Washington State Drug-Free Business Initiative
12729 NE 20th St, Suite 17
Bellevue, WA 98005
(425) 451-4771

WEST VIRGINIA

CSAP RADAR NETWORK STATE CENTER
J.D. Waggoner
West Virginia Library Commission Cultural Center
1900 Kanawha Blvd. East
Charleston, WV 25305-0620
(304) 558-2041 Fax: (304) 558-2044

STATE OF WEST VIRGINIA
West Virginia contracts with the AFL-CIO Appalachian Council to provide employee assistance programs, endorsed by both labor and management, to individuals in the workforce. The goal of the Council is to make all workers aware of services available to assist individuals experiencing any type of personal difficulties. Representatives visit worksites and conduct employee training sessions on the problems and symptoms of drug and alcohol abuse. Posters are placed throughout the worksite to reinforce worker awareness, and information is mailed out to all employees listing centers where troubled individuals can self-refer for confidential counseling or treatment. The state's Behavioral Health Service also provides funding to the Council for other workplace substance abuse initiatives, including technical assistance to firms wishing to establish workplaces free of substance abuse.

Frank C. Fantauzzo
AFL-CIO Appalachian Council, Inc.
501 Broad Street

Charleston, WV 25301
(304) 345-5811

Joe Kiger
AFL-CIO Appalachian Council, Inc.
Employee Assistance Program
Route 2, Box 241A
Washington, WV 26181
(304) 863-8264

Don Griffin
Trans-Potomac Prevention Coalition
285 Rock Cliff Drive
Martinsburg, WV 25401
(304) 264-0944

U.S. DRUG ENFORCEMENT ADMINISTRATION
DEMAND REDUCTION FIELD OFFICE
Special Agent Mark Warpness
Drug Enforcement Administration
801 I Street N.W. Room 514
Washington, D.C. 20024
(202) 305-8639 Fax: (202) 307-5823

WEST VIRGINIA NATIONAL GUARD
COUNTERDRUG PROGRAM
Drug Demand Reduction Administrator
1703 Coonskin Drive
Charleston, WV 23511-1085
(304) 341-6460 Fax: (304) 341-6095

WISCONSIN

CSAP RADAR NETWORK STATE CENTER
Steve Braunginn
Wisconsin Clearinghouse
1552 University Ave. Department 7A

P.O. Box 1468
Madison, WI 53701-1468
(608) 263-2797 (608) 263-6886 Fax: (608) 262-6346

DRUG-FREE WORKPLACE NETWORK
No state programs have been reported. But a coalition of over
ten labor groups, chambers of commerce and the Greater
Milwaukee Committee is working with the DRUG-FREE
WORKPLACE NETWORK in providing employers, especially
small employers, assistance in developing workplace
substance abuse programs. The network offers a kit
explaining workplace substance abuse issues, consultation on
drug testing, supervisory training, employee education, EAPs,
and general program design.
Jerome Houfek
DRUG-FREE WORKPLACE NETWORK
1126 S. 70th St., Suite 116
West Allis, WI 53214
(414) 475-2310

U.S. DRUG ENFORCEMENT ADMINISTRATION
DEMAND REDUCTION FIELD OFFICE
Special Agent Michael Zawadzki
Drug Enforcement Administration
230 South Dearborn Street, 12th Floor
Chicago, IL 60604
(312) 353-1427 Fax: (312) 353-1476

WISCONSIN NATIONAL GUARD DRUG CONTROL
PROGRAM
Drug Demand Reduction Administrator
PO Box 8111
Madison, WI 53708-8111
(608) 242-3548 Fax: (608) 242-3546

RESOURCES

WYOMING

CSAP RADAR NETWORK STATE CENTER
Janette Morris
Wyoming Care Program
College of Education Room 35
Laramie, WY 82071-3374
(307) 766-4119

STATE OF WYOMING
The Office of Substance Abuse in the Division of Behavioral
Health distributes information packets to employers who
request assistance in addressing workplace substance abuse.
Included in the packet is information on federal requirements
for a workplace substance abuse program as well as federal
publications regarding the establishment of a workplace
substance abuse program. The Office also provides limited
consultation to large and small businesses in Wyoming
regarding workplace substance abuse issues. If extended
technical assistance or training is required, the Office can help
link businesses with local service providers.
Dr. James R. Lewis
State of Wyoming Office of Substance Abuse
Division of Behavioral Health
Hathaway Building, Rm. 452
Cheyenne, WY 82002
(307) 777-6493

U.S. DRUG ENFORCEMENT ADMINISTRATION
DEMAND REDUCTION FIELD OFFICE
Special Agents Ron Hollingshead and/or Dennis Follett
Drug Enforcement Administration
115 Inverness Drive East
Englewood, CO 80112-5116
(303) 705-7317 Fax: (303) 705-7414

WYOMING NATIONAL GUARD DRUG DEMAND
REDUCTION PROGRAM
Drug Demand Reduction Administrator
5500 Bishop Blvd.
Cheyenne, WY 82009-3320
(307) 772-5957
E-mail: harding@wy-150.army.mil

Other State and Local Resources

Alcohol Policy Network of Alameda County
2512 Ninth Street, Suite 3
Berkeley, CA 94710
Phone: (510)548-9822
Fax: (510) 548-0485
E-mail: jlkiley@pacbell.net
Subject areas: Environmental prevention strategies,
advertising, availability, policy, underage drinking.
Services or materials provided: Copies of ordinances,
newsletter, training and technical assistance. Environmental
prevention strategies refer to approaches that focus on
environmental factors which may contribute to alcohol
problems. Examples include restricting alcohol advertising,
reducing alcohol outlet density or alcohol availability,
increasing alcohol taxes, and promoting responsible beverage
service programs. These approaches are distinguished from
prevention strategies which focus on the individual, such as
treatment.

Berkeley Media Studies Group
2140 Shattuck Avenue, Suite 804
Berkeley, CA 94704
Phone: (510) 204-9700
Fax: (510) 204-9710

RESOURCES

E-mail: bmsg@bmsg.org
Subject areas: Media studies, policy.
Services or materials provided: Media advocacy, training and technical assistance.

California Council on Alcohol Policy (Cal Council)
2512 Ninth Street, Suite 3
Berkeley, CA 94710-2542
Phone: (510) 653-6864
Fax: (510) 548-0485
E-mail: jlkiley@pacbell.net
Subject areas: Statewide network of local policy advocates, environmental prevention strategies, policy, underage drinking.
Services or materials provided: Legislative updates/action alerts, training, and technical assistance.

California Latino Alcohol and Other Drugs Coalition (CAL-LADCO)
27287 Patrick Avenue, Suite 9
Hayward, CA 94541-4405
Phone: (510) 785-8372, Ext. 2
Fax: (510) 785-8677
E-mail: cal-ladco@juno.com
Subject areas: Facilitating a statewide network of Latino communities and developing environmental prevention strategies for Latino communities.
Services or materials provided: Brochures, technical assistance.

CalPartners Coalition
909 - 12th Street, Suite 205
Sacramento, CA 95814
Phone: (916) 442-3760
Fax: (916) 447-7052
E-mail: calpartners@calpartners.org
Web: http://www.calpartners.org

Subject areas: Statewide coalition - alcohol industry practices, environmental prevention strategies (advertising, availability), violence, Latino communities.
Services or materials provided: Fact sheets/data and statistics/research summaries, legislative updates/action alerts, media advocacy, links to funding sources, publications, training and technical assistance.

Center on Alcohol Advertising
c/o Trauma Foundation
San Francisco General Hospital
Building One, Room 300
San Francisco, CA 94110
Phone: (415) 821-8209
Fax: (415) 282-2563
E-mail: alcoholads@traumafdn.org
Web: http://www.traumafdn.org/alcohol/ads/index.html
Subject areas: Environmental prevention strategies (advertising), underage drinking. Services or materials provided: Advocates' stories, fact sheets/data and statistics/research summaries, media advocacy.

Community Coalition for Substance Abuse Prevention and Treatment
8101 South Vermont Avenue
Los Angeles, CA 90044
Phone: (213) 750-9087
Fax: (213) 750-9640
Subject areas: Economic development, environmental prevention strategies (advertising, availability), underage drinking.
Services or materials provided: Community organizing, issue development, leadership development, treatment referrals, youth leadership programs.

Community Wellness Partnership
640 South Garey Avenue
Pomona, CA 91766

Phone: (909) 469-2299
Fax: (909) 469-2298
Subject areas: Environmental prevention strategies
(advertising, availability, alcohol industry targeting of youth
and communities of color).
Services or materials: Newsletter, training and technical
assistance, youth leadership program.

Connecticut Coalition to Stop Underage Drinking
30 Arbor Street
Hartford, CT 06106
Phone: (860) 523-8042, Ext. 12 or 14
Fax: (860) 236-9412

Connecticut Clearinghouse
334 Farmington Avenue
Plainville, CT 06062
Phone: (800) 232-4424 or (860) 793-9791
Fax: (860) 793-9813
E-mail: info@ctclearinghouse.org
Web:http://www.ctclearinghouse.org
Subject areas: Crime, underage drinking, violence.
Services or materials provided: Audio/Visual Materials
(available to Connecticut residents only), fact sheets/data and
statistics/research summaries, library (available to Connecticut
residents only), publications.

Georgia Alcohol Policy Partnership
2045 Peachtree Rd, Suite 605
Atlanta, GA 30309
Phone: (404) 351-1800
Fax: (404) 351-2840
Web: http://www.gapp.org

Indiana Coalition to Reduce Underage Drinking
29 Boone Village
Zionsville, IN 46077
Phone: (317) 873-3900

Fax: (317) 873-0993
E-mail: icrud@indy.net

Institute for the Study of Social Change
2198 Sixth Street, Suite 201
Berkeley, CA 94710
Phone: (510) 540-4717
Fax: (510) 540-4731
E-mail: fwittman@uclink4.berkeley.edu
Subject areas: Environmental prevention strategies
(advertising, availability/zoning).
Services or materials provided: Publications, training and
technical assistance.

Interfaith Network
27287 Patrick Avenue
Hayward, CA 94544-4405
Phone: (510) 785-8372
Fax: (510) 785-8677
E-mail: interfaithnetwork@juno.com
Subject areas: Environmental prevention strategies
(advertising, availability), underage drinking, violence.
Services or materials provided: Facilitates local and statewide
connections between congregations, and between
congregations and community; newsletters, training and
technical assistance.

Louisiana Alliance to Prevent Underage Drinking
5700 Florida Blvd., Suite 604
Baton Rouge, LA 70896
Phone: (504) 926-0807
Fax: (504) 926-3842
E-mail: lacoalition@eatel.net

Maryland Underage Drinking Prevention Coalition
2620 Riva Road
Annapolis, MD 21401
Phone: (410) 573-9792

RESOURCES

E-mail: info@mudpc.org
Web: http://www.mudpc.org
Subject areas: Statewide coalition - environmental prevention strategies, underage drinking.
Services or materials provided: Audio/Visual materials, legislative updates/action alerts, media advocacy, publications, training andtechnical assistance, youth leadership program.

Metropolitan Atlanta Council on Alcohol and Drugs
2045 Peachtree Road, N.E., Suite 605
Atlanta, GA 30309-1410
Phone: (404) 351-1800
Fax: (404) 351-2840
E-mail: www@macad.org
Web: http://www.macad.org
Subject areas: Policy, prevention, underage drinking.
Services or materials provided: Audio/Visual materials, legislative updates/action alerts, publications, training and technical assistance, youth leadership program.

Minnesota Prevention Research Center (MPRC)
2829 Verndale Avenue
Anoka, MN 55303
Outside Minnesota: (800) 782-1878
Within Minnesota: (612) 427-5310 or (800) 247-1303
Fax: (612) 427-7841 or (612) 427-1084
Web: http://www.miph.org/mprc/
Subject areas: College binge drinking, injury, underage drinking, violence.
Services or materials provided: Audio/Visual materials, fact sheets/data and statistics/research summaries, publications.

Minnesota Join Together Coalition to Reduce Underage Alcohol Use
2829 Verndale Avenue
Anoka, MN 55303
Phone: (612) 427-5310

Fax: (612) 427-7841

Missouri Association of Community Task Forces
1648B East Elm Street
Jefferson City, MO 65101
Phone: (573) 635-6669
Fax: (573) 635-5731

Narcotics Education League
Centro de Juventud
3209 Galindo Street
Oakland, CA 94610
Phone: (510) 532-5995
Fax: (510) 532-4451
Subject areas: Environmental prevention strategies
(advertising, availability), violence, youth advocacy.
Services or materials provided: Case studies, copies of
ordinances, newsletters/brochures, training and technical
assistance.

North Carolina Initiative to Reduce Underage Drinking
200 Park Offices, Suite 212
P.O. Box 13374
Research Triangle Park, NC 27709
Phone: (919) 990-9550
Fax: (919) 990-9518
E-mail: initiative@mindspring.com
Web: http://www.initiative.org

Oregon Coalition to Reduce Underage Drinking (OCRUD)
4520 SW Water, Suite 201
Portland, OR 97201
Phone: (503) 279-9209
Fax: (503) 827-3902
E-mail: ocrud@triax.com

Pennsylvanians Against Underage Drinking (PAUD)
Bureau of Alcohol Education, PLCB

Northwest Office Building, Room 602
Harrisburg, PA 17124-0001
Phone: (717) 705-0859
Fax: (717) 783-2612
E-mail: coalition@lb2rscs.lcb.state.pa.us
Web: http://www.lcb.state.pa.us/edu/community-paud.htm

Puerto Rico Coalition to Reduce Underage Drinking
(COPRAM)
P.O. Box 29132
65 Infantry Station
San Juan, PR 00929-1032
Phone: (787) 768-1985, ext 301 or 302
Fax: (787) 257-2725
E-mail: aspirapr@worldnet.att.net

Texans Standing Tall: A Statewide Coalition to Prevent
Underage Drinking
611 South Congress Avenue
Austin, TX 78704
Phone: (512) 445-4976
Fax: (512) 445-4979
E-mail: maddtx@eden.com

Washington, DC:
National Capital Coalition to Prevent Underage Drinking
1015 15th Street, NW, Suite 409
Washington, DC 20005
Phone: (202) 216-0671
Fax: (202) 371-0243
E-mail: nccpud@erols.com

Learning the Boulder Way/A Matter of Degree
The University of Colorado at Boulder
Baker Hall, Suite 119
Campus Box 31
Boulder, CO 80309
Phone: (303) 492-4278

Fax: (303) 492-3267
Web: http://patch.Colorado.EDU/sacs/ralphie/a/Alcohol.html

A Matter of Degree
The University of Delaware
Center for Counseling and Student Development
261 Perkins Student Center
Newark, DE 19716
Phone: (302) 831-8107
Fax: (302) 831-2148

Partnership for Alcohol Responsibility/A Matter of Degree
Florida State University
Thagard Student Health Center
Room 455, Department of Health Enhancement
Tallahassee, FL 32306-2140
Phone: (850) 644-6489
Fax: (850) 644-8958
E-mail: dskiles@admin.fsu.edu
Web: http://www.fsu.edu

A Matter of Degree
Georgia Institute of Technology
Office of the Dean of Students
283 9th Street
Atlanta, GA 30309
Phone: (404) 894-6367
Fax: (404) 894-9928
E-mail: gail.disabantino@vpss.gatech.edu

Stepping Up Program/A Matter of Degree
University of Iowa
100 Currier
Iowa City, IA 52242
Phone: (319) 335-1349
Fax: (319) 335-2979

RESOURCES

Campus Community Coalition for Change/A Matter of Degree
Louisiana State University and Agricultural and Mechanical
College
Student Health Center
Infirmary Road at West Chimes
Baton Rouge, LA 70803
Phone: (504) 388-5650
Fax: (504) 388-5655
E-mail: mathews@lsu.edu
Web: http://www.students.lsu.edu/shc

A Matter of Degree
University of Nebraska at Lincoln
12C University Health Center
Lincoln, NE 68588-0618
Phone: (402) 472-7440
E-mail: lmajor1@unl.edu

A Matter of Degree
Lehigh University
29 Trembley Drive
Bethlehem, PA 18015
Phone: (610) 758-3890
Fax: (610) 758-6132

A Matter of Degree
University of Vermont
41 S. Prospect Street
Burlington, VT 05405
Phone: (802) 656-3380
Fax: (802) 656-8191

Wisconsin Clearinghouse for Prevention Resources/A Matter
of Degree
University of Wisconsin
1552 University Avenue
Madison, WI 53705
Phone: (608) 262-9007

Fax: (608) 262-6346
Web: http://www.uhs.wisc.edu/rwj/rwjhome.htm

Alcohol Epidemiology Program
University of Minnesota
http://EPIHUB.EPI.UMN.EDU/alcohol/default.htp
Subject areas: Incidence and prevalence, program/policy
evaluation, motor vehicle crashes and injuries, underage
drinking.
Services or materials provided: Fact sheets/data and
statistics/research summaries, model ordinances, publications.

Alcohol Research Group
2000 Hearst Avenue, Suite 300
Berkeley, CA 94709-7175
Phone: (510) 642-5208
Fax: (510) 642-7175
E-mail: amitchell@arg.org
Web: http://www.arg.org
Subject areas: Attitudes, evaluation, history, incidence and
prevalence, international studies, legal aspects, policy,
prevention, special populations, treatment.
Services or materials provided: Library services (non-lending;
not online, but accessible by phone or e-mail), publications.

Alcohol-Related Injury and Violence (ARIV) Project
c/o Trauma Foundation
San Francisco General Hospital
Building One, Room 300
San Francisco, CA 94110
Phone: (415) 821-8209
Fax: (415) 282-2563
E-mail: ariv@traumafdn.org
Web: http://www.traumafdn.org/alcohol/ariv
Subject areas: Costs, economic development, environmental
prevention strategies, incidence and prevalence, injury,
underage drinking, violence.

RESOURCES

Services or materials provided: Fact sheets/data and statistics/research summaries, library services (online and available by phone or e-mail) advocates' stories.

American Public Health Association
1015 - 15th Street, NW
Washington, DC 20005-2605
Phone: (202) 789-5600
Fax: (202) 789-5661
Web: http://www.apha.org
Subject areas: Alcohol (Alcohol, Tobacco and Other Drugs section), injury and violence (Injury Control and Emergency Health Services section).
Services or materials provided: Newsletters, publications, training and technical assistance.

Bacchus and Gamma Peer Education Network
P.O. Box 100430
Denver, CO 80250-0430
Phone: (303) 871-0901
Fax: (303) 871-0907
E-mail: bacgam@aol.com
Web: http://www.bacchusgamma.org
Subject areas: College binge drinking, underage drinking.
Services or materials provided: Fact sheets, statistics, research summaries, publications, training, and technical assistance.

Bureau of Justice Statistics Clearinghouse
P.O. Box 179, Dept. BJS
Annapolis Junction, MD 20701-0179
Web: http://www.ojp.usdoj.gov/bjs
Subject areas: incidence and prevalence, injury, violence, crime.
Services or materials provided: Fact sheets, statistics, research summaries, publications.

Center of Alcohol Studies
Rutgers University

607 Allison Road
Smithers Hall - Busch Campus
Piscataway, NJ 08854-8001
Phone: (908) 445-4442
Fax: (908) 445-5944
Subject areas: Incidence and prevalence, injury, violence, women.
Services or materials provided: Fact sheets, statistics, research summaries, library services (not online, but accessible by phone or e-mail), publications.

Center for Science in the Public Interest (CSPI)
Alcohol Policies Project
1875 Connecticut Avenue N.W., #300
Washington, DC 20009
Phone: (202) 332-9110, ext. 385
Fax: (202) 265-4954
Web: http://www.cspinet.org/booze
Subject areas: College binge drinking, environmental prevention strategies (advertising, availability), underage drinking, warning labels.
Services or materials provided: Fact sheets, statistics, research summaries, legislative updates/action alerts, publications.

Center for Substance Abuse Prevention (CSAP) (a project of the Substance Abuse and Mental Health Services Administration - separate listing for SAMHSA is listed separately below)
5600 Fishers Lane, Rockwall II
Rockville, MD 20857
Phone: (301) 443-0364
E-mail: nnadal@samhsa.gov
Web: http://www.samhsa.gov/csap/index.htm
Subject areas: Crime, prevention, violence
Services or materials provided: Fact sheets/data and statistics/research summaries, publications, technical assistance and training.

RESOURCES

Order CSAP publications through the National Clearinghouse for Alcohol and Drug Information.

Center for Substance Abuse Research (CESAR)
University of Maryland, College Park
4321 Hartwick Road, Suite 501
College Park, MD 90740
Phone: (301) 403-8329
Fax: (301) 403-8342
E-mail: cesar@cesar.umd.edu
Web: http://www.cesar.umd.edu
Subject areas: Incidence and prevalence, prevention, treatment, underage drinking.
Services or materials provided: Fact sheets/data and statistics/research summaries, publications, technical assistance and training.

CLEW Associates
2198 Sixth Street, Suite 201
Berkeley, CA 94710
Phone: (510) 540-4717
Fax: (510) 540-4731
E-mail: CLEW_Associates@msn.com
Subject areas: Environmental prevention strategies (availability), local planning and mapping information system.
Services or materials provided: Architectural programming, software and services to assist with the mapping of AOD problems, training and technical assistance.

Community Anti-Drug Coalitions of America (CADCA)
900 North Pitt Street, Suite 300
Alexandria, VA 22314
Phone: (703) 706-0563
Fax: (703) 706-0565
Web: http://www.cadca.org
Subject areas: National network of community coalitions - underage drinking, violence.

Services or materials provided: Leadership development, legislative updates/action alerts, links to funding sources, training and technical assistance.

Core Institute
Center for Alcohol and Other Drug Studies
Student Health Programs
Southern Illinois University
Carbondale, IL 62901-6802
Phone: (618) 453-4366
E-mail: coreinst@siu.edu
http://www.siu.edu/departments/coreinst/public_html/index.html
Subject areas: College binge drinking, incidence and prevalence, underage drinking.
Services or materials provided: Fact sheets/data and statistics/research summaries, publications.

Facing Alcohol Concerns through Education (FACE)
105 West Fourth Street
Clare, MI 48617
Phone: (toll free) (888) 822-3223
Fax: (517) 386-3532
E-mail: FACE@glccomputers.com
Web: http://FACEproject.org
Subject areas: College binge drinking, environmental prevention strategies (advertising, availability, taxes, packaging), policy, underage drinking, violence.
Services or materials provided: Audio/Visual materials, media advocacy, publications, training and technical assistance.

The Higher Education Center for Alcohol and Other Drug Prevention
Education Development Center, Inc.
55 Chapel Street
Newton, MA 02158-1060
Phone: (800) 676-1730
Fax: (617) 928-1537

E-mail: HigherEdCtr@edc.org
Web: http://www.edc.org/hec/
Subject areas: College binge drinking, environmental prevention strategies, underage drinking.
Services or materials provided: Fact sheets/data and statistics/research summaries, publications, training and technical assistance.

Join Together
441 Stuart Street, 7th Floor
Boston, MA 02116
Phone: (617) 437-1500
Fax: (617) 437-9394
E-mail: info@jointogether.org
Web: http://www.jointogether.org
Subject areas: College binge drinking, links to funding sources, prevention, treatment, underage drinking.
Services or materials provided: Audio/visual materials, fact sheets/data and statistics/research summaries, publications.

The Marin Institute for the Prevention of Alcohol and Other Drug Problems
24 Belvedere Road
San Rafael, CA 94901
Phone: (415) 456-5692
Fax: (415) 456-0941
Web: http://www.marininstitute.org
Subject areas: Economic development, environmental prevention strategies (advertising, availability, alcohol industry practices), international issues, legal policy, underage drinking, violence.
Services or materials provided: Training center, technical assistance, community organizing, audio/visual materials, fact sheets/data and statistics/research summaries, leadership development, model ordinances, publications, resource center (online and available by phone).

Mothers Against Drunk Driving (MADD)
(To find your local chapter, write to the address below or visit MADD's Web site)
P.O. Box 541688
Dallas, TX 75354-1688
Web: http://www.madd.org
Subject areas: Environmental prevention strategies, motor vehicle crashes and injuries, underage drinking.
Services or materials provided: Audio/Visual materials, fact sheets/data and statistics/research summaries, legislative updates/action alerts, publications, youth leadership program.

National Council on Alcoholism and Drug Dependence, Inc. (NCADD)
12 West 21st Street
New York, NY 10010
Phone: (212) 206-6770
Fax: (212) 645-1690
Web: http://www.ncadd.org
Subject areas: National network of affiliates - college binge drinking, environmental prevention strategies (advertising, taxes), motor vehicle crashes and injuries, public education, treatment, underage drinking.
Services or materials provided: Legislative updates/action alerts, publications, national referral network.

National Highway Traffic Safety Administration (NHTSA)
400 Seventh Street, SW
Washington, DC 20590
Phone from outside Washington, DC: (800) 424-9393
Phone from within Washington, DC: (202) 366-0123
Web: http://www.nhtsa.dot.gov
Subject areas: Prevention, motor vehicle crashes and injuries.
Services or materials provided: Fact sheets/data and statistics/research summaries, publications.

RESOURCES

National Clearinghouse for Alcohol and Drug Information
(NCADI)
P.O. Box 2345
Rockville, MD 20847-2345
Fax: 301-468-6433
E-mail: info@health.org
Web: http://www.health.org (to access Prevline, which is
NCADI's online service)
Subject areas: Prevention, treatment, underage drinking.
Services or materials provided: Audio/Visual materials, fact
sheets/data and statistics/research summaries, links to funding
sources, publications.

National Criminal Justice Reference Service
Justice Information Center
P.O. Box 6000
Rockville, MD 20849-6000
Phone: (800) 851-3420 or (301) 519-5500
E-mail: askncjrs@ncjrs.org
Web: http://www.ncjrs.org/homepage.htm
Subject areas: Crime, incidence and prevalence, victim
services, underage drinking.
Services or materials provided: Fact sheets/data and
statistics/research summaries, links to funding sources,
publications.

National Institute on Alcohol Abuse and Alcoholism (NIAAA)
6000 Executive Boulevard, Willco Building
Bethesda, Maryland 20892-7003
Web: http://www.niaaa.nih.gov
Subject areas: Costs, incidence and prevalence, injury,
violence, prevention, treatment, underage drinking.
Services or materials provided: Database of publications
(ETOH), fact sheets/data and statistics/research summaries,
funding, publications.

National Institute on Drug Abuse (NIDA)
Division of Epidemiology and Prevention Research

5600 Fishers Lane
Rockville, MD 20857
E-mail: Information@lists.nida.nih.gov
Web: http://www.nida.nih.gov/NIDAHome.html
Subject areas: Costs, incidence and prevalence, prevention, treatment, underage drinking.
Services or materials provided: Fact sheets/data and statistics/research summaries, funding, publications.

Office of Juvenile Justice and Delinquency Prevention (OJJDP)
810 Seventh Street, NW
Washington, DC 20531
Phone: (202) 307-5911
E-mail: AskJJ@ojp.usdoj.gov
Web: http://www.ncjrs.org/ojjhome.htm
Subject areas: Crime, underage drinking.
Services or materials provided: Funding, publications, training and technical assistance.

Prevention Research Center
2150 Shattuck Avenue, Suite 900
Berkeley CA 94704
Phone: (510) 486-1111
Fax: (510) 644-0594
E-mail: center@prev.org
Subject areas: Beliefs, attitudes and values, college binge drinking, environmental prevention strategies (advertising, availability, responsible beverage service), Latino comm-unities, motor vehicle crashes and injuries, public policy, underage drinking, violence in the workplace.
Services or materials provided: Publications.

Regional Alcohol and Drug Awareness Resource (RADAR)
Network c/o Center for Substance Abuse
Prevention (CSAP)
5600 Fishers Lane, Rockwall II
Rockville, MD 20857

RESOURCES

Web: http://www.ctclearinghouse.org/lncadi.htm
Further information and a list of RADAR Network Centers in every state are available through the National Clearinghouse for Alcohol and Drug Information.
Subject areas: National network of information centers - dissemination, prevention.
Services or materials provided: Fact sheets/data and statistics/research summaries, links to funding sources, publications, training and technical assistance.

Substance Abuse and Mental Health Services Administration (SAMHSA)
Phone: (301) 443-8956
E-mail: info@samhsa.gov
Web: http://www.samhsa.gov
Subject areas: Incidence and prevalence, prevention, treatment, underage drinking.
Services or materials provided: Fact sheets/data and statistics/research summaries, funding, publications.

Alcohol Policy Network
Ontario Public Health Association
468 Queen Street East, Suite 202
Toronto, Ontario CANADA
M5A 1T7
Phone: (416) 367-3313, ext. 27 or 23, or (800) 267-6817
Fax: (416) 367-2844
E-mail: apn@web.net
Web: http://sano.arf.org/apn/apolnet.htm
Subject areas: Policy, prevention.
Services or materials provided: Media advocacy, publications, training and technical assistance.

Alcohol Concern
32-36 Loman Street
London SE1 0EE
United Kingdom
Phone: (+44) 0171-928-7377

Fax: (+44) 0171-928-4644
E-mail: alccon@popmail.dircon.co.uk
Web: http://www.alcoholconcern.org.uk/achome.htm
Subject areas: Policy, prevention, motor vehicle crashes and injuries, treatment, workplace.
Services or materials provided: Fact sheets/data and statistics/research summaries, library, media advocacy, publications, training and technical assistance.

Alcohol Advisory Council of New Zealand (ALAC)
National and Central Regional Office
Level 3, National Insurance House
119-123 Featherston Street
PO Box 5023
Wellington, New Zealand
Phone: 04-472-0997
Fax: 04-473-0890
E-mail: central@alac.org.nz
Web: http://www.alcohol.org.nz
Subject areas: Evaluation research, policy.
Services or materials provided: Fact sheets/data and statistics/research summaries, library, publications.

Centre for Addiction and Mental Health
Public Affairs
33 Russell Street
Toronto, Ontario
Canada M5S 2S1
Phone: (416) 595-6878
Fax: (416) 595-6881
Web: http://www.camh.net
Subject areas: Cultural competency, crime, treatment, underage drinking.
Services or materials provided: Fact sheets/data and statistics/research summaries, publications.

Eurocare
Web: http://www.eurocare.org

RESOURCES

Eurocare Secretariat
1 The Quay
St. Ives, Cambridgeshire
PE17 4AR
United Kingdom
E-mail: eurocare@bbs.eurocare.org
-or-
Eurocare EU Liaison Office
Rue des Confédérés 96-98
B-1000 Brussels, Belgium
E-mail: eurocare@club.innet.be
Subject areas: Cultural competency, incidence and prevalence, international issues, policy, prevention, treatment.
Services or materials provided: Fact sheets/data and statistics/research summaries, publications, training and technical assistance.

Institute of Alcohol Studies
12 Caxton Street
London SW1H OQS
United Kingdom
Phone: (+44) 171-222-4001
Fax: (+44) 171-799-2510
E-mail: info@ias.org.uk
Web: http://www.ias.org.uk
Subject areas: Prevention, workplace.
Services or materials provided: Fact sheets/data and statistics/research summaries, library, publications, training and technical assistance.

International Council on Alcohol and Addictions (ICAA)
Conseil International sur les Problèmes de l Alcoolisme et des Toxicomanies (CIPAT)
E-mail: icaa@pingnet.ch
Web: http://www.icaa.ch
Subject areas: Cultural competence, international issues, policy, prevention, underage drinking.

Services or materials provided: Audio/Visual materials, fact sheets/data and statistics/research summaries, legislative updates/action alerts, library (not online, but accessible by e-mail), publications.

Web Sites

AA World Services
  http://www.alcoholics-anonymous.org/
Addiction Research Foundation
  http://www.arf.org/
Addiction Technology Transfer Centers
  http://views.vcu.edu/nattc/
American Medical Association
  http://www.ama_assn.org/special/aos/resource.htm
American Psychiatric Association
  http://www.psych.org/
American Psychological Association
  http://www.apa.org/
American Society of Addiction Medicine
  http://www.asam.org
APA Newsletter
  http://www.kumc.edu/addictions_newsletter/
Center for Mental Health Services
  http://www.samhsa.gov/cmhs/cmhs.htm
Center for Substance Abuse Prevention
  http://www.samhsa.gov/csap/index.htm
Center for Substance Abuse Research
  http://www.bsos.umd.edu/cesar/cesar.html
Center for Substance Abuse Treatment
  http://www.samhsa.gov/csat/csat.htm
CSAT by Fax
  http://www.health.org/daatpp.htm
Ctr for Educ & Drug Research

RESOURCES

http://www.eval.srv.cis.pitt.edu/~mmv/cedar.html
Department of Health and Human Services
    http://www.os.dhhs.gov:80/
Drug Abuse Warning Network
    http://www.health.org/pubs/dawn/index.htm
Drug Enforcement Administration
    http://www.usdoj.gov/dea/index.htm
Education Center for Alcohol and Drug Prevention
    http://www.edc.org/hec/
Food and Drug Administration
    http://www.fda.gov/fdahomepage.html
Health Care Financing Administration
    http://www.hcfa.gov/
Healthfinder
    http://www.healthfinder.gov/
HHS Partner Gateway
    http://www.os.dhhs.gov:80/partner/
ICRC on Alcohol and Other Drug Abuse
    http://www.realsolutions.org/icrc.htm
Internet Alcohol Recovery Center
    http://www.med.upenn.edu/recovery
Join Together Online
    http://www.jointogether.org/jtc
Justice Information Center
    http://www.ncjrs.org/
Knowledge Exchange Network
    http://www.mentalhealth.org/
Library of Congress
    http://lcweb.loc.gov/homepage/lchp.html
Managed Behavioral Care
    http://www.samhsa.gov/mc/mcmtgs.htm
Monitoring the Future
    http://www.isr.umich.edu/src/mtf/index.html
NAADA Counselors
    http://www.naadac.org/index.html
Narcotics Anonymous
    http://www.wsoinc.com/basic.htm

NASADAD
> http://www.nasadad.org/default.htm

National Association of Social Workers (NASW)
> http://www.naswdc.org

National Families in Action (NFIA)
> http://www.emory.edu/NFIA/

National Inhalant Prevention Coalition
> http://www.inhalants.org/

National Institute on Drug Abuse
> http://www.nida.nih.gov/

National Treatment Consortium
> http://www.ntc_usa.org/index.html

National Evaluation Data and Technical Center
> http://www.calib.com/nedtac/index.htm

National Technical Center for Substance Abuse
> http://www.tiac.net/users/ntc/

NCADI Online Catalog
> http://www.health.org/pubs/catalog/

NCASA
> http://www.casacolumbia.org/home.htm

NIAAA
> http://www.niaaa.nih.gov/

ONDCP Clearinghouse
> http://www.ncjrs.org/drgshome.htm

ONDCP Statistics Briefing Room
> http://www.whitehouse.gov/fsbr/ssbr.html

Partnership for a Drug-Free America
> http://www.drugfreeamerica.org/

Prevline
> http://www.health.org/

Research Institute on Addictions
> http://www.ria.org/

Research Society on Alcoholism (RSA)
> http://www.sci.sdsu.edu/RSA/

SAMHSA Home Page
> http://www.samhsa.gov/

The Web of Addictions
> http://www.well.com/user/woa/

Appendix C

Sample Policies

Sample Policy #1

The Company recognizes that when a behavioral/medical problem related to drug dependency is diagnosed and properly treated at an early stage, the afflicted employee is more likely to recover with less damage to personal health and family well-being.

It is the purpose of this policy, and of the control measures for implementing it, to provide a basis for in-plant action concerning behavioral/medical problems in a manner that will:

Encourage the earliest possible diagnosis, treatment, and other appropriate help in all situations where employee health and work performance have been affected.

Assure consistency in neither providing more help nor condoning more delay in seeking help than would be the general in-plant practice in comparable situations involving non-stigmatized illnesses, and

Coordinate in-plant and community-helping services so that, insofar as is possible, employees seeking help can benefit from the best combination of helping and therapeutic services appropriate to various behavioral/medical conditions available in the community.

The decision to seek diagnosis and accept treatment for any illness is the responsibility of the individual. It will be the Company's policy that the same individual responsibility applies to behavioral/medical problems, since the Company views these as treatable illnesses insofar as personnel administrative practices are concerned.

Further, it will be the responsibility of the employee to comply with the referrals for diagnosis and to cooperate with the prescribed therapy.

Unsatisfactory job performance will be handled under the rules pursuant to labor agreements covering union-affiliated employees and under rules of conduct covering other groups.

Sample Policy #2

PURPOSE

The Company recognizes that the state of an employee's health affects his job performance, the kind of work he can perform, and may affect his opportunities for continued employment. The Company also recognizes that drug abuse ranks as one of the major health problems

338

in the world. It is the intent of this policy to provide employees with the company's viewpoint on drug abuse disorders, to encourage an enlightened attitude toward these disorders, and to provide guidelines for consistent handling throughout the Company regarding drug abuse situations.

POLICY

The Company gives the same consideration to employees with drug dependencies as it does to employees having other diseases. The Company is concerned only with those situations where use of drugs seriously interferes with an employee's health and job performance, adversely affects the performance of other employees, or is considered so serious as to be detrimental to the Company's business. There is no intent to intrude upon the private lives of employees.

Early recognition and treatment of drug dependency problems is important for successful rehabilitation, economic return to the Company, and reduced personal, family, and social disruption. The Company supports sound treatment efforts, and an employee's job will not be jeopardized for conscientiously seeking assistance. Constructive disciplinary measures may be utilized to provide motivation to seek assistance. Normal Company benefits, such as sick leave and the group medical plan, are available to give help in the rehabilitation process.

LEGAL DRUGS

The use of any legally obtained drug, to the point where such use adversely affects the employee's performance, is prohibited. This prohibition covers arriving on Company premises under the effects of any drug which adversely affects the employee's job performance, including the use of prescribed drugs under medical direction. Where physician-directed use of drugs adversely affects job performance, it is in the best general interest of the employee, co-workers, and the Company that sick leave be utilized.

SAMPLE POLICIES

ILLEGAL DRUGS

Illegal drugs, for the purpose of this policy, include (a) drugs which are not legally obtainable, and (b) drugs which are legally obtainable but have been obtained illegally.

The sale, purchase, transfer, use, or possession of illegal drugs, as defined above, by employees on Company premises or while on Company business is prohibited. Arriving on Company premises under the influence of any drug to the extent that job performance is adversely affected is prohibited. This prohibition applies to any and all forms of narcotics, depressants, stimulants, or hallucinogens whose sale, purchase, transfer, use or possession is prohibited or restricted by law.

Any employee engaging in the sale of such illegal drugs on Company premises or while on Company business will be suspended immediately pending investigation.

Any employee found purchasing, transferring, possessing, or using illegal drugs on Company premises or while on Company business is subject to disciplinary action, up to and including termination. It is the intent of the Company, however, to encourage and assist such employees in treatment or rehabilitation whenever appropriate.

SCOPE

This policy is to be implemented in world-wide operations. Where legal or extralegal obligations or common business practices in international operations conflict with the scope of this policy, the principles and intent of the policy should be followed as closely as possible.

Sample Policy #3

I. POLICY

The Company is committed at all of its facilities to achieving a safe work environment free from drug abuse through education, intervention and, if appropriate, disciplinary measures. The Company prohibits the use, possession, or sale of illicit drugs in the workplace or when conducting Company business, and requires its employees to be free from illicit drugs in order to assure the safety of its operations, employees, and communities in which it operates, and to protect the Company's assets.

II. BUSINESS UNIT IMPLEMENTATION

A. Education:

Supervisors and other management personnel are to be trained in:

- detecting the signs and behavior of persons who are under the influence of illicit drugs;

- confidential assistance available to them, and

- consequences of continued abuse.

B. Intervention:

The Company recognizes the benefits of rehabilitation of employees who become victims of drug abuse and is supportive of rehabilitation efforts.

Cooperation by the employee is expected during rehabilitation. Following a medical release to return to work, a condition of

341

reinstatement at the workplace is agreement to periodic drug testing. Rehabilitated employees must remain free of illicit drugs as a condition of continuing employment.

It is the responsibility of each employee to remain free of illicit drugs when at work, and to seek assistance for addictive illnesses.

All medical information will be protected as confidential unless otherwise required by law, overriding public health and safety concerns, or with a signed authorization by the employee.

If evidence of the use of illicit drugs is discovered among applicants for employment, either through urine testing or other methods, the employment process shall be suspended.

Current employees whose work assignments are at high risk for safety or production reasons will be administered periodic urine tests.

Employees suspected for cause to be under the influence of drugs shall be provided transportation to a medical facility, where the employee will undergo a health evaluation and appropriate biological testing, and to the employee's home.

Employees who distribute, sell, or transfer illegal drugs or controlled substances will be terminated without offer of rehabilitation.

Illegal drugs or controlled substances found on Company property will be turned over and cooperation given to the appropriate law enforcement agency.

C. Discipline:

Employees are prohibited and will be subject to discipline up to and including discharge for the use, sale, attempt to sell, possession, or distribution of illegal drugs or controlled substances, and the paraphernalia associated with such, on Company premises including parking lots or during Company business.

Entry onto Company property constitutes consent to and recognition of the right of the Company and its authorized agents to search persons, vehicles, lockers and other property while individuals are entering, on, or leaving Company property.

Employees who engage in the sale, attempted sale, distribution, or transfer of illegal or controlled drugs on or off Company property will be discharged:

- If on Company property, discharge will be immediate.

- If off Company property and/or not on Company business, the employee will be placed on "leave without pay" pending the outcome of criminal proceedings. Upon resolution of the criminal proceedings and following a full review of all evidence, a determination will be made as to the employee's status.

An employee who is suspected with cause to be under the influence of drugs, and refuses to take a health evaluation and/or biological testing is subject to discipline up to and including discharge.

Sample Policy #4

I. PURPOSE

The Company desires to and actually engages in programs designed to maintain a safe, healthy, lawful, and productive working environment for all employees. Illegal use of drugs and controlled substances increases the potential for accidents, absenteeism, tardiness, sloppy and indifferent performance, inefficiency, poor employee morale, and damage to the Company's reputation. Therefore, in the interest of the health and welfare of all employees, illegal use of drugs and controlled substances will not be tolerated on any Company site or in any work situation involving the Company and its employees, customers, or suppliers.

SAMPLE POLICIES

II. SCOPE

This policy applies to all employees of the Company. Whenever the term "Company" is used herein, it shall be deemed to include domestic and foreign subsidiaries and affiliated firms in which the Company has a direct or indirect controlling interest. No employee shall undertake any conduct indirectly or directly proscribed by this policy.

III. DEFINITIONS

Legal Drug

A "legal drug" is a prescribed drug or over-the-counter drug which has been legally obtained and is being used for the purpose for which it was prescribed or manufactured.

Illegal Drug

An "illegal drug" or "controlled substance" is any drug or controlled substance which (1) is not legally obtainable, or (2) is legally obtainable but was not legally obtained. Illegal drugs include but are not limited to: marijuana, hashish, cocaine, PCP, LSD, heroin, Dilaudid, Quaalude, and methamphetamine.

IV. POLICY

On-the-job use, possession, or distribution of illegal drugs or controlled substances is prohibited. Consumption, use, manufacture, possession, transfer, sale, or distribution of any illegal drug or controlled substance on Company premises or property while performing Company business or during work breaks (including lunch and/or dinner breaks) is prohibited. In addition, the presence of any detectable amount of an illegal drug or controlled substance in any employee while conducting Company business or on Company premises is prohibited. Violation of this policy is cause for disciplinary action up to and including termination.

All persons being considered for employment with the Company shall submit to a drug test as part of the pre-employment medical evaluation. Acceptability for employment is conditional upon passing the drug test.

V. PROCEDURE

Searches

The Company may conduct searches without prior notice on Company premises for drugs, drug paraphernalia, and controlled substances, including searches of employee personal property such as vehicles, packages, briefcases, purses, lunch boxes, and pockets, and searches of Company property such as desks, file cabinets, and lockers. Such searches may be conducted with the assistance of specially trained dogs.

Each employee is expected to cooperate and to consent to such a search as a condition of continued employment with the Company. Refusal to consent is cause for termination.

Testing for Illegal Drugs and Controlled Substances

The Company and/or its customers, without prior notice, may require employees to submit to blood and/or urine tests to determine possible use of an illegal drug or controlled substance. Each employee is expected to cooperate and consent as a condition of continued employment. Refusal is cause for termination.

VI. RESPONSIBILITY

Each Division President, Corporate Department Head, or other Company unit manager is responsible for assuring compliance with this policy by all employees within his or her organization, and may at his or her discretion institute a control program for compliance.

VII. IMPLEMENTATION

Drug testing programs will be developed by each division based upon perceived operating or customer requirements. Plans to implement drug testing programs will be submitted to the Company's Corporate Office of General Counsel and the Corporate Office of Employee Relations for review prior to implementation. It will also be the responsibility of each division to implement pre-employment drug testing for all job applicants.

VIII. EMPLOYEE ASSISTANCE

Company assistance will be provided to any employee who voluntarily asks the Company for help in resolving a drug use problem. For assistance to be given by the Company, the employee's request must have been made prior to any detection of the employee's drug use.

An after-the-fact request for assistance from an employee discovered to be in violation of this policy will not be a consideration when determining disciplinary action.

Sample Policy #5

I. STATEMENT

A. General

1. It is the policy of the Company to achieve and maintain a safe working environment free from the influence of drug abuse through education, rehabilitation and, where appropriate, disciplinary measures in order to assure the safety and protection of its employees, non-employees, operations, assets and the localities in which it functions. The Company prohibits the possession, use, distribution or sale of illicit drugs in the workplace or when conducting company business, and requires employees and non-employees to be free from illicit drugs upon entering Company owned, leased, or operated premises.

B. Definitions

1. The term "illicit drugs" is meant to include any and all illegal drugs, including so-called look-alike and designer drugs; legally obtained drugs which are used in a manner other than that prescribed by a physician; and any substance which can affect a person's perceptions or motor functions. Some examples of illicit drugs are cannabis (marijuana) substances, cocaine, heroin, phencyclidine, and alcohol.

2. The term "possession" is meant to also include the presence in the body system of any detectable amount of illicit drug.

3. The term "biological testing" is meant to include the collection and analysis of urine, blood, saliva, hair, tissue, and other specimens of the human body.

4. The term "for cause" is meant to include accidents, near accidents, erratic conduct suggestive of drug use, and similar performance behaviors.

C. Exception

1. On-the-job possession and use of a legally obtained prescription medicine shall be permitted provided that:

- the person to whom the medicine is prescribed informs the supervisor prior to possessing or using the medicine on the job.

- the medicine is in the original vial/container in which it was dispensed and that the vial/container bears the original label

347

reflecting the employee's name, physician's name, name of medicine, dosage, dispensary, and date dispensed.

- the date dispensed is within the past twelve months.

2. The Company at all times reserves the right to judge the effect that a prescription medicine may have upon work performance and to restrict the using employee's work activity or presence at the worksite accordingly.

II. IMPLEMENTATION

A. Education

1. Supervisors and other management personnel are to be trained in:

- detecting the signs and behavior of persons who may be under the influence of illicit drugs;

- counseling these employees to seek professional evaluation and assistance; and

- recognizing these activities as a direct job responsibility.

2. Employees are to be informed of:

- signs of drug abuse;

- confidential employee assistance programs available to them, including medical rehabilitation; and

- health and disciplinary consequences of abuse.

B. Intervention

1. The Company recognizes the benefits of medical rehabilitation of employees who become victims of drug abuse, and is highly supportive of rehabilitation efforts. Rehabilitation is limited to a single

effort through a professionally recognized treatment program, covered under the employee's Sick Pay Plan.

2. An employee will be placed on leave without pay during the rehabilitation period.

3. Cooperation by the employee is expected during rehabilitation. Following a medical release to return to work, a condition of reinstatement at the workplace is agreement to periodic drug testing. Rehabilitated employees must remain free of illicit drugs as a condition of continued employment.

4. It is the responsibility of each employee to remain free of illicit drugs when at work, and to seek rehabilitative assistance.

5. The Company may perform biological testing of its employees for the presence of illicit drugs under the following circumstances:

- For cause;

- Medical surveillance following rehabilitation;

- Periodic screening to assure safe operations; and/or

- Assure protection of Company assets and reputation.

6. All employee information relating to rehabilitation and biological testing will be protected by the Company as confidential unless otherwise required by law, overriding public health and safety concerns, or authorized in writing by the employee.

7. All applicants for employment will be subject to urine testing. If evidence of the use of illicit drugs by an applicant is discovered, either through urine testing or other means, the employment process shall be suspended. If the applicant refuses to take a urine test, the employment process will be suspended.

8. When biological testing is deemed appropriate in "for cause" situations, employees shall be provided transportation to a medical facility where the employee will undergo a health evaluation. Biological testing will be conducted as part of the health evaluation.

After the employee has been evaluated, he or she will be transported home or to a treatment facility.

9. Illicit drugs found on Company property may be turned over and cooperation given to the appropriate law enforcement agency.

10. If an employee is the subject of investigation by the Company or by a law enforcement agency, the employee may be suspended without pay pending completion of the investigation.

C. Discipline

1. Any employee who engages in the sale, attempted sale, distribution, or transfer of illicit drugs on Company property or on Company business will be discharged.

2. Any employee who refuses to undergo a health evaluation and/or biological testing is subject to discipline up to and including discharge.

3. An employee who refuses to enter rehabilitation after having been found to be in violation of this policy shall be subject to termination.

Sample Policy #6

The Company has a vital interest in maintaining safe, healthful and efficient working conditions for its employees. Being under the influence of a drug on the job may pose serious safety and health risks not only to the user but to all those who work with the user. The possession, use or sale of an illegal drug in the workplace may also pose unacceptable risks for safe, healthful, and efficient operations.

The Company recognizes that its own health and future are dependent upon the physical and psychological health of its employees. Accordingly, it is the right, obligation and intent of the Company to maintain a safe, healthful and efficient working environment for all of its employees and to protect Company property, equipment, and operations.

DEFINITIONS

For the purposes of this policy,

"Under the influence" means that the employee is affected by a drug in any detectable manner. The symptoms of influence are not confined to those consistent with misbehavior, nor to obvious impairment of physical or mental ability, such as slurred speech or difficulty in maintaining balance. A determination of influence can be established by a professional opinion, a scientifically valid test, and in some cases by the opinion of a layperson.

"Legal drug" includes prescribed drugs and over-the-counter drugs which have been legally obtained and are being used for the purpose for which they were prescribed or manufactured.

"Illegal drug" means any drug which is not legally obtainable or which is legally obtainable but has not been legally obtained. The term includes prescribed drugs not legally obtained and prescribed drugs not being used for prescribed purposes. It also includes cannabis substances such as marijuana and hashish.

PRE-EMPLOYMENT SCREENING

The Company will maintain pre-employment screening practices designed to prevent hiring individuals who use illegal drugs or individuals whose use of illegal drugs indicates a potential for impaired or unsafe job performance.

SAMPLE POLICIES

ON-THE-JOB USE, POSSESSION, OR SALE OF DRUGS

Except as provided below, the use or being under the influence of any legally obtained drug by any employee while performing Company business or while in a Company facility is prohibited to the extent that such use or influence may affect the safety of co-workers or members of the public, the employee's job performance, or the safe or efficient operation of the Company facility. An employee may continue to work, even though under the influence of a legal drug, if Management has determined, after consulting with the Medical Department and Employee Relations, that the employee does not pose a threat to his or her own safety or the safety of co-workers and that the employee's job performance is not significantly affected by the legal drug. Otherwise, the employee may be required to take leave of absence or comply with other appropriate action determined by Management.

The use, sale, purchase, transfer, or possession of an illegal drug by any employee while in a Company facility or while performing Company business is prohibited. The presence in any detectable manner of any illegal drug in an employee while performing Company business or while in a Company facility is prohibited.

DISCIPLINARY ACTION

Violation of this policy can result in disciplinary action, up to and including termination, even for a first offense.

FACILITY WORK RULES

Nothing in this policy precludes Management of any particular Company facility from establishing work rules which apply to that facility. Except as provided below, such work rules cannot be less stringent than this policy. Where any law imposes restrictions on implementation of this policy, Management will modify the policy in accord with such restrictions.

SEARCHES

The Company may conduct unannounced searches for illegal drugs in Company facilities. Employees are expected to cooperate.

Searches of employees and their personal property may be conducted when there is reasonable suspicion to believe that the employee or employees are in violation of this policy.

Searches of employees and their personal property may be conducted when circumstances or workplace conditions justify them.

An employee's consent to a search is required as a condition of employment and the employee's refusal to consent may result in disciplinary action, including termination, even for a first refusal.

Searches of Company facilities and property can be conducted at any time and do not have to be based on reasonable suspicion.

DRUG TESTING

The Company may require a urine test, blood test, or other test of those persons suspected of using or being under the influence of a drug or where circumstances or workplace conditions justify it. An employee's consent to submit to such a test is required as a condition of employment and the employee's refusal to consent may result in disciplinary action, including termination, for a first refusal or any subsequent refusal.

CONTRACT PERSONNEL

The provisions of this policy relating to (1) On-the-Job Use, Possession or Sale of Drugs and (2) Searches are applicable to contract personnel. Violation of these provisions or refusal to cooperate with implementation of this policy can result in barring of contract personnel from Company facilities or participating in Company operations.

REQUIREMENT TO REPORT USE OF LEGAL DRUGS

For certain job positions, an employee's use of a legal drug can pose a significant risk to the safety of the employee or others. Employees who believe or have been informed that the use of a legal drug may present a safety risk are to report such drug use to the Medical Department to determine job related consequences. Supervisors who are aware of such a situation are to instruct the employee to inform the Medical Department.

EMPLOYEE ASSISTANCE PROGRAM (EAP)

The Company maintains an Employee Assistance Program which provides help to employees who suffer from drug abuse and other problems. However, it is the responsibility of each employee to seek assistance from the EAP before a drug problem leads to disciplinary action. Once a violation of this policy occurs, any subsequent use of the EAP on a voluntary basis will not necessarily lessen disciplinary action and may, in fact, have no bearing on the determination of appropriate disciplinary action.

The employee's decision to seek EAP help prior to detection of a drug problem will not be used as the basis for disciplinary action and will not be used against the employee in any disciplinary proceeding. On the other hand, using the EAP will not be a defense to the imposition of disciplinary action where facts proving a violation of this policy are obtained outside the EAP.

Sample Policy #7

POLICY STATEMENT

The Company has a responsibility to its employees and stockholders to maintain a safe and productive work environment free from the influences of drug abuse.

The possession, use, sale, attempted sale or distribution of marijuana, illegal drugs, or the paraphernalia associated with such activities on Company-owned or Company-operated premises is prohibited.

Additionally, the Company requires that employees in the workplace be free of the effects of drug use and accordingly prohibits employees, while under the influence of drugs, from entering its owned or operated premises.

Company premises include Company-provided transportation, work areas, living accommodations, recreation areas, and all other owned, leased, or operated facilities.

IMPLEMENTATION

Entry onto Company premises constitutes acceptance of this policy and consent to the right of the Company and its authorized agents to search persons, automobiles, lockers, desks, living quarters, and other individual property while entering, on, or leaving Company premises. Such searches may include, where appropriate, biological testing.

The possession, use, sale, or attempted sale or distribution of marijuana or illegal drugs on Company premises will subject the employee to disciplinary action up to and including discharge.

Employees on Company premises while under the influence or demonstrating the symptoms of drug use or whose job performance or work habits are affected by drug use will be required as a condition of continued employment to fully cooperate with the Company in securing rehabilitation treatment. Failure to fully cooperate or repetition will result in discipline up to and including discharge.

Sample Policy #8

STATEMENT

The purpose of this policy is to help, in a positive manner, employees from becoming ineffective, both on or off the job, due to the use of drugs or alcohol. The Company recognizes its obligation to protect the health and safety of its employees, to provide safe and effective operations for the public, and to protect the assets and image of the company for its stockholders. Therefore, the Company is committed to achieving a safe work environment free of alcohol and drug abuse through education, intervention and, if appropriate, disciplinary measures. Accordingly, the following policy will be enforced:

1. The use, sale, attempt to sell, possession, or distribution of illegal drugs, alcohol or controlled substances (unless prescribed by a licensed physician for medical reasons), and the paraphernalia associated with such on Company premises, including parking areas, are prohibited. Employees under the influence of alcohol, non-medical controlled substances or illegal drugs are prohibited from Company property. Employees under the influence of illegal drugs, alcohol, or controlled substances while at work will be subject to disciplinary action, including discharge. Employees selling, attempting to sell, transferring or distributing illegal drugs or controlled substances will be discharged.

2. Entry onto Company property constitutes consent to and recognition of the right of the Company and its authorized agents to search persons, automobiles, lockers and other property of individuals while entering, on, or leaving Company property.

3. If an employee is the victim of alcohol or drug usage, the Company will cooperate with the employee in attempted rehabilitation, provided the employee fully cooperates with such rehabilitative efforts and provided rehabilitative efforts were not attempted in the past. The Company will not attempt rehabilitation of employees who distribute, sell or transfer illegal drugs or controlled substances. The medical information will be treated as confidential in accordance with existing Company policy.

ADMINISTRATION

All employees should take seriously the dangers inherent in the consumption of alcohol and drugs not only from the standpoint of their personal health but also the safety and potential property damage to themselves, others and the effects on their families. The consistent and proper administration of the Company's policy is necessary to ensure its effectiveness and enforceability before any reviewing authorities. Set forth below are administrative guidelines to be utilized by all management personnel with regard to the alcohol and drug abuse policy of the Company.

SALE, ATTEMPTED SALE, DISTRIBUTION OR TRANSFER OF ILLEGAL OR CONTROLLED DRUGS

The sale, attempted sale, distribution or transfer of illegal or controlled drugs are serious offenses and violations of the state and federal laws. Furthermore, an employee who engages in such activities represents a potential danger in that he or she may involve other employees in the illegal use of drugs. Accordingly, any employee will be dismissed who engages in the sale, attempted sale, distribution or transfer of illegal or controlled drugs on Company premises or while off Company premises whether or not on Company business. It is not the policy of

357

the Company to attempt rehabilitation of employees who sell, attempt to sell, distribute or transfer illegal or controlled drugs. If an employee is suspected of engaging in the sale, attempted sale, transfer or distribution of illegal or controlled drugs, the details should be reviewed with appropriate line management and the Human Resources Manager. If it appears that the suspicions reported have substance, the situation must be reviewed with the Law Department and Corporate Security Department. Cooperation should be given to appropriate law enforcement officers in connection with investigations they may undertake. In those cases where our first knowledge of any illegal activity by the employee is as a result of an arrest, the matter should be referred to the appropriate line management and the Human Resources Manager, who must review the situation with the Law Department and the Corporate Security Department before taking any action. After all Company investigations have been completed and all available facts have been reviewed, the employee will be dismissed if the evidence substantiates that the employee has been involved in the distribution, sale, attempted sale, or transfer of illegal or controlled drugs. If the distribution, sale, attempted sale or transfer occurred on Company property or on Company business, the employee's dismissal should not be delayed awaiting any court determination in the matter. If the distribution, sale, attempted sale or transfer of illegal or controlled drugs occurred while off Company property and not on Company property and not on Company business, the employee should be placed on leave without pay pending the resolution of criminal proceedings. Upon resolution of the criminal proceedings a determination will be made as to the employee's status, following a full review of all evidence with the Law Department.

USE OR POSSESSION OF DRUGS OR ALCOHOL IN THE WORKPLACE OR REPORTING TO WORK UNDER THE INFLUENCE

Any employee who is found drinking or in possession of alcoholic beverages on Company premises, including Company parking lots, or in Company operated vehicles, or coming or returning to work in an apparent intoxicated condition (e.g., stumbling, slurred speech, unusual behavior, bloodshot pupils, alcohol smell on breath, etc.) is subject to disciplinary action up to and including dismissal. Such an employee must be removed from the job at once and required to undergo health evaluations and/or biological testing such as urinalysis, saliva testing, and blood analysis. The employee should not be returned to work until a determination of what disciplinary action, if any, is merited. Where an employee is being required to undergo the health evaluations and/or biological testing, the supervisor must make sure the employee understands that the requirement to take the test is a direct and proper instruction from the supervisor with no other alternatives available except to refuse a direct instruction. The supervisor should advise the employee that a refusal to take the test as directed will be considered as a refusal of a direct order and such refusal may result in disciplinary action up to and including discharge. If illegal or controlled drugs (unless prescribed by a licensed physician for medical reasons) are found in an employee's possession on Company premises, such drugs should be turned over to law enforcement officials. The employee should be disciplined upon satisfactory proof that the drug is an illegal drug or controlled substance (unless prescribed by a licensed doctor for medical reasons). Any employee who is found receiving or purchasing illegal or controlled drugs on Company premises or while on Company business is subject to disciplinary action up to and including discharge.

SUSPECTED ALCOHOL OR DRUG ABUSE AND REHABILITATION

Supervisors must be as knowledgeable as possible concerning the signs and symptoms of drug or alcohol dependency (including but not limited to such things as absenteeism, tardiness, change in physical appearance, disinterest in work, or change in personality). Suspected problems must be referred to appropriate line management and the Human Resources Manager before any action is taken. Since diagnosis is complex and a false accusation must be avoided, supervisors should not undertake the counseling or rehabilitation of an employee suspected of misusing drugs without the advice and assistance of health professionals but rather should report a suspected problem promptly, as a delay can be dangerous for the employee, other employees and the Company.

SAMPLE POLICIES

When drug or alcohol misuse is suspected, the following steps should be followed carefully:

1. The employee's behavior and symptoms must be reported to appropriate line management and the Human Resources Manager.

2. It is important that each suspicion of drug or alcohol misuse be carefully investigated and documented. Therefore, line management, in conjunction with the Human Resources Manager, must conduct an immediate and thorough investigation before any action is taken.

3. If the investigation indicates a possible health related problem and/or the presence of a work related problem which has not been corrected, a meeting should be conducted between the employee and a supervisor. The supervisor should discuss with the employee any unsatisfactory behavior and performance, citing specific reasons, such as absenteeism, tardiness, physical appearance, disinterest in work, and failure to complete assignments. The supervisor should make no suggestion of suspected drug or alcohol misuse during this discussion. If the employee refuses to agree to the referral to the company physician and/or a contract employee assistance program, the supervisor should explain that such a refusal may be grounds for dismissal. Before the employee's visit to the Company physician and/or the contract employee assistance program, the Human Resource Manager should give the physician and/or the contract employee assistance program representative all the facts of the case and the employee should be told that the information has been made available to the physician and/or the contract employee assistance program representative.

4. After the medical examination, if alcohol or drug abuse is indicated:

The employee will be referred to a professionally recognized treatment program by the Company physician and/or the contract employee assistance representative. Rehabilitated employees will then be expected to achieve and maintain a standard level of productivity and remain substance-free when at work.

If rehabilitation has previously proved ineffective, or if the employee has not cooperated, or refuses to participate in rehabilitation, disciplinary action should be taken. It may be desirable to first suspend the employee as a warning concerning the seriousness of the offense, but our position of refusing to retain habitual drug or alcohol abusers should be made quite clear to the employee.

Employees who have undergone substance abuse rehabilitation may be required to submit periodically, without prior notice, to test procedures. Under these circumstances, positive results may be a basis for termination.

RESPONSIBILITY

Recognition of alcohol or drug abuse as a medical problem is not intended to inhibit or restrict disciplinary action that is clearly warranted. Reporting to work under the influence of such substances and usage or possession of illicit drugs on the job cannot be condoned. However, alertness to these problems is the supervisor's responsibility, and it may be possible to help an employee, thereby salvaging an individual for family and community life, and retaining an experienced worker for the Company.

Appendix D

Announcement Aids

Substance Abuse Testing

The abuse of alcohol and drugs is a significant issue in today's society, and our Company is not exempt from the problem. Management has the responsibility to take reasonable measures sufficient to assure that drug or alcohol use by employees does not jeopardize the safety of operations or otherwise adversely affect the Company, its employees, customers, or the community.

ANNOUNCEMENT AIDS

After careful consideration of the many issues involved, management has decided to initiate a substance abuse testing program. Beginning immediately all new hires will be tested for illegal drugs in conjunction with their normal pre-employment physical examinations. Individuals with confirmed positive results will not be hired. In addition, beginning immediately existing employees will be subject to testing in limited "for cause" situations in which their behavior or performance creates a reasonable concern that drug or alcohol abuse may be a factor. Widespread testing of large groups of employees on a periodic or random basis is not planned, but the Company reserves the right to do so if circumstances indicate a need for such testing.

The testing program will complement existing rehabilitation efforts and be augmented by expanded awareness training for supervisors to better recognize substance abuse problems. Considerable effort has gone into ensuring the testing itself is accurate and the program fairly administered. Specific questions concerning the program should be addressed to your Employee Relations contact.

The Company recognizes that alcoholism and drug dependencies are self-induced, chronic, and complex diseases and that they are treatable illnesses. Programs are already in place to assist employees and their dependents in the diagnosis and treatment of these serious illnesses.

ABC Manufacturing, Inc.
9834 Alabama Avenue
Somewhere, US 12345

Mr. William Doe
1234 Main Street
Anytown, US 56708

Dear Mr. Doe:

As I am sure you are aware, the abuse of drugs has become widespread in America and has received a great deal of recent publicity. The problem is no longer confined to a relative few but has expanded into all areas of our lives. Its cost is staggering in terms of increased health risks, personal injury, property damage, family and social problems, and reduced productivity on the job. We would be naive to think that our Company is insulated from this problem.

Because of our concern for the safety of our employees, property, and the public and our concern about the productivity of our workforce, the Company has adopted a new corporate policy that deals with drug abuse. It is applicable to all U.S. dollar payroll employees. Our purpose in adopting this policy, which restates the Company's long standing prohibition against the presence of drugs in our offices and workplaces, is to further the Company's goal of establishing and maintaining a work environment free from the adverse effects of drug abuse.

In connection with the above-described policy, a formal drug testing program will begin 30 days from the date of this letter. Under this program, drug tests will be included in all pre-employment medical examinations. In addition, current employees who are required to take mandatory medical examinations will be tested for drugs on an annual basis. Expatriate employees and their dependents will be tested for drugs in connection with initial transfer outside the United States and during mandatory annual medical examinations because of the significant risks associated with drug use in many foreign countries and the detrimental consequences of drug abuse to an expatriate community.

Annual drug testing for employees required to take physical examinations has been adopted because these employees, by the nature of their jobs, could pose an immediate safety risk to themselves, fellow employees, property, and/or the general public of working under the influence of drugs. In addition, employees who, in the judgment of management, may be working under the influence of drugs will be subject to a medical examination which includes drug testing without prior notice. This includes employees who are not part of the annual testing program. As in the past, if an employee's performance is deteriorating, management may require the employee to undergo a medical examination. Beginning 30 days from the date of this letter, such examinations will include drug testing.

The policy also provides that the Company may conduct inspections, as well as medical examinations, at its discretion to determine if an employee is in violation of the policy. Such actions will not be undertaken indiscriminately, but only when there is a reasonable suspicion of a violation.

We are aware that for those individuals who engage in the occasional use of illicit drugs on their own time, adoption of these policies may lead to positive test results. Even though occasional use may not appear to interfere with work performance and/or safety on the job, we nevertheless believe that the weight of available evidence suggests that the use of drugs by employees will, over time, increase our risk of accidents and adversely affect our overall productivity. Neither of these potential consequences is acceptable to us.

The Company believes this program addresses a legitimate business concern and is sensitive to the issue of employee privacy. One laboratory will analyze all samples company-wide and will retain those that test positive. The laboratory utilizes state of the art technology, ensuring the accuracy of test results.

Positive drug test results will be dealt with through the administration of appropriate disciplinary actions. I encourage any employee with a drug problem to get help now, rather than wait for a positive test result.

Yours very truly,

Harrison Smith

ABC Manufacturing, Inc.
9834 Alabama Avenue
Somewhere, US 12345
XYZ Contractors, Inc.
1234 Main Street
Plant City, US 56789

Dear Sir:

This is to inform you of our Company's drug abuse policy. The policy applies to contractor employees as well as our own employees.

The simple observance of the policy, as set forth below, will help ensure the continued well-being and safety of all personnel and property. Adherence is mandatory and violation of it by any of your employees will not be tolerated. The policy provides that the use, possession, sale, transfer, or being under the influence of illegal drugs or other intoxicants on Company premises or while conducting Company business is forbidden.

Violations of this policy by an employee of a contractor will be cause for immediately removing and barring that contractor's employee from any Company premises.

To enforce this policy, the Company may at any time conduct searches upon its premises. Searches may include but not be limited to persons, personal effects, and personal vehicles wherever located on Company premises. Refusal by persons in your employ to cooperate or submit to searches will be cause for immediately removing and barring such persons from any Company premises.

Entry by any person into Company premises constitutes consent to and recognition of the right of our Company and its authorized representatives to conduct searches.

Please acknowledge acceptance of these conditions by return letter at your very earliest convenience.

Sincerely,

James Wilson

NOTICE

The use, transfer, possession or sale of illegal or unauthorized materials on the premises of the Company, or at any workplaces on which the company has contracted to perform its work IS PROHIBITED. The intent is to maintain a safe and healthy work environment for employees and other personnel at the workplace, and to protect company property and other property for which the company is liable. Searches of individuals, their personal effects, lockers, and vehicles may be conducted at such times and places as necessary to obtain compliance.

Prohibited articles include stolen and misappropriated Company property and materials, illegal and unauthorized drugs, alcoholic beverages, firearms, explosives, weapons and hazardous substances or articles.

Illegal drugs include (but are not limited to) marijuana, heroin, cocaine, and prescription drugs (in the possession of the individual but not prescribed by a licensed physician for use by the individual). Unauthorized drugs include excessive quantities of prescribed drugs which may adversely influence performance or behavior.

If any of the above prohibited articles are found, the individual possessing the articles will be subject to disciplinary action. Any of the above articles discovered through searches will be taken into custody, when appropriate, and may be turned over to the proper law enforcement authorities.

Authorized personnel may conduct the searches without prior announcement, and at such times and places on premises or work locations as considered appropriate by the Company. Urine samples may be requested in conjunction with the searches. Entry onto premises or work locations is consent to, and recognition of, the right of the Company and its authorized representatives to conduct the unannounced searches and to obtain urine samples for analysis.

NOTICE

Company-wide policy includes the requirement that strict regulations shall exist relative to controlled substances and weapons on Company property. The use and/or possession of illegal drugs, drug paraphernalia, alcoholic beverages, firearms or other weapons is strictly prohibited. Employees will not be allowed to work under the influence of alcohol or drugs. Those found to be in violation of this policy are subject to immediate dismissal.

It is the policy of the Company to maintain a safe work environment and to provide protection against loss, theft and damage of property belonging to the Company, employees and other persons and companies present at the plant site. To this end, the use, possession, transportation or sale of any illegal drug, drug paraphernalia (marijuana clips, syringes, etc.), alcoholic beverages, explosives, weapons or any other similar item or substance which could cause or contribute to injury to personnel or damage to Company property is strictly prohibited on or in connection with the real or personal property of the Company, at the property of the Company's affiliates, partners, contractors, or subcontractors used in connection with the plant's operations. Possession of another's property without the effective consent of the owner is similarly prohibited.

This policy will be implemented by such reasonable means as may be determined by the Company at its sole discretion. These means include but are not limited to the search of persons and their personal effects. Such searches may be made from time to time without prior announcement and may include the person and personal effects such as lockers, lunch boxes, purses, personal belongings, vehicles and other similar items. Contraband items discovered through these searches will be taken into custody and may be turned over to law enforcement authorities.

Legally prescribed drugs will be allowed. Prescription numbers may be recorded during a search and verified through the doctor or pharmacy issuing the prescription. It is prohibited to have more than one type of medication in any single container, to have medications in unlabeled containers or in containers with anyone else's name, or to possess non-prescribed medications other than as immediately needed.

NOTICE

In accordance with Company policy, this is to notify all employees and employees of contractors and other companies that illegal and unauthorized drugs, drug paraphernalia, alcohol, and firearms are not permitted on Company premises or property. The Company regards the possession, use, or distribution of such items by any person on any Company premises or property as posing a serious threat to the safety of employees, invitees, and operations.

The Company reserves the right at all times, without prior announcement, to conduct urinalysis tests, blood tests, and searches of employees' personal effects, lockers, baggage, vehicles, and quarters for the purpose of determining if any employees are under the influence of or have recently used drugs or alcohol, or are in possession of any unauthorized items. The purpose of these actions is to provide a safe and healthy working environment.

Any Company employee who refuses to submit to a urinalysis test, blood test, search, or is found to have recently used or is under the influence of drugs or alcohol, or is in possession of unauthorized items without an explanation satisfactory to the Company will be subject to disciplinary action up to and including immediate discharge. Any employee of a contractor having business with the company who refuses to submit to a urinalysis test, blood test, or search, or who is likewise found to be in violation of this Company policy will be removed from and not allowed to return to Company premises or properties.

Unauthorized items discovered as a result of a search may be taken into custody and may be turned over to the appropriate law enforcement authority.

WARNING PRIOR TO ENTRY

Nonprescription drugs and alcohol are prohibited on any property owned or controlled by the company.

For safety and security reasons, entry to or exit from any property owned or controlled by the company is conditioned upon the company's right to search persons and personal effects, including vehicles.

Anyone entering, on, or leaving company premises is subject to search at anytime.

REMINDER TO ALL EMPLOYEES

It is the policy of the Company to maintain a safe work environment. Accordingly, use, possession, transportation, or sale of any suspected illegal drug, drug paraphernalia (such as marijuana clips, incense, syringes, etc.), alcoholic beverages, or weapons on work locations, owned or leased property, and adjacent areas of the Company is strictly prohibited.

This is a condition of employment. Persons suspected of being in violation of this prohibition will be immediately terminated.

As a safety precaution, entry into, presence upon, or leaving any work location, owned or leased property, or adjacent area is conditioned upon the right of the Company to search the person and personal effects for suspected illegal drugs, drug paraphernalia, intoxicating beverages, or weapons. All persons, while on Company work locations, owned or leased property, or adjacent areas or while entering or leaving same, may be subject to searches of lockers, packages, carried items and vehicles. Such searches may be made from time to time, and without prior announcement, and may include employees of other organizations doing business with or for the Company.

Suspected items discovered through searches may be turned over to the proper law enforcement authorities.

Any employee of the Company who refuses to consent to such searches may be immediately terminated.

Certain legally prescribed drugs will be allowed provided the quantity does not exceed 2 days use, and provided the prescription is not dated more than 90 days old. Each such prescription number may be recorded and the drug and prescription verified through the doctor or pharmacy issuing the prescription. It is prohibited to have more than one type of medication in any single container, to have medications in unlabeled containers or in containers with anyone else's name, or to possess non-prescribed medications.

I have read and understand the above. I understand that strict compliance is a condition of employment or of being allowed on Company property.

Signature: _____ Date _____

NOTICE TO EMPLOYEES AND NON-EMPLOYEES

It is the policy of the Company and its subsidiary and affiliated companies to maintain a safe work environment at all its facilities and locations. To this end, the possession of any illegal drug, drug paraphernalia, alcoholic beverage, explosive, weapon or any other similar item or substance which could cause or contribute to injury to Company personnel or damage to its property is strictly prohibited at work locations or other business premises of the Company. This policy may be implemented by such reasonable means as may from time to time be determined appropriate, including searches of the person and personal effects of any persons as a condition to entering, remaining in, or leaving a work area.

Compliance with this policy is a condition of employment for employees of the Company. Employees who decline to be searched or who are otherwise found in violation of this policy will be subject to immediate termination. Non-employees who decline to be searched or are otherwise found in violation of this policy will be excluded from the Company's work areas.

Acknowledgment

I have read and understand the above Company policy. I understand that compliance with the above policy is a condition of entry to the Company's premises.

Signature: _____ Date: _____

ACKNOWLEDGMENT AND CONSENT

I, _____, have read and understand the Company policy on contraband, such as firearms, alcoholic beverages, and illegal drugs. I also understand that this policy will be enforced and that personal searches and drug tests may be used to enforce the policy.

I understand completely that termination action will be taken in the event I am found to have an illegal drug in my system, or if I am found to possess, use, or distribute contraband at a Company work location.

I further understand that termination action will be taken if I refuse to take the drug test, or if my test result indicates a positive presence of illegal drugs or if I refuse to be searched or cooperate with detection procedures.

I hereby grant permission for any hospital, physician, or the Company to take urine samples, to have these samples analyzed for drugs, and

ANNOUNCEMENT AIDS

to report the results to the Company. I understand that refusal to sign this document will result in termination of my employment.

Signature: _____ Date: _____

ACKNOWLEDGMENT BY A NON-EMPLOYEE

I understand that in the interest of providing a safe and efficient environment the Company has and enforces a policy designed to control drug abuse on Company premises.

I understand that this policy is implemented from time to time by a variety of reasonable means. Such means include searches of persons, personal effects, and personal vehicles entering, on, or departing Company premises. The Company may also require non-employees on Company premises to provide urine specimens for drug testing purposes.

I understand that any non-employee who declines to be searched or declines to provide a urine specimen may be escorted from the Company's premises, barred from re-entry, and may be excluded from any future participation in Company operations.

I have read this policy (or it has been explained to me) and I understand the provisions of it that apply to me as a non-employee on Company premises or engaged in Company business.

I agree to comply with this policy and understand that compliance is a condition of my being permitted to be on the Company's premises or my participation in Company operations.

Signature: _____ Date: _____

ACKNOWLEDGMENT

This is to inform you that the Company conducts testing to identify job applicants and current employees who may be abusing drugs and/or alcohol.

A copy of the Company's policy on this matter is either attached to this notice or will be given to you upon request.

You have the right to refuse to undergo testing. However, the consequences of refusal to undergo testing or a refusal to cooperate in testing by an applicant will result in the termination of the pre-employment selection process, and the consequences of refusal to undergo testing or a refusal to cooperate in testing by an employee will result in disciplinary action up to and including discharge.

An applicant who fails a test will not be hired and an employee who fails a test will be subject to disciplinary action up to and including discharge.

I acknowledge receipt and understanding of the above written notice.

_____   _____

(Signature)   (Date Signed)

Appendix E

Employee Awareness Aids

Crack and Cocaine

Cocaine is a powerfully addictive drug of abuse. Once having tried cocaine, an individual cannot predict or control the extent to which he or she will continue to use the drug.

The major routes of administration of cocaine are sniffing or snorting, injecting, and smoking (including free-base and crack cocaine). Snorting is the process of inhaling cocaine powder through the nose where it is absorbed into the bloodstream through the nasal tissues. Injecting is the act of using a needle to release the drug directly into the bloodstream. Smoking involves inhaling cocaine vapor or smoke into the lungs followed by absorption into the bloodstream.

Crack is the street name given to cocaine that has been processed from cocaine hydrochloride to a free base for smoking. Rather than requiring the more volatile method of processing cocaine using ether, crack cocaine is processed with ammonia or sodium bicarbonate (baking soda) and water and heated to remove the hydrochloride, thus producing a form of cocaine that can be smoked. The term crack refers to the crackling sound heard when the mixture is heated.

There is great risk whether cocaine is ingested by inhalation, injection, or smoking. It appears that compulsive cocaine use may develop even more rapidly if the substance is smoked rather than snorted. Smoking allows extremely high doses of cocaine to reach the brain very quickly and brings an intense and immediate high. The injecting drug user is at risk for transmitting or acquiring HIV infection/AIDS if needles or other injection equipment are shared.

HEALTH HAZARDS

Cocaine is a strong central nervous system stimulant that interferes with the reabsorption process of dopamine, a chemical messenger associated with pleasure. Dopamine is released as part of the brain's reward system and is involved in the high that characterizes cocaine consumption.

Physical effects of cocaine use include constricted peripheral blood vessels, dilated pupils, and increased temperature, heart rate, and blood pressure. The duration of cocaine's immediate euphoric effects, which include hyperstimulation, reduced fatigue, and mental clarity, depends on the route of administration. The faster the absorption, the more intense the high. On the other hand, the faster the absorption, the shorter the duration of action. The high from snorting may last 15 to 30 minutes, while that from smoking may last 5 to 10 minutes. Increased use can reduce the period of stimulation.

Some users of cocaine report feelings of restlessness, irritability, and anxiety. An appreciable tolerance to the high may be developed, and many addicts report that they seek but fail to achieve as much pleasure as they did from their first exposure. Scientific evidence suggests that the powerful neuropsychologic reinforcing property of cocaine is responsible for an individual's continued use, despite harmful physical and social consequences. In rare instances, sudden death can occur on the first use of cocaine or unexpectedly thereafter. However, there is no way to determine who is prone to sudden death.

High doses of cocaine and/or prolonged use can trigger paranoia. Smoking crack cocaine can produce a particularly aggressive paranoid behavior in users. When addicted individuals stop using cocaine, they often become depressed. This also may lead to further cocaine use to alleviate depression. Prolonged cocaine snorting can result in ulceration of the mucous membrane of the nose and can damage the nasal septum enough to cause it to collapse. Cocaine-related deaths are often a result of cardiac arrest or seizures followed by respiratory arrest.

COCAETHYLENE

When people mix cocaine and alcohol, they compound the danger each drug poses. Researchers have found that the human liver combines cocaine and alcohol and manufactures a third substance, cocaethylene, that intensifies cocaine's euphoric effects, while possibly increasing the risk of sudden death.

TREATMENT

The widespread abuse of cocaine has led to extensive efforts to develop treatment programs for this type of drug abuse. A top research priority is to find a medication to block or greatly reduce the effects of cocaine. Researchers are also looking at medications that help alleviate the severe craving that people in treatment for cocaine addiction often experience. Several medications are currently being investigated to test their safety and efficacy.

In addition to treatment medications, behavioral interventions, particularly cognitive behavioral therapy, can be effective in decreasing drug use by patients in treatment for cocaine abuse. Providing the optimal combination of treatment services for each individual is critical to successful treatment outcome.

Inhalant Abuse

About 17 percent of adolescents in this country say that at least once in their lives they have sniffed inhalants, usually volatile solvents such as spray paint, glue, or cigarette lighter fluid. Results from a number of surveys suggest that among children under 18, the level of use of inhalants is comparable to that of stimulants and is exceeded only by the level of use of marijuana, alcohol, and cigarettes.

Inhalant abuse, however, is a stepchild in the war on drugs. The abuse of inhalants, which includes a broad array of cheap and easily obtainable household products, is not viewed in the same high-risk category as drugs such as alcohol, cocaine, and heroin. Some people tend to view inhalant sniffing, snorting, bagging (fumes inhaled from a plastic bag), or huffing (inhalant-soaked rag in the mouth) as a kind of childish fad.

But inhalant abuse is deadly serious. Sniffing volatile solvents, which includes most inhalants, can cause severe damage to the brain and nervous system. By starving the body of oxygen or forcing the heart to beat more rapidly and erratically, inhalants can kill sniffers, most of whom are adolescents.

Survey data on the prevalence of inhalant abuse are difficult to obtain for a number of reasons, and information that does exist may under-emphasize the severity of the situation. No one knows how many adolescents and young people die each year from inhalant abuse, in part because medical examiners often attribute deaths from inhalant abuse to suffocation, suicide, or accidents. What's more, no national system exists for gathering data on the extent of inhalant-related injuries. Although medical journals have described the situation as serious, some researchers warn that doctors and emergency medical personnel are not adequately trained to recognize and report symptoms of inhalant abuse.

With so many substances lumped together as inhalants, research data describing frequency and trends of inhalant abuse are uneven and sometimes contradictory. However, evidence indicates that inhalant abuse is more common among all socioeconomic levels of American youth than is typically recognized by parents and the public.

A major roadblock to recognizing the size of the inhalant problem is the ready availability of products that are inhaled. Inhalants are cheap and can be purchased legally in retail stores in a variety of seemingly harmless products. As a result, adolescents who sniff inhalants to get high don't face the drug procurement obstacles that confront abusers of other drugs.

TYPES OF INHALANTS

Inhalants can be broken down into three major categories: volatile solvents, nitrites, and anesthetics. Volatile solvents are either gases, such as butane gas fumes, or liquids, such as gasoline or paint thinner, that vaporize at room temperature. Products that contain volatile solvents are numerous. Besides gasoline and paint thinner, products with volatile solvents include spray paint, paint and wax removers, hair spray, odorants, air fresheners, cigarette lighter fuels, analgesic sprays, and propellant gases used in aerosols such as whipped cream dispensers.

Volatile solvents produce a quick form of intoxication and excitation followed by drowsiness, disinhibition, staggering, lightheadedness, and agitation. Because many inhalant products contain more than one volatile solvent, it is difficult to clearly identify in humans the specific chemical responsible for subsequent brain or nerve damage or death.

Some volatile solvents are inhaled by abusers because of the effects produced not by the product's primary ingredient but by propellant gases, like those used in aerosols such as hair spray or spray paint. Other volatile solvents found in aerosol products, such as gold and silver spray paint, are sniffed not because of the effects from propellant gases but because of the psychoactive effects caused by the specific solvents necessary to suspend metallic paints in the spray.

Nitrites historically have been used by certain groups, largely gay men, to enhance sexual experience and pleasure. Often called poppers, some nitrite products are sold as room odorizers. But use of nitrites has fallen off dramatically in recent years. This may be partly because products containing butyl, propyl, and certain other nitrites have been banned, although products using chemical variants of the banned substances are still sold.

Within the other major category of inhalants, the anesthetics, the principal substance of abuse is nitrous oxide. A colorless, sweet-tasting gas used by doctors and dentists for general anesthesia, nitrous oxide is called laughing gas because it often induces a state of giggling and laughter. Recent anecdotal reports indicate that nitrous oxide is being sold illicitly to teenagers and young adults at outdoor events such as rock concerts. Nitrous oxide often is sold in large balloons from which the gas is released and inhaled for its mind-altering effects. But nitrous oxide is no laughing matter. Inhaling the gas may deplete the body of oxygen and can result in death; prolonged use can result in peripheral nerve damage.

Heroin

Heroin is a highly addictive drug, and its use is a serious problem in America. Current estimates indicate that nearly 600,000 people need treatment for heroin addiction. Recent studies suggest a shift from injecting heroin to snorting or smoking because of increased purity and the misconception that these forms of use will not lead to addiction.

Heroin is processed from morphine, a naturally occurring substance extracted from the seed pod of the Asian poppy plant. Heroin usually appears as a white or brown powder. Street names associated with heroin include smack, H, skag, and junk. Other names may refer to types of heroin produced in a specific geographical area, such as Mexican black tar.

HEALTH HAZARDS

Heroin abuse is associated with serious health conditions, including fatal overdose, spontaneous abortion, collapsed veins, and infectious diseases, including HIV/AIDS and hepatitis.

The short-term effects of heroin abuse appear soon after a single dose and disappear in a few hours. After an injection of heroin, the user reports feeling a surge of euphoria accompanied by a warm flushing of the skin, a dry mouth, and heavy extremities. Following this initial euphoria, the user goes on the nod, an alternately wakeful and drowsy state. Mental functioning becomes clouded due to the depression of the central nervous system.

Long-term effects of heroin appear after repeated use for some period of time. Chronic users may develop collapsed veins, infection of the heart lining and valves, abscesses, cellulitis, and liver disease. Pulmonary complications, including various types of pneumonia, may result from the poor health condition of the abuser, as well as from heroin's depressing effects on respiration.

In addition to the effects of the drug itself, street heroin may have additives that do not readily dissolve and result in clogging the blood vessels that lead to the lungs, liver, kidneys, or brain. This can cause infection and death of small patches of cells in vital organs.

TOLERANCE, ADDICTION, AND WITHDRAWAL

With regular heroin use, tolerance develops. This means the abuser must use more heroin to achieve the same intensity or effect. As higher doses are used over time, physical dependence and addiction develop. With physical dependence, the body has adapted to the presence of the drug and withdrawal symptoms may occur if use is reduced or stopped.

Withdrawal, which in regular abusers may occur as early as a few hours after the last administration, produces drug craving, restlessness, muscle and bone pain, insomnia, diarrhea, vomiting, cold flashes with goose bumps, kicking movements, and other symptoms. Major withdrawal symptoms peak between 48 and 72 hours after the last dose and subside after about a week. Sudden withdrawal by heavily dependent users who are in poor health is occasionally fatal, although heroin withdrawal is considered much less dangerous than alcohol or barbiturate withdrawal.

TREATMENT

There is a broad range of treatment options for heroin addiction, including medications as well as behavioral therapies. Science has taught us that when medication treatment is integrated with other supportive services, patients are often able to stop heroin (or other opiate) use and return to more stable and productive lives.

Methadone, a synthetic opiate medication that blocks the effects of heroin for about 24 hours, has a proven record of success when prescribed at a high enough dosage level for people addicted to heroin. LAAM, also a synthetic opiate medication for treating heroin addiction, can block the effects of heroin for up to 72 hours. Other approved medications are naloxone, which is used to treat cases of overdose, and naltrexone, both of which block the effects of morphine, heroin, and other opiates. Several other medications for use in heroin treatment programs are under study.

There are many effective behavioral treatments available for heroin addiction. These can include residential and outpatient approaches. Several new behavioral therapies are showing particular promise for heroin addiction. Contingency management therapy uses a voucher-based system in which patients earn points based on negative drug tests. Points can be exchanged for items that encourage healthful living. Cognitive-behavioral interventions are designed to help modify the patient's thinking, expectancies, and behaviors and to increase skills in coping with various life stressors.

Quantitative indicators and field reports continue to suggest an increasing incidence of new heroin snorters in the younger age groups, often among women. One concern is that snorters may shift to needle injecting because of increased tolerance, nasal soreness, or declining or unreliable purity. Injection use would place them at increased risk of contracting HIV/AIDS.

LSD

LSD is one of the major drugs making up the hallucinogen class. LSD is one of the most potent mood-changing chemicals. It is manufactured from lysergic acid, which is found in ergot, a fungus that grows on rye and other grains.

LSD, commonly referred to as acid, is sold on the street in tablets, capsules, and, occasionally, liquid form. It is odorless, colorless, and has a slightly bitter taste and is usually taken by mouth. Often LSD is added to absorbent paper, such as blotter paper, and divided into small decorated squares, with each square representing one dose.

HEALTH HAZARDS

The effects of LSD are unpredictable. They depend on the amount taken; the user's personality, mood, and expectations; and the surroundings in which the drug is used. Usually, the user feels the first effects of the drug 30 to 90 minutes after taking it. The physical effects include dilated pupils, higher body temperature, increased heart rate and blood pressure, sweating, loss of appetite, sleeplessness, dry mouth, and tremors.

Sensations and feelings change much more dramatically than the physical signs. The user may feel several different emotions at once or swing rapidly from one emotion to another. If taken in a large enough dose, the drug produces delusions and visual hallucinations. The user's sense of time and self changes. Sensations may seem to "cross over," giving the user the feeling of hearing colors and seeing sounds. These changes can be frightening and can cause panic.

Users refer to their experience with LSD as a trip and to acute adverse reactions as a bad trip. These experiences are long; typically they begin to clear after about 12 hours.

Some LSD users experience terrifying thoughts and feelings, fear of losing control, fear of insanity and death, and despair while using LSD. Some fatal accidents have occurred during states of LSD intoxication.

Many LSD users experience flashbacks, recurrence of certain aspects of a person's experience, without the user having taken the drug again. A flashback occurs suddenly, often without warning, and may occur within a few days or more than a year after LSD use. Flashbacks usually occur in people who use hallucinogens chronically or have an underlying personality problem; however, otherwise healthy people who use LSD occasionally may also have flashbacks. Bad trips and flashbacks are only part of the risks of LSD use. LSD users may manifest relatively long-lasting psychoses, such as schizophrenia or severe depression. It is difficult to determine the extent and mechanism of the LSD involvement in these illnesses.

Most users of LSD voluntarily decrease or stop its use over time. LSD is not considered an addictive drug since it does not produce compulsive drug-seeking behavior as do cocaine, amphetamine, heroin, alcohol, and nicotine. However, like many of the addictive drugs, LSD produces tolerance, so some users who take the drug repeatedly must take progressively higher doses to achieve the state of intoxication that they had previously achieved. This is an extremely dangerous practice, given the unpredictability of the drug.

Marijuana

Marijuana is a green or gray mixture of dried, shredded flowers and leaves of the hemp plant Cannabis sativa. There are over 200 slang terms for marijuana including pot, herb, weed, boom, Mary Jane, gangster, and chronic. It is usually smoked as a cigarette (called a joint or a nail) or in a pipe or bong. In recent years, it has appeared in blunts. These are cigars that have been emptied of tobacco and re-filled with marijuana, often in combination with another drug such as crack. Some users also mix marijuana into foods or use it to brew tea.

THC (delta-9-tetrahydrocannabinol) is the principal active chemical in marijuana. Membranes of certain nerve cells contain protein receptors that bind THC. Once securely in place, THC kicks off a series of cellular reactions that ultimately lead to the high that users experience when they smoke marijuana. The short term effects of marijuana include problems with memory and learning; distorted perception; difficulty in thinking and problem-solving; loss of coordination; and increased heart rate, anxiety, and panic attacks.

Scientists have found that whether an individual has positive or negative sensations after smoking marijuana can be influenced by heredity. One study demonstrated that identical male twins were more likely than non-identical male twins to report similar responses to marijuana use, indicating a genetic basis for their sensations. Identical twins share all of their genes, and fraternal twins share about half.

EFFECTS OF MARIJUANA ON THE BRAIN

Researchers have found that THC changes the way in which sensory information gets into and is acted on by the hippocampus. This is a component of the brain's limbic system that is crucial for learning, memory, and the integration of sensory experiences with emotions and motivations. Investigations have shown that neurons in the information processing system of the hippocampus and the activity of the nerve fibers are suppressed by THC. Researchers have discovered that learned behaviors, which depend on the hippocampus, also deteriorate.

Recent research findings also indicate that long-term use of marijuana produces changes in the brain similar to those seen after long-term use of other major drugs of abuse.

EFFECTS ON THE LUNGS

Someone who smokes marijuana regularly may have many of the same respiratory problems that tobacco smokers have. These individuals may have daily cough and phlegm, symptoms of chronic bronchitis, and more frequent chest colds. Continuing to smoke marijuana can lead to abnormal functioning of lung tissue injured or destroyed by marijuana smoke.

Regardless of the THC content, the amount of tar inhaled by marijuana smokers and the level of carbon monoxide absorbed are three to five times greater than among tobacco smokers. This may be due to the marijuana users inhaling more deeply and holding the smoke in the lungs.

EFFECTS ON HEART RATE AND BLOOD PRESSURE

Recent findings indicate that smoking marijuana while shooting up cocaine has the potential to cause severe increases in heart rate and blood pressure. In one study, experienced marijuana and cocaine users were given marijuana alone, cocaine alone, and then a combination of both. Each drug alone produced cardiovascular effects; when they were combined, the effects were greater and lasted longer. The heart rate of the subjects in the study increased 29 beats per minute with marijuana alone and 32 beats per minute with cocaine alone. When the drugs were given together, the heart rate increased to 49 beats per minute, and the increased rate persisted for a longer time. The drugs were given with the subjects sitting quietly. In normal circumstances, an individual may smoke marijuana and inject cocaine and then do something physically stressful that may significantly increase risks of overload on the cardiovascular system.

EFFECTS OF HEAVY MARIJUANA USE ON LEARNING AND SOCIAL BEHAVIOR

A study of college students has shown that critical skills related to attention, memory, and learning are impaired among people who use marijuana heavily, even after discontinuing its use for at least 24 hours. Researchers compared 65 "heavy users," who had smoked marijuana a median of 29 of the past 30 days, and 64 "light users," who had smoked a median of 1 of the past 30 days. After a closely monitored 19- to 24-hour period of abstinence from marijuana and other illicit drugs and alcohol, the undergraduates were given several standard tests measuring aspects of attention, memory, and learning. Compared to the light users, heavy marijuana users made more errors and had more difficulty sustaining attention, shifting attention to meet the demands of changes in the environment, and in registering, processing, and using information. The findings suggest that the greater impairment among heavy users is likely due to an alteration of brain activity produced by marijuana.

Longitudinal research on marijuana use among young people below college age indicates those who used have lower achievement than the non-users, more acceptance of deviant behavior, more delinquent behavior and aggression, greater rebelliousness, poorer relationships with parents, and more associations with delinquent and drug-using friends.

Research also shows more anger and more regressive behavior (thumb sucking, temper tantrums) in toddlers whose parents use marijuana than among the toddlers of non-using parents.

EFFECTS ON PREGNANCY

Any drug of abuse can affect a mother's health during pregnancy. Drugs of abuse may interfere with proper nutrition and rest, which can affect good functioning of the immune system. Some studies have found that babies born to mothers who used marijuana during pregnancy were smaller than those born to mothers who did not use the drug. In general, smaller babies are more likely to develop health problems.

A nursing mother who uses marijuana passes some of the THC to the baby in her breast milk. Research indicates that the use of marijuana by a mother during the first month of breast-feeding can impair the infant's motor development (control of muscle movement).

ADDICTIVE POTENTIAL

A drug is addicting if it causes compulsive, often uncontrollable drug craving, seeking, and use, even in the face of negative health and social consequences. Marijuana meets these criteria. More than 120,000 people seek treatment per year for their primary marijuana addiction. In addition, animal studies suggest marijuana causes physical dependence, and some people report withdrawal symptoms.

Questions and Answers About Marijuana

What is it?

Marijuana is a green, brown, or gray mixture of dried, shredded leaves, stems, seeds, and flowers of the hemp plant. You may hear marijuana called by street names such as pot, herb, weed, grass, boom, Mary Jane, gangster, or chronic. There are more than 200 slang terms for marijuana. Sinsemilla, hashish, and hash oil are stronger forms of marijuana. All forms of marijuana are mind-altering. In other words, they change how the brain works. They all contain THC (delta-9-tetrahydrocannabinol), the main active chemical in marijuana. They also contain more than 400 other chemicals. Marijuana's effects on the user depend on the strength or potency of the THC it contains.

How long does it stay in the user's body?

THC in marijuana is strongly absorbed by fatty tissues in various organs. Generally, traces (metabolites) of THC can be detected by standard urine testing methods several days after a smoking session. However, in heavy chronic users, traces can sometimes be detected for weeks after they have stopped using marijuana.

What happens if you smoke marijuana?

The effects of the drug on each person depend on the user's experience, as well as to: how strong the marijuana is (how much THC it has); what the user expects to happen; where (the place) the drug is used; how it is taken; and whether the user is drinking alcohol or using other drugs. Some people feel nothing at all when they smoke marijuana. Others may feel relaxed or high. Sometimes marijuana makes users feel thirsty and very hungry, an effect called the munchies. Some users can get bad effects from marijuana. They may suffer sudden feelings of anxiety and have paranoid thoughts. This is more likely to happen when a more potent variety of marijuana is used.

What are the short-term effects?

The short-term effects of marijuana include: problems with memory and learning; distorted perception (sights, sounds, time, touch); trouble with thinking and problem-solving; loss of coordination; and increased heart rate and anxiety. These effects are even greater when other drugs are mixed with marijuana; users do not always know what drugs are given to them.

Does marijuana affect work?

Marijuana affects memory, judgment and perception. Workers on marijuana tend to make mistakes, lose their timing and eye-hand coordination, and lose interest in what they are doing.

What are the long-term effects?

Findings so far show that regular use of marijuana or THC may play a role in some kinds of cancer and in problems with the respiratory, immune, and reproductive systems. It's hard to know for sure whether regular marijuana use causes cancer. But it is known that marijuana contains some of the same, and sometimes even more, of the cancer-causing chemicals found in tobacco smoke. Studies show that someone who smokes five joints per week may be taking in as many cancer-causing chemicals as someone who smokes a full pack of cigarettes every day. People who smoke marijuana often develop the same kinds of breathing problems that cigarette smokers have. They tend to have more chest colds than nonusers. They are also at greater risk of getting lung infections like pneumonia. Animal studies have found that THC can damage the cells and tissues in the body that help protect people from disease.

How can you tell if someone has been using marijuana?

If someone is high on marijuana, he or she might seem dizzy and have trouble walking; seem silly and giggly for no reason; have very red, bloodshot eyes; and have a hard time remembering things that just happened. When the early effects fade, over a few hours, the user can become very sleepy.

Is marijuana used as a medicine?

There has been much talk about the possible medical use of marijuana. Under U.S. law, marijuana is a Schedule I controlled substance. This means that the drug, at least in its smoked form, has no commonly accepted medical use. THC, the active chemical in marijuana, is manufactured into a pill available by prescription that can be used to treat the nausea and vomiting that occur with certain cancer treatments and to help AIDS patients eat more to keep up their weight. According to scientists, more research needs to be done on marijuana's side effects and potential benefits before it is used medically with any regularity.

How does marijuana affect driving?

Marijuana has serious harmful effects on the skills required to drive safely: alertness, the ability to concentrate, coordination, and the ability to react quickly. These effects can last up to 24 hours after smoking marijuana. Marijuana use can make it difficult to judge distances and react to signals and sounds on the road. Marijuana may play a role in car accidents. In one study, researchers found that of 150 reckless drivers who were tested for drugs at the arrest scene 33 percent tested positive for marijuana, and 12 percent tested positive for both marijuana and cocaine. Data have also shown that while smoking marijuana, people show the same lack of coordination on standard drunk driver tests as do people who have had too much to drink.

If a woman is pregnant and smokes marijuana, will it hurt the baby?

Doctors advise pregnant women not to use any drugs because they could harm the growing fetus. One animal study has linked marijuana use to loss of the fetus very early in pregnancy. Some scientific studies have found that babies born to marijuana users were shorter, weighed less, and had smaller head sizes than those born to mothers who did not use the drug. Smaller babies are more likely to develop health problems. There are also research data showing nervous system problems in children of mothers who smoked marijuana. Researchers are not certain whether a newborn baby's health problems, if they are caused by marijuana, will continue as the child grows. Preliminary research shows that children born to mothers who used marijuana regularly during pregnancy may have trouble concentrating.

What does marijuana do to the brain?

Some studies show that when people have smoked large amounts of marijuana for years, the drug takes its toll on mental functions. Heavy or daily use of marijuana affects the parts of the brain that control memory, attention, and learning. A working short-term memory is needed to learn and perform tasks that call for more than one or two steps. Smoking marijuana causes some changes in the brain that are like those caused by cocaine, heroin, and alcohol. Some researchers believe that these changes may put a person more at risk of becoming addicted to other drugs such as cocaine or heroin.

Can people become addicted to marijuana?

Yes. While not everyone who uses marijuana becomes addicted, when a user begins to seek out and take the drug compulsively, that person is said to be dependent or addicted to the drug. Many people entering drug treatment programs report marijuana as their primary drug of abuse, showing they need help to stop using the drug. According to one study, marijuana use by teenagers who have prior serious antisocial problems can quickly lead to dependence on the drug. Some frequent, heavy users of marijuana develop a tolerance for it. Tolerance means that the user needs larger doses of the drug to get the same desired results previously obtained from smaller amounts.

What if a person wants to quit using the drug?

Up until a few years ago, it was hard to find treatment programs specifically for marijuana users. Now researchers are testing different ways to help marijuana users abstain from drug use. There are currently no medications for treating marijuana addiction. Treatment programs focus on counseling and group support systems.

How is marijuana used?

Most users roll loose marijuana into a cigarette (called a joint or a nail) or smoke it in a pipe. One well-known type of water pipe is the bong. Some users mix marijuana into foods or use it to brew a tea. Another method is to slice open a cigar and replace the tobacco with marijuana, making what's called a blunt. When the blunt is smoked with a 40 ounce. bottle of malt liquor, it is called a B-40. Marijuana cigarettes or blunts often include crack cocaine, a combination known by various street names, such as primos or woolies. Joints and blunts often are dipped in PCP and are called happy sticks, wicky sticks, love boat, or tical.

Do marijuana users lose their motivation?

Some frequent, long-term marijuana users show signs of a lack of motivation (amotivational syndrome). Their problems include not caring about what happens in their lives, no desire to work regularly, fatigue, and a lack of concern about how they look. As a result of these symptoms, some users tend to perform poorly at work.

Ecstasy

MDMA, called ecstasy or XTC on the street, is a synthetic, mind-altering drug with hallucinogenic and amphetamine-like properties. Its chemical structure is similar to two other synthetic drugs, MDA and methamphetamine, which are known to cause brain damage.

EMPLOYEE AWARENESS AIDS

Beliefs about ecstasy are reminiscent of similar claims made about LSD, which proved to be untrue. According to its proponents, MDMA can make people trust each other and can break down barriers between therapists and patients, lovers, and family members.

Many problems users encounter with MDMA are similar to those found with the use of amphetamines and cocaine. Problems include psychological difficulties, such as confusion, depression, sleep problems, drug craving, severe anxiety, and paranoia, during and sometimes weeks after taking MDMA. Physical problems include muscle tension, involuntary teeth-clenching, nausea, blurred vision, rapid eye movement, faintness, and chills or sweating. MDMA also increases heart rate and blood pressure, special risks for people with circulatory or heart disease.

MDA, the parent drug of MDMA, is an amphetamine-like drug that has also been abused and is similar in chemical structure to MDMA. Research shows that MDA destroys serotonin-producing neurons, which play a direct role in regulating aggression, mood, sexual activity, sleep, and sensitivity to pain. It is probably this action on the serotonin system that gives MDA its purported properties of heightened sexual experience, tranquility, and conviviality.

MDMA also is related in structure and effects to methamphetamine, which has been shown to cause degeneration of neurons containing the neurotransmitter dopamine. Damage to these neurons is the underlying cause of the motor disturbances seen in Parkinson's disease.

In laboratory experiments, a single exposure to methamphetamine at high doses or prolonged use at low doses destroys up to 50 percent of the brain cells that use dopamine. Although this damage may not be immediately apparent, scientists believe that with aging or exposure to other toxic agents, Parkinsonian symptoms may eventually emerge. These symptoms begin with lack of coordination and tremors and may eventually result in a form of paralysis.

PCP (Phencyclidine)

PCP (phencyclidine) was developed as an intravenous anesthetic. Use of PCP in humans was discontinued after it was found that patients often became agitated, delusional, and irrational while recovering from its anesthetic effects. PCP is illegally manufactured in laboratories and is sold on the street by such names as angel dust, ozone, wack, and rocket fuel. Killer joints and crystal supergrass are names that refer to PCP combined with marijuana. The variety of street names for PCP reflects its bizarre and volatile effects.

PCP is a white crystalline powder that is readily soluble in water or alcohol. It has a distinctive bitter chemical taste. PCP can be mixed easily with dyes and turns up on the illicit drug market in a variety of tablets, capsules, and colored powders. It is normally used in one of three ways: snorted, smoked, or eaten. For smoking, PCP is often applied to a leafy material such as mint, parsley, oregano, or marijuana.

PCP is addicting. Its use often leads to psychological dependence, craving, and compulsive PCP-seeking behavior. It was first introduced as a street drug and quickly gained a reputation as a drug that could cause bad reactions and was not worth the risk. Many people, after using the drug once, will not knowingly use it again. Yet others use it consistently and regularly. Some persist in using PCP because of its addicting properties. Others cite feelings of strength, power, invulnerability, and a numbing effect on the mind as reasons for their continued PCP use.

Many PCP users are brought to emergency rooms because of PCP's unpleasant psychological effects or because of overdoses. In a hospital or detention setting, they often become violent or suicidal, and are very dangerous to themselves and to others.

At low to moderate doses, physiological effects of PCP include a slight increase in breathing rate and a more pronounced rise in blood pressure and pulse rate. Respiration becomes shallow, and flushing and profuse sweating occur. Generalized numbness of the extremities and muscular incoordination also may occur. Psychological effects include distinct changes in body awareness, similar to those associated with alcohol intoxication.

At high doses of PCP, there is a drop in blood pressure, pulse rate, and respiration. This may be accompanied by nausea, vomiting, blurred vision, flicking up and down of the eyes, drooling, loss of balance, and dizziness. High doses of PCP can also cause seizures, coma, and death (though death more often results from accidental injury or suicide during PCP intoxication). Psychological effects at high doses include illusions and hallucinations. PCP can cause effects that mimic the full range of symptoms of schizophrenia such as delusions, paranoia, disordered thinking, a sensation of distance from one's environment, and catatonia. Speech is often sparse and garbled.

Pain Medications

Pain is the most common reason people visit a doctor. When treating pain, physicians have long wrestled with a dilemma: How can a doctor relieve a patient's suffering while avoiding the potential for that patient to become addicted to a powerful, opiate pain medication?

Today, the medical profession has concluded that many doctors under-prescribe powerful painkillers because they overestimate the potential for patients to become addicted to these painkillers, which include opiates, such as morphine and codeine, and substances that are structurally related to morphine. The term opioids is used to describe the entire class (both synthetic and natural) of chemicals structurally similar to morphine. Although these drugs carry an extreme risk of addiction, many physicians are not aware that these drugs are rarely abused when used for medicinal purposes.

Years of research have uncovered three categories of opioids:

- Agonists, such as Demerol and methadone, that mimic the effects of opioids that naturally occur in the body;

- Antagonists, such as naloxone, that block certain effects of opioids.

- Mixed agonist-antagonist opioid agents, such as buprenorphine and nalbuphine, that both activate and block specific opioid effects. These partial agonists minimize the agonists' negative side effects, including sedation, respiratory problems, and abuse potential, while relieving pain.

Opiates, including morphine and codeine, and synthetic opioids, such as Demerol and fentanyl, work by mimicking the pain-relieving chemicals produced in the body. These chemicals bind to opiate receptors, activating pain-relieving systems in the brain and spinal cord. But opioids can cause undesirable side effects such as nausea, sedation, confusion, and constipation. With prolonged use of opiates and opioids, individuals become tolerant to the drugs, require larger doses, and can become physically dependent on them.

Ritalin

Ritalin, the trade name for methylphenidate, is a medication prescribed for children with an abnormally high level of activity or with attention-deficit hyperactivity disorder (ADHD) and is also occasionally prescribed for treating narcolepsy.

Although not fully understood as to how it works, Ritalin has a notably calming effect on hyperactive children and a focusing effect on those with ADHD. When taken as prescribed, Ritalin is a valuable medicine. Further, research has shown that people with ADHD do not get addicted to their stimulant medications at treatment dosages.

Because of its stimulant properties, in recent years there have been reports of its abuse by people for whom it is not a medication. Users mix Ritalin with heroin, or with both cocaine and heroin for a more potent effect. Others crush and inhale the drug or take the pill orally. Ritalin's potential for abuse has caused the U.S. Drug Enforcement

Administration (DEA) to impose stringent controls such as special licenses and restrictions on prescription refills. Some states impose further regulations such as limiting the number of dosage units per prescription.

Rohypnol and GHB

ROHYPNOL

Rohypnol, the trade name for flunitrazepam, has been a concern for the last few years because of its abuse and reputation as a "date rape" drug. People may unknowingly be given the drug which, when mixed with alcohol, can incapacitate a victim and prevent them from resisting sexual assault. Also, Rohypnol may be lethal when mixed with alcohol and/or other depressants.

Rohypnol produces sedative-hypnotic effects including muscle relaxation and amnesia; it can also produce physical and psychological dependence.

Rohypnol is not approved for use in the United States, and its importation is banned. Illicit use of Rohypnol began in Europe and spread to the United States where it became known as rophies, roofies, roach, rope, and the date rape drug.

Another very similar drug is clonazepam, which is marketed in the U.S. as Klonopin and in Mexico as Rivotril.

GHB

GHB (gamma- hydroxybutyrate) is abused for its euphoric, sedative, and anabolic (body building) effects. As with Rohypnol and clonazepam, GHB has been associated with sexual assault.

Reports indicate liquid GHB is being used in nightclubs for effects similar to those of Rohypnol. It is known in the club scene as liquid ecstacy, somatomax, scoop, or grievous bodily harm.

Coma and seizures can occur following abuse of GHB and, when combined with methamphetamine, there appears to be an increased risk of seizure. Combining use with other drugs such as alcohol can result in nausea and difficulty breathing. GHB may also produce withdrawal effects, including insomnia, anxiety, tremors, and sweating. Concern about Rohypnol, GHB, and other similarly abused sedative-hypnotics, led Congress to pass the Drug-Induced Rape Prevention and Punishment Act. This legislation increased federal penalties for use of any controlled substance to aid in sexual assault.

Steroids

Anabolic steroids are synthetic derivatives of the male hormone testosterone. The full name is androgenic (promoting masculine characteristics) anabolic (building) steroids (the class of drugs). These derivatives of testosterone promote the growth of skeletal muscle and increase lean body mass. Anabolic steroids were first abused by athletes seeking to improve performance. Today, others use anabolic steroids to improve physical appearance.

Anabolic steroids are taken orally or injected, and athletes and other abusers take them typically in cycles of weeks or months, rather than continuously, in patterns called cycling. Cycling involves taking multiple doses of steroids over a specific period of time, stopping for a period, and starting again. In addition, users frequently combine several different types of steroids to maximize their effectiveness while minimizing negative effects, a process known as stacking.

HEALTH HAZARDS

Reports indicate that use of anabolic steroids produces increases in lean muscle mass, strength, and ability to train longer and harder, but long-term, high-dose effects of steroid use are largely unknown. Many health hazards of short-term effects are reversible. In addition, people who inject anabolic steroids run the added risk of contracting or transmitting hepatitis or the HIV virus that leads to AIDS.

The major side effects of anabolic steroid use include liver tumors, jaundice (yellowish pigmentation of skin, tissues, and body fluids), fluid retention, and high blood pressure; others are severe acne and trembling. Additional side effects include for men shrinking of the testicles, reduced sperm count, infertility, baldness, and development of breasts. For women the effects include growth of facial hair, changes in or cessation of the menstrual cycle, enlargement of the clitoris, and deepened voice. For adolescents the effects are growth halted prematurely through premature skeletal maturation and accelerated pubertal changes.

Research shows that aggression and other psychiatric side effects may result from anabolic steroid abuse. Many users report feeling good about themselves while on anabolic steroids, but researchers report that anabolic steroid abuse can cause wild mood swings including manic-like symptoms leading to violent, even homicidal, episodes. Depression often is seen when the drugs are stopped and may contribute to steroid dependence. Researchers reported also that users may suffer from paranoid jealousy, extreme irritability, delusions, and impaired judgment stemming from feelings of invincibility.

Barbiturates

WHAT ARE THEY?

The barbiturates are depressant drugs. In small doses they are effective in relieving anxiety and tension. In large doses they are used to induce sleep. Barbiturates are used to treat epilepsy and for intravenous anesthesia. When large doses are not followed by sleep, signs of mental confusion, euphoria, and even stimulation may occur, similar to that produced by alcohol.

WHAT ARE THE EFFECTS?

The effects are similar to the effects of alcohol. Small amounts produce calmness and relax muscles. Somewhat larger doses can cause slurred speech, staggering gait, poor judgment, and slow, uncertain reflexes. These effects make it dangerous to drive a vehicle or operate machinery. Large doses can cause unconsciousness and death.

POTENTIATION

Barbiturates are often used by persons seeking effects similar to those produced by alcohol, often combining the two. Because alcohol potentiates, or increases the barbiturate effects, this practice is extremely hazardous.

Users also take them in combination with or as a substitute for other depressants, such as heroin. They are often taken alternately with amphetamines, as they tend to enhance the euphoric effects of amphetamines while calming the overwrought nervous states they produce. Barbiturates can cause poisoning, coma, respiratory and kidney failure, and death.

DEPENDENCE

How much and how often these drugs are taken determine how fast the user develops tolerance and whether withdrawal will occur. Withdrawal is often more severe than heroin withdrawal. People who have difficulty dealing with stress or anxiety or who have trouble sleeping may overuse or become dependent.

BARBITURATES KILL

Barbiturate overdose is implicated in nearly one-third of all reported drug-induced deaths. Accidental deaths may occur when a user takes an unintended larger or repeated dose because of confusion or impairment in judgment caused by the drug.

Depressants

WHAT ARE THEY?

Depressants are drugs which depress or sedate the central nervous system. They are sometimes called sedatives or sedative-hypnotics because they include drugs which calm the nerves (sedation) and produce sleep (hypnotic effect). Depressants are also widely called tranquilizers and sleeping pills. There are three categories of depressants: barbiturates, nonbarbiturates, and benzodiazepines.

BARBITURATES

The barbiturates are the largest and most common category. They can produce mental confusion, euphoria, and even stimulation may occur, similar to that produced by alcohol. Barbiturates are often used with alcohol, and because alcohol potentiates, or increases barbiturate effects, this practice is extremely hazardous.

Users also take barbiturates in combination with or as a substitute for other depressants, such as heroin, and are often taken alternately with amphetamines, as they tend to enhance the euphoric effects of amphetamines while calming the nervousness they produce.

NONBARBITURATES

This category of depressants includes a large number of commonly abused synthetic drugs that are prescribed to help people sleep. Among them are Doriden, Miltown, Noludar, Placidyl, Sopor, and Quaalude.

BENZODIAZEPINES

This category of depressants is a family of four very similar tranquilizers sold as Valium, Serax, Librium and Tranxene. They differ mainly in respect to duration of action.

ARE THEY DANGEROUS?

Depressants kill. Barbiturate overdose is implicated in nearly one-third of all reported drug-induced deaths. Accidental deaths may occur when a user takes an unintended larger or repeated dose because of confusion or impairment in judgment caused by initial intake of the drug.

Drugs and Driving

ALCOHOL AND CAFFEINE

Alcohol works as a sedative. It affects judgment and coordination, and is a factor in more than half of America's highway deaths. Alcohol increases the sleep-inducing effects of tranquilizers and barbiturates. Mixing these drugs while driving is often fatal.

The effects of caffeine relate to the amount taken and the individual. When a person drinks two cups of coffee, the effects begin in 15-30 minutes. The person's metabolism, body temperature, and blood pressure may increase. Other effects can include hand tremors and a loss of coordination. Extremely high doses, such as can be found in caffeine tablets, may cause nausea, diarrhea, sleeplessness, trembling, headache, and nervousness. These symptoms can directly affect a person's ability to drive or operate machinery.

MARIJUANA

This drug can greatly reduce a driver's ability to react, stay in lane through curves, and maintain speed and proper distance relative to other vehicles. Marijuana delays a person's response to sights and sounds so that it takes a driver longer to react to a dangerous situation. The ability to perform sequential tasks can also be affected. As a result, a marijuana smoker's biggest driving problems occur when faced with unexpected events, such as a car approaching from a side street or a child running from between parked cars. The greater the demands of the driving situation, the less able the marijuana user will be to cope.

The driver who doesn't feel high may still be under the influence for a long time after the high has passed. A normal level of driving performance is not regained for at least 4-6 hours after smoking a single marijuana cigarette.

COMBINING MARIJUANA AND ALCOHOL

The combined use of marijuana and alcohol is more hazardous than the use of either alone. But combined use is becoming widespread. Studies have reported that nearly half of the regular users combine alcohol with marijuana, and that 60-80 percent of users drive while under the influence.

Marijuana and Learning

THC

The chief mind-altering ingredient in marijuana is called THC. By comparison with alcohol on a molecule for molecule basis, THC is 10,000 times stronger in its ability to produce intoxication.

In recent years the average strength of marijuana has greatly increased. In 1975, samples exceeding 1 percent THC content were rare; by 1980 a 5 percent content was common; and today it is not unusual for street marijuana to contain 7 percent THC.

THE EFFECTS

Most users of marijuana experience an increase in heart rate, reddening of the eyes, and dryness in the mouth and throat. Studies of marijuana's mental effects have revealed that the drug temporarily impairs short-term memory, alters sense of time, and reduces the ability to perform tasks requiring concentration, swift reactions, and coordination.

Many users feel that their hearing, vision, and skin sensitivity are enhanced by the drug, although these reports have not been objectively confirmed by research. The most commonly reported immediate adverse effect is acute panic anxiety reaction. This is usually described as an intense fear of losing control and going crazy.

Marijuana does not directly cause mental disorders, but it brings to the surface emotional problems and can even trigger more severe disturbances, particularly schizophrenia. People suffering from depression or other emotional problems who use marijuana to feel better often make the condition worse.

LEARNING PROBLEMS

Research shows that the effects of marijuana can impair thinking, reading comprehension, verbal skills, and arithmetic skills. Researchers also believe that the drug may interfere with the development of social skills and may encourage a person to want to escape from reality.

Opiates and Pregnancy

WHAT ARE THEY?

Opiates, sometimes called narcotics, are a group of drugs which are used medically to relieve pain, but also have a high potential for abuse. Some opiates come from a resin taken from the seed of the Asian poppy. This category of opiates includes opium, morphine, heroin, and codeine. Other types of opiates are synthetically or chemically manufactured.

THE EFFECTS

Opiates tend to relax the user. When injected, the user feels an immediate "rush." The user may go "on the nod," moving back and forth from alertness to drowsiness. With very large doses, the user cannot be awakened, pupils become smaller, and the skin becomes cold, moist, and bluish in color. Breathing slows down and death may occur.

ADDICTION

Dependence is very likely, especially when a person takes large doses or even takes small doses over an extended period. When a person becomes dependent, finding and taking the drug becomes the main focus in life. As more and more of the drug is taken over time, larger amounts are needed to get the same pleasant effects.

OPIATES AND PREGNANCY

Researchers estimate that nearly half of the women who are dependent on opiates suffer anemia, heart disease, diabetes, pneumonia, or hepatitis during pregnancy and childbirth. They have more spontaneous abortions, breech deliveries, caesarian sections, premature births, and stillbirths. Infants born to these women often have withdrawal symptoms which may last several weeks or months. Many of these babies die.

THE DANGERS

Most of the dangers are caused by taking too much of the drug at one time, using unsterile needles, contamination of the drug itself, or combining the drug with other substances. Opiate users may eventually develop infections of the heart lining and valves, skin abscesses, and congested lungs.

Peyote, Mescaline, and Psilocybin

WHAT ARE THEY?

These three substances are hallucinogens. They affect perception, sensation, thinking, self-awareness and emotion. Changes in time and space perception, delusions, and hallucinations may be mild or overwhelming, depending on dose and quality of the drug taken.

Effects will vary from one person to another and from one occasion to another. Because hallucinogens affect the mind, they are sometimes called psychedelics.

PEYOTE

Peyote is a small cactus which grows wild in the northeastern part of Mexico and the Rio Grande valley of Texas. The dried bulb of the plant, called a peyote button, induces a psychedelic effect on the user. There has been very little illegal use made of the peyote because it has an obnoxious taste and causes nausea. It has been used by Mexican Indians for hundreds of years in ritual ceremonies.

MESCALINE

Mescaline is a chemical extracted from peyote buttons and its effects are similar to those of LSD. It is obtainable in gelatin capsules, as a powder to be mixed with water, or as a liquid.

PSILOCYBIN

Psilocybin is an active ingredient of the psilocybin mushroom (grown in Mexico) and, like peyote and mescaline is used in traditional Indian rites. When eaten, these "sacred" or "magic" mushrooms affect mood and perception in a manner similar to LSD.

EFFECTS

Hallucinogens like these may cause the user to experience nausea, chills, flushes, irregular breathing, sweating, and trembling. The user's mood and behavior will vary from a trance-like state to great agitation and fear.

Phencyclidine and Bizarre Behavior

WHAT IS IT?

Phencyclidine, or PCP, was developed in the late 1950s as a surgical anesthetic. Because of its unusual and unpleasant side effects in human patients (delirium, extreme excitement, and visual disturbances), PCP was restricted for use as a veterinary anesthetic and tranquilizer. Most, if not all, PCP on the illicit market is produced in hideaway laboratories.

WHAT ARE THE EFFECTS?

Effects of PCP vary according to dosage levels. Low doses may provide the usual releasing effects of many psychoactive drugs, such as a floating euphoria and a feeling of numbness. Increased doses produce an excited, confused intoxication, which may include muscle rigidity, loss of concentration and memory, visual disturbances, delirium, feelings of isolation, convulsions, speech impairment, violent behavior, fear of death, and changes in perception.

Research shows that PCP seems to scramble the brain's ability to function normally. Everyday activities, such as driving or even walking, can be a task for the PCP user.

PCP IS DANGEROUS

PCP intoxication can produce violent and bizarre behavior even in mild-mannered people. Violence may be directed at themselves or others and often account for serious injuries or death. Bizarre behavior by PCP users has produced deaths by drowning, burning, falling from high places, driving accidents, and overdoses.

A temporary, schizophrenic-like psychosis, which can last for days or weeks, has also occurred in users of moderate and higher doses. During a psychotic episode the user can be excited, incoherent and aggressive or exactly the opposite - depressed and withdrawn. Paranoia, a state in which a person feels he is persecuted, will often accompany a psychotic episode. Long-term PCP users also report hearing voices and having memory and speech problems.

Most experts believe that PCP poses greater risks to the user than any other drug of abuse.

412

Stimulants

WHAT ARE THEY?

Stimulants, or uppers, are a class of drugs which stimulate the central nervous system, producing an increase in alertness and activity. The stimulants include cocaine, amphetamines, and caffeine.

THE LEGITIMATE USES

Current medical use of amphetamines is usually restricted to the treatment of narcolepsy, a rare disorder marked by an uncontrollable requirement for sleep, and for minor brain damage in children. Amphetamines are also prescribed for short-term appetite control.

Caffeine naturally occurs in coffee, tea, and in over-the-counter preparations designed to help people overcome drowsiness.

The only legitimate medical use of cocaine in the United States is as a local anesthetic.

OVERUSE AND ABUSE

Overuse and abuse are associated with all of the stimulants, but the risks are greatest with amphetamines and cocaine. Although caffeine represents a health risk when overused and abused, it has no comparison to the risks of amphetamines and cocaine.

AMPHETAMINES

Two trade names stand out in the amphetamine class: Benzedrine and Dexedrine. Because tolerance often develops, the user will take increasingly large doses to achieve the desired result. Hallucinations can occur with excessive use. For example, a driver who takes "bennies" to reduce sleepiness while driving runs the risk of an accident by reacting to something that is not there.

PSYCHOSIS

Amphetamines can accumulate in the user's body over a period of time, resulting in a poisoning of the body's system. This toxic condition can produce what is known as amphetamine psychosis, an extremely paranoid and suspicious state of mind which can erupt in bizarre, violent conduct.

Marijuana and Fertility

USE BY WOMEN

A recent study revealed that female users of marijuana had defective menstrual cycles three times more frequently than a similar group of nonusers. The defective cycles involved either a failure to ovulate or a shortened period of fertility - findings which suggest that regular marijuana use may reduce fertility in women.

Laboratory tests using female monkeys, whose reproductive organs are very similar to humans, showed that THC-treated monkeys were four times more likely than untreated monkeys to abort or have stillborn infants.

Males born of the THC-treated monkeys weighed less than average at birth. Scientists believe that marijuana has a poisonous effect on embryos and fetuses.

Research findings also suggest that marijuana may be especially harmful to the human reproductive system during the teen years, a period when the body undergoes rapid physical and sexual development.

USE BY MEN

Studies of adult males have found that chronic users had lower levels of testosterone (the principal male sex hormone) than nonusers and that giving up marijuana after heavy use reversed the condition. Other research has shown that the sperm count diminishes as marijuana use increases, and still other studies have shown that some of the sperm of chronic users are defective and nonfunctional.

OTHER DANGERS

Burnout is the user's term to describe the effect of prolonged marijuana smoking. Burned-out users are dull, slow moving, and inattentive. They are sometimes so unaware of their surroundings that they do not respond to normal conversation. This form of mental impairment may not be completely reversible.

Marijuana use increases heart rate as much as 50 percent depending on the amount of THC. It brings on chest pain in people who have a poor blood supply to the heart.

Drug Myths

WHAT IS BELIEVED

Drugs have been and probably always will be surrounded by myth. Many widely held beliefs about drugs and users have been proved untrue, but continue to persist. Heroin and cocaine have been called nonaddictive but are in fact highly addictive; LSD and peyote have been called "mind expanders" but work more like "mind destroyers"; marijuana has been touted as a "sex enhancer" although there is evidence to show that it reduces sexual desires and fertility. Marijuana is also commonly referred to as a "safe" drug even though it has been linked to medical problems.

WHAT IS KNOWN

The short-term effects of drugs on a user reflect both physical and physiological factors. These include the types and quantities of drugs consumed; the user's personal level of tolerance; the method of taking (swallowing, injecting, or inhaling); and the user's psychological state at the time of consumption. The immediate impact to a user will vary according to the factors. For example, a healthy individual who swallows a small amount of LSD at a party may experience no immediate health damage. However, if the user at the time of consumption is depressed or takes a larger dose there is a risk of mental breakdown.

The immediate outcomes of drug use may range from the user's passing out, experiencing mood changes, engaging in violence, suffering perceptual distortions, and losing control of body functions. These conditions make a person unable to judge time and distance, make sensible decisions, and operate vehicles or machinery. Thus a user poses a danger to himself and those around him.

The long-term effects come with repeated use. Addiction is destructive to the user, the family, and society as a whole.

Another reality is the connection between abuse and crime. Drugs and crime are often linked. A recent national survey reported that almost one-third of all inmates of state prisons were under the influence of a drug just before they committed their crimes. It's also known that abusers are not "mellow, happy dreamers," but are likely to commit violent crimes.

Inhalants Are Everywhere

WHAT ARE THEY?

Inhalants are breathable substances that can be sniffed or inhaled. Most are legal and many are found in everyday household products.

AEROSOLS

Anything in an aerosol can - especially spray paint - is a likely product for abuse. Other commonly abused spray products are vegetable oil and hair spray.

TOLUENES

The compound toluene is a favorite. It is found in gasoline, transmission fluid, model airplane glue and other glues, nail polish, nail polish remover, and a variety of ordinary substances found around the house.

EMPLOYEE AWARENESS AIDS

The term "glue sniffing" is associated with the abuse of toluenes. In this very dangerous practice, the user places airplane glue in a paper sack and holds it over the nose while inhaling the fumes. Many teenagers have sustained brain damage in this way.

NITRITES

Amyl nitrite is used for treating heart patients. When placed under the patient's nose, blood vessels dilate and the heart beats faster. It is sold in a cloth-covered plastic bulb. When the bulb is broken, it makes a snapping sound (thus the nickname "snapper" or "popper"). Butyl nitrite also affects blood pressure and heart rate, and is abused for the instant "rush" it gives.

OTHER INHALANTS

Other kinds of inhalants include nitrous oxide (laughing gas), dry cleaning fluids, and room deodorizers.

THE RISKS

There is a high risk of sudden death from spray inhalation because the spraying effect can either interfere directly with breathing, or produce irregular heart beats. The risk is increased when the fumes are concentrated, as would be the case when they are sniffed from a paper bag.

LSD: The Ultimate Flashback

WHAT IS IT?

LSD is an hallucinogen, i.e., a drug that affects perception, sensation, thinking, self-awareness, and emotion. Changes in time and space perception, delusions, and hallucinations can range from mild to overwhelming, depending on dose and quality of the LSD taken. Effects will vary from one person to another and from one occasion to another. Because LSD affects the mind, it is sometimes called a psychedelic drug.

LSD is man-made or synthetic. It is usually manufactured as a white, odorless powder taken orally. Basically, LSD causes changes in sensation. Users have described changes in vision, depth perception, and in the meanings of perceived objects. Sense of time and of self are altered. The user may see music or hear color.

Physical reactions range from minor changes such as dilated pupils; a rise in body temperature, heartbeat, or blood pressure; tremors; and unconsciousness.

FLASHBACK

A flashback is a recurrence of some features of a previous LSD experience. A flashback may be spontaneous - just happen - or it may be triggered by physical or psychological stress, by prescribed medications, or by marijuana. A flashback can cause great anxiety, and heavy use seems to produce them more frequently.

419

WHAT ARE THE DANGERS?

After taking LSD, a person loses control over normal thought processes. Although some perceptions are pleasant, others may cause panic or may make a person believe that he or she cannot be hurt. The long-term harmful reactions include anxiety and depression, and breaks from reality which may last from a few days to months.

The exact relationship between LSD and emotional disruption is not known, but it is suspected that when a person has suffered from an emotional disturbance prior to using LSD, the drug may cause a breakdown.

Ice (Crystal Methamphetamine)

Ice get its name from both its ice-like appearance and the belief among users that it is a "cool" smoke. It is actually crystal methamphetamine, a highly addictive drug. Like the name suggests, it is in the family of amphetamines, meaning that ice is a stimulant. Even the mildest amphetamines are well-known for causing personality changes, aggressive behavior, hallucinations, and paranoia.

Methamphetamine is super-potent and fast-acting. In its crystal form, the potency and rapidity of effects are even more pronounced.

MORE DANGEROUS THAN CRACK?

An easy way to understand ice is to compare it to crack. In fact, ice is to methamphetamine what crack is to cocaine. They both come in the form of clumpy crystals that look like rock salt or chips of ice. Ice and crack are colorless, odorless, smokable, and inhalable. They both act quickly and produce a powerful, euphoric or "floating" high. In one respect, ice is superior because the high will last for 12 to 24 hours, compared to a 30-minute high for crack.

Like crack, ice is highly addictive and even small dosages can cause serious health damage, even death.

A DANGEROUS NEW FAD FOR THE YOUNG

Ice is currently used mostly by the young - teenagers and people in their early 20s. Many of these users have suffered severe damage to vital organs such as the heart and brain, and many became addicted after a single use.

Body tolerance of ice occurs fairly quickly. Soon the user has to smoke more to get high. As use increases, toxic amounts of the drug accumulate in the body. Hallucinations then begin and the user falls into a psychotic condition in which brain functions can break down, often irreversibly.

Ice can over-stimulate the heart and raise blood pressure to an abnormally high level. Even a healthy body may not be able to ward off or survive a heart attack or a seizure of the arterial system.

Prescription Drugs

MISUSE IS COMMON

The average American uses more than 7 medications per year, and about 2 out of every 3 persons who visit the doctor's office will leave with a prescription in hand. Although prescription medications are often valuable in making the difference between comfort and pain, the widespread practice of dispensing medicines creates a high potential for drug misuse and abuse.

People with chronic, long-term health problems often require medications all of their lives. These persons are particularly vulnerable to drug misuse, not because they are seeking to get "high," but because their need to reduce pain leads them to greater and greater dosages until finally they develop a dependency or addiction. Many of these people become impaired because they take too much medication or take it at the wrong intervals.

Another misuse is taking drugs that have been prescribed for someone else. Using drugs that have been in the medicine cabinet for an extended period of time or combining an old prescription drug with a new prescription drug is risky. Misuse can have dangerous and even fatal outcomes.

WHAT CAN BE DONE?

Specific questions need to be asked when receiving a prescription. The answers may have an impact in the workplace. For example:

- What are the effects of the drug? Will it cause fainting, drowsiness or agitation?

- How and when should it be taken? For how long?

- What should not be done while taking the medicine?

HOSPITAL STATISTICS

It is well-known in the medical profession that misuse of prescription drugs is a major health problem. A large number of emergency room cases are related to improper self-administration of medications. When taken with care, prescription drugs can improve the quality of a person's life, but when misused they can severely damage and even bring an end to life.

Drugs and Stress

Millions of Americans who suffer from stress needlessly turn to prescription and non-prescription remedies. Headache sufferers alone spend more than $1.5 billion a year on aspirin and other over-the-counter products, and yet they often fail to find relief.

The majority of stress-related or tension headaches are caused by muscle contractions. Pain and tightness across the forehead or at the neck will produce a dull ache. Many of these headaches are triggered by fatigue. Physical stress, such as leaning over a machine or work table for several hours can cause muscles to tighten. When muscles in the head, neck, upper back or face are tense for a long period, a headache is apt to set in.

A stress-related headache differs from a migraine. A migraine is often so intense as to produce nausea and vomiting. Whether stress-related or migraine, the chance of a headache being related to an organic problem, such as a tumor, is less than one-half of one percent.

THE RISK OF USING DRUGS

Some people automatically head to the medicine cabinet when stress shows up, and in so doing they may be creating a separate problem. Aspirin, one of the most widely used pain relievers, can cause kidney damage and stomach irritation, and excessive amounts of the commonly used non-aspirin remedies are known to be harmful to the liver.

A frequent user of prescription and non-prescription pain relievers will eventually build up a tolerance in which the medications lose their effectiveness, requiring the user to take more and more in order to achieve the same level of relief. The result can be a dependency just as real and just as dangerous as a dependency on cocaine or heroin.

WHAT CAN BE DONE?

Relief from stress without the use of drugs can often be obtained by doing something simple. Moving around, changing posture, taking a rest break, or moving to a comfortable chair may be all that is required.

Simple relaxation exercises can also help, such as breathing deeply and flexing the muscles while imagining a peaceful scene.

Drugs and Accidents

More than half of America's highway deaths involve drugs, and drugs are a major contributor of on-the-job injuries and deaths caused by workers operating motor vehicles and working with dangerous machinery while impaired. Many different types of drugs are involved but three stand out: alcohol, caffeine and marijuana.

ALCOHOL

Alcohol is well known as an intoxicating substance. It also works as a sedative, affecting judgment and coordination. Alcohol causes sleepiness and increases the sleep-inducing effects of depressants, such as tranquilizers and barbiturates. Mixing these drugs while driving or operating equipment can be fatal to the operator and others.

CAFFEINE

The effects of caffeine relate to the amount taken and the individual. When a person drinks two cups of coffee, the effects begin in 15-30 minutes. The person's metabolism, body temperature, and blood pressure may increase.

Other effects can include hand tremors and a loss of coordination. Extremely high doses, such as can be found in caffeine tablets, may cause nausea, diarrhea, sleeplessness, trembling, headache, and nervousness.

MARIJUANA

This drug can greatly reduce a driver's ability to react, stay in lane through curves, and maintain speed and proper distance relative to other vehicles. Marijuana delays a person's response to sights and sounds so that it takes a driver longer to react to a dangerous situation.

The ability to perform sequential tasks can also be affected. As a result, a marijuana smoker's biggest driving problems occur when faced with unexpected events, such as a car approaching from a side street or a child running from between parked cars. The greater the demands of the driving situation, the less able the marijuana user will be to cope.

The driver who doesn't feel high may still be under the influence for a long time after the high has passed. A normal level of driving performance is not regained for at least 4-6 hours after smoking a single marijuana cigarette.

The Truth About Drugs

THE MYTH

Drugs have been and probably always will be surrounded by myth. Many widely held beliefs about drugs and users have been proved untrue, but continue to persist. Heroin and cocaine have been called nonaddictive but are in fact highly addictive; LSD and peyote have been called mind expanders but work more like mind destroyers; marijuana has been touted as a sex enhancer although there is evidence to show that it reduces sexual desires and fertility. Marijuana is also commonly referred to as a safe drug even though it has been linked to medical problems.

THE TRUTH

The short-term effects of drugs on a user reflect both physical and physiological factors. These include the types and quantities of drugs consumed; the user's personal level of tolerance; the method of taking (swallowing, injecting, or inhaling); and the user's psychological state at the time of consumption. The immediate impact to a user will vary according to the factors. For example, a healthy individual who swallows a small amount of LSD at a party may experience no immediate health damage. However, if the user at the time of consumption is depressed there is a risk of mental breakdown.

The immediate outcomes of drug use may range from the user's passing out, experiencing mood changes, engaging in violence, suffering perceptual distortions, and losing control of body functions. These conditions make a person unable to judge time and distance, make sensible decisions, and operate vehicles or machinery. Thus a user poses a danger to himself and those around him.

The long-term effects come with repeated use. Addiction is destructive to the user, the family, and society as a whole.

Another reality is the connection between abuse and crime. Drugs and crime are often linked. A recent national survey reported that almost one-third of all inmates of state prisons were under the influence of a drug just before they committed their crimes. It's also known that abusers are not mellow, happy dreamers, but are likely to commit violent crimes.

Look-Alike and Act-Alike Drugs

Look-alikes are drugs manufactured to look like and imitate the effects of real drugs. Most of the look-alikes are made to imitate amphetamines, or "uppers," and will often contain stimulants such as caffeine and other non-prescription drugs.

There are also cocaine look-alikes. When cocaine is in low supply and the buyer demand for it is high, look-alikes are apt to appear for sale on the street. Cocaine look-alikes are sometimes the substances used to dilute real cocaine, such as flour, talcum powder, baking soda and sugar. In some cases, chemicals will be added to the look-alike to give it a stimulating effect.

Act-alikes generally contain the same drugs as look-alikes. However, they are made with no attempt to make them look like the drug they are designed to imitate. The purpose behind making them look different is to give the manufacturer, who is usually an unlicensed chemist, a defense against laws that prohibit the manufacture and sale of look-alikes.

Act-alikes are often sold on the street as "speed" and "uppers." Even though they are not as strong as amphetamines, they represent a health danger to users who are led to believe they are safe.

Look-alikes and act-alikes are also called "ripoff drugs" and "phony dope." The street seller will represent the product as cocaine, amphetamines, or a popular drug, such as Quaalude. With cocaine, the buyer has no way of telling if the white powder being offered is in fact cocaine or some other white powder substance. Even with amphetamines and Quaalude, which can be bought with a prescription, the buyer can be tricked when the tablets or capsules bear counterfeit markings.

The negative effects of these drugs include anxiety, restlessness, weakness, throbbing headache, difficulty in breathing, and a rapid heart beat. Persons with high blood pressure can suffer brain hemorrhage and death. In an overdose situation it can happen that the attending physician will misidentify the drug causing the overdose, and as a result the emergency treatment will be ineffective or harmful.

The greatest risk associated with look-alikes and act-alikes is that the user will be led into a pattern of drug use which he or she believes is safe. Once started, the user is likely to switch to more dangerous drugs. This is a common pattern seen in teenagers and young adults.

Mixing Drugs

Illegal drugs, such as crack and marijuana, are easily available to anyone who wants to obtain them. Even more easily available are the hundreds of legal drugs that can be purchased at the local drug store or can be found in medicine cabinets in homes all across the United States.

Another drug that is common to our everyday style of living is alcohol. Alcohol and all forms of legal and illegal drugs produce effects that alter the way we feel, think and act. When alcohol and a drug are taken together, each of them will exert certain influences on the brain and the central nervous system. Oftentimes, these influences are increased beyond the normal strength of the two substances working alone, or the influences compete against each other and cause the user's body to react in unpredictable and risky ways.

The things we eat and drink are chemically processed within our bodies and eventually leave our bodies as waste. This process is called metabolism. The more rapidly a drug is metabolized, the less impact it has. When a drug is forced to compete with another drug, the metabolic process is slowed down, and sometimes short-circuited. In other words, the body's natural functions are disturbed and the result can be injury to health or life itself.

A heavy drinker runs a risk when taking a depressant to treat a medical condition. This is so because the heavy drinker will most likely consume alcohol before the depressant completely wears off. The combined effect of the depressant and the alcohol may place the body's system into an overdosed condition. Further, while in a stupor, the heavy drinker may forget that he has already consumed the medication and take another dose. This is not an unusual thing to happen, and many people have died or become seriously ill in this way.

Without a doubt, the greatest danger that comes from mixing alcohol and drugs relates to accidents. A very high percentage of injuries and deaths that occur in the workplace, at home, and on the highway is the result of doing three things in combination: drinking alcohol, taking one or more legal or illegal drugs, and operating a vehicle or equipment that can kill. There are two special dimensions to the tragedy of such accidents. The first is that accidents involving drugs and alcohol should not happen at all, and the second is that the victims of these unnecessary accidents are often innocent persons, such as co-workers, friends or family members.

Appendix F

Supervisor Aids

Drug Abuse at Work

ECONOMIC COSTS

Studies consistently indicate that drug abuse carries an extremely high cost to American industry. Why is drug abuse costly to business? The answer is that employees who use drugs have higher rates of absenteeism, turnover, sick days off, medical claims, and accident rates. Drug-abusing employees are associated with lower productivity, product loss and waste, as well as the use of poor judgment. Drug abusers also cause a greater number of problems for supervisors, such as insubordination and stealing to support a habit.

HUMAN COSTS

But drug abuse in the workplace cannot be looked at in just economic terms. The problem has a human side. There is the health damage to the user, and the neglect, shame and loss of affection within the user's family. There are the injuries and deaths inflicted upon employees by drug-impaired co-workers who cause accidents, and the maiming and killing of innocent people on the highways by workers who operate motor vehicles.

In some industries there is great potential for widespread damage to the public health and ecology. The incidents at Bhopal, Chernobyl and Valdez prove that human failure can produce catastrophic results, and this should force all of us to ask a fundamental question, "Can we afford to allow on-the-job drug abuse to be a contributing factor to human failure?"

DRUG ABUSE AFFECTS EVERYONE

Back in the 1960s and 1970s drug abuse was largely associated with the hippie life style. Not today. Drug abuse cuts across all segments of society - young and old, male and female, rich and poor, black and white. Drugs are just as likely to be taken at work or before going to work as at any other place or time.

The preferences for drugs have also changed. Although marijuana continues to be the most widely abused drug among the total population of users, cocaine has become the preferred drug of many. "Crack," an inexpensive but potent and potentially lethal form of cocaine, is becoming a favorite of the young and of those who cannot afford more expensive drugs.

Dimensions of Workplace Drug Abuse

Drug abuse has three dimensions that impact the workplace. First, and most importantly, is the effect of drugs on the health and personal life of the drug-abusing employee. Second is the accident risk that impairment poses to the drug-abusing employee, co-workers and others. Third is the loss of efficiency and productivity in work performance.

HEALTH AND PERSONAL LIFE

Abuse is the excessive use of drugs. Dependency and addiction are much more serious. Long before the abuser hits bottom, the body suffers serious deterioration. The signs can be memory loss; lack of interest in food, sex, and personal hygiene; and mood swings ranging from lethargy to hyperactivity.

On a personal level, a drug abuser will cause damage to the family unit and social relationships. The destruction of the home and social environment often begins with bickering in the home; followed by bitter arguments; neglect and mistreatment of children; and embarrassment among relatives and caring friends. Finally, the abuser will organize his or her life around drugs, and being in the company of other abusers.

SAFETY

The employer is expected to maintain a safe working environment for employees, people who enter the work premises, and for anyone who could be affected by the work or the persons who do the work. The use of drugs by an employee can have an impairing effect on the

433

employee's ability to think clearly and perform tasks that call for attention to safety. Statistics point clearly to a connection between the abuse of drugs and on-the-job injuries, deaths and major losses.

EFFICIENCY AND PRODUCTIVITY

An employee who regularly uses drugs cannot perform at full capacity, and is often someone who cannot get along with others. Abuse is linked with mistakes in judgment, loss and waste, theft, tardiness, absenteeism, turnover, and insurance costs. It usually begins with arriving on the job late and leaving early; followed by absenteeism; a productivity decline; judgment failure; and difficulties with co-workers and supervisors.

Right and Wrong Actions

RIGHT ACTIONS

- Look for the performance and behavior indicators of drug abuse.

- Confront the offending employee in a non-accusing way. Describe the unacceptable performance or behavior, explain why it cannot be tolerated, and allow the employee to give a reason for it.

- Advise the employee to obtain professional assistance when the problem appears to be drug related. Remind the employee that a failure to correct the basic problem could lead to discipline.

- Keep detailed records of what was observed and what was done in the way of intervention.

- Report observations and intervention actions.

- Insist that professional help be obtained when the employee has admitted an abuse problem.

- Ensure that the employee is making positive use of any assistance received as the result of a referral to professional help.

- Take immediate action to remove an employee from a work situation where drug abuse has damaged or poses a danger to safety, production, or property.

WRONG ACTIONS

- Do not accuse an employee of abuse.

- Do not raise the subject of abuse directly.

- Do not be drawn into a protective or confidential relationship with an employee.

- Do not discuss actual or suspected abusing employees with other workers.

- Do not use derogatory terms when referring to a suspected drug abuser.

The Tell-Tale Signs of Drug Abuse

The supervisor is the person most likely to detect changes in the performance and behavior patterns of an abusing employee, and is the person responsible for initiating action to correct the problem. The supervisor is also in the best position to follow up and determine if the problem has been corrected.

Some common signs point to the presence of drug abuse. These signs may appear to result from other causes, but when examined closely the connections to abuse are often apparent.

- A record of no-shows and lateness.

- Prolonged absences from the workstation.

- Frequent telephone calls, perhaps for the purpose of arranging to meet with a supplier.

- Frequent and long visits to the rest room or locker room, perhaps to take a drug.

- Visits to the employee by strangers or other employees for matters unrelated to the job.

- Unexplained nervousness.

- Deviations from work rules and standards.

- An unexplained change in disposition in a short period of time.

- Weight loss and loss of appetite.

- Withdrawal symptoms, such as a runny nose, sniffling, red eyes, trembling of hands or mouth, unsteady gait and a general tiredness.

- Symptoms of being under the influence.

Indicators and Intervention

When substance abuse is believed to be contributing to an employee's deteriorating performance, ignoring the situation won't help. It may be the employee who has an alcohol or drug problem or it may be a family member. No matter who has a problem, it will likely only get worse and have costly consequences unless action is taken.

RECOGNIZING THE INDICATORS

Clinical diagnosis of an alcohol or other drug problem is not the job of the supervisor, but work performance is. A key part of every supervisor's job is to remain alert to changes in employee performance and to work with employees who are having problems so that performance improves.

The following list of performance and behavior problems are common to many substance-abusing employees. However, it is important to remember that these symptoms do not necessarily indicate that the employee has a substance abuse problem.

PERFORMANCE INDICATORS

- Inconsistent work quality

- Poor concentration

- Lowered productivity

- Increased absenteeism

- Unexplained disappearances from the jobsite

- Carelessness and mistakes

- Errors in judgment

- Needless risk-taking

- Disregard for safety

- Extended lunch periods and early departures

BEHAVIOR INDICATORS

- Frequent financial problems

- Avoiding friends and colleagues

- Blaming others for own problems and shortcomings

- Complaints about problems at home

- Deteriorating personal appearance

- Complaints and excuses of vaguely-defined illnesses

WHEN AND HOW TO INTERVENE

When an employee's performance begins to deteriorate for whatever reason, the supervisor has the right and responsibility to intervene. The supervisor does not need to be an expert on alcohol and other drugs to intervene appropriately if substance abuse is suspected; the intervention should be focused on the performance problem.

PRINCIPLES OF INTERVENTION

- Stick to the facts as they affect work performance.

- Don't rely on memory; have all supporting documents and records available.

- Do not discuss alcohol or drug use.

- Be clear and firm:

  - Explain company policy concerning performance.

  - Explain company substance abuse policy.

  - Explain consequences if performance expectations are not met.

- Be supportive but avoid emotional involvement:

- Offer help in resolving performance problems.

- Identify resources where the employee can obtain help.

Appendix G

Aids to Drug Testing

Instructions for Persons to Be Tested

Your appointment for drug and/or alcohol testing has been set for:

_____(time)   on _____(date)

The appointment place is: _____

AIDS TO DRUG TESTING

Please keep the appointment and be on time. Only a valid emergency supported by documentation and verified by your supervisor will be an accepted reason for not appearing or not appearing on time.

Bring to the appointment a form of official identification that bears your photograph.

Do not bring packages or items that could be thought to conceal substitute urine.

Please cooperate with the testing personnel.

If this will be your first experience with testing, do not be concerned. You will be treated with respect and not asked to do anything unreasonable. Steps will be taken by the testing personnel to guard against substitution or contamination of specimens, but they will not intrude on your privacy or personal dignity.

If something occurs while you are being processed which you feel could affect the test result, you should report this to the person who scheduled your appointment.

Please take this form with you to the testing appointment.

Test Consent in Reasonable Cause and Post-Accident Situations

PART I. NOTICE TO EMPLOYEE

The Company's policy provides that an employee may be required to submit to drug or alcohol testing (1) when the employee's performance or behavior on the job provides reasonable cause to believe that the employee is under the influence of a drug or alcohol, or (2) when an employee has been involved in an accident that requires further inquiry.

Reasonable cause has been shown to believe that you may be under the influence of a drug or alcohol, or that you have been directly involved in an accident that requires further inquiry.

PART II. EMPLOYEE'S ACKNOWLEDGMENT AND CONSENT

I am aware of the Company's policy referred to above. I understand that I cannot be compelled to submit to a drug or alcohol test, but that if I refuse I may be subject to disciplinary action, including discharge. I understand that if the results of such a test reveals an unexplained presence of a drug or alcohol in my body I may be subject to disciplinary action, including discharge.

I hereby consent to the testing, and I give consent to the Company and its agents, including the collecting and testing agencies, to disclose and discuss the results of testing for official purposes.

_____   _____

(Signature of Employee)   (Date)

Return to Duty Test Consent

PART I. NOTICE TO PERSON RETURNING TO DUTY

Company policy provides that an employee suspended for having in his or her body system an unexplained presence of a prohibited drug may be required as a condition of reinstatement to enter a Company-approved rehabilitation program.

An element of a rehabilitation program may require the suspended employee to undergo, cooperate with, and successfully complete an approved course of therapy as a condition of reinstatement. Further, if reinstated, the employee may be required to remain enrolled in the

443

program for the purpose of receiving follow-up, reinforcing, or maintenance therapy.

If you are reinstated, you will be expected to remain drug-free and you may from time to time be asked on an unannounced basis to provide specimens for drug testing. If you refuse to provide specimens when requested to do so or if such specimens reveal an unexplained presence of a prohibited drug, you may be subject to disciplinary action, including discharge.

PART II. RESPONSE OF PERSON RETURNING TO DUTY

I have read and understand the provisions regarding reinstatement following a violation of the Company's policy. I agree to comply with those provisions.

I specifically consent at this time to give specimen(s) for testing purposes. I also give consent to the Company and its agents, including the collecting and testing agencies, to disclose and discuss the results of such testing.

_____   _____

(Signature of Consenting Person)   (Date)

Applicant's Consent to Be Tested

I understand it is the policy of the Company to conduct urine tests of job applicants for the purpose of detecting drug abuse, and that one of the requirements for consideration of employment with the Company is the satisfactory passing of the Company's urine test.

For the purpose of being further considered for employment, I hereby agree to provide a specimen of my urine so that it may be analyzed for the presence of drugs.

I understand that a favorable test result will not necessarily guarantee that I will be employed by the Company.

If I am accepted for employment, I agree to take drug and/or alcohol tests whenever requested by the Company, and I understand that the taking of such tests is a condition of my continued employment.

I also give consent to the drug testing agency to release to the Company and other officially interested parties the results of the tests made of my urine specimen.

At this time I consent to the drug test.

_____   _____

(Signature of Applicant)   (Date Signed)

Employee's Consent to Be Tested

I have been made aware of and I understand my employer's policy concerning drug and/or alcohol abuse. I understand that the policy authorizes testing to ensure compliance.

I understand that I cannot be compelled to give specimens, but that giving specimens and cooperating in the testing is a condition of my continued employment. I understand that if I refuse to provide specimens I will be subject to disciplinary action up to and including discharge.

I understand that if I give specimens, such as urine, breath or blood specimens, they will be analyzed for the presence of drugs and/or alcohol, and that a positive test will subject me to disciplinary action up to and including discharge.

I understand I am now being asked to give a specimen of my:

AIDS TO DRUG TESTING

[ ] Urine

[ ] Breath

[ ] Blood

I understand the reason for the testing is related to:

[ ] A reasonable cause determination that I may be impaired by a drug and/or alcohol.

[ ] The investigation of a work-related accident or incident.

[ ] Random testing to assure safe operations.

[ ] Periodic testing conducted incident to health or fitness for duty evaluations.

[ ] Testing conducted following release from a program of rehabilitation.

[ ] My assignment to a position that requires testing as a pre-assignment condition.

[ ] Other:_____

I understand the testing is being done pursuant to:

[ ] DOT regulations

[ ] My employer's authority

I authorize the officers, employees and agents of my employer, the specimen collecting agency, the drug testing laboratory, the medical review officer, and other officially interested parties to communicate among themselves for official purposes my drug and/or alcohol test results, both orally and in writing, and to communicate such test results at any official, administrative or judicial proceeding.

I also authorize the above named parties to have continued access to my test specimens for the purpose of conducting any further analyses or studies that may be necessary.

At this time I consent to provide the specimen(s) for testing.

Employee's Voluntary Notice of Legal Drug Use

Please be advised that I am currently taking the following prescription drug which has been prescribed to me for a valid medical purpose:

Name of drug: _____

Prescription No: _____   Prescription Date: _____

Prescribing Physician's Name: _____

Prescribing Physician's Phone Number: _____

My use of this drug is:

    [ ] Temporary and expected to end on or about _____

    [ ] Indefinite

I hereby give my consent to the above named prescribing physician to answer the Company's questions about my use of this drug.

_____   _____

(Signature of Employee)   . (Date Signed)

Notice of Positive Test Result

This is to inform you that the urine, breath or blood specimen that you presented for drug testing was found to be positive for:

[ ] Cannabinoids (a marijuana substance)

[ ] Cocaine

[ ] Amphetamines

[ ] Phencyclidine (PCP)

[ ] Opiates

     [ ] Codeine

     [ ] Morphine

     [ ] Heroin

[ ] Methadone

[ ] Methaqualone

[ ] Benzodiazepines

[ ] Barbiturates

[ ] Propoxyphene

[ ] Other: _____

Annual Summary of Test Results for Pipeline Operations

1. The total number of persons who were tested: _____

2. The total number of persons who tested negative: _____

3. The total number of persons who tested positive: _____

4. The number of tests by category and positive results:

CATEGORY	# OF TESTS	# OF POSITIVES
Pre-employment	_____	_____
Periodic	_____	_____
Reasonable Cause	_____	_____
Random	_____	_____
Post-accident	_____	_____

5. The disposition of each person who failed a drug test:

a. Not hired: _____

b. Terminated: _____

c. Assigned to non-DOT duties: _____

d. Referred to Rehabilitation: _____

e. Leave of Absence or Layoff: _____

6. The number of tests positive in screening: _____

7. The number of tests that were positive in the confirmatory test and positive upon review by the MRO: _____

8. The number of positive tests that were reported to the MRO by drug category:

a. Marijuana _____

b. Cocaine _____

c. Opiates _____

d. Amphetamines _____

e. Phencyclidine (PCP) _____

Urine Specimen Collection Handbook for Federal Workplace Drug Testing Programs

CONTENTS

- Collection Steps

- Blind Samples

- Documentation Errors/Fatal Flaws

- Regulated and Nonregulated Employers

- "Shy Bladder" Collection

- Direct Observed Collections

- Dealing With Problems

INTRODUCTION

On September 15, 1986, President Ronald Reagan signed Executive Order 12564 establishing the goal of a Drug-Free Federal Workplace. The Order required the head of each Executive agency to establish a program to test for the use of illegal drugs by federal employees in sensitive positions and required the Secretary of Health and Human Services to promulgate scientific and technical guidelines for drug testing programs. The Executive Order also required the Department of Health and Human Services (HHS) to assist the Office of Personnel Management to develop and improve training programs for federal supervisors and managers on illegal drug use and to mount an intensive drug awareness campaign throughout the federal workforce.

Public Law 100-71 (July 11, 1987) requires HHS to do the following: (1) certify that each agency has developed a plan for achieving a drug-free workplace in accordance with Executive Order 12564 and applicable provisions of law, and (2) publish Mandatory Guidelines that (a) establish comprehensive standards for all aspects of laboratory drug testing and laboratory procedures to be applied in carrying out the Executive Order, including standards that require the use of the best available technology for ensuring the full reliability and accuracy of drug tests and strict procedures governing the chain of custody of specimens collected for drug testing; (b) specify the drugs for which federal employees may be tested; and (c) establish standards and procedures for periodic review of laboratories and criteria for certification and revocation of certification of laboratories to perform drug testing in carrying out the Executive Order.

This handbook provides guidance to collectors who will be collecting urine specimens in accordance with the Mandatory Guidelines for Federal Workplace Drug Testing Programs. The collector is key to the success of a drug testing program and is the one individual with whom all donors will have direct, face-to-face contact. If the collector does not ensure the integrity of the specimen and adhere to the collection process, the specimen may not be considered a valid piece of evidence. If a specimen is reported positive for a drug or metabolite, the entire collection process must be able to withstand the closest scrutiny and all challenges to its integrity.

This guidance is intended to supplement the information provided in the Mandatory Guidelines.

Note: All collectors must understand and follow the collection procedures.

There may be intermediaries, such as consortia, contractors, clinics, or doctors, who act as agency representatives and who conduct collections. While an agency can contract for such functions, it is the agency's responsibility to ensure that the collection procedures comply with the Mandatory Guidelines.

THE COLLECTOR

The collection site person performs essential steps in conducting a federal agency urine specimen collection for drug testing. The Mandatory Guidelines define a collection site person as "a person who instructs and assists individuals at a collection site and who receives and makes an initial examination of the urine specimen provided by those individuals."

The following individuals may serve as collectors:

1. Agency employees who have received training in collecting urine specimens in accordance with the Mandatory Guidelines.

2. Non-medical and medical personnel (e.g., nurses, medical technicians, physicians, physicians' assistants) contracted by an agency who have received training in collecting urine specimens in accordance with the Mandatory Guidelines.

Note: An individual working for an HHS- certified drug testing laboratory will not be allowed to serve as a collector of a regulated specimen if that individual can link the donor with the specimen drug test result or laboratory report. To allow such an individual to collect such a specimen would compromise the confidentiality of the donor's test result.

A donor cannot serve as the collector of his or her own urine specimen. The supervisor of a donor should not serve as the collector unless there is no feasible alternative.

In general, an employee who is subject to the Federal Workplace Drug Testing Program should not be a collector or an observer for co-workers who are in the same testing pool or who work together with that employee on a daily basis. This is to preclude any potential appearance of conflict of interest.

When a collection is required to be performed under direct observation, the collector must be the same gender as the donor. There is no exception to this requirement.

Note: Instructions describing the collection procedure must be available at the collection site for reference by the collector.

THE COLLECTION SITE

A collection site may be a permanent or temporary facility located either at the worksite or at a remote site. A collection site must at a minimum:

1. Allow the donor to have privacy while providing the urine specimen.

2. Have a source of water or moist towelettes for washing hands.

3. Have a work area for the collector.

4. Allow the collector to restrict access to the site during the collection.

Note: The term "collection site" refers to the entire facility used to collect the urine specimen, that is, the rest room or toilet stall and the work area used by the collector.

Any of the following could be used to collect urine specimens provided the area can be arranged to satisfy the minimum requirements listed above:

1. All types of rest rooms (e.g., male or female, employee, doctor's office, hospital, clinic, hotel/motel, public)

2. Mobile facility (e.g., a vehicle with an enclosed toilet)

Note: The collector's work area must be located outside the rest room. However, if there is no appropriate space available outside the rest room to serve as a work area and the rest room is large enough to accommodate a work area, the work area may be located inside the rest room as long as the donor has privacy while providing a urine specimen and the collector is the same gender as the donor.

With regard to security at a collection site while collections are being conducted, the following measures should be taken:

1. Restrict access to only authorized personnel.

2. Restrict access to collection materials/supplies.

Note: The collector should ensure that the donor does not have access to items that could be used to adulterate or dilute the specimen (e.g., soap, disinfectants, personal hygiene products, water).

3. Prohibit unobserved entrance/exit from the site.

4. Provide for secure handling/storage of specimens from collection until shipment.

Note: Security and specimen handling procedures may vary significantly depending on whether the collection site is at a permanent or temporary location. When the collection site is a permanent facility that is used primarily for collections, all materials and supplies are readily available and there will normally be cabinets, lockers, or refrigerators that can be used to secure specimens prior to shipment to the laboratory. Additionally, all records are maintained at the permanent site with appropriate copies of documents being sent to the laboratory, agency, and Medical Review Officer (MRO). For temporary or remote collection sites, all supplies are brought to the site and then the site is returned to its normal use. In these cases, the collector will normally transport the records and specimens (i.e., unless the specimens are shipped to the laboratory directly from the temporary collection site) to another location. This other location will then be used to store records, prepare specimens for shipment to the laboratory (if applicable), and distribute documents as required. With the transfer of records and specimens that may occur when a temporary site is used, a primary concern for collectors is to ensure that chain of custody is maintained for the specimens.

In final preparation of the site, any water supply available in the collection site must be controlled to prevent the donor from attempting to dilute the specimen. This includes any water supply in an immediate adjacent area to which the donor may have access prior to handing the specimen to the collector. Whenever possible, bluing or other color appropriate agents must be added to any tank or toilet bowl that is accessible to the donor.

The following are acceptable ways to control access to a water supply:

1. Use tape to prevent opening/turning faucet handles.

2. Close the shutoff valve for the water supply.

Note: If access to a water supply in the rest room cannot be controlled, the collector may tell the donor that he or she will be listening at the entrance to the rest room for any sounds associated with the donor attempting to use the available sources of water. Alternatively, the collector may enter the rest room with the donor if the collector is the same gender as the donor, but remains outside the toilet stall.

AIDS TO DRUG TESTING

COLLECTION SUPPLIES

Once a site has been selected, the collector must ensure that the following supplies are available to conduct proper collections:

1. Clean, single-use, wrapped or sealed specimen bottles with appropriate caps/lids.

2. Clean, single-use, wrapped or sealed collection containers for each donor to urinate into. Use of a collection container is optional, but highly recommended if the specimen bottle neck or opening is small.

3. Temperature strips that can be attached to the exterior surface of collection containers or specimen bottles to measure the temperature within 4 minutes after the donor gives the specimen container/bottle to the collector.

Note: If the temperature strip does not appear to be working properly, the collector must take the specimen temperature with a temperature measuring device that has a sterile sleeve or other methodology to prevent possible contamination of the specimen.

4. Appropriate temperature measuring device that can be used to measure a donor's body temperature if the temperature of the specimen is outside of the range listed in the Mandatory Guidelines.

5. Office of Management and Budget (OMB) approved Custody and Control Forms (CCFs).

6. Tamper-evident labels/seals for the specimen bottles that have the same preprinted specimen I.D. number that appears on the CCF. The appropriate labels/seals are provided with each CCF.

Note: The tamper-evident seal also serves as a label; therefore, it will be referred to either as the tamper-evident label/seal or as the label/seal.

7. Separate supply of tamper-evident seals.

Note: Occasionally, the tamper-evident label/seal provided with the CCF will not properly adhere to the specimen bottle because of environmental conditions (e.g., moisture, temperature, specimen bottle material). When this occurs, the collector should have a separate tamper-evident seal that can be used to seal the specimen bottle.

8. Leak-proof plastic bags in which sealed specimen bottles are placed prior to shipment to the laboratory.

9. Absorbent material that is placed inside the leak-proof plastic bag in case the specimen bottle leaks during shipment.

10. Shipping containers/mailers that can be labeled for transporting specimens to the laboratory and that can be securely sealed to eliminate the possibility of undetected tampering.

Note: Generally, the above items are supplied as collection kits, i.e., each collection kit contains the items needed to collect a specimen from a donor and send it to a laboratory for testing.

11. Bluing or other coloring agent to add to the toilet bowl or tank to discourage adulteration/dilution of the specimen.

12. Collector should have appropriate identification. The collector is required to provide his or her identification (or collection company identification) if requested by the donor. There is no requirement for the collector to have a picture I.D. or to provide his or her driver's license with an address. Also, the collector is not required to provide any certification or other documentation to the donor proving the collector's training in the collection process.

Note: Although not required, it would benefit the collector to have the agency representative's name and telephone number to call should unusual situations arise during the collection process.

13. Storage box, area, or place where specimens can be stored before shipment to the laboratory.

Note: If a specimen is not immediately prepared for shipment after collection, chain of custody must be maintained by placing the specimen in a secured temporary location (e.g., inside a refrigerator that can be secured, inside a cabinet that can be secured, an unsecured temporary storage area that is always maintained within the line of sight of the collector to ensure that no one has access to the specimen).

AIDS TO DRUG TESTING

Note: Collectors should use single-use disposable gloves while handling specimens. The Occupational Safety and Health Administration has specific guidelines addressing protection of employees who are exposed to potentially infectious body fluids.

CUSTODY AND CONTROL FORM

All urine specimens must be collected while maintaining chain of custody. Chain of custody is the term used to describe the process of documenting the handling of a specimen from the time a donor gives the specimen to the collector, during the testing at the laboratory, and until the results are reported by the laboratory.

For specimens collected under federal regulations, an Office of Management and Budget (OMB) approved Custody and Control Form (CCF) must be used to document the collection of a specimen at the collection site. The OMB-approved CCF can be supplied by a number of different sources (e.g., laboratories, collectors, MROs) without being modified; however, it is usually provided by the laboratory.

Note: There is a space provided at the top of the form to allow the laboratory to preprint its name and address. If the form does not have the preprinted laboratory name and address, the collector must ensure that the name and address of the laboratory receiving the specimen are printed on the top of the form.

Note: If the CCF uses a barcode for the specimen identification number, there must be a human readable number associated with the barcode.

Note: The OMB number must appear on each copy of the CCF.

The CCF consists of the following seven copies with the color of each copy noted in parentheses:

Copy 1. Original must accompany specimen to laboratory (White)

Copy 2. Second original must accompany specimen to laboratory (White)

Copy 3. Split specimen copy must accompany split specimen to laboratory (White)

Copy 4. Medical Review Officer copy (Pink)

Copy 5. Donor copy (Green)

Copy 6. Collector copy (Yellow)

Copy 7. Employer copy (Blue)

Note: Copy 3 is discarded for single specimen collections.

The reverse side of Copy 7 gives instructions on completing the CCF. The CCF is completed as follows:

Step 1. This step is completed by the collector or agency. The following information is required: name, address, and identification number (if applicable) of the employer; specific name and address of the MRO; donor's social security number or other employee identification number; reason for the test; and tests to be performed.

Note: The agency will most likely provide all the necessary information when the collector is notified that an individual has been selected for testing. The notification should also normally indicate the time the donor should arrive at the site or when the collector should come to the site to collect the specimen.

Step 2. This step is completed by the collector. The collector is required to measure the temperature of the specimen within 4 minutes after receiving the specimen from the donor. If the temperature is within the acceptable range, the "Yes" box is checked. If the temperature is outside the acceptable range, the "No" box is checked and the actual temperature is recorded. When this occurs, it may only be possible to indicate that the actual temperature is greater than or less than the highest or lowest temperature indicated on the measuring device.

Step 3. This step is completed by the collector and donor.

Step 4. This step is completed by the donor. On Copy 4 of the CCF, the donor provides a daytime phone number, evening phone number, date of birth, printed name, signature, and date of collection.

Note: The donor should read the statement on the CCF before providing a signature.

Note: In the event that the donor refuses to sign Copy 4, the collector must provide an appropriate comment on the "REMARKS" line in Step 5 on the CCF.

Step 5. This step is completed by the collector. The following information is provided: name and address of the collection facility, collector's business phone number, printed name and signature of the collector, date of collection, time of collection, and a block to check whether the collection was a single or split specimen collection. This section also has a "REMARKS" line to allow the collector to annotate any problems that may have occurred during the collection.

Step 6. This step is started by the collector and completed as necessary thereafter. This section is used to document the transfer and handling of the specimen at the collection site. The first transfer of the specimen occurs when the donor gives the specimen container/bottle to the collector. On the first line, the collector records the date and prints and signs his or her name in the column labeled "SPECIMEN RECEIVED BY." The collector should complete the first line immediately after receiving the specimen from the donor.

Note: The collector may delay documenting the chain of custody until after the temperature of the specimen is measured to ensure that it is measured within 4 minutes after receiving the specimen. After the specimen/split specimen bottles are properly sealed and the donor has initialed the label/seal on each bottle, one or more of the following actions may occur:

A. Specimen/split specimens are immediately placed in a leak-proof plastic bag and sealed in a shipping container/package for shipment to the laboratory.

The collector must complete the second line of Step 6. The collector records the date of shipment, signs his or her name in the column labeled "SPECIMEN RELEASED BY," prints name of carrier in the column labeled "SPECIMEN RECEIVED BY," and prints "Ship to Lab" in the column labeled "PURPOSE OF CHANGE." The leak-proof plastic bag containing the specimen/split specimens and appropriate copies of the CCF are sealed in a shipping container/package for shipment to the laboratory.

Note: If a collector is collecting specimens from several donors during a short period of time and the collector intends to place all of the specimens in a single shipping container, the collector may complete each CCF indicating that the specimen has been released to a specific carrier and place each specimen bottle in its separate leak-proof plastic bag along with the Copy 1 and Copy 2 of the CCF. To use this procedure, the collector must maintain visual contact of each plastic bag until all plastic bags are sealed in the shipping container.

B. Specimen/split specimens are placed in temporary storage before being prepared for shipment to the laboratory.

The collector places the specimen/split specimens and the CCF in temporary storage until the collector or other individual has an opportunity to place the specimen/ split specimens in leak-proof plastic bags and to seal the bags in a shipping container/package. The collector records the date of transfer, prints and signs his or her name in the column labeled "SPECIMEN RELEASED BY," prints "Temporary Storage" in the column labeled "SPECIMEN RECEIVED BY," and in the column labeled "PURPOSE OF CHANGE" prints the reason for the specimen transfer. After an individual removes the specimen/split specimens from temporary storage, the individual records the date of transfer, prints "Temporary Storage" in the column labeled "SPECIMEN RELEASED BY," prints and signs his or her name in the column labeled "SPECIMEN RECEIVED BY," and in the column labeled "PURPOSE OF CHANGE" prints the reason for the specimen transfer (e.g., Prepare for Shipment). On the fourth line, the individual who is placing the specimen/split specimens in a leak-proof plastic bag and then placing and sealing the plastic bags in the shipping container/package records the date of shipment, signs his or her name in the column labeled "SPECIMEN RELEASED BY," prints the name of the carrier in the column labeled "SPECIMEN RECEIVED BY," and prints "Ship Specimen" in the column labeled "PURPOSE OF CHANGE."

Note: While a specimen is in temporary storage, the storage area must be secured, or someone must be constantly present at the site, to prevent anyone from gaining access to the specimen or split specimens being stored.

AIDS TO DRUG TESTING

C. Specimen/split specimens are transferred to another individual.

The collector transfers the specimen/ split specimens and the copies of the CCF to another individual who prepares the specimen/split specimens for shipment to the laboratory or to another individual who will hand carry the specimen/split specimens directly to the laboratory. On the second line, the collector records the date of transfer and prints and signs his or her name in the column labeled "SPECIMEN RELEASED BY." The receiving individual prints and signs his or her name in the column labeled "SPECIMEN RECEIVED BY" and in the column labeled "PURPOSE OF CHANGE" prints the reason for the specimen transfer (e.g., Prepare for Shipment, Deliver to Lab).

If the "PURPOSE OF CHANGE" is to prepare the specimen/split specimens for shipment to the laboratory, the receiving individual records on the third line the date of shipment, signs his or her name in the column labeled "SPECIMEN RELEASED BY," prints name of carrier in the column labeled "SPECIMEN RECEIVED BY," and prints "Ship Specimen" in the column labeled "PURPOSE OF CHANGE." If the "PURPOSE OF CHANGE" is that the receiving individual will personally deliver the specimen/split specimens to the laboratory, after arriving at the laboratory, the receiving individual records the date of delivery, prints and signs his or her name in the column labeled "SPECIMEN RELEASED BY." An individual at the laboratory will print and sign his or her name in the column labeled "SPECIMEN RECEIVED BY" and in the column labeled "PURPOSE OF CHANGE" prints the reason for the specimen transfer (e.g., Receipt of Specimen for Testing).

Note: The individual receiving the specimen/split specimens from the collector is responsible for placing the specimen/split specimens in a leak-proof plastic bag before sealing the plastic bag containing the specimen/split specimens in the shipping container/package or personally delivering the specimen/split specimens to the laboratory.

Note: The "PURPOSE OF CHANGE" block is used only for documenting the transfer of specimens and must not be used for other purposes (e.g., to indicate the condition of the specimen bottle seal(s)).

Note: After the shipping container/package is sealed, there is no requirement for couriers, express carriers, or Postal Service personnel to document chain of custody for the specimens during transit because they do not have access to the specimen/split specimens or the CCF. Chain of custody annotations resume when the shipping container/package is opened and an individual has access to the specimen/split specimens and the CCF.

Step 7. This step is completed by the laboratory. When the laboratory receives the specimen bottle(s) and the CCF, discrepancies noted in completion of the CCF must be documented by the laboratory on the "REMARKS" line in Step 7.

Note: When a specimen with a discrepancy is received with a discrepancy, the laboratory should immediately contact the collection site to determine if the discrepancy can be recovered. If the collection site can provide a Memorandum For Record (MFR) (see Appendix B for a sample MFR) to recover the discrepancy, the laboratory is permitted to test the specimen, but must hold the results until the MFR is received. If the discrepancy cannot be recovered by an MFR from the collection site, the laboratory may not test the specimen and must indicate the reason on the "REMARKS" line. This notification also alerts the collection site that an error has been made and that the collection site must implement corrective action to prevent the recurrence of the discrepancy. The laboratory should include a copy of the MFR with its report to the MRO to ensure that the MRO is aware that the discrepancy has been recovered.

DONOR IDENTIFICATION

The donor must be positively identified as the individual selected for testing. Acceptable methods of identification are

1. Photo identification (e.g., driver's license, employee badge).

2. Positive identification by an agency representative.

3. Any identification allowed under an agency's workplace drug testing plan.

The following are not acceptable ways to identify the donor:

AIDS TO DRUG TESTING

1. Identification by a co-worker or another donor.

2. Single non-photo identification card (e.g., social security card, credit card, union or other membership cards, pay vouchers, voter registration card).

Note: If the donor has no photo identification, the collector should record on the "REMARKS" line that photo identification was not available. The collector may proceed with the collection if the donor can provide two items of identification bearing his or her signature. After the donor signs the certification statement, the collector should compare the donor's signature with signatures on the identification that was presented. If the signatures match, the collector lists on the "REMARKS" line the two items of identification used to identify the donor and states the "signature identification was confirmed." The collector then continues with the collection process. If the signature does not match the signatures on the two items of identification presented, the collector should state on the "REMARKS" line that "signature identification is unconfirmed," discontinue the collection, and notify the collection site supervisor and the agency.

In situations where the donor does not have either a photo identification or two other appropriate items of identification that could be used to verify identity and signature, this should not be automatically considered a refusal to test. The collector should remember that his or her primary function is to obtain a specimen that can be tested for drugs. The collector should provide sufficient information on the "REMARKS" line to help the MRO and the agency make a determination regarding the validity of the specimen and the collection process.

COLLECTION STEPS

The following steps describe a typical urine collection procedure under the Mandatory Guidelines:

Note: Changes in the sequence of the steps, errors, or omissions in some of the steps may result in a specimen being unacceptable for testing at the laboratory or the results being declared invalid upon review by the MRO.

Step 1. After preparing the collection site and verifying the identification of the donor, the collector ensures that the required information is provided in Step 1 of the CCF. This includes:

a. Agency's name, address, and I.D. number (if applicable).

b. MRO name and address.

Note: A specific physician's name and address must appear on the form rather than the name of the clinic or medical facility.

c. Donor's social security number or employee I.D. number (e.g., badge number or other employee number).

d. Reason for test (i.e., random, pre- employment, etc.).

e. Tests to be performed (i.e., drugs for which the specimen will be tested).

Note: The collector should request the donor to review the instructions on the back of the CCF to ensure that the donor knows what to expect while at the collection site.

Step 2. The collector asks the donor to remove any unnecessary outer clothing (e.g., coat, jacket, hat, etc.) and to leave any briefcase, purse, or other personal belongings he or she is carrying with the outer garments. The donor may retain his or her wallet.

Step 3. The donor must not be asked to empty his or her pockets or to remove other articles of clothing, such as shirts, pants, dresses, or underwear. Additionally, the donor must not be requested or required to remove all clothing and wear a hospital or examination gown.

Note: If a collector, during the course of a collection procedure, notices any unusual behavior to indicate that a donor may attempt to tamper with or adulterate a specimen (e.g., as evidenced by a bulging or overstuffed pocket), the collector may request that the donor empty his or her pockets, display the items, and explain the need for such items during the collection. This procedure may be done only when

AIDS TO DRUG TESTING

individual suspicion exists that a donor may tamper with or adulterate a specimen.

Step 4. The collector instructs the donor to wash and dry his or her hands, preferably under the collector's observation. The donor should not be allowed any further access to water or other materials that could be used to adulterate/dilute the specimen.

Step 5. The collector either gives the donor or allows the donor to select the collection container or specimen bottle to be used from the available supply. If the container or specimen bottle is wrapped or sealed, either the collector may unwrap or break the seal in the donor's presence or the donor may unwrap or break the seal in the collector's presence.

Note: The collection containers and specimen bottles must be wrapped/sealed separately.

Step 6. If the donor is going to use the collection container, only the collection container should be unwrapped at this time. The specimen bottle should be unwrapped in the donor's presence when the donor gives the specimen in the collection container to the collector.

Note: For a single specimen collection, if the collection container and specimen bottle are wrapped/sealed together, only the collection container or specimen bottle (whichever is selected by the donor) should be taken into the rest room. If the donor selected the collection container, the collector must maintain custody of the specimen bottle. If the donor selected the specimen bottle, the collector may discard the collection container. If the collection kit contains two specimen bottles, the collector can dispose of the unused specimen bottle. If the extra specimen bottle is returned empty to the laboratory, the laboratory may interpret this to be a split specimen collection in which the split was not collected (i.e., unless a comment is made to this effect on the "REMARKS" line).

Note: For a split specimen collection, if the collection container and two specimen bottles are wrapped/sealed together, only the collection container or one of the specimen bottles (whichever is selected by the donor) should be taken into the rest room. If the donor selected the collection container, the collector must maintain custody of the specimen bottles. If the donor selected a specimen bottle, the collector may discard the collection container but maintain custody of the

466

second specimen bottle. Under no circumstance is the donor allowed to take the second specimen bottle into the rest room even if the donor wants to urinate directly into a specimen bottle. This ensures that the donor will not split the specimen while in the rest room.

Note: A federal agency will normally be using the single specimen collection procedure unless the agency has elected to use the optional split specimen collection procedure.

Step 7. The donor takes the collection container/specimen bottle into the rest room, toilet stall, or partitioned area to provide the specimen in private. The collector instructs the donor not to flush the toilet or to use any source of water that could not be secured.

Note: The collector should remind the donor to leave the rest room, toilet stall, or partitioned area as quickly as possible after the donor has voided into the collection container/specimen bottle. Since the collector is required to measure the temperature of the specimen to determine if it is in the acceptable range, this request should ensure that the donor minimizes the time between voiding into the collection container/specimen bottle and leaving the rest room, toilet stall, or partitioned area.

Note: The donor is always permitted to provide a specimen in private unless a direct observed collection has been authorized.

Step 8. The donor gives the specimen to the collector immediately upon leaving the rest room, toilet stall, or partitioned area.

Note: Both the collector and donor will maintain visual contact of the specimen until the label/seal is placed over the specimen bottle cap/lid.

Step 9. The collector performs the following checks:

a. Checks the specimen volume to ensure there is at least 30 mL. If it is a split specimen collection, a minimum of 45 mL is required.

Note: For a single specimen collection, if the volume is less than 30 mL, the action taken will depend on the temperature of the specimen. If the temperature is within the acceptable range (i.e., 32 to 38 degrees Celsius or 90 to 100 degrees Fahrenheit), the specimen is discarded and a second specimen is collected. The donor may be given a reasonable amount of liquid to drink to provide a second specimen. The collector may use the same CCF for the second specimen, but should use new specimen collection containers and bottles. If the donor fails for any reason to provide 30 mL of urine for the second specimen collected, the collector will contact the agency to obtain guidance on the action to be taken. If the temperature is outside the acceptable range, a second specimen is collected under direct observation and both specimens are sent to the laboratory for testing. The collector must use a separate CCF for each specimen and provide an appropriate comment on each CCF to indicate why two specimens were collected. The donor may be given a reasonable amount of liquid to drink to provide a second specimen. If the donor fails for any reason to provide 30 mL of urine for the second specimen collected, the collector will contact the agency to obtain guidance on the action to be taken.

Note: For a split specimen collection, if the volume is less than 30 mL, the action taken will depend on the temperature of the specimen.

If the temperature is within the acceptable range, the specimen is discarded and a second specimen is collected. The donor may be given a reasonable amount of liquid to drink to provide a second specimen. The collector may use the same CCF for the second specimen, but should use new specimen collection containers and bottles. If the donor fails to provide 45 mL for the split specimen collection, the donor forfeits the use of a split specimen collection procedure. If the donor fails for any reason to provide at least 30 mL of urine for the second specimen collected, the collector will contact the agency to obtain guidance on the action to be taken.

If the temperature is outside the acceptable range, a second specimen is collected under direct observation and both specimens are sent to the laboratory for testing. The collector must use a separate CCF for each specimen and provide an appropriate comment on each CCF to indicate why two specimens were collected. The donor may be given a reasonable amount of liquid to drink to provide a second specimen. If the donor fails to provide 45 mL for the split specimen collection, the donor forfeits the use of a split specimen collection procedure. If the donor fails for any reason to provide 30 mL of urine for the second specimen collected, the collector will contact the agency to obtain guidance on the action to be taken.

Note: For a split specimen collection, if the volume is between 30 and 45 mL, the action taken will depend on the temperature of the specimen.

If the temperature is within the acceptable range, all of the urine should be poured into or remain in the specimen bottle (Bottle A). Bottle A is sent to the laboratory along with the CCF. The collector should provide an appropriate comment on the "REMARKS" line that the donor did not provide a sufficient volume of urine for Bottle B. The donor forfeits the use of a split specimen collection procedure. If the temperature is outside the acceptable range, a second specimen is collected under direct observation and both specimens are sent to the laboratory for testing. The collector must use a separate CCF for each specimen and provide an appropriate comment on each CCF to indicate why two specimens were collected. The donor may be given a reasonable amount of liquid to drink to provide a second specimen.

If the donor fails for any reason to provide at least 30 mL of urine for the second specimen collected, the collector will contact the agency to obtain guidance on the action to be taken. If the donor fails to provide 45 mL for the split specimen collection, the donor forfeits the use of a split specimen collection procedure.

Note: Under no circumstance is the collector permitted to collect and add or combine urine from two separate voids.

b. Reads the specimen temperature within 4 minutes of receiving the specimen and checks/marks the box on the custody and control form if the temperature is in the acceptable range or records the actual temperature on the custody and control form (CCF, Step 2). If the donor voids into a collection container, the collector affixes a temperature strip to the collection container and reads the temperature before pouring the specimen into the specimen bottle. If the donor voids into a specimen bottle, the collector affixes a temperature strip to the specimen bottle and reads the temperature.

Note: If the temperature of the specimen is clearly below the acceptable temperature range, there is reason to believe that the donor may have adulterated or diluted the specimen. The collector records on the "REMARKS" line that the specimen temperature was below the acceptable temperature range and completes the collection procedure for this specimen. The collector may be authorized to collect a second specimen using direct observation.

If the temperature of the specimen is clearly above the acceptable temperature range, the collector should offer the donor an opportunity to have his or her body temperature taken. A donor's body temperature may serve as an explanation for the temperature of the specimen being above the upper limit. The collector records on the "REMARKS" line that the specimen temperature was above the acceptable temperature range, including the donor's actual body temperature, and then completes the collection procedure for this specimen. If the donor's body temperature does not provide an explanation for the elevated specimen temperature, a direct observed collection may be authorized. The collector will obtain, in advance of any direct observed collection, the review and concurrence of a collection site supervisor or the agency that the facts support the decision and requirement to conduct a direct observed collection. Any required second collection under direct observation should be conducted before the donor departs the collection site. Each specimen will be sent to the laboratory with its own CCF.

Note: If a temperature strip is not available, the collector may use another temperature measuring device to determine the specimen's temperature. This must be accomplished in such a way that the device will not contaminate the specimen.

c. Inspects the specimen for unusual color, odor, or other signs of adulteration.

Note: If it is apparent on visual inspection that the donor has adulterated the specimen (for example, blue dye is in the specimen), the collector will proceed to collect another specimen under direct observation following the above steps and both specimens will be forwarded to the laboratory for testing. See Chapter 12 for additional instructions on conducting a direct observed collection.

Step 10. If a collection container is used, the collector pours the specimen from the collection container into a specimen bottle, places the lid/cap on the bottle, and uses the "A" bottle, label/seal. If a split specimen collection procedure is used, the collector pours 30 mL of urine into a bottle, places the lid/cap on the bottle, and uses the "A" bottle label/seal. The collector then pours the remaining urine (at least

15 mL) into a second bottle, places the lid/cap on the bottle, and uses the "B" bottle label/seal.

If a specimen bottle is used by the donor to provide a specimen, the collector pours at least 15 mL into the second bottle, which is labeled with the "B" bottle label/seal. The original bottle (into which the donor provided the specimen) is labeled with the "A" bottle label/seal. The collector should make sure that at least 30 mL (or more) remains in the original "A" bottle.

Note: The label/seal must be placed over the lid/cap to ensure that the lid/cap cannot be removed without destroying the label/seal. The donor must be present to observe the sealing of the specimen bottle(s).

Step 11. The collector writes the date on the CCF label(s)/seal(s). The collector will place the CCF label/seal on the specimen bottle. The donor is requested to initial the CCF label(s)/seal(s).

Note: Occasionally, the tamper-evident label/seal provided with the CCF will not properly adhere to the specimen bottle because of environmental conditions (e.g., moisture, temperature, specimen bottle material). When this occurs, the collector should still apply the tamper-evident label/seal provided with the CCF and then apply a second, separate tamper-evident seal to seal the specimen bottle. This second seal should be placed perpendicular to the CCF label/seal to avoid obscuring information on the CCF label/seal. This second seal must be initialed and dated by the collector and should be initialed by the donor.

BLIND SAMPLES

The Mandatory Guidelines require each agency to include blind samples in its workplace drug testing program. As stated in the Guidelines, the agencies shall only purchase blind quality control materials that (a) have been certified by immunoassay and gas chromatography/mass spectrometry and (b) have stability data which verify those materials' performance over time.

471

AIDS TO DRUG TESTING

In addition, each agency is required to ensure that at least 20 percent of the total number of specimens submitted are blind samples (up to a maximum of 200 blind samples) during the initial 90-day period of any new drug testing program and a minimum of 3 percent blind samples (up to a maximum of 100 blind samples) are submitted per quarter thereafter. The blind samples are either purchased by the agency for use with its program and transferred to the collector or the collector or MRO purchases the samples for the agency and submits the samples along with donor specimens.

In either case, a blind sample is submitted using the same CCF as that used for a donor specimen. The collector provides the required information to ensure that the CCF has been properly completed as well as using fictitious initials on the specimen bottle label/seal. In addition, since there is no donor, the collector must indicate that the sample is a blind sample in Step 4 on Copy 4 of the CCF.

Note: Since there is no donor for a blind sample, Copy 5 of the CCF (i.e., the donor copy) may be discarded by the collector or retained at the collection site.

Note: If an agency has elected to collect split specimens for its program, the blind samples should also be submitted as "split specimens."

DOCUMENTATION ERRORS/FATAL FLAWS

When an HHS-certified laboratory receives a donor specimen, it checks for discrepancies in the documentation.

The following errors or omissions are considered "fatal flaws" and should result in a specimen being rejected for drug testing by the laboratory:

1. The preprinted specimen I.D. number on the CCF does not match the specimen I.D. number on the specimen bottle label/seal.

2. There is no specimen I.D. number on the specimen bottle label/seal.

3. There is an insufficient quantity of urine for the laboratory to complete all tests.

4. The specimen bottle label/seal is missing, broken, or shows evidence of tampering.

5. The specimen is obviously adulterated (e.g., color, foreign objects, unusual odor), and it may contain something that will likely affect the performance of laboratory instruments.

Note: When a specimen contains an adulterant that may affect the performance of the instruments used to test for drugs, the laboratory may decide not to test the specimen for drugs but may only conduct adulteration tests to show that a problem exists with the specimen.

Other errors or omissions may be "fatal flaws" unless the information can be recovered and/or provided by the collector to the laboratory in a written MFR. Examples of errors or omissions that could be recovered using an MFR are as follows:

1. The collector failed to sign the collector certification statement (e.g., the collector did sign the chain of custody block, but mistakenly forgot to sign the certification statement).

2. There was an incomplete chain of custody block (e.g., the collector did not sign the "SPECIMEN RECEIVED BY" block, but was the only individual involved with collecting specimens that day).

3. The donor's social security number or I.D. number is omitted on the CCF, and the collector did not state that the "donor refused to provide information" on the "REMARKS" line (e.g., the collector could provide an MFR explaining that the information was mistakenly omitted on the "REMARKS" line). If an MFR cannot be provided by the collector to recover the missing information or to correct an error, the laboratory will reject the specimen for testing. Specimen test results reviewed by the MRO will be canceled by the MRO when the following errors occur (i.e., unless an MFR has been provided to correct the error):

1. The donor certification statement on Copy 4 of the CCF is not signed, and there is no indication on the "REMARKS" line that the donor refused to sign the certification statement.

2. The laboratory's certifying scientist failed to sign the certification statement on Copy 2 of the CCF.

HHS recommends that laboratories retain specimens for a minimum of 5 days to allow the collector to provide an MFR (if possible). Therefore, the laboratory should immediately contact the collector after a specimen is received to determine whether the collector can provide an MFR that would recover an error or omission on the CCF. If the collector indicates that the information can be recovered, the laboratory may test the specimen, but may not report the results until the MFR is received.

"SHY BLADDER" COLLECTION

Occasionally, a donor is unable to provide a specimen upon arrival at the collection site because he or she either urinated recently or has a "shy bladder." Generally, the term "shy bladder" refers to an individual who is unable to provide a sufficient specimen either upon demand or when someone is nearby during the attempted urination. If the donor tells the collector upon arrival at the collection site that he or she cannot provide a specimen, the collector should

1. Continue the collection procedures by requesting the donor to try to provide a specimen.

Note: The donor demonstrates his or her inability to provide a specimen when the donor provides either no specimen or a specimen of insufficient quantity.

2. Maintain a record of each attempt (i.e., record the time of each attempt and whether there was an insufficient quantity of specimen or no specimen provided).

3. Discard any inadequate specimen and the specimen bottle or collection container that was used for the void, but retain the CCF.

Note: If there was actually no specimen provided on an attempt, the specimen bottle/collection container may be used for the next attempt.

4. Direct the donor to remain at the collection site and to drink fluids (e.g., 8 ounces of fluid every 30 minutes up to a maximum of 24

ounces or until the donor has provided a sufficient urine specimen, whichever occurs first).

Note: The donor should remain under the direct observation of the collector or an agency representative to prevent the donor from possibly compromising the collection process (e.g., drinking excessive fluids to "flush" his or her system and urinate prior to providing the specimen for a urine drug test, obtaining "clean" urine, or obtaining adulterants).

Note: With regard to giving the donor fluids to drink in order to provide a specimen, the example given is only a guide for the collector. The donor and collector may vary the amounts and the frequency. However, the maximum of 24 ounces should not be exceeded to avoid the possible risk of water intoxication.

5. Inform the donor to let the collector know when the donor can provide a sufficient quantity of specimen. The collector continues with the collection process at that time. The collector uses the CCF from the first attempt.

Note: It is recommended that the collector allow sufficient time to have only one additional attempt rather than having to document several unsuccessful attempts.

Note: The collector should provide an appropriate comment on the "REMARKS" line to indicate the number of attempts that were made to collect the specimen and the appropriate total ounces of fluids that were given to the donor.

6. If after a period of 2 hours (i.e., from the time the donor first demonstrated that he or she was unable to provide a sufficient quantity of specimen) the donor is still unable to provide an adequate specimen, the collection process must be discontinued and the agency is notified of a potential shy bladder situation.

Note: The agency should arrange to have the donor evaluated, as soon as practical after the attempted collection, by a licensed physician to determine whether the donor's inability to provide a specimen is for a genuine medical reason or constitutes a refusal to provide a specimen.

Note: In a collection for a pre-employment test, if the agency chooses not to select the applicant, the agency does not need to have the donor evaluated for shy bladder.

7. Copies of the CCF with a shy bladder annotation on the "REMARKS" line should be distributed as follows: Copies 1, 2, 3-Discarded

Copy 4: Sent to the MRO

Copy 5: Given to the donor

Copy 6: Retained by the collector

Copy 7: Sent to the employer

DIRECT OBSERVED COLLECTIONS

A direct observed collection (i.e., the collector or agency designated representative accompanies the donor into the stall/toilet area and observes the act of urination) may occur only under very specific circumstances.

Note: A direct observed collection must be conducted by a collector of the same gender as the donor even if a collector of the opposite gender has a medical background/training.

The Mandatory Guidelines allow an immediate second collection under direct observation in the following circumstances:

1. The temperature of the specimen is outside the acceptable temperature range and the donor either refuses to allow the collector to measure his or her body temperature or the donor's body temperature does not explain the specimen temperature.

Note: If the donor's body temperature is sufficiently different from the expected temperature, the difference may explain why the temperature of the specimen was outside the acceptable range.

2. The collector believes the donor adulterated or substituted the specimen provided (e.g., there is blue dye in the specimen, the collector hears or smells something unusual while the donor is

providing the specimen, the collector sees an adulterating substance on the floor).

Note: In both of the above described circumstances, the collector must obtain the concurrence of the collector's supervisor or the designated agency representative that the facts support the need to conduct a direct observed collection. The collector is not to proceed with a direct observed collection unless concurrence is obtained from the collector's supervisor or designated agency representative. If concurrence is obtained, the Guidelines require that an observed collection be conducted immediately, i.e., as soon as the donor is able to provide another specimen.

Note: Since the collector is required to send the possible adulterated/substituted specimen from the first collection to the laboratory, the laboratory is most likely going to test the "suspect" specimen. To ensure that the laboratory and the MRO are aware that the first specimen is a possible adulterated/substituted specimen and that a second specimen was collected using direct observation, the collector must provide an appropriate comment on the "REMARKS" line on the CCFs (Step 5) for both specimens. Additionally, the collector must ensure that the comments appear on all copies of the CCFs.

The Mandatory Guidelines permit a direct observed collection when the collector is notified of this requirement by the agency. The agency may authorize a direct observed collection under the following conditions:

1. The specimen provided by the donor on a previous drug test was reported by the laboratory to have been diluted, adulterated, or the test was not performed (i.e., because the specimen was unsuitable for testing). In addition, the MRO has determined, based on information provided by the donor, that no medical explanation exists for the specimen's unsuitability.

2. The agency believes that the donor may alter or substitute the specimen to be provided.

Note: In the above situations, the decision to conduct a direct observed collection during a subsequent collection is made by the agency, not the collector. It is the responsibility of the agency to notify the collector when a direct observed collection is justified.

Note: If a specimen (negative or positive) is reported by the laboratory as having been diluted/adulterated/test not performed, the agency or MRO is not authorized to direct the donor to immediately provide another specimen for analysis. It only allows the agency to authorize that option the next time the donor is selected for a drug test. A diluted/adulterated/test not performed specimen is not sufficient to permit collecting another specimen for reasonable suspicion/cause.

CHAIN OF CUSTODY FOR A DIRECT OBSERVED COLLECTION

There may be instances when the collector is not able to serve as a direct observer (e.g., when the gender of the collector is different from that of the donor). In these instances, the collector must call upon another designated individual to act as the observer. When this occurs, the procedure for completing the chain of custody block on the CCF may be different from that used for a typical collection.

When the observer is not the collector, the following alternatives are acceptable:

1. If the observer actually receives the specimen from the donor, the observer must be included in the chain of custody block (CCF, Step 6) under the "SPECIMEN RECEIVED BY" block. When the observer gives the specimen to the collector, the observer releases the specimen to the collector (i.e., signs the "SPECIMEN RELEASED BY" block) and the collector indicates receiving the specimen from the observer (i.e., signs the "SPECIMEN RECEIVED BY" block).

Note: This approach adds an additional transaction to the chain of custody block compared with the transactions on a chain of custody block from an unobserved collection.

2. If the observer does not "physically" handle the specimen, Step 6 of the CCF must be completed by the collector as usual. The name of the observer and the reason for an observed collection may be annotated on the "REMARKS" line in Step 5 of the CCF, documented in a separate log that is maintained at the collection site, or documented on a separate sheet that is attached to the CCF.

DEALING WITH PROBLEMS

1. Only a public rest room is available for a specimen collection. Comment: A public rest room may be used in the collection of specimens provided it has been secured during the collection process as specified in Chapter 3.

2. The collector does not have any bluing agent. Comment: Use other materials to color the water, if possible (e.g., ink, food coloring, etc.). Cut off the water supply during each collection; turn on for flushing of the toilet after each collection. If materials other than a bluing agent are used, the resultant color should not be yellow or orange. If other than blue, the collector should annotate on the "REMARKS" line the color that was actually substituted for the bluing agent.

3. The temperature strip does not give a measurable reading.

Comment: The temperature strip may be defective or the specimen temperature is actually outside the acceptable range. If the specimen bottle feels within the normal range, the collector should immediately use another temperature strip to measure the specimen temperature. This second attempt may verify that the original temperature strip was defective. If the specimen bottle feels too cold or too hot, the collector may use an alternative temperature measuring device to measure the actual temperature of the specimen, contacts a supervisor, and annotates the circumstances on the "REMARKS" line.

4. The collector or donor accidentally spills the specimen before it is sealed in the specimen bottle.

Comment: The collector should attempt another collection using a new collection kit (collection container, bottles, etc.) and provide an appropriate statement on the "REMARKS" line.

5. The donor refuses to provide his or her social security number.

Comment: Request that the donor provide an alternate identification number (e.g., badge number, payroll number, etc.). If the donor does not provide an I.D. number, record "donor refuses to provide I.D. number" on the "REMARKS" line. This is not a refusal if the donor subsequently provides a specimen. Proceed with the collection.

6. The collector requests the donor to wear a hospital gown. Comment: Collections for workplace drug testing will not require or allow disrobing.

7. The donor refuses to wash his or her hands prior to the collection. Comment: Record that the donor refused to wash his or her hands on the "REMARKS" line and proceed with the collection.

8. The donor provides a specimen less than 30 mL (or 45 mL for a split specimen collection) and leaves the collection site to drink fluids and returns to attempt another void. Comment: The donor must remain within visual control of the collector, the collector's supervisor, or an agency representative. This is to ensure that the donor does not leave the collection site to obtain a clean specimen, drink excessive fluids, or perform other actions that could compromise the integrity of the specimen. If the donor leaves the collection area after he or she is told to remain at the site, this may be considered a refusal.

9. The donor provides a 30 mL specimen, but the agency has decided to use the split specimen collection procedure for its employees (45 mL). The donor wants to remain at the collection site to attempt a second void. Comment: Since 30 mL is considered a sufficient quantity for a single specimen collection, the specimen is processed for testing and the collector provides an appropriate comment on the "REMARKS" line stating that there was an insufficient quantity provided for a Bottle B specimen. At this time, the collector informs the donor that he or she has forfeited the opportunity to provide a second void of sufficient quantity (i.e., 45 mL) for split specimens. Additionally, under no circumstance is the collector permitted to collect and add or combine urine from two separate voids.

10. The collector suspects that the specimen has been adulterated or substituted and contains less than 45 mL of volume.

Comment: Record on the "REMARKS" line that the specimen is possibly adulterated and process the specimen for shipment to the laboratory regardless of the quantity. Obtain the concurrence from a supervisor or agency representative that conditions exist to obtain a second specimen using direct observation.

11. The specimen's temperature is "out of range," and a second specimen has been collected under direct observation. What happens to the first specimen? Comment: Mark the CCF of the first specimen

indicating the specimen was out of the temperature range and record on the "REMARKS" line that a second specimen was collected using direct observation. On the "REMARKS" line of the second specimen indicate that this specimen was collected using direct observation. Send both specimens and the CCFs to the laboratory in one shipping container, if possible.

12. The donor has an indwelling catheter or other medical device and cannot provide a freshly voided specimen. Comment: If a freshly voided specimen cannot be obtained, the collection should not be conducted. Notify the agency representative immediately of the inability to conduct a specimen collection.

13. The specimen is being stored prior to shipment.

Comment: After the specimen bottle has been sealed in a shipping container, the package should be stored in a secure place and preferably refrigerated if storage for several days is anticipated. The use of a log book or other documentation is recommended to track specimen storage, possible transfer to other locations, and final shipment to the laboratory.

14. The collector requests a donor to list any medications he or she is currently taking.

Comment: The collector may not require a donor to provide any information regarding medications or other medical information in conjunction with a specimen collection. However, the collector may suggest to a donor that such information be recorded on the donor copy of the CCF (Copy 5) or on another piece of paper that the donor retains for his or her own use. This would assist a donor in recalling any medications he or she may have been taking at the time of a collection should a positive result be reported.

15. The collector requires a donor to sign a consent form. Comment: A collection facility or laboratory (but not an agency site) may use a donor consent form in conjunction with the specimen collection. However, such a consent form will not indemnify or "hold harmless" the collection site or laboratory. If the donor refuses to sign the consent form, the collection facility or laboratory must have procedures in place to accomplish the collection within a reasonable time. The collection cannot be postponed to another day. Refusal by the donor to sign the consent form cannot be interpreted as refusal to

provide a specimen. Use of a consent form by the agency is not required under the Mandatory Guidelines.

16. The donor requests to keep his or her wallet on his or her person during the collections. Comment: The donor may keep his or her wallet during the specimen collection process.

17. The donor requests to have a union or legal representative present during the collection. Comment: If the agency's policy permits such practice, it is permissible, as long as the union or other representative does not disrupt or interfere with the collection process or cause any delay in the collection process. Any representative must remain outside the stall or rest room when the donor is providing the specimen and should not "participate" in any way in the collection process itself.

18. Two or more donors are present at the same time at a collection site.

Comment: The collector may initiate the collection process for each donor, but only one donor at a time is permitted to use the enclosed area designated for providing the specimen.

19. The donor tells the collector he or she cannot provide a specimen. When does the "shy bladder" procedure start?

Comment: If the donor tells the collector when he or she reports for a collection that he or she cannot provide a specimen, the collector should continue the collection process and request the donor to try again. In many cases, the donor may, in fact, be able to provide the minimum quantity required. If the donor attempts to urinate, but comes back with no specimen or less than the required quantity, the collector should inform the donor and annotate on the form that a shy bladder condition exists and note the time. The advantage of this procedure is that the collector will have documentation of an attempted collection and the time that it was attempted. The collector must ensure that the donor clearly understands the need to collect a valid specimen within a reasonable period of time.

20. The collection site only has a six-part custody and control form, and a split specimen collection is required. Comment: Split specimen collections cannot be collected using a six-part form. Do not start the collection process, but notify the collection site supervisor or the

agency representative. The seven-part OMB-approved CCF must be used for a split specimen collection.

21. The agency policy uses single specimen collection procedures, but the collector only has the seven-part CCF. Comment: The collector can perform a single specimen collection using the seven-part OMB-approved CCF. Copy 3 for the split specimen is discarded by the collector and the "NO" box is checked for a split specimen collection on the CCF.

22. The donor is not present when the collector seals the shipping container. Comment: The donor does not have to be present when the specimen bottle and CCF are placed in the shipping container. The donor must, however, observe the collector placing the tamper-evident label/seal on the specimen bottle. The donor's initials on the bottle label/seal and signature on the CCF attest to the accuracy of the information and the correctness of the collection process to this point.

23. The collector wants to use a "code" name or pseudonym on the CCF. Comment: The use of a "code" name, pseudonym, collector I.D. number, or other substitute for the collector's real name is not acceptable. The collector's name should be the same as that appearing on the identification each collector is required to make available upon the donor's request. (The use or lack of a middle initial does not invalidate the collection.)

24. After the specimen bottles were sealed in the shipping container, the collector realizes that he or she failed to mark on the CCF that the temperature was within the acceptable range. Comment: The collector should note this omission in a log book and/or annotate it on the "REMARKS" line of the collector's copy of the CCF. Also, the collector should send an MFR to the laboratory explaining the inadvertent omission.

25. The collector inadvertently collects a split specimen when a split specimen was not required. Comment: This is not a fatal flaw. If the collector discovers that the split was collected inappropriately, he or she may discard the split specimen if it has not been sealed in the leak-proof plastic bag (i.e., within the secondary seal). The collector then provides an appropriate comment on the "REMARKS" line of the CCF. If the specimen bottles are already sealed within the leak-proof

plastic bag or shipping container, the collector should annotate the circumstances of this collection on his or her copy of the CCF.

26. The donor goes into the rest room and does not come out in a reasonable period of time. Comment: In general, the collector should tell the donor that if he or she cannot provide a specimen within 2 minutes, that the donor should come out of the rest room and inform the collector of the inability to provide a specimen. If a donor remains in the rest room an excessive length of time (e.g., 5 minutes), the collector should knock on the door and request the donor to come out. The collector should try to solicit some type of response from the donor that would indicate that the donor heard the collector's request.

27. The donor provides a specimen that appears to have been adulterated and departs the collection site before the required observed collection is conducted. Comment: If the collector (with concurrence of the collection site supervisor or the designated agency representative) determines that an observed collection is required and unequivocally indicates this to the donor and the donor leaves the site, this may be considered a refusal by the donor. If the donor leaves the site prior to the collector indicating that an observed collection must be conducted, the donor should be recalled as soon as possible for the observed collection.

Appendix H

EAP Aids

Statement of Employee Assistance Program

The Company maintains an employee assistance program (EAP) for employees and supervisors. The EAP includes:

An education and training component of not less than 60 minutes for all employees, including supervisors and managers, which:

- Addresses the effects and consequences of drug and alcohol use on health, safety, and the work environment.

- Displays and distributes hot-line telephone numbers for obtaining help related to drug and alcohol use.

- Displays and distributes the Company's policy regarding the use of drugs and alcohol.

A training component of not less than 60 minutes duration for supervisors and managers which addresses:

- The specific contemporaneous, physical, behavioral, and performance indicators of probable drug use.

- Intervention tactics.

- How to make reasonable cause determinations, including the two supervisors rule.

- Post-accident testing procedures.

- Supervisory responsibilities for carrying out the Company's policy on drug and alcohol use.

The education and training component for all employees is designed to discourage drug and alcohol abuse by employees.

The training component for supervisors and managers is designed to develop skills and knowledge in:

- Detecting the signs and behaviors of persons who may be impaired by drugs or alcohol.

- Intervening in on-the-job situations that appear to involve persons impaired by drugs or alcohol.

- Recognizing, as a job responsibility, the special role played by supervisors and managers in carrying out the Company's policy on drug and alcohol use.

Directory of EAP Services

ADA-EAP CONSULTING
P.O. Box 60348
Sacramento, CA 95860
Telephone: 916-974-1436
Licenses and Certifications: CEAP
Services Provided: EAP, DFW, TR, OC
Geographic Area Served: National

ACCESS USA
16720 Steubner Airline Suite 138
Spring, TX 77379
Telephone: 800-203-4002
Licenses and Certifications: CEAP, LCDC, CADAC, TRT
Services Provided: EAP, DFW, TR, OC
Geographic Area Served: National

ADDCARE COUNSELING, INC.
11 Point Circle
Greenville, SC 29615
Telephone: 864-467-1319
Fax: 864-467-0241
Licenses and Certifications: CEAP, State License, MA
Services Provided: EAP, MC, TR, OC, DFW
Geographic Area Served: National

ADDIS AND ASSOCIATES, INC.
Hooker-Fulton Building
125 Main St., Suite 602-606
Bradford, PA 16701
Telephone: 814-362-2136
Fax: 814-362-2468
Licenses and Certifications:
Services Provided: EAP, TR, OC
Geographic Area Served: International

EAP AIDS

AFTER-LOSS ASSOCIATES
P.O. Box 3085
Gloucester, MA 01931
Telephone: 978-282-4633
E-mail: afterlos@ix.netcom.com
Licenses and Certifications: LICSW
Services Provided: EAP
Geographic Area Served: National

THE ALLEN GROUP
2965 W. State Road. 434 Suite 100
Longwood, FL 32779
Telephone: 800-272-7252 or 407-788-8822
Fax: 407-862-1477
E-mail: dcurto@theallengroup.com
Licenses and Certifications: CEAP
Services Provided: EAP, DFW, MC, TR, OC
Geographic Area Served: International

ALTERNATIVE RESOURCES
2848 Longhorn St.
Ontario, CA 91761
Telephone: 800-879-0219
Fax: 909-948-5199
Licenses and Certifications: CEAP
Services Provided: EAP, DFW, TR, OC
Geographic Area Served: National

ANIEBONA ASSOCIATES
Jean M. Aniebona
210 East 15th Street
New York, NY 10003
E-mail: janiebona@aol.com
Telephone: 212-475-8458
Fax: 212-677-3130
Licenses and Certifications: CSW
Services Provided: EAP, DFW, MC, TR, OC
Geographic Area Served: International

ANN EVINS DOAK, INC.
115 Castle Heights Ave. North Suite 101
Lebanon, TN 37087

Telephone: 615-449-2265
Fax: 615-449-2410
Geographic Area Served: National

AMERICAN HEALTHCARE PARTNERS
Weslayan Tower
24 Greenway Plaza, Suite 450
Houston, TX 77046
Telephone: 713-892-8700
Fax: 713-892-8799
E-mail: info@ahphelp.com
Licenses and Certifications: CEAP
Services Provided: EAP, DFW, MC, TR, OC
Geographic Area Served: International

APPLIED SOLUTIONS
1120 G St., NW, Suite 550
Washington, DC 20005
Telephone: 202-628-5109
Fax: 202-628-5111
Licenses and Certifications: CEAP, CAS
Services Provided: DFW, TR, DC
Geographic Area Served: International

ARCHEUS, LTD.
140 Broadway, 15th Floor
New York, NY 10005-1193
Telephone: 212-809-5099
Fax: 212-809-5497
Licenses and Certifications: CEAP
Services Provided: EAP
Geographic Area Served: National

ASSOCIATED COUNSELING SERVICES
1520 120th Avenue
Amery, WI 54001
Telephone: 715-483-9354
Fax: 715-483-1302
E-mail: creative@bucky.win.bright.net
Licenses and Certifications: MAC, MSM, CCDCR
Services Provided: TR, Consulting
Geographic Area Served: National

EAP AIDS

BEHAVIOR MANAGEMENT ASSOCIATES, INC
IMPACT Employee Assistance Program
Four Commerce Park Square
23200 Chagrin Blvd., Suite 325
Cleveland, OH 44122-5402
Telephone: 216-292-6007
Fax: 216-292-7352
Licenses and Certifications: Ph.D., Psy.D., LISW, LSW, LPCC, CCDC
III, CEAP, M.Ed., M.A.
Services Provided: EAP, MC, TR, OC
Geographic Area Served: National

BEHAVIORAL HEALTH CARE MANAGEMENT, INC.
470 Hastings Square Plaza Ste. #8
Hackettstown, NJ 07840
Telephone: 908-852-6350
Fax: 908-852-6380
E-mail: bhcmgt@aol.com
Licenses and Certifications: CEAP, CSW, MA
Services Provided: EAP, DFW, MC, TR, OC
Geographic Area Served: National

BEHAVIORAL HEALTH MARKETING SYSTEMS
P.O. Box 2096
Wickenburg, AZ 85358
Telephone: 520-684-2607
Fax: 520-684-3378
E-mail: clnnsbr@primenet.com
Licenses and Certifications:
Services Provided: Consulting, Training
Geographic Area Served: National

BENSINGER, DUPONT & ASSOCIATES
20 N. Wacker Suite 920
Chicago, IL 60606
Telephone: 312-726-8620 800-227-8620
Fax: 312-726-1061
Licenses and Certifications: CEAP, LCSW, LSW, CADC, RN, Ph.D.
Services Provided: EAP, DFW, MC, TR, OC
Geographic Area Served: International

CANDACE BIBBY, EAP CONSULTANT
14081 Yorba St., Suite 217
Tustin, CA 92680
Telephone: 714-832-6368
Fax: 619-340-0410
Licenses and Certifications: CEAP
Services Provided: EAP, DFW, TR, OC
Geographic Area Served: National

ROBERT BOWEN
2009 Arbor Forest Drive
Marietta, GA 30064
Telephone: 770-988-8333 or 404-234-3434
Licenses and Certifications: LPC, CAC II
Services Provided: EAP, TR, OC
Geographic Area Served: International

BURKE-TAYLOR ASSOCIATES, INC.
P.O. Box 12692
Research Triangle Park, NC 27709
Telephone: 919-941-5512
Fax: 919-941-5242
Licenses and Certifications: CEAP
Services Provided: EAP, DFW, MC, TR, OC
Geographic Area Served: National

BUSINESS PSYCHOLOGY ASSOCIATES
1501 Tyrell Ln.
Boise, ID 83706
Telephone: 800-486-4372
Fax: 208-344-7430
E-mail: patnckg@buspsych.com
Licenses and Certifications:
Services Provided: EAP, MC
Geographic Area Served: National

CARE PLUS SOLUTIONS
28 Oregon Ave.
Bronxville, NY 10708
Telephone: 914-723-3554 800-765-8263
Fax: 914-723-3544
Licenses and Certifications: CEAP, CSW, MBA

Services Provided: EAP, DFW, MC, TR
Geographic Area Served: National

CB CONSULTING CO.
P.O. Box 75
Rehrersburg, PA 19550
Telephone: 800-921-5433
Licenses and Certifications: CEAP
Services Provided: EAP, TR
Geographic Area Served: International

CENTER FOR FAMILIES & CHILDREN
EASE Family Dependent Care
1468 W. 9th Street Suite 225
Cleveland, OH 44113
Telephone: 216-241-6400
Fax: 216-241-4034
Licenses and Certifications: LISW, LPCC, CCDC, CEAP
Services Provided: EAP, DFW, TR, OC
Geographic Area Served: National

CHILD & ELDER CARE INSIGHTS, INC.
19111 Detroit Rd. Suite 104
Rocky River, OH 44116
Telephone: 440-356-2900
Fax: 440-356-2919
E-mail: ceci@CareReports.com
Licenses and Certifications:
Services Provided: EAP
Geographic Area Served: International

CHILD AND FAMILY GUIDANCE CENTERS EAP
8915 Harry Hines Blvd.
Dallas, TX 75235
Telephone: 214-351-3490
Fax: 214-352-0871
E-mail: maustin@gtemail.net
Licenses and Certifications: Ph.D., LMSW-ACP, LPC, LCDC
Services Provided: EAP, TR, OC
Geographic Area Served: National

ANN CLARK ASSOCIATES
8910 University Center La., Suite 850
San Diego, CA 92122
Telephone: 619-452-1254 800-932-0034
Fax: 619-452-7819
Licenses and Certifications: CEAP, MFCC, LCSW, Ph.D
Services Provided: EAP, DFW, MC, TR, OC
Geographic Area Served: International

COMMUNITYCARE EAP
218 W. 5th Street 8th Floor
Tulsa, OK 74119
Telephone: 918-594-5232 or 800-221-3976
Fax: 918-594-5230
Licenses and Certifications: CEAP, MS, CTS, CCJS-MAC
Services Provided: EAP
Geographic Area Served: National

ComPsych CORPORATION
NBC Tower
455 Cityfront Plaza, Floor 24
Chicago, IL 60611
Telephone: 312-595-4000
Fax: 312-595-4029
E-mail: info@compsych.com
Licenses and Certifications: CEAP, MSW, LPC, Ph.D., RN, CMHC,
LCSW, ACSW, LMHC, LICSW, CSACII, NCACII, CAC, MFCC
Services Provided: EAP, MC, TR, OC
Geographic Area Served: International

CONCERN EMPLOYEE ASSISTANCE PROGRAM
8280 Montgomery Road
Cincinnati, OH 45236
Telephone: 513-891-1627
Fax: 513-891-0838
E-mail: judie-garvin@trihealth.com
Licenses and Certifications: JCAHO
Services Provided: EAP, DFW, MC, TR, OC
Geographic Area Served: National

CONSULTATION, EDUCATION, & RESEARCH ASSOCIATES, INC.
1717 East La Rua Street
Pensacola, FL 32501
Telephone: 904-476-7707
Fax: 904-438-4232
E-mail: cera@cerainc.com
Licenses and Certifications: Licensed, Board Certified Physician
Services Provided: EAP, DFW, MC, TR, OC
Geographic Area Served: International

CORPCARE ASSOCIATES, INC.
7000 Peachtree Dunwoody Rd.
Building 4, Suite 300
Atlanta, GA 30328
Telephone: 770-396-5253
Fax: 770-396-9522
E-mail: corpcareap@aol.com
Licenses and Certifications: CEAP, AAMFT
Services Provided: EAP, DFW, MC, TR, OC
Geographic Area Served: National

CORPORATE CARE WORKS, INC.
4190 Belfort Road, Suite 140
Jacksonville, FL 32216
Telephone: 904-296-9436
Fax: 904-296-1511
E-mail: ckpersico@aol.com
Licenses and Certifications:
Services Provided: EAP, TR
Geographic Area Served: National

THE COUNSELING CONNECTION, INC.
P.O. Box 1935
Woodstock, GA 30189
Telephone: 770-516-0941
Fax: 770-517-6650
E-mail: schauf@randomc.com
Licenses and Certifications: CEAP, LPC
Services Provided: EAP, DFW, TR, OC
Geographic Area Served: National

COUNSELING AND REFERRAL
1931 Jefferson Davis Highway
Room C-25 Crystal Mall 3
Arlington, VA 22202
Telephone: 703-413-0755
Fax: 703-413-0757
E-mail: jneassociates@erois.com
Licenses and Certifications:
Services Provided: EAP, MC, TR, OC
Geographic Area Served: National

CRISIS SOLUTIONS, INC.
Dorothy B. Mayer
70 West Burton Pl. Suite 1901
Chicago, IL 60610-1430
Telephone: 312-280-9005
Fax: 312-280-9052
E-mail: dottym9005@aol.com
Licenses and Certifications: CEAP, LCSW, CSADC, BCD
Services Provided: EAP, DFW, TR, OC
Geographic Area Served: International

DEGRANDE AND ASSOCIATES
641 Roslyn Rd.
Grosse Pointe Woods, MI 48236
Telephone: 313-556-0683
Fax: 313-974-9720
Licenses and Certifications: CEAP, ACSW
Services Provided: EAP, DFW, TR, OC
Geographic Area Served: National

DOR AND ASSOCIATES, INC.
430 1st Ave. North #216
Minneapolis, MN 55401
Telephone: 612-332-4805
Fax: 612-342-2422
E-mail: doreap@doreap.com
Licenses and Certifications: CEAP, MS, LICSW, LP, Ph.D.
Services Provided: EAP, DFW, DOT, OC, TR
Geographic Area Served: National

ROBERT T. DORRIS & ASSOCIATES, INC.
5210 Lewis Road Suite 7
Agoura Hills, CA 91301
Telephone: 800-436-7747
Fax: 818-707-0496
E-mail: info@dorris.com
Licenses and Certifications: Ph.D., LCSW, MFCC, CEAP
Services Provided: EAP, DFW, DAP, MC, TR, OC
Geographic Area Served: National

DOVETAIL, INC.
60B W. Terra Cotta Ave., Suite 227
Crystal Lake, IL 60014
Telephone: 815-356-9630
Fax: 815-356-9828
E-mail: dovetail@mc.net
Licenses and Certifications: Ph.D., LCSW, CADC, CEAP
Services Provided: EAP, DFW, MC, TR, OC
Geographic Area Served: National

EAP SYSTEMS
500 West Cummings Park
Suite 6000
Woburn, MA 01801
Telephone: 781-935-8850
Fax: 781-935-2594
E-mail: info@eapsystems.com
Licenses and Certifications: Ph.D., LICSW, CEAP
Services Provided: EAP, DFW, TR, OD, Executive Coaching
Geographic Area Served: National

EHPAssist
P.O. Box 1670
Bethesda, MD 20872
Telephone: 301-571-0067
Fax: 301-571-0146
Licenses and Certifications: CEAP, LCSW
Services Provided: EAP, DFW
Geographic Area Served: National

496

EmployASSIST
3175 S. Congress Ave. Suite 210
Lake Worth, FL 33461
Telephone: 561-967-8025
Fax: 561-967-4543
E-mail: eas@gate.net
Licenses and Certifications: CEAP, CAP, NCACII, ICADC
Services Provided: EAP, DFW, SAP, DOT Driver/Supervisor
Training
Geographic Area Served: National

EMPLOYEE ASSISTANCE CENTER
2204 Timberloch #100
Woodlands, TX 77380
Telephone: 281-363-1633
Fax: 281-363-3898
Licenses and Certifications: CEAP, NCC, CADAC, LPC
Services Provided: EAP, DFW, OC
Geographic Area Served: National

EMPLOYEE ASSISTANCE PROGRAMS, INC.
410 17th Street, Suite 2000
Denver, CO 80202
Telephone: 800-970-6255
Fax: 303-615-9758
E-mail: jcollins@eapinc.com
Licenses and Certifications:
Services Provided: EAP, DFW, MC, TR, OC
Geographic Area Served: International

EMPLOYEE ASSISTANCE SERVICE, INC.
7918 Jones Branch Dr., Suite 230
McLean, VA 22102
Telephone: 703-448-8101
Fax: 703-448-8674
Licenses and Certifications: CEAP, LCSW, LCSW-C, LPC, CAC, NCC,
CCDC
Services Provided: EAP, DFW, MC, TR, OC
Geographic Area Served: International

EAP AIDS

EMPLOYEE ASSISTANCE SERVICES ENTERPRISES
1650 NW Front Ave. Suite 220
Portland, OR 97209
Telephone: 800-854-9968
Fax: 503-228-7197
E-mail: ease@worldaccess.com
Licenses and Certifications: CEAP
Services Provided: EAP, DFW, TR, OC
Geographic Area Served: National

EMPLOYEE COUNSELING PROGRAM
4623 Falls Road
Baltimore, MD 21209-4914
Telephone: 410-366-1980 ex: 278, 279
Fax: 410-366-8530
E-mail: ecp.fcs@juno.com
Licenses and Certifications: MSW, LCSW-C, Accredited: Council on
Accreditation of Services for Families and Children
Services Provided: EAP, DFW, TR, OC
Geographic Area Served: National

EMPLOYEE & FAMILY RESOURCES: EAP Division
505 5th Ave, Suite 600
Des Moines, IA 50309
Telephone: 515-244-6090
Fax: 515-284-5201
E-mail: eapinfo@efr.org
Licenses and Certifications: EASNA, CEAP, LMHC, LMFT, LISW,
CACI
Services Provided: EAP, DFW, MC, Student Assistance Program
Geographic Area Served: National

EMPLOYEE HEALTH PLUS
1661 Garden Hwy.
Sacramento, CA 95833
Telephone: 916-929-1365
Fax: 916-927-5368
Licenses and Certifications: CEAP
Services Provided: EAP, DFW, MC, TR
Geographic Area Served: National

EMPLOYEE SUPPORT SYSTEMS COMPANY.
309 N. Rampart Street, Suite A
Orange, CA 92868
Telephone: 714-978-7915
Fax: 714-634-1621
E-mail: info@dorris.com
Licenses and Certifications: CEAP, Ph.D., MFCC, LCSW, ARM,
CCIDC Critical Incident Debriefings
Services Provided: EAP, DFW, TR, OC
Geographic Area Served: National

FAMILY & CHILDREN'S SERVICES, INC.
2712 S. Calhoun
Fort Wayne, IN 46807
Telephone: 219-744-4326
Fax: 219-744-0188
Licenses and Certifications: CEAP
Services Provided: EAP, SAP, DFW, TR, OC
Geographic Area Served: National

FAMILY SOCIAL & PSYCHOLOGICAL SERVICES, LLC
13255 West Bluemound Rd., Suite 101
Brookfield, WI 53005
Telephone: 417-797-2803
Fax: 414-797-2805
Licenses and Certifications: CEAP, MPA
Services Provided: EAP, DFW, MC, TR, OC
Geographic Area Served: National

FAUECAST
P.O. Box 756
New Brunswick, NJ 08903
Telephone: 908-359-3686
Fax: 908-359-8575
E-mail: jfaue@tapnet.net
Licenses and Certifications: CEAP, ACSW, LCSW
Services Provided: EAP, TR, OC
Geographic Area Served: National

FLETCHER RESOURCE ASSOCIATES
2254 Petworth Ct.
Naperville, IL 60565

Telephone: 708-416-3254
Licenses and Certifications: CEAP
Services Provided: EAP, DFW, TR, OC
Geographic Area Served: National

THE GOOD HOPE CENTER
P.O. Box 470
East Greenwich, RI 02818
Telephone: 800-752-4673
Fax: 401-397-0093
E-mail: goodhopecenter@home.com
Licenses and Certifications: State of Rhode Island
Services Provided: EAP, MC, TR, OC
Geographic Area Served: National

GREENLEAF SERVICES
P.O. Box 80338 602 Beivoir Ave.
Chattanooga, TN 37414
Telephone: 615-624-6964
Fax: 615-624-6967
Licenses and Certifications: CEAP
Services Provided: EAP, MC
Geographic Area Served: National

KATHLEEN GREER ASSOCIATES
161 Worcester Rd.
Framingham, MA 01701
Telephone: 508-879-2093
Fax: 508-875-5574
E-Mail: KGA4EAP@aol.com
Licenses and Certifications: LICSW, LCSW, LMHC, CEAP, CAC
Services Provided: EAP, Training, Consulting
Geographic Area Served: National

H & H HEALTH ASSOCIATES
(Hobart & Associates, Inc.)
11132 South Towne Square Suite 107
St. Louis, MO 63123
Telephone: 800-832-8302 or 314-845-8302
Fax: 314-845-8087
E-mail: hhhealth@stlnet.com

Licenses and Certifications: CEAP, LCSW, LPC, Ph.D., CSACII, RN, M.P.H., OHC, MBA
Services Provided: EAP, DFW, MC, TR, OC
Geographic Area Served: National

KATHLEEN M. HANES
256 Bunn Dr. Suite 4
Princeton, NJ 08540
and
712 East Main St. Suite 2B
Moorestown, NJ 08057
Telephone: 609-452-1110 #3
Licenses and Certifications: CEAP, LPC, MCAT, MS, NCC
Services Provided: EAP, MC, TR, OC
Geographic Area Served: National

HHRC
A division of Integrated Insights
9370 Sky Park Court, Suite 140
San Diego, CA 92123
Telephone: 619-571-1698
Fax: 619-571-1868
E-mail: eap@hhrc.com
Licenses and Certifications: CAEP, Knox-Keene Licensure
Services Provided: EAP, DFW, DAP, MC, TR, OC
Geographic Area Served: International

HEALTH & HUMAN SERVICES GROUP
25108 Marguerite Pkwy., Suite B142
Mission Viejo, CA 92692
Telephone: 800-275-7460
Fax: 714-768-6224
Licenses and Certifications:
Services Provided: EAP, DFW, TR, OC
Geographic Area Served: International

HEALTH MANAGEMENT CENTER, INC.
10391 Miralago Pi.
Santa Ana, CA 92705
Telephone: 714-505-3172
Fax: 310-860-1059
Licenses and Certifications: CEAP

EAP AIDS

Services Provided: EAP, DFW, MC, TR, OC
Geographic Area Served: National

HEALTH MANAGEMENT SYSTEMS OF AMERICA
20811 Kelly Road
Eastpointe, MI 48021
Telephone: 800-847-7240
Fax: 810-773-3000
E-mail: hmsa@hmsanet.com
Licenses and Certifications:
Services Provided: EAP, DFW, TR, MC, OC
Geographic Area Served: National

HEALTH PROMOTION SERVICES
730 Holiday Dr., Foster Plaza 8
Pittsburgh, PA 15220
Telephone: 412-937-8011
Fax 412-928-0552
Licenses and Certifications: CEAP, RN
Services Provided: EAP, DFW, TR, OC
Geographic Area Served: National

HELPNET, INC.
P.O. Box 3217
Long Beach, CA 90803-0217
Telephone: 800-443-5766
800-435-7638 From CA, FL
Fax: 562-498-6873
E-mail: info@hnweb.com
Licenses and Certifications: MFCC, LCSW, Cl. Psychologist, MD
(Psychiatrist)
Services Provided: EAP, TR, OC
Geographic Area Served: National

PERCY HOLLINS
3114 Jacqueline Ct.
St. Louis, MO 63114
Telephone: 314-423-9149
Licenses and Certifications: CEAP
Services Provided: EAP, TR
Geographic Area Served: National

HUMAN AFFAIRS INTERNATIONAL
955 Chesterbrook Blvd., Suite 120
Wayne, PA 19087
Telephone: 610-251-6436
Fax: 610-644-5082
Licenses and Certifications:
Services Provided: EAP, DFW, MC, TR, OC
Geographic Area Served: International

HUMAN AFFAIRS INTERNATIONAL
5801 South Fashion Blvd.
Salt Lake City, UT 84107
Telephone: 801-578-7332
Fax: 801-578-7669
Licenses and Certifications: CEAP
Services Provided: EAP, DFW, MC, TR
Geographic Area Served: International

HUMAN MANAGEMENT SERVICE, INC.
930 East Lancaster Ave.
Exton, PA 19341
Telephone: 800-343-2186
Fax: 610-594-9824
E-mail: hms@worldlynx.net
Licenses and Certifications: CAC, CEAP, ACSW, LSW
Services Provided: EAP, DFW, TR, OC
Geographic Area Served: International

INOVA EMPLOYEE ASSISTANCE
5400 Shawnee Road, Suite 208
Alexandria, VA 22312
Telephone: 703-914-6719
Fax: 703-914-6718
E-mail: pflench@inovaeap.com
Licenses and Certifications: CEAP, LCSW, LICSW, LPC, LMFC, CCAC, CCDAC
Services Provided: EAP, DFW, TR, OC
Geographic Area Served: International

INTERFACE EAP, INC.
7670 Woodway Suite 350
Houston, TX 77063

EAP AIDS

Telephone: 713-781-3364
Fax: 713-781-4954
E-mail: info@ieap.com
Licenses and Certifications: Various
Services Provided: EAP, MC, TR, OC
Geographic Area Served: National

INTERPERSONAL DYNAMICS, INC.
2265 Teton Plaza
Idaho Falls, ID 83404
Telephone: 208-529-1737
Fax: 208-529-1757
E-mail: idynamic@srv.net
Licenses and Certifications: CEAP
Services Provided: EAP, DFW, TR, OC, MC
Geographic Area Served: National

INTERVENTION STRATEGIES INTERNATIONAL, INC.
265 Cedar Lane
Teaneck, NJ 07666
Telephone: 201-836-0404
Fax: 201-836-3932
E-mail: intstrat@ix.netcom.com
Licenses and Certifications: C.A.C
Services Provided: EAP, TR, OC
Geographic Area Served: International

JANUS ASSOCIATES, INC.
711 West 40th St., Suite 207
Baltimore, MD 21211
Telephone: 800-942-6640
Fax: 410-889-7397
Licenses and Certifications: Ph.D., CAS, LCSW-C, CAC, CPC
Services Provided: EAP, DFW, TR, OC, SAP, PTI, CISD, MC
Geographic Area Served: National

JONES & CLARKE ASSOCIATES, EAP/SAP
1130 Ten Rod Road Suite A102
North Kingstown, RI 02852
Telephone: 401-295-2230
Fax: 401-783-9365
E-mail: rj@netsense.net

Licenses and Certifications: MA, CEAP, CAS, M.Ed., LMHC, CCMHC, MAC, SAP
Services Provided: EAP, MC, TR, OC
Geographic Area Served: National

KEEPING TRACK, INC.
4355 North High St., Suite 101
P.O. Box 14468
Columbus, OH 43214-0468
Telephone: 612-267-3272
Licenses and Certifications:
Services Provided: TR, OC
Geographic Area Served: National

JULIE KELLY AND ASSOCIATES
One Linda Vista
East Tiburon, CA 94920-1918
Telephone: 415-435-4882
Licenses and Certifications: CEAP
Services Provided: OC
Geographic Area Served: National

LAUPHEIMER ASSOCIATES, INC.
571 White Plains Rd.
East Chester, NY 10707
Telephone: 914-337-6858
Fax: 914-337-3481
Licenses and Certifications:
Services Provided: EAP
Geographic Area Served: National

LIFE CHANGES EAP
1045 Main St. Suite 2
Danville, VA 24541
Telephone: 800-776-3022
Fax: 804-797-5947
E-mail: lifechanges@dancom.com
Licenses and Certifications: CEAP, MAC, CSAC, NCACII
Services Provided: EAP, DFW, MC, TR
Geographic Area Served: National

EAP AIDS

LIFE CHANGES EAP
2505 South 17th Street
Wilmington, NC 28401
Telephone: 800-776-3022
Fax: 804-797-5947
E-mail: gene.smith@dancom.com
Licenses and Certifications: CEAP, MAC, CSAC, NCACII
Services Provided: EAP, DFW, MC, TR
Geographic Area Served: National

LIFEWORKS BEHAVIORAL HEALTH SYSTEM
26-A Hill Rd.
Parsippany, NJ 07054
Telephone: 201-402-1015
Fax: 201-402-9092
Licenses and Certifications:
Services Provided: EAP, MC, TR, OC
Geographic Area Served: National

SHARON LIGEFT CONSULTANT
618 Central Ave.
Wilmette, IL 60091
Telephone: 708-251-2822
Fax: 708-251-2978
Licenses and Certifications: CEAP, LCSW, BSN
Services Provided: EAP, TR, OC
Geographic Area Served: National

LITTLE GAFFNEY & ASSOCIATES, INC.
9441 Silver King Ct.
Fairfax, VA 22031
Telephone: 703-359-8311
Fax: 703-359-7024
Licenses and Certifications: CEAP
Services Provided: EAP, TR, OC
Geographic Area Served: National

LONDON ASSOCIATES INTERNATIONAL
18062 Irvine Boulevard Suite 200
Tustin, CA 92780-3328
Telephone: 714-505-0873
Fax: 714-505-0874

E-mail: lai@londonassocintl.com
Licenses and Certifications: ABPP, ABPH, ABPS, BCD, DCSW
Services Provided: EAP, DFW, MC, TR, OC
Geographic Area Served: International

LONGVIEW ASSOCIATES, INC.
222 Mamaroneck Avenue Suite 301
White Plains, NY 10605
Telephone: 800-666-5327
Fax: 914-683-0037
E-mail: lindseyrjl@aol.com
Licenses and Certifications: M.Ed., CEAP
Services Provided: EAP, DFW, TR, OC
Geographic Area Served: National

THE LYTLE GROUP
15 S. Montgomery Street
Hollidaysburg, PA 16648
Telephone: 814-698-1147
Fax: 814-696-1156
E-mail: 105326.2506@compuserve.com
Licenses and Certifications: CEAP, CAC, LSW, R.N., C.I.S.D.
Services Provided: EAP, DFW, TR, MC, OC
Geographic Area Served: National

MCC
11095 Viking Dr.
Eden Prairie, MN 55344
Telephone: 612-996-2487
Fax: 612-996-2722
Licenses and Certifications: CEAP
Services Provided: EAP, DFW, MC, TR, OC
Geographic Area Served: National

MASCHHOFF, BARR & ASSOCIATES
1501 Market St., Suite 200
Tacoma, WA 98402
Telephone: 800-523-5668
Fax: 206-596-5656
Services Provided: EAP, DFW, MC, TR, OC
Geographic Area Served: International

EAP AIDS

MASI RESEARCH CONSULTANTS, INC.
2301 E St., NW, Suite 209
Washington, DC 20037
Telephone: 202-223-2399
Fax: 202-223-2392
Licenses and Certifications: CEAP, MSW, DSW
Services Provided: EAP, DFW, MC, TR, DC
Geographic Area Served: International

THE MEADOWS
P.O. Box 97
Wiekenburg, AZ 85358
Telephone: 602-684-3926 Ext. 133
Fax: 602-684-3935
Services Provided: OC
Geographic Area Served: International

MEDICAL BUSINESS MANAGEMENT, INC.
3490 Independence Dr.
Birmingham, AL 35209
Telephone: 800-925-5327
Licenses and Certifications: CEAP, Ph.D.
Services Provided: EAP, DFW, MC, TR, OC
Geographic Area Served: National

MERIDIAN RESOURCE CORPORATION
401 West Michigan St.
Milwaukee, WI 53203
Telephone: 414-226-5619
Fax: 414-226-5109
Licenses and Certifications: CEAP, ACSW, CICSW
Services Provided: EAP, DFW, MC, TR, OC
Geographic Area Served: National

MIDDEL & ASSOCIATES
1425 West Outer Dr.
Traverse City, MI 49684
Telephone: 616-929-3617
Licenses and Certifications: CEAP, ACSW
Services Provided: TR, OC
Geographic Area Served: International

MUSTARD SEED, INC.
Neshaminy Plaza One
3070 Bristol Pike, Suite 102
Bensalem, PA 19020
Telephone: 215-638-2273
Fax: 215-638-2952
Licenses and Certifications:
Services Provided: EAP, DFW, MC, TR, OC
Geographic Area Served: National

NATIONAL EMPLOYEE ASSISTANCE SERVICES, INC.
20225 Watertower Blvd. Suite 400
Brookfield, WI 53045
Telephone: 800-634-6433
Fax: 414-798-3928
E-mail: info@neas.com
Licenses and Certifications: MSW, Ph.D., CEAP, CADC II,
CADC III, CMFT, AMFT, CTS
Services Provided: EAP, MC, TR, OC
Geographic Area Served: International

NEWBRIDGE CONSULTATION
585 Steward Ave., Suite L-70
Garden City, NY 11530
Telephone: 516-222-1221
Fax: 516-222-2915
Licenses and Certifications: CEAP
Services Provided: EAP, DFW, MC, TR, OC
Geographic Area Served: National

NORTH, CLAWSON & BOLT, LTD.
66 East Main St.
P.O. Box 593
Moorestown, NJ 08057-0593
Telephone: 609-273-8118
Fax: 609-273-6656
Licenses and Certifications: CEAP
Services Provided: EAP, DFW, MC, OC, TR
Geographic Area Served: National

EAP AIDS

OCCUPATIONAL HEALTH CONSULTANTS OF AMERICA
3428 West Market
Akron, OH 44333
Telephone: 800-955-6422 or 330-836-2754
Fax: 800-742-1830 or 330-836-3022
Licenses and Certifications: CEAP, LPCC, CCDCII, LISW, Ph.D.
Services Provided: EAP, DFW, MC, TR, OC
Geographic Area Served: National

OCCUPATIONAL HEALTH CONSULTANTS OF AMERICA
3401 West End Ave.
Nashville, TN 37203
Telephone: 800-955-6422 or 615-292-4327
Fax: 615-292-0512
Licenses and Certifications: CEAP
Services Provided: EAP, MC
Geographic Area Served: National

ON-CALL
A division of Life Crisis Services
1423 S. Big Bend Blvd.
St. Louis, MO 63117
Telephone: 314-647-3100
Fax: 314-647-1762
E-mail: info@on-call.org
Licenses and Certifications: MSW, LCSW, LPC
Services Provided: EAP, TR, OC
Geographic Area Served: International

J.M. OHER & ASSOCIATES
10 Tanglewild Pl.
Chappaqua, NY 10514-2528
Telephone: 914-238-0607
Fax: 914-238-3161
Licenses and Certifications: CEAP
Services Provided: EAP, DFVV, MC, TR, OC
Geographic Area Served: International

PARTNERSHIP EAP, INC.
29 City Centre Plaza
Middletown, OH 45042
Telephone: 513-423-3327

Fax: 513-423-3676
Licenses and Certifications: CEAP
Services Provided: EAP, SAP, DFW, TR, OC
Geographic Area Served: National

PEAK PERFORMANCE STRATEGIES
28241 Fontana Dr.
Southfield, MI 48076-5432
Telephone: 810-356-0018
Licenses and Certifications: CEAP, CSW, ACSW
Services Provided: DFW, TR
Geographic Area Served: National

PEOPLE RESOURCES, INC.
10900 Manchester Road, Suite 203
St. Louis, MO 63122
Telephone: 314-822-8210
Fax: 314-822-4419
E-mail: prieap@primary.net
Licenses and Certifications: Ph.D., LCSW, LPC, LCPC, CEAP,
CCDC III, ACSW, LISW, MAD
Services Provided: EAP, MC, TR, OC
Geographic Area Served: International

PERSPECTIVES, LTD.
111 North Wabash, Suite 1620
Chicago, IL 60602
Telephone: 800-456-6327
Fax: 312-558-1570
Licenses and Certifications: LCSW, CSADC, CEAP
Services Provided: EAP, DFW, MC, TR, OC
Geographic Area Served: National

PHILLIPS & ASSOCIATES
2515 Liberty Pkwy.
Baltimore, MD 21222
Telephone: 410-284-6175
Fax: 202-628-5111
Licenses and Certifications: CEAP
Services Provided: DFW, TR, OC
Geographic Area Served: National

EAP AIDS

PPC INTERNATIONAL, LLC
315 J.S. McDonnell Blvd.
Building 305 2-East
Hazelwood, MO 63042
Telephone: 314-214-8900
Fax: 314-214-8910
E-mail: ppcint@stlnet.com
Licenses and Certifications: ISO9002
Services Provided: EAP
Geographic Area Served: International

PRIME EAP, INC.
214 North Charles St.
Baltimore, MD 21201
Telephone: 410-547-6650
Fax: 410-727-6723
Licenses and Certifications: CEAP
Services Provided: EAP, DFW, TR, OC
Geographic Area Served: National

PROCESS DYNAMICS, LTD.
Londonderry Office Park
5786 Lincoln Dr.
Edina, MN 55436
Telephone: 612-936-7730
Fax: 612-936-9156
Licenses and Certifications: CEAP, MS, LICSW, CCDP, LP, PhD,
ACSW
Services Provided: EAP, DFW, TR
Geographic Area Served: National

PROFESSIONAL EMPLOYEE ASSISTANCE CONSULTING
6345 Balboa Blvd., Suite 205
Encino, CA 91316
Telephone: 800-527-7322 800-423-8666 (outside CA)
Fax: 818-345-7672
E-mail: peac97@aol.com
Licenses and Certifications: CEAP
Services Provided: EAP, DFW, MC, TR, OC
Geographic Area Served: National

PROGRESSIVE CORPORATE CARE
5225 Sheridan Dr.
Williamsville, NY 14221
Telephone: 716-626-9976
Licenses and Certifications:
Services Provided: EAP
Geographic Area Served: National

PSYCH CARE, INC.
2850 Douglas Rd.
Coral Gables, FL 33134
Telephone: 800-962-4404 Ext. 368
Fax: 800-370-1116
E-mail: alcblanc@vincam.com
Licenses and Certifications: MSW, LCSW, CCM, ABQAURP
DIPLOMATE
Services Provided: EAP, DFW, MC, TR
Geographic Area Served: National

PSYCHOLOGY SYSTEMS, INC.
615 South Main St.
Milpitas, CA 95035
Telephone: 408-263-8046
Fax: 408-942-0264
Licenses and Certifications: PhD
Services Provided: EAP, DFW, MC
Geographic Area Served: National

PSYCHWORKS, INC.
3111 University Drive Suite 725
Coral Springs, FL 33065
offices also in Ft. Lauderdale & North Miami
Telephone: 954-344-2022
Fax: 954-753-3585
E-mail: info@psychworks.com
Licenses and Certifications: CEAP, CRC, CAC, LMHC, CHE
Services Provided: EAP, DFW, MC, TR, OC
Geographic Area Served: National

REACH, INC.
98 Floral Ave., P.O. Box 807
Murray Hill, NJ 07974

Telephone: 800-USA-REACH 908-665-8050
Fax: 908-665-8282
E-mail: GillianRB@aol.com
Licenses and Certifications: CEAP
Services Provided: EAP, MC, TR, OC
Geographic Area Served: National

DAVID REED & ASSOCIATES
23046 Avenida Carlota #600
Laguna Hills, CA 92653
Telephone: 800-664-5090
Fax: 714-460-6482
E-mail: eap@reedassoc.com
Licenses and Certifications: Psychologist, LCSW, MFCC, CEAP
Services Provided: EAP, DFW, TR, OC
Geographic Area Served: National

RESOURCE EAP, INC.
1046 Riverside Ave.
Jacksonville, FL 32204
Telephone: 904-634-1700
Fax: 904-634-8812
Licenses and Certifications: CEAP, MSH
Services Provided: EAP, DFW
Geographic Area Served: National

RESOURCE INTERNATIONAL
120 Centerville Road
Warwick, RI 02886
Telephone: 800-833-0453
Fax: 401-732-3730
E-mail: ecomp@msn.com
Licenses and Certifications: CEAP, LICSW, ACSW, LCDP, LCSW,
CADAC, CD, RN
Services Provided: EAP, DFW, TR, OC
Geographic Area Served: National

RESOURCE MANAGEMENT CONSULTANTS
59 Stiles Rd.
Salem, NH 03079
Telephone: 800-332-7998
Fax: 603-890-8806

Services Provided: EAP, DFW, MC, TR, OC
Geographic Area Served: National

RESOURCE MANAGEMENT SERVICES, INC.
4516 N. Sterling, Suite 200
Peoria, IL 61615
Telephone: 309-681-5652
Fax: 309-681-5658
E-mail: tchapin@bitwisesystems.com
Licenses and Certifications: CEAP, American Society of Training
and Development, Professional Association of Resume Writers,
Institute of Management Consultants
Services Provided: EAP, DFW, MC, TR, OC
Geographic Area Served: National

LLOYD REYNOLDS ASSOCIATES
733 Elmer St.
Vineland, NJ 08360
Telephone: 609-692-4486
Licenses and Certifications: CEAP, NCACII, CADC
Services Provided: EAP, DFW, MC, TR, OC
Geographic Area Served: National

RLM CONSULTING, INC.
3243 East Calhoun Pkwy.
Minneapolis, MN 55408-3311
Telephone: 612-827-4147
Fax: 612-827-1886
Licenses and Certifications: CEAP
Services Provided: EAP, DFW, TR, OC, DOT
Geographic Area Served: National

ST. ELIZABETH MEDICAL CENTER
Employee Assistance Program
P.O. Box 7501
Lafayette, IN 47903-7501
Telephone: 765-423-6918
Fax: 765-742-2213
Licenses and Certifications: CEAP, MS
Services Provided: EAP, DFW, TR, OC
Geographic Area Served: National

EAP AIDS

ST. MARY'S HOSPITAL
56 Franklin Street
Waterbury, CT 06706
Telephone: 203-574-6070
Fax: 203-597-3741
Licenses and Certifications: CEAP, Ph.D.
Services Provided: EAP, SAP, DFW, TR, OC
Geographic Area Served: National

SARMUL CONSULTANTS
1 Strawberry Hill Ct.
Stamford, CT 06902
Telephone: 203-327-1596
Services Provided: EAP, TR, OC
Geographic Area Served: National

THE SAND CREEK GROUP, LTD.
333 N. Main St. #203
Stillwater, MN 55082
Telephone: 612-430-3383 800-632-7643
Fax: 612-430-9753
Licenses and Certifications: CEAP, CCDC-R, ICADC
Services Provided: EAP, DFW, MC, TR, OC
Geographic Area Served: International

SIMMS SERVICES
36 Carriage La.
Newark, DE 19711
Telephone: 302-368-4101
Licenses and Certifications:
Services Provided: DFW, TR, OC
Geographic Area Served: International

SOUTHERN EMPLOYEE ASSISTANCE PROGRAMS
P.O. Box 8037
Madeira Beach, FL 33738-8037
Telephone: 813-975-1672
Fax: 813-398-2945
Licenses and Certifications: CEAP
Services Provided: EAP, DFW, MC, TR, OC
Geographic Area Served: National

SPECTRUM HEALTH
233 Fulton NE, Suite 209
Grand Rapids, MI 49503
Telephone: 616-391-3910
Fax: 616-391-8874
Licenses and Certifications: CEAP, CAC
Services Provided: EAP, OC
Geographic Area Served: National

STUECKER & ASSOCIATES, INC.
1169 Eastern Parkway, Suite 2243
Louisville, KY 40217
Telephone: 502-452-9227
Fax: 502-452-1529
E-mail: stueckerandassoc@ka.net
Licenses and Certifications: CEAP, LCSW, Ph.D.
Services Provided: EAP, DFW, MC, TR, OC
Geographic Area Served: International

SUPPORTIVE SYSTEMS, LLC
539 Turtle Creek Drive South, Suite 12
Indianapolis, IN 46227
Telephone: 800-660-6645 or 317-788-4111
Fax: 317-788-7783
E-mail: ssllc@aol.com
Licenses and Certifications: CEAP, Advanced CISM staff, LCSW,
LMFT
Services Provided: EAP, DFW, TR, OC, MC
Geographic Area Served: National

TRANSITIONS, INC. ELDERCARE CONSULTING
1121 Douglas Ave. South
Minneapolis, MN 55403
Telephone: 612-377-1865
Fax: 612-377-1865
E-mail: sudeka@asktransitions.com
Licenses and Certifications: NAPGCM, LGSW
Services Provided: EAP, TR, OC
Geographic Area Served: International

EAP AIDS

THE UNIVERSITY OF TEXAS EAP
7000 Fannin #1670
Houston, TX 77030
Telephone: 800-346-3549 or 713-500-3327
Fax: 713-500-3330
E-mail: hdunagin@admin4.hsc.uth.tmc.edu
Licenses and Certifications: CEAP, CDC, CADAC, LPC, LMSW, LMFT, ACRPS, CISD
Services Provided: EAP, DFW, TR, OC
Geographic Area Served: National

U.S. BEHAVIORAL HEALTH
2000 Powell St.
Suite 1180
Emeryville, CA 94608-1832
Telephone: 510-601-2255
Fax: 510-547-2336
Licenses and Certifications:
Services Provided: EAP, MC, TR
Geographic Area Served: National

VALUE BEHAVIORAL HEALTH
27300 West Eleven Mile Rd.
Suite 1000
Southfield, MI 48034
Telephone: 800-1447-0166
Fax: 810-948-8488
Licenses and Certifications: CEAP, MA, LLP
Services Provided: EAP, DFVV, MC, TR, OC
Geographic Area Served: International

THE WELLNESS CORP.
512 West Main Street
Shrewsbury, MA 01545
Telephone: 508-842-2780
Fax: 508-842-6068
Licenses and Certifications: CEAP
Services Provided: EAP, MC
Geographic Area Served: International

THE WELLSPRING GROUP
2840 Northup Way
Bellevue, WA 98004
Telephone: 425-827-1990
Fax: 425-822-4813
E-mail: wellspring@emh.com
Licenses and Certifications:
Services Provided: EAP, DFW, TR, OC
Geographic Area Served: National

WGI CONSULTING & TRAINING
24800 Denso Drive, Suite 255
Southfield, MI 48034-7449
Telephone: 800-336-1491 or 248-351-7890
Fax: 248-351-7896
E-mail: wellnessgroup@compuserve.com
Licenses and Certifications: CEAP, Psychology, Law, Medical
Services Provided: EAP, DFW, TR, OC
Geographic Area Served: International

WHEELER EAP
91 Northwest Drive
Plainville, CT 06062
Telephone: 800-522-3271
Fax: 800-793-3554
E-mail: eap@connix.com
Licenses and Certifications: CEAP
Services Provided: EAP, DFW, TR, OC
Geographic Area Served: International

WISCONSIN COMMUNITY MENTAL
HEALTH COUNSELING CENTERS
155 East Capitol Dr.
Hartland, WI 53029
Telephone: 414-375-5540
Fax: 414-473-6188
Licenses and Certifications: NCC, CCMHC, CMP
Services Provided: EAP, DFW, MC, TR, OC
Geographic Area Served: National

WORKPLACE WELLNESS, INC.
P.O. Box 51
Montrose, AL 36559
Telephone: 800-748-1170
Fax: 334-621-1672
E-mail: dmdaniell@msn.com
Licenses and Certifications: CEAP
Services Provided: EAP, TR, OC
Geographic Area Served: National

Directory of Substance Abuse Professionals

THE ALLEN GROUP
2965 W. State Road. 434 Suite 100
Longwood, FL 32779
Telephone: 800-272-7252 or 407-788-8822
Fax: 407-862-1477
E-mail: dcurto@theallengroup.com
Geographic Area Served: International

AMERICAN HEALTHCARE PARTNERS
Weslayan Tower
24 Greenway Plaza, Suite 450
Houston, TX 77046
Telephone: 713-892-8700
Fax: 713-892-8799
E-mail: info@ahphelp.com
Geographic Area Served: International

ANIEBONA ASSOCIATES
Jean M. Aniebona
210 East 15th Street
New York, NY 10003
E-mail: janiebona@aol.com
Telephone: 212-475-8458

Fax: 212-677-3130
Geographic Area Served: International

ASSOCIATED COUNSELING SERVICES
1520 120th Avenue
Amery, WI 54001
Telephone: 715-483-9354
Fax: 715-483-1302
E-mail: creative@bucky.win.bright.net
Geographic Area Served: National

BEHAVIOR MANAGEMENT ASSOCIATES, INC
IMPACT Employee Assistance Program
Four Commerce Park Square
23200 Chagrin Blvd., Suite 325
Cleveland, OH 44122-5402
Telephone: 216-292-6007
Fax: 216-292-7352
Geographic Area Served: National

BEHAVIORAL HEALTH CARE MANAGEMENT, INC.
470 Hastings Square Plaza Ste. #8
Hackettstown, NJ 07840
Telephone: 201-984-6155
Fax: 201-984-0244
E-mail: bhcmgt@aol.com
Geographic Area Served: National

BENSINGER, DUPONT & ASSOCIATES
20 N. Wacker Suite 920
Chicago, IL 60606
Telephone: 312-726-8620 800-227-8620
Fax: 312-726-1061
E-mail: bdaapke@worldnet.att.net
Geographic Area Served: International

ROBERT BOWEN
2009 Arbor Forest Drive
Marietta, GA 30064
Telephone: 770-988-8333 or 404-234-3434
Geographic Area Served: International

EAP AIDS

CARE PLUS SOLUTIONS
28 Oregon Ave.
Bronxville, NY 10708
Telephone: 914-723-3554 800-765-8263
Fax: 914-723-3544
Geographic Area Served: National

CENTER FOR FAMILIES & CHILDREN
EASE Family Dependent Care
1468 W. 9th Street Suite 225
Cleveland, OH 44113
Telephone: 216-241-6400
Fax: 216-241-4034
Geographic Area Served: National

CHILD AND FAMILY GUIDANCE CENTERS EAP
8915 Harry Hines Blvd.
Dallas, TX 75235
Telephone: 214-351-3490
Fax: 214-352-0871
E-mail: maustin@gtemail.net
Geographic Area Served: National

ComPsych CORPORATION
NBC Tower
455 Cityfront Plaza, Floor 24
Chicago, IL 60611
Telephone: 312-595-4000
Fax: 312-595-4029
E-mail: info@compsych.com
Geographic Area Served: International

CONCERN EMPLOYEE ASSISTANCE PROGRAM
8280 Montgomery Road
Cincinnati, OH 45236
Telephone: 513-891-1627
Fax: 513-891-0838
E-mail: judie-garvin@trihealth.com
Geographic Area Served: National

CONSULTATION, EDUCATION, & RESEARCH ASSOCIATES, INC.
1717 East La Rua Street
Pensacola, FL 32501
Telephone: 904-476-7707
Fax: 904-438-4232
E-mail: cera@cerainc.com
Geographic Area Served: International

CORPCARE ASSOCIATES, INC.
7000 Peachtree Dunwoody Rd.
Building 4, Suite 300
Atlanta, GA 30328
Telephone: 770-396-5253
Fax: 770-396-9522
E-mail: corpcareap@aol.com
Geographic Area Served: National

THE COUNSELING CONNECTION, Inc.
P.O. Box 1935
Woodstock, GA 30189
Telephone: 770-516-0941
Fax: 770-517-6650
E-mail: schauf@randomc.com
Geographic Area Served: National

COUNSELING AND REFERRAL
1931 Jefferson Davis Highway
Room C-25 Crystal Mall 3
Arlington, VA 22202
Telephone: 703-413-0755
Fax: 703-413-0757
E-mail: jneassociates@erois.com
Geographic Area Served: National

CRISIS SOLUTIONS, INC.
Dorothy B. Mayer
70 West Burton Pl. Suite 1901
Telephone: 312-280-9005
Fax: 312-280-9052
E-mail: dottym9005@aol.com
Geographic Area Served: International

DOR AND ASSOCIATES, INC.
430 1st Ave. North #216
Minneapolis, MN 55401
Telephone: 612-332-4805
Fax: 612-342-2422
E-mail: doreap@doreap.com
Geographic Area Served: National

ROBERT T. DORRIS & ASSOCIATES, INC.
5210 Lewis Road Suite 7
Agoura Hills, CA 91301
Telephone: 800-436-7747
Fax: 818-707-0496
E-mail: info@dorris.com
Geographic Area Served: National

DOVETAIL, INC.
60B W. Terra Cotta Ave., Suite 227
Crystal Lake, IL 60014
Telephone: 815-356-9630
Fax: 815-356-9828
E-mail: dovetail@mc.net
Geographic Area Served: National

EHPAssist
P.O. Box 1670
Bethesda, MD 20872
Telephone: 301-571-0067
Fax: 301-571-0146
Geographic Area Served: National

EmployASSIST
3175 S. Congress Ave. Suite 210
Lake Worth, FL 33461
Telephone: 561-967-8025
Fax: 561-967-4543
E-mail: eas@gate.net
Geographic Area Served: National

EMPLOYEE ASSISTANCE CENTER
2204 Timberloch #100
Woodlands, TX 77380

Telephone: 281-363-1633
Fax: 281-363-3898
Geographic Area Served: National

EMPLOYEE ASSISTANCE PROGRAMS, INC.
410 17th Street, Suite 2000
Denver, CO 80202
Telephone: 800-970-6255
Fax: 303-615-9758
E-mail: jcollins@eapinc.com
Geographic Area Served: International

EMPLOYEE ASSISTANCE SERVICES ENTERPRISES
1650 NW Front Ave. Suite 220
Portland, OR 97209
Telephone: 800-854-9968
Fax: 503-228-7197
E-mail: ease@worldaccess.com
Geographic Area Served: National

EMPLOYEE COUNSELING PROGRAM
4623 Falls Road
Baltimore, MD 21209-4914
Telephone: 410-366-1980 ex: 278, 279
Fax: 410-366-8530
E-mail: ecp.fcs@juno.com
Geographic Area Served: National

EMPLOYEE & FAMILY RESOURCES: EAP DIVISION
505 5th Ave, Suite 600
Des Moines, IA 50309
Telephone: 515-244-6090
Fax: 515-284-5201
E-mail: eapinfo@efr.org
Geographic Area Served: National

EMPLOYEE SUPPORT SYSTEMS COMPANY.
309 N. Rampart Street, Suite A
Orange, CA 92868
Telephone: 714-978-7915
Fax: 714-634-1621
E-mail: info@dorris.com

EAP AIDS

Geographic Area Served: National

FAMILY & CHILDREN'S SERVICES, INC.
2712 S. Calhoun
Fort Wayne, IN 46807
Telephone: 219-744-4326
Fax: 219-744-0188
Geographic Area Served: National

FAUECAST
P.O. Box 756
New Brunswick, NJ 08903
Telephone: 908-359-3686
Fax: 908-359-8575
E-mial: jfaue@tapnet.net
Geographic Area Served: National

THE GOOD HOPE CENTER
P.O. Box 470
East Greenwich, RI 02818
Telephone: 800-752-4673
Fax: 401-397-0093
E-mail: goodhopecenter@home.com
Geographic Area Served: National

H & H HEALTH ASSOCIATES
(Hobart & Associates, Inc.)
11132 South Towne Square Suite 107
St. Louis, MO 63123
Telephone: 800-832-8302 or 314-845-8302
Fax: 314-845-8087
E-mail: hhhealth@stlnet.com
Geographic Area Served: National

KATHLEEN M. HANES
256 Bunn Dr. Suite 4
Princeton, NJ 08540
and
712 East Main St. Suite 2B
Moorestown, NJ 08057
Telephone: 609-452-1110 #3
Geographic Area Served: National

HHRC
A division of Integrated Insights
9370 Sky Park Court, Suite 140
San Diego, CA 92123
Telephone: 619-571-1698
Fax: 619-571-1868
E-mail: eap@hhrc.com
Geographic Area Served: International

HEALTH MANAGEMENT SYSTEMS OF AMERICA
20811 Kelly Road
Eastpointe, MI 48021
Telephone: 800-847-7240
Fax: 810-773-3000
E-mail: hmsa@hmsanet.com
Geographic Area Served: National

HUMAN MANAGEMENT SERVICE, INC.
930 East Lancaster Ave.
Exton, PA 19341
Telephone: 800-343-2186
Fax: 610-594-9824
E-mail: hms@worldlynx.net
Geographic Area Served: International

INOVA EMPLOYEE ASSISTANCE
5400 Shawnee Road, Suite 208
Alexandria, VA 22312
Telephone: 703-914-6719
Fax: 703-914-6718
E-mail: pflench@inovaeap.com
Geographic Area Served: International

THE INSTITUTE FOR STAGED RECOVERY
85 Fifth Avenue Suite 900
New York, NY 10003
Telephone: 212-242-5052
Fax: 212-242-5052
Geographic Area Served: National

EAP AIDS

INTERFACE EAP, INC.
7670 Woodway Suite 350
Houston, TX 77063
Telephone: 713-781-3364
Fax: 713-781-4954
E-mail: info@ieap.com
Geographic Area Served: National

INTERPERSONAL DYNAMICS, INC.
2265 Teton Plaza
Idaho Falls, ID 83404
Telephone: 208-529-1737
Fax: 208-529-1757
E-mail: idynamic@srv.net
Geographic Area Served: National

INTERVENTION STRATEGIES INTERNATIONAL, INC.
265 Cedar Lane
Teaneck, NJ 07666
Telephone: 201-836-0404
Fax: 201-836-3932
E-mail: intstrat@ix.netcom.com
Geographic Area Served: International

JANUS ASSOCIATES, INC.
711 West 40th St., Suite 207
Baltimore, MD 21211
Telephone: 800-942-6640
Fax: 410-889-7397
Geographic Area Served: National

JERRY A. JOHNSON, CCDCR, NCACI
P.O. Box 424
St. Cloud, MN 56302
Telephone: 320-240-6576
Fax: 320-240-6576
E-mail: ccdcr@aol.com
Geographic Area Served: National

JONES & CLARKE ASSOCIATES, EAP/SAP
1130 Ten Rod Road Suite A102
North Kingstown, RI 02852

Telephone: 401-295-2230
Fax: 401-783-9365
E-mail: rj@netsense.net
Geographic Area Served: National

LIFE CHANGES EAP
1045 Main St. Suite 2
Danville, VA 24541
Telephone: 800-776-3022
Fax: 804-797-5947
E-mail: lifechanges@dancom.com
Geographic Area Served: National

LIFE CHANGES EAP
2505 South 17th Street
Wilmington, NC 28401
Telephone: 800-776-3022
Fax: 804-797-5947
E-mail: gene.smith@dancom.com
Geographic Area Served: National

LONDON ASSOCIATES INTERNATIONAL
18062 Irvine Boulevard Suite 200
Tustin, CA 92780-3328
Telephone: 714-505-0873
Fax: 714-505-0874
E-mail: lai@londonassocintl.com
Geographic Area Served: International

THE LYTLE GROUP
15 S. Montgomery Street
Hollidaysburg, PA 16648
Telephone: 814-698-1147
Fax: 814-696-1156
E-mail: 105326.2506@compuserve.com
Geographic Area Served: National

OCCUPATIONAL HEALTH CONSULTANTS OF AMERICA
3428 West Market
Akron, OH 44333
Telephone: 800-955-6422 or 330-836-2754
Fax: 800-742-1830 or 330-836-3022

EAP AIDS

Geographic Area Served: National

OHCA
Occupational Health Consultants of America
3401 West End Ave.
Nashville, TN 37203
Telephone: 615-292-4327
Fax: 615-292-0512
Geographic Area Served: National

PARTNERSHIP EAP, INC.
29 City Centre Plaza
Middletown, OH 45042
Telephone: 513-423-3327
Fax: 513-423-3676
Geographic Area Served: National

PEOPLE RESOURCES, INC.
10900 Manchester Road, Suite 203
St. Louis, MO 63122
Telephone: 314-822-8210
Fax: 314-822-4419
E-mail: prieap@primary.net
Geographic Area Served: International

PERSPECTIVES, LTD.
111 North Wabash, Suite 1620
Chicago, IL 60602
Telephone: 800-456-6327
Fax: 312-558-1570
Geographic Area Served: National

PROFESSIONAL EMPLOYEE ASSISTANCE CONSULTING
6345 Balboa Blvd., Suite 205
Encino, CA 91316
Telephone: 800-527-7322 800-423-8666 (outside CA)
Fax: 818-345-7672
E-mail: peac97@aol.com
Geographic Area Served: National

PSYCHWORKS, INC.
3111 University Drive Suite 725
Coral Springs, FL 33065
Also offices in Ft. Lauderdale & North Miami
Telephone: 954-344-2022
Fax: 954-753-3585
E-mail: info@psychworks.com
Geographic Area Served: National

REACH, INC.
98 Floral Ave., P.O. Box 807
Murray Hill, NJ 07974
Telephone: 800-USA-REACH 908-665-8050
Fax: 908-665-8282
E-mail: GillianRB@aol.com
Geographic Area Served: National

DAVID REED & ASSOCIATES
23046 Avenida Carlota #600
Laguna Hills, CA 92653
Telephone: 800-664-5090
Fax: 714-460-6482
E-mail: eap@reedassoc.com
Geographic Area Served: National

RESOURCE MANAGEMENT SERVICES, INC.
4516 N. Sterling, Suite 200
Peoria, IL 61615
Telephone: 309-681-5652
Fax: 309-681-5658
E-mail: tchapin@bitwisesystems.com
Geographic Area Served: National

ST. MARY'S HOSPITAL
56 Franklin Street
Waterbury, CT 06706
Telephone: 203-574-6070
Fax: 203-597-3741
Geographic Area Served: National

EAP AIDS

ST. ELIZABETH MEDICAL CENTER
Employee Assistance Program
P.O. Box 7501
Lafayette, IN 47903-7501
Telephone: 765-423-6918
Fax: 765-742-2213
Geographic Area Served: National

THE SAND CREEK GROUP, LTD.
333 N. Main St. #203
Stillwater, MN 55082
Telephone: 612-430-3383 800-632-7643
Fax: 612-430-9753
Geographic Area Served: International

SPECTRUM HEALTH
233 Fulton NE, Suite 209
Grand Rapids, MI 49503
Telephone: 616-391-3910
Fax: 616-391-8874
Geographic Area Served: National

STUECKER & ASSOCIATES, INC.
1169 Eastern Parkway, Suite 2243
Louisville, KY 40217
Telephone: 502-452-9227
Fax: 502-452-1529
E-mail: stueckerandassoc@ka.net
Geographic Area Served: International

SUPPORTIVE SYSTEMS, LLC
539 Turtle Creek Drive South, Suite 12
Indianapolis, IN 46227
Telephone: 800-660-6645 or 317-788-4111
Fax: 317-788-7783
E-mail: ssllc@aol.com
Geographic Area Served: National

THE UNIVERSITY OF TEXAS EAP
7000 Fannin #1670
Houston, TX 77030
Telephone: 800-346-3549 or 713-500-3327

Fax: 713-500-3330
E-mail: hdunagin@admin4.hsc.uth.tmc.edu
Geographic Area Served: National

THE WELLNESS CORP.
512 West Main Street
Shrewsbury, MA 01545
Telephone: 508-842-2780
Fax: 508-842-6068
Geographic Area Served: International

WGI CONSULTING & TRAINING
24800 Denso Drive, Suite 255
Southfield, MI 48034-7449
Telephone: 800-336-1491 or 248-351-7890
Fax: 248-351-7896
E-mail: wellnessgroup@compuserve.com
Geographic Area Served: International

WHEELER EAP
91 Northwest Drive
Plainville, CT 06062
Telephone: 800-522-3271
Fax: 800-793-3554
E-mail: eap@connix.com
Geographic Area Served: International

WORKPLACE WELLNESS, INC.
P.O. Box 51
Montrose, AL 36559
Telephone: 800-748-1170
Fax: 334-621-1672
E-mail: dmdaniell@msn.com
Geographic Area Served: National

Appendix I

Glossary

abuser. A person who uses drugs in ways that threaten personal health or impair social or economic functioning.

accuracy. Ability to get the correct or true drug testing result.

addiction. A chronic, relapsing disease, characterized by compulsive drug-seeking and use and by neurochemical and molecular changes in the brain. The point at which a person's chemical usage causes repeated harmful consequences and the person is unable to stop using the drug of choice. Medically, the term implies that withdrawal will take place when the mood-changing chemical is removed from the body.

agonist. A chemical compound that mimics the action of a natural neurotransmitter.

GLOSSARY

alcoholism. A treatable illness brought on by harmful dependence upon alcohol, which is physically and psychologically addictive. As a disease, alcoholism is primary, chronic, progressive, and fatal.

aliquot. A portion of a specimen used for testing.

amphetamines. Synthetic amines (uppers) that act with a pronounced stimulant effect on the central nervous system.

amyl nitrite. Ampules sold on the street as poppers and snappers.

analog. A chemical compound that is similar to another drug in its effects but differs slightly in its chemical makeup.

anesthetic. An agent that causes insensitivity to pain.

antagonist. A drug that counteracts or blocks the effects of another drug.

antidepressants. A group of drugs used in treating depressive disorders.

assay. The measurement of the quantity of a chemical component.

barbiturates. A class of drugs used in medicine as hypnotic agents to promote sleep or sedation. Some are also useful in the control of epilepsy. All are central nervous system depressants and are subject to abuse. Depending upon their potency, they are classified as Schedule I or Schedule II drugs.

batch reporting. Reporting of results of drug tests conducted of urine specimens that were sent to the testing laboratory in groups or "batches." Test results are generally reported on all specimens in a batch simultaneously, rather than reporting the negative results first then, after a delay while they are confirmed, reporting the positive results. Batch reporting improves confidentiality by helping to avoid identifying those individuals whose test must be confirmed.

benzodiazepines. A class of drugs used in medicine as minor tranquilizers which is frequently prescribed to treat anxiety. They are central nervous system depressants and are subject to abuse.

binge drinking. The consumption of five or more alcoholic drinks in a row on at least one occasion.

blank. A biological specimen with no detectable drugs added, routinely analyzed by a drug testing laboratory to ensure that no false-positive results are obtained.

blind sample. A specimen submitted to a laboratory for quality control testing purposes, with a fictitious identifier, so that the laboratory cannot distinguish it from employee specimens, and which is spiked with known quantities of specific drugs or which is blank, containing no drugs.

blood alcohol concentration (BAC). The amount of alcohol in the bloodstream measured in percentages. A BAC of 0.10 percent means that a person has 1 part alcohol per 1,000 parts blood in the body.

buprenorphine. A mixed agonist/antagonist medication being studied for the treatment of heroin addiction.

butyl nitrite. A drug packaged in small bottles and illegally sold. Street names include bolt, bullet, climax, locker room, and rush.

cannabinoids. The psychoactive substances found in the common hemp plant, or Cannabis Sativa. Most of the psychological effects are produced by delta-9-tetrahydrocannabinol.

certified laboratory. A laboratory which has met certain minimum performance standards set by an accrediting agency, and has received a certificate to verify this fact.

chain-of-custody. Procedures to account for the integrity of each urine specimen by tracking its handling and storage from point of specimen collection to final disposition of the specimen. Documentation of this process must include the date and purpose each time a specimen is handled or transferred, and identification of each individual in the chain-of-custody.

chemical dependency. A harmful dependence on mood-changing chemicals.

chromatography. Any of a variety of techniques used to separate mixtures of drugs and their metabolites and other chemicals into individual components based on differences in their relative affinities for two different media, i.e., a mobile phase and a stationary phase. In gas chromatography, the mobile phase is inert gas such as nitrogen or helium and the stationary phase is a high-boiling liquid bound to fine particles packed in a glass column, or bound to the inner surface of a glass capillary column.

coca. The plant, Erythroxylon, from which cocaine is derived. Also refers to the leaves of this plant.

cocaethylene. A potent stimulant created when cocaine and alcohol are used together.

cocaine. An alkaloid, methylbenzoylecgonine, obtained from the leaves of the coca tree (Erythroxylon). It is a central nervous system stimulant that produces euphoric excitement.

collection site. A place designated where individuals present themselves for the purpose of providing a specimen of their urine to be analyzed for the presence of drugs.

concentration. The amount of drug in a unit volume of biological fluid expressed as weight/volume. Urine concentrations are expressed in nanogram/milliliter, as micrograms/milliliter or milligrams/liter.

confirmatory test. A second analytical procedure to identify the presence of a specific drug which is independent of the initial drug test and which uses a different technique and chemical principle in order to ensure reliability and accuracy.

crack. A smokable form of cocaine.

craving. A powerful, often uncontrollable desire for drugs.

cutoff level. The defined concentration of an analyte in a specimen at or above which the test is called positive and below which it is called negative. This concentration is usually significantly greater than the sensitivity of the assay. Also called threshold.

depressants. Drugs that reduce the activity of the nervous system (e.g., alcohol, downers, and narcotics).

designer drug. An analog of a restricted drug that has psychoactive properties. To circumvent legal restrictions, underground chemists modify the molecular structure of certain illegal drugs to produce analogs known as designer drugs. Many of the so- called designer drugs are related to amphetamines and have mild stimulant properties but are mostly euphoriants. They can produce severe neurochemical damage to the brain.

detection limit. The lowest concentration of a drug that can be reliably detected.

detoxification. A process of allowing the body to rid itself of a drug while managing the symptoms of withdrawal. It is often the first step in a drug treatment program.

dopamine. A neurotransmitter present in regions of the brain that regulate movement, emotion, motivation, and the feeling of pleasure.

downers. Barbiturates, minor tranquilizers, and related depressants.

drug abuse. Pathological use of a prescribed or unprescribed chemical substance.

drug. Any chemical substance that alters mood, perception, or consciousness.

employee assistance program (EAP). A program designed to assist employees with drug abuse, or other problems, by mean of counseling, treatment, or referral to more specific resources.

enabling. Allowing irresponsible and destructive behavior patterns to continue by taking responsibility for others, not allowing them to face the consequences of their own actions.

ethyl alcohol. The member of the alcohol series of chemicals which is used in alcoholic beverages. It is less toxic than other members of this series, but it is a central nervous system depressant and has a high abuse potential.

false negative. A test result which states that no drug is present when, in fact, a tested drug or metabolite is present in an amount greater than the threshold or cut-off amount.

GLOSSARY

false positive. A test result which states that a drug or metabolite is present when, in fact, the drug or metabolite is not present or is in an amount less than the threshold or cut-off value.

fentanyl. A medically useful opioid analog that is 50 times more potent than heroin.

GC/MS (gas chromatography/mass spectroscopy). The instrumental technique which couples the powerful separation potential of gas chromatography with the specific characterization ability of mass spectroscopy.

habituation. The result of repeated consumption of a drug which produces psychological but no physical dependence. The psychological dependence produces a desire (not a compulsion) to continue taking drugs for the sense of improved well-being. Also called psychological dependence.

hallucinogens. Drugs that stimulate the nervous system and produce varied changes in perception and mood.

hashish. The concentrated resin of the marijuana plant.

heroin. A semisynthetic derivative of morphine originally used as an analgesic and cough depressant. In harmful doses it induces euphoria and tends to make the user think he or she is removed from reality, tension, and pressures.

immunoassay. The measurement of an antigen-antibody interaction utilizing such procedures as immunofluorescence, radioimmunoassay, enzyme immunoassay or other nonradioisotopic techniques. In drug testing, the antigen is a drug or metabolite and its corresponding labeled analog; the antibody is a protein grown in an animal and directed towards a specific drug, metabolite, or group of similar compounds.

inhalants. Inhalants include a variety of psychoactive substances which are inhaled as gases or volatile liquids. Many are readily available in most households and are inexpensive. They include paint thinner, glue, gasoline, and other products that are not considered to be drugs.

initial test. A preliminary or screening test used to identify those specimens which are negative for the presence of drugs or their metabolites. These specimens need no further examination and need not undergo a more costly confirmation test.

levo-alpha-acetyl-methadol (LAAM). An FDA-approved medication for heroin addiction.

LSD. A drug that distorts perception of time and space, and creates illusions and hallucinations. It comes in liquid form and most often is swallowed after being placed on a sugar cube or blotting paper. LSD increases blood pressure, heart rate, and blood sugar. Nausea, chills, flushes, irregular breathing, sweating, and trembling can occur.

marijuana. A drug prepared by crushing the dried flowering cannabis top and leaves into a tealike substance, which is usually rolled into a cigarette (a joint) and smoked. The effects are felt within minutes. The user may experience a distorted sense of time and distance, suffer reduced attention span, and loss of memory. Higher doses also cause impaired judgment, slowed reaction time, limited motor skills, confusion of time sense, and short-term memory loss.

mass spectrometry. Analysis using an analytical instrument that provides information about the molecular mass and structure of complex molecules. This technique can identify and quantify extremely small amounts of drugs or metabolites by their mass-fragment spectrum.

medical review officer (MRO). A licensed physician responsible for receiving laboratory results generated by a drug testing program who has knowledge of substance abuse disorders and has appropriate medical training to interpret and evaluate an individual's positive test result together with his or her medical history and any other relevant biomedical information.

meperidine. A medically approved opioid available under various brand names, e.g., Demerol.

metabolite. A compound produced from chemical changes of a drug in the body.

methadone. A long-acting synthetic medication shown to be effective in treating heroin addiction. It has an action similar to that of morphine and heroin except that withdrawal is more prolonged and less severe. It is used in methadone maintenance programs as a substitute for heroin in the treatment of addicts.

methaqualone. A hypnotic drug unrelated to the barbiturates but used as a sedative and sleeping aid. It is also known by its trade name Quaalude.

narcotics. A class of depressant drugs derived from opium or related chemically to compounds in opium.

neuron. A nerve cell in the brain.

on-site screening. A preliminary immunoassay test conducted at the worksite.

opiates. Drugs derived from opium such as morphine and codeine.

passive inhalation. Exposure of non-smoking subjects to side-stream smoke from active smokers, thereby raising the possibility that a non-user may test positive.

pharmacodynamics. The study of the relationship of drug concentration to drug effects.

pharmacokinetics. The study of the time course of the processes (absorption, distribution, metabolism, and excretion) that a drug undergoes in the body.

phencyclidine (PCP). A synthetic substance chemically related to ketamine, widely used in anesthesia. Intoxication may result in blurred vision, diminished sensation, muscular rigidity, muteness, confusion, anxious amnesia, distortion of body image, thought disorder, auditory hallucinations, and variable motor depression or stimulation, which may include aggressive or bizarre behavior.

physical dependence. An adaptive physiological state that occurs with regular drug use and results in a withdrawal syndrome when drug use is stopped. It occurs when a person cannot function normally without the repeated use of a drug. If the drug is withdrawn, the person has severe physical and psychic disturbances.

polydrug use. The consumption of more than one drug at the same time.

precision. A measurement of the agreement between repeated measurements.

pre-employment testing. Drug testing of applicants for jobs.

psychoactive drugs. Drugs that affect the mind, especially mood, thought, or perception.

qualitative analysis. A measurement that determines the presence or absence of specific drugs or metabolites in a specimen.

quality assurance (QA). A program by which technical procedures are provided to ensure good quality laboratory services. These procedures include pre-analytical conditions and variables, analytical variables, and control of the analytical quality by statistical methods.

quality control (QC). A system instituted to maintain the output of a technical operation at a level that has been established as acceptable. It involves the setting of quality standards, continual appraisal of conformance to these standards, and in the absence of conformance, taking corrective action to establish or maintain the predetermined levels of performance.

quantitative analysis. The accurate determination of the quantity of drug or metabolite present in a specimen

random testing. Unannounced, random selection of candidates to be tested.

reasonable suspicion testing. Testing conducted when reason exists to believe that a person may be using illegal drugs. The belief is based on specific objective facts and reasonable inferences. Also called for-cause testing.

rush. A surge of euphoric pleasure that rapidly follows administration of a drug.

safety-sensitive position. An occupational position deemed acutely sensitive to safety considerations such as an airline pilot, a nuclear reactor operator, etc.

GLOSSARY

Schedule I Drugs. Drugs in Schedule I of the Controlled Substances Act, i.e., substances that have a high potential for abuse, no currently acceptable medical use in treatment, and which lack any accepted safe use under medical supervision.

Schedule II Drugs. Drugs in Schedule II of the Controlled Substances Act, i.e., substances that have a high potential for abuse with severe liability to cause psychic or physical dependence, but have some approved medical use.

sensitive position. A job that involves activities affecting public health or safety, national defense, or other functions requiring a high degree of trust and confidence.

sensitivity. The smallest concentration of a drug or metabolite which can be reliably detected by a particular assay method.

specific gravity. The ratio of the density of urine to the density of water at a specified temperature. The specific gravity of random urine specimens ranges between 1.002 and 1.030 at body temperature, depending on fluid intake.

specificity. The ability of a particular test to identify a drug or metabolite without interference or cross reaction.

specimen. The entire quantity of material (e.g., urine and blood) collected for analysis.

split specimen. A specimen that has been divided into two portions, one of which may be submitted for analysis and the other preserved by freezing for the purpose of confirmation analysis or reanalysis.

standard. An authentic sample of the analyte of known purity, or a solution of the analyte of a known concentration.

steroids. A large family of pharmaceutical drugs related to the adrenal hormone cortisone.

stimulants. Drugs that increase the activity of the nervous system, causing wakefulness.

sudden sniffing death. A death, usually due to heart failure, within minutes of using an inhalant.

544

Texas Shoe Shine. Spray paint containing toluene.

THC. Delta-9-tetrahydrocannabinol, the most active cannabinoid.

tolerance. A condition in which higher doses of a drug are required to produce the same effect as during initial use. It refers to a state in which the body becomes used to the presence of a drug in given amounts and eventually fails to respond to ordinarily effective dosages. Hence, increasingly larger doses are necessary to produce desired effects.

torch breathing. Igniting exhaled volatile gas, such as propane or butane.

uppers. Stimulants.

vertigo. The sensation of dizziness.

whippet. A balloon or plastic bag filled with nitrous oxide.

withdrawal. A variety of symptoms that occur after use of an addictive drug is reduced or stopped.

Index

547

INDEX

INDEX

torch breathing, 545
training component, 71, 72, 485, 486
training outcomes, 128

U.S. Department of Health and Human Services, 55, 218
U.S. Department of Transportation, 17, 31, 61, 218

unannounced search, 55, 353, 368
urinalysis, 8, 82, 135, 359, 370

verified positive test result, 149, 150
vertigo, 545

what to look for, 21, 99
whippet, 545